Raising a Nation

The Speeches of
Xanana Gusmão
2011-2014

LONGUEVILLE
MEDIA

Originally published in 2015 by
Longueville Media
PO Box 205
Haberfield NSW 2045 Australia
www.longmedia.com.au
info@longmedia.com.au

Copyright © Kay Rala Xanana Gusmao 2015

All rights reserved. No part of this publication may be reproduced or transmitted in any form or by any means, electronic or mechanical, including photocopying, recording or by any information storage and retrieval system, without the prior permission in writing from the author, publisher and copyright holders.

For the National Library of Australia Cataloguing-in-Publication entry visit www.nla.gov.au

Print ISBN: 978-1-920681-99-9
POD ISBN: 978-1-7635361-2-8

Contents

Forewords

Fr Frank Brennan SJ AO — vii
Major General Mick Slater — x

Poems
A Fighter Who Fell — xii
Grandfather Crocodile — xiii

2011 – IV Constitutional Government — 1

Bali Democracy Forum IV – 'Enhancing Democratic Participation in a Changing World: Responding to Democratic Voices' — 2

2012 – IV Constitutional Government — 11

Opening of the Forum on Inclusive Growth — 12
Opening of the Conference '10 Years On: The Contribution of Social Programmes to the Construction of the Social State in Timor-Leste' — 17
Opening of the Timor 1942 Exhibition at the Anzac Memorial, Hyde Park, Sydney — 21
Australia Timor-Leste Business Council Reception — 23
Second Jakarta International Defence Dialogue (JIDD): 'Military Operations other than War: Regional and National Perspectives' — 27
Graduation Ceremony for Senior Students of Universidade Nacional Timor Lorosa'e (UNTL) — 33
Opening Session of the ICAPP-CAPDI Joint Conference on Peace and Reconciliation in Asia — 36
Timor-Leste and Development Partners Meeting: 'State Building 10 Years On: A Reflection on Timor-Leste' — 42

2012 – V Constitutional Government — 52

Swearing-in of the V Constitutional Government	53
g7+ Fragility Assessment Workshop	62
Presenting the Program for the V Constitutional Government to the National Parliament	64
Celebration of the 1st Anniversary of the Central Bank of Timor-Leste	77
67th Session of The United Nations General Assembly	81
High Level Event on 'Peacebuilding: Way Towards Sustainable Peace and Security'	88
Reception to Launch The United Nations Secretary General's Education First Initiative	91
g7+ High Level Side Event of the United Nations General Assembly	93
Ceremony Marking the end of the Operational Activity of the ISF and UNPOL	96
Bali Democracy Forum V: 'Advancing Democracy Principles at the Global Setting'	99
g7+ Haiti Ministerial Retreat	106
End of Mission of the International Stabilisation Force	111
Graduation Ceremony for the Finalist Students of UNTL	113

2013 – V Constitutional Government   118

Presentation of the Draft Budget Law for 2013	119
2013 World Summit on 'Peace, Security and Human Development'	135
Opening of the International Conference on the Post-2015 Development Agenda	140
Public Private Partnership Investor Conference	144
Third Jakarta International Defence Dialogue: 'Defence and Diplomacy in the Asia-Pacific Region'	148
69th Session of the Economic and Social Commission for Asia and the Pacific	156
International Conference on Decentralization and Local Government	160
Twelfth International Institute for Strategic Studies Asia Security Summit. The Shangri-la Dialogue, Second Plenary Session: 'Defending National Interest, Preventing Conflict'	164
Lecture on Timor-Leste's Role and Future in a Rising Asia-Pacific – The S. Rajaratnam School of International Studies	169
Lecture at the Lee Kuan Yew School of Public Policy at the National University of Singapore: Peace Building and State Building: From Fragility to Resilience	177
Address at the Thomson Reuters Asia Petroleum Lunch	184

Address at the UP College of Law, University of the Philippines: 'Peace and Reconciliation – The Timorese Experience'	189
Opening Session of the 2013 Timor-Leste Development Partners Meeting – 'State Building for the Next Decade: A Reflection on Timor-Leste's Experiences and Expectations in State Building'	197
Closing of the Timor-Leste and Development Partners Meeting	206
Forum for Economic and Trade Cooperation Between China and Portuguese Speaking Countries: 'A New Investment Paradigm in Timor-Leste'	209
Reflecting on the State of the Nation	215
Opening Session of the Pacific Islands Development Forum: 'Leadership, Innovation and Partnership for Green / Blue Pacific Economies', Keynote Address	236
Lecture at the Viet Nam National University on State Building: 'The Timor-Leste Experience in a Southeast Asian Context'	246
Conference on 'Harnessing Natural Resource Wealth For Inclusive Growth and Economic Development', Keynote Address	256
Workshop on Peacekeeping Transitions: Lessons Learned From The UN Missions in Timor-Leste: 'Timor-Leste on the Verge of the Transition', Opening Address	262
Bali Democracy Forum VI: 'Consolidating Democracy in a Pluralistic Society'	268
Lecture at the University of Juba on 'Sharing Experiences'	275
United Nations Economic and Social Commission of Asia and the Pacific Ministerial Conference on 'Regional Economic Cooperation and Integration in Asia and the Pacific'	280

2014 – V Constitutional Government 285

Dinner to Welcome and Honour Her Royal Highness Princess Maha Chakri Sirindhorn of the Kingdom of Thailand	286
2014 Jakarta International Defence Dialogue: 'Building Maritime Collaboration for Security and Stability'	289
Forum on Trade and Investment Opportunities in Timor-Leste	295
Address upon Receiving an Honorary PhD in International Relations: 'Timor-Leste and ASEAN: Perspectives And Challenges'	300
Address at a Western Australia Business Lunch Hosted by DLA Piper	311
Special Event SAS Charity Dinner	314
Boao Forum for Asia Annual Conference 2014 – 'Asia's New Future: Identifying Growth Drivers'	319

Boao Forum for Asia Annual Conference 2014 – 'Asia's New Future: Identifying New Growth Drivers', Session 12, 'Reviving The Silk Road: A Dialogue with Asian Leaders'	322
Address at the Hunan (China) Timor-Leste Investment Cooperation Conference	326
Address at the g7+ Ministerial Meeting in Togo	328
International Scientific Conference on the Investigation, Education, Cooperation and Development in the Community of Portuguese Language Countries: 'Timor-Leste's Policy During its Leadership of the CPLP: A Globalised Vision for the Future'	332
Seminar on Economic Globalisation and Investment Opportunities: The CPLP and the Asia-Pacific Region – 'Timor-Leste's Presidency of the CPLP: A Vision Towards the Future'	341
2014 Timor-Leste Development Partners' Meeting	346
70th Session of The United Nations Economic and Social Commission for Asia and the Pacific, Keynote Address	352
Address at the World Summit 2014: 'Peace, Security and Human Development'	357
Address to a Business and Investment Lunch Hosted by DLA Piper	362
High-level Ministerial Lunch Meeting on Peace and Capable Institutions as Stand-alone Goals in the Post-2015 Development Agenda	365
International Conference: INTERFET, Reflections on the 1999 East Timor Crisis	368
Order of Solidarity Medal Awards Ceremony, Queen's Hall, Parliament House, Victoria	377
United Nations Third International Conference on Small Island Developing States: 'The Sustainable Development of Small Island States through Genuine and Durable Partnerships'	380
United Nations Climate Change Summit	383
69th Session of The United Nations General Assembly	385
Acceptance Speech for the Conferral of the Highest Indonesia Medal of Honour, 'Bintang Republik Indonesia Adipurna' by H.E. President of The Republic of Indonesia	393

Forewords

Fr Frank Brennan SJ AO

This is the third volume of Xanana Gusmão's collected speeches, and yet as he reminds one of his many university audiences, he never attended university. The reader needs to remember that this orator won the Timor poetry prize as a young man. His poetic flourishes are still evident even in his formal prime ministerial prose. Reflecting on how Nehru in 1947 had issued the challenge to Asia and the Far East to face up to the new economic challenges, Gusmão recalls, 'I have to say, in 1947, I was 1 year old, and my people were trying to dry out the tears of the devastation of the Second World War'.

This volume contains speeches from 2011-2014, mostly those delivered in his second term as prime minister. Here we read the deliberations of the mature statesman who has developed a deep perspective on his nation's history and struggle, together with a reconciled understanding of his own battles as a guerrilla leader, emerging politician and then role model for his people. At the time of Nelson Mandela's death he recalls how Mandela gave hope 'in Timor-Leste's darkest moments in our struggle for liberation, as we were fighting in the mountains and the valleys of our homeland'. Looking back almost 500 years to the arrival of the Portuguese in 1515, he rejoices in 'this meeting of civilisation and cultures that shaped the destiny of a People, a country and a nation – with a history and a culture that are unique in the region'.

Embracing the mantra, 'Good-bye Conflict, Welcome Development', he constantly asks his people to face the continuing challenges of the newly independent Timor-Leste which is one of the UN's 49 least developed countries and one of the World Bank's 30 fragile states on their critical list. He is rightly proud that there has been 11.9% economic growth per annum since 2007, with life expectancy increasing from 35 years to 63 years in just 32 years. But he keeps reminding his people that there is so much more to be done to lift the country out of abject poverty and to provide basic health, housing and education for all.

In many speeches he outlines his government's bold vision for economic development, including the responsible exploitation of oil and gas reserves which are rightly theirs. But he does not shy away from what a poison chalice oil has been for other developing countries which have failed to develop other industries and to build other needed infrastructure. Reflecting on state building for the next decade, he reminds development partners: 'In many parts of the world some countries, with enormous reserves of natural resources (exploited by multinationals), face serious problems of fragility and insecurity, when their resources could make them viable and economically sustainable. It is a pity that after so many dozens of years, the international community has still not managed to resolve the root problems of those countries and instead maintains their fragility.'

Gusmão outlines his vision for getting right the international settings, as well as domestic governance. He has pioneered Timor-Leste's full compliance with the Extractive Industries Transparency Initiative. He has travelled the region constantly putting Timor-Leste's case for ASEAN membership. He has led the g7+ initiative which brings together the governments of 20 countries which have been affected by conflict and which are now in the next stage of development. Fulfilling his g7+ responsibilities, he delivers speeches in countries as various as Haiti and South Sudan calling everyone to their finest instincts of service for those in desperate need.

While lamenting Timor-Leste's failure to match the 2015 Millennium Development Goals, he is proud that Emilia Pires is serving as a member of a high level panel of the UN discerning how to move the international community to embrace the post-2015 goals. Insisting that Timor-Leste give back to the international community after what it has received in recent years, he joyfully espouses the role of José Ramos-Horta as special representative for the Secretary General of the UN in Guinea-Bissau. He concedes, 'It may seem strange that Timor-Leste, one of the poorest nations in the world, is providing aid to Guinea-Bissau but we remember the generosity of the many nations around the world that supported our nation as we started on the path to peace and stability. And we know that democracy is worth the investment.'

Having been a guerrilla fighter against the Indonesians and having been their political prisoner, he is the embodiment of reconciliation in his relationship with, and genuine affection, for President Yodhoyono. Speaking in South Korea, he told the World Summit on Peace, Security and Human Development: 'More than a close neighbour, Indonesia is an inspiration for our Nation. Under the wise leadership of His Excellency Susilio Bambang Yudhoyono, we witnessed the construction of a modern democracy that encompasses progress and the promotion of peace at national, regional and international level. We wish that the peaceful transition to President Joko Widodo will contribute to the success of this great nation.'

Gusmão does not disguise his disappointments and frustrations with Australia. But he delights in the reported observation of Julie Bishop: 'The best is yet to come'. While adversely contrasting Australia's behaviour with that of Singapore when Indonesia invaded East Timor, he nonetheless builds on the abundant good will first expressed and shared during World War II and consolidated by all that Australia has contributed since independence. Gusmão, the gracious warrior and the mature statesman, is at his best when he addresses the Australian SAS Charity Dinner in Perth. He honestly expresses the betrayal and hurt caused by Australia's support for the Indonesian occupation in 1975 just 32 years after 60,000 Timorese had been killed by the Japanese for standing by the Australians of the 2/2nd and 2/4th Independent Companies. He speaks personally about the courage and dedication of the SAS who were at his people's side after the chaos following the 1999 vote for independence: 'We will always remember that, at this very difficult time, when we were taking our first steps as a free people, the SAS and the Australian Defence Forces were with us'.

These are the writings and speeches of a reconciler who has fought the good fight and of a nation's founder who has given his all to the next, more difficult stage of national development and growth. He does it with grace and simplicity as when he tells yet another group of high level investors visiting Díli to return home to work on their mutually agreed projects 'stimulated by the best coffee in the world, our coffee!' May these speeches long inspire those committed to 'Ba dame' – opting for peace, and to working for the development and human dignity of all persons including those in the least developed countries and in fragile states.

Fr Frank Brennan SJ AO
14 September 2014

Major General Mick Slater

The wisdom and experience of a soldier, a diplomat and a statesman fill the speeches made by Xanana Gusmão throughout his public life. This volume contains many of his significant addresses from the period 2010 to 2012 and evidence of his clarity of vision and strength of commitment is abundant in every message that he has delivered. He has been acclaimed on stages from the villages in his struggling country of Timor-Leste to the United Nations. He has brought conflicting groups together to resolve their differences, provided reasoned guidance on political and economic developments and contributed to international stability and progress.

Readers will observe in this volume how one man's tremendous love of country fires his passion and drives his thinking. His public appearances have, since 1999 been positive and optimistic, giving hope and confidence to a society suffering the growing pangs of early nationhood.

Throughout his public life Xanana Gusmão, in the period covered by these speeches, campaigned for growth and cooperation in the areas of social, economic, institutional and regional stability. His accumulated life experience gained from an austere childhood, time in prison, human rights activistism and political leadership have taught him the value and necessity of inclusiveness when uniting people. Whether in small villages or on national or international stages he has urged understanding, cooperation and at times forgiveness to ensure that all people's views, needs and voices are heard and considered. Wisely he has demonstrated the need for understanding and unity if solutions to social and political problems are to be found. His words are skillfully crafted to bring people together, break down barriers and provide an atmosphere to look forward to a better future for all people. He does not see a future where people are divided between "Haves and Have Nots."

For those fortunate enough to have heard these speeches and others who now read them, Xanana Gusmão is heard to describe in detail the support provided to his country from the international community. He strategically acknowledges and thanks other countries for this costly support and contribution to the success of Timor-Leste. He consciously avoids claiming personal or even national level Timor-Leste responsibility for the success of his country since 1999. Further, he gives many examples of where the people, Government and other public institutions have stumbled along the way to becoming a self-reliant democratic society. Along with optimism, the perennial theme of acknowledging others who have supported along with his society's failures can teach some indispensable lessons to anyone who aspires to become a uniting leader.

Xanana Gusmão has stood strongly but gently on many international stages where his influence has reached well beyond the shores of his beloved Timor-Leste. He has used the trauma, suffering and success of his small country to inspire more influential audiences to listen and to think differently and work more cooperatively with each other to resolve international problems.

Unfortunately, this book cannot showcase the raw strength of commitment, passion and deep emotion that are always the foundation of an address by Xanana Gusmão where crowds in their thousands stand silently mesmerized, hanging on his every word or are applauding and yelling at the top of their voices 'Xanana Xanana Xanana...'

Major General Mick Slater AO, DSC, CSC

Meeting with the people as Prime Minister in May 2010
when travelling amongst the villages of Timor-Leste.

With good friend, former President of the Republic of Indonesia, H.E. Susilo Bambang Yudhoyono, on a visit to Indonesia, 22nd March, 2011.

With the President of the People's Republic of China, H.E. Xi Jinping in Bejing, China, 8th April 2014.

Leaving the g7+ High Level Side Event at the United Nations in New York City after leading the panel with the President of Liberia, H.E. Ellen Johnson Sirleaf, 26th September 2012.

Celebrating with the children of Malou Village in Jonglei State, Bor County, Republic of South Sudan, 4th December 2013.

Meeting with Governor-General of Australia, His Excellency General the Honourable Sir Peter Cosgrove AK MC (Ret'd), at the INTERFET 15th Anniversary Conference, Melbourne, September 2014.

Press conference with then US Secretary of State Hillary Rodham Clinton at the State Department, Washington DC, February 24, 2011.

A Fighter Who Fell

High on the mountain peaks of Timor
The grass grows
And warms the fractured bones
Of a fighter who fell

Down on the grassy plains of Timor
A flower shows
And beautifies the bones
Of a fighter who fell

This is the hopeful life that grows
From life's release
The life that every woman knows
Who calls for peace
With every waking breath
But not the peace of death

Throughout the peaks and plains of Timor
The life-blood flows
And animates the bones
Of the fighters who fell

Xanana Gusmão
English translation by Agio Pereira & Rob Wesley-Smith; versification by Peter Wesley-Smith

Grandfather Crocodile

For Marta B. Neves, Lisbon

The legend says
and who am I to disbelieve!

The sun perched atop the sea
opened its eyes
and with its rays
indicated a way

From the depths of the ocean
a crocodile in search of a destiny
spied the pool of light, and there he surfaced

Then wearily, he stretched himself out
in time
and his lumpy hide was transformed
into a mountain range
where people were born
and where people died

Grandfather crocodile

— the legend says
and who am I to disbelieve
that he is Timor!

Xanana Gusmão
English translation by Kirsty Sword & Ana Luisa Amaral

These speeches were compiled and published when His Excellency Xanana Gusmão was Prime Minister of the Democratic Republic of Timor-Leste and comprises the speeches given during the IV and V Constitutional Governments.

His Excellency announced his resignation as Prime Minister on 6 February 2015.

IV Constitutional Government

Bali Democracy Forum IV – 'Enhancing Democratic Participation in a Changing World: Responding to Democratic Voices'

Nusa Dua, Bali, 8 December 2011

Your Excellency the President of the Republic of Indonesia, Dr Susilo Bambang Yudhoyono

Your Excellency, the Co-Chair, the Prime Minister of the People's Republic of Bangladesh, Sheikh Hasina Wajed

Your Excellencies the Heads of State and Government

Distinguished Participants

Ladies and Gentlemen,

I must again give praise, Mr President, for the persistence and dedication that you have shown to this noble cause.

Those of us that for the last four years have witnessed the growing participation, and the increasing intensity and depth of discussions, at the annual Bali Democracy Forum must congratulate its organisers, the Institute for Peace and Democracy.

It is a great honour for me to be once again side by side with my dear friend the President of Indonesia, Dr Susilo Bambang Yudhoyono, and to be able to contribute to a future of democracy, freedom and dignity in our region.

As the world's third largest democracy and with a huge emerging economy, Indonesia's pragmatic outlook and national vision is becoming an important international reference. Timor-Leste is inspired by this neighbour's growth and its promotion of a successful democracy.

The history of Timor-Leste will be forever connected with that of Indonesia. The victory of democracy and of the democratic voices of our people, have helped shape not only our nations but our region of South East Asia.

It was in 1999 that the democratic voices finally started to be heard. The Indonesian people and the Timorese people began together a new chapter – when they voted for democracy, they voted for respect for human rights, they voted for freedom and they voted for social and economic development.

Today's times give us confidence in important initiatives such as this Forum. As I said at the Third BDF, it is these meetings that stimulate reflection, encourage dialogue ... and lead to change.

The year of 2011 will be recorded in history, written in many languages and with different narratives.

Ladies and Gentlemen,

Every day we see crowds of people agitating with feverish passion and enthusiasm for the profound changes taking place in the world.

We see other groups, however, expressing their despair with a world facing enormous challenges and we feel suffocated by these emotions and feelings.

There is something wrong in all of this.

We see victories achieved through the might of weapons, we see the despair of hunger, we see post-election violence, we see veiled threats at the polls, we see fear in the faces of people living with the presence of foreign troops, we see repression of peaceful demonstrators by police in democratic countries, we see world leaders powerless to find a solution for our economic and environmental problems, we see leaders from developing countries holding absolute power, we see intransigency in postures that dignify no one.

And no one is pleased with this imbalance of values. There is something wrong in all of this.

It turns out that, after all, the world is not changing. The world is saturated with problems that world leaders have always avoided rather than tackled. It is People that are trying to change the world, while leaders refuse to heed their demands.

World leaders believe they represent the views of their people when they proclaim so-called 'national interest' as if they were representing the real national interests of the people.

In this way, the leaders of many countries believe that their own interests are also the interests of the people they rule, if not oppress.

World problems are systemic, after all. Most of humanity remains illiterate, barefoot, ignorant of their rights, homeless and living in misery.

Universal standards, criteria and human rights are introduced as ends in themselves, as if selling cheap products from the civilized world and those who do not purchase them are shunned as not being part of the group of well behaved children, as measured by indicators set by experts who live in skyscrapers and work for CEOs.

Elections are proclaimed as ends in themselves; and then we watch an Italian model of non-elected government composed of technocrats and another government simply tailored with a Greek suit which offend common standards and sensitivities that would, if occurring in a developing country, be considered unpalatable and raise human rights hackles everywhere from Brussels to Geneva, from the capitals of democracy to the Security Council in New York.

We are witnessing an orchestra playing without a conductor, as no one is able to pick up the baton. And the problem is not political or economic or even social. This is a problem of the system.

There is something wrong in all of this, and no one wants to take the blame.

We are at a particular conjuncture where it is much easier to make small repairs than to promote long term solutions. It is much easier to demand from others that are weaker and poorer than to demand from one self.

The result of this is an accumulation of contradictions and problems which are becoming unsolvable, and this affects everyone. In every summit... of the powerful, solutions are always 'too little' and, in the end, we all reach the conclusion that it is all 'too late'. And this is making people truly exasperated!

And in their speeches they bring the same tone of doubt, of distrust, of rivalry – with a mix of politics, economics and ideology, of human rights and supremacy, of trade and security, of intelligence and defence, all in a desperate search for justifications to impose upon others.

The mentality of the Cold War will continue to be the main obstacle in this Millennium.

Ladies and Gentlemen

But let us talk of ourselves, because we need to take care of ourselves.

Allow me to say a few words on the interaction of the concept of 'democratic participation'.

I will divide this in two levels, as the Institute for Peace and Democracy has done so well.

One of the fundamental problems of developing countries is the State building process. This process is vital for the establishment of a multi-party constitutional system, with properly defined checks and balances, with clear medium and long term plans that, with well prepared human resources, are guaranteed to be implemented, and with all the necessary conditions to enable effective performance delivery.

Only a gradual but efficient implementation of a well designed plan can inspire trust in society and give governance credibility.

The State must legislate to ensure the transparency of its acts and the accountability of public accounts, which can be viewed by all. This is the only way for citizens to have confidence in the future of the Nation.

Technology provides the means for the State to assist society in the monitoring of government at all times, through the use of internet based transparency portals which include procurement, revenue, State budget execution and project implementation websites.

This is the way in which we can ensure good governance.

On the other hand, there is a need to balance the demands of society with the responses by the State.

This is the challenge of leadership in setting action plans and the challenge between understanding the totality of the needs of the country and the demands of its parts, so that there can be consensual acceptance of the annual programs of government according to national and sector priorities.

Civil society must have an overall understanding of the problems of the country and of the effort made by the State if it is to make a constructive contribution and a critical interpretation of the acts undertaken by leaders and undertake a mediating role instead of a disruptive one that would distort democracy.

The challenge ahead of us is how to change the mentality of our societies, which are fond of copying models from highly industrialized countries and supposed role models of democracy.

In changing mentalities in our societies, it is important to clarify that duties and rights go hand in hand. Citizenship is a coin with two sides: rights and duties. In young democracies it is common for people to focus on rights and to forget that they also have the duty to do something positive for the country, without demanding extra benefits from the State.

I believe that the substance of democratic participation by the State and by society is as follows:

- Collective responsibilities towards the Nation, in terms of commitments and duties;
- National Reconciliation, in the search for truth, tolerance and peace;
- A critical society under a constructive ideal, in the collective search for solutions and defending national identity;
- Safeguarding national interests, without gross chauvinism or deceitful alienations.

In young democracies, people in society tend to consider themselves 'independent', that is operating 'outside the State', in the sense that they are more of an activist than they are a citizen, or better yet, that they are the citizens of the international organisations that pay them so handsomely, and defend them so well, rather than a citizen defending their own country.

We also have the opposite phenomenon, where false nationalism feeds a feeling of unbridled aversion to that which is foreign, sometimes for no valid reason at all, merely to cover up the lack of a mature national perspective in regard to the social and economic development of the country. In short, through such attitudes, they attempt to cover up the lack of political development.

Ladies and Gentlemen

These are the lessons we are taking from the world's 50 Least Developed Countries and from the g7+ group that fragile nations established and which represents over 350 million people who live in a situation of political, social and economic fragility.

The true challenge is in our hands, in each of our countries, in each of our societies, in each of our peoples. Most of all, the challenge is in the hands of the country leaders, which can make their countries either stronger or weaker.

We need to be the agents of our own processes. A process is only genuine and able to produce positive results, in the medium and long term, if it is promoted mainly by internal factors. Whenever a process is led from outside it invariably suffers uncontrollable convulsions and distortions, causing much more damage than gain.

Across the world there are 1.5 billion people living in States that are fragile and affected by conflicts. Over 70% of these fragile States have been enduring conflict since 1989.

30% of International Aid (ODA) is provided towards fragile States, and yet they are very far from meeting the MDG targets for 2015.

Consequently, Mr President,

While Indonesia is leading, with courage and conviction, the concept of relationship between 'democracy and development', Timor-Leste is leading the relationship between 'Peace building' and 'State building'.

As I have announced at this Forum previously, Timor-Leste co-chaired the First International Dialogue on 'Peace building and State building' which took place in Díli, in 2010, as well as the second Dialogue which was held in Monrovia, Liberia, in 2011.

Along with this International Dialogue, the g7+ group is also a space for fragile States (a term not appreciated by some) to share experiences and be heard as one voice by the international community, in a collective attempt to build States, build Democracies and build Peace.

Timor-Leste is proud of its leadership and establishment of the g7+ as a permanent forum. For a small and young Nation, being able to participate in the consolidation of this group and to give voice to States that by themselves would be voiceless is also giving expression to democracy.

We started as a group of 7 countries that, when coming together to discuss issues related to Good International Engagement in Fragile States and Situations, found that despite coming from different contexts and continents and having different languages and cultures, we had the same types of challenges.

Currently we represent 19 countries, after the recent admissions of Equatorial Guinea and Togo, which discuss amongst ourselves and with international donors to improve the principles for good international engagement in regard to development assistance.

Recently I had the opportunity to visit Juba, on the occasion of the g7+ Inter-Ministerial Retreat. When we arrived, the Southern Sudanese were reflecting on their first 100 days as an independent State, happy to be able to so soon host an international event that would also discuss their State building challenges.

Let us have no illusions – for countries that have to deal with poverty, instability and violent conflicts, taking charge of their own development is no easy task. The people that suffer yearn for democracy because they believe it will mitigate their suffering. The benefits of democracy, however, take time to be reaped.

The democratic formulas of the West do not always work when carbon copied to other countries. And furthermore, the democratic experience of developed countries is not always appropriate to fragile States. These are countries traumatised by war and devastated by poverty, often instigated by interests of economic supremacy.

Additionally, international aid has always followed unacceptably strict criteria and 'one size fits all' standards. Democratic values are universal; however, the specific circumstances of each country and the manner in which those values are assimilated are individual. It is necessary to consider the historical, social and cultural context of each country before attempting to implement a development program, without ever losing sight of human dignity.

For poor countries, aid is often a matter of survival – lives depend on that aid!

Still, the debate on international aid is almost as old as the debate on democracy. International aid and lessons of democracy from developed countries go hand in hand almost every time, but, nevertheless, thousands of people remain in poverty. Sometimes, if not most times, when a large volume of aid comes close to the population of a country it becomes poorer than before the arrival of that aid.

Poor countries are accused of corruption and blamed for international failures. However, do rich countries have effective mechanisms of transparency and accountability for the failure of international aid?

It will be difficult to meet the Millennium Development Goals for 2015. Donor countries feel frustrated and I believe that their taxpayers question the amounts channelled into international aid when, during this time of global economic crisis, those very taxpayers are enduring hardship.

These are all the issues that should be discussed within the scope of democracy.

For all this I say: fighting poverty, hunger, disease and ignorance is promoting democracy!

And I will add: promoting peace and promoting a more active and understanding international diplomacy is investing in the democratic process at a global level. Here I would like to commend the US Secretary of Defence, Luis Panetta, when he urges

Israel to break its auto-isolationism and to sit at the table with its neighbours... to talk... for the good of humanity! It is high time for us all to honour universal values with the same commitment!

Your Excellencies

Ladies and Gentlemen,

Last week, at the opening session of the Fourth International Forum on International Aid Effectiveness, held in Busan, South Korea, the Secretary General of the United Nations said that international aid is not charity but rather an intelligent investment in security and prosperity.

I agree. And as a result of the Juba Inter-Ministerial Retreat the g7+ presented, in Busan, its New Deal for Engagement in Fragile States. 34 countries and international agencies immediately endorsed this New Deal.

This is an important landmark in the relationship between fragile States and partner organisations. This is an honest attempt to understand better the challenges inherent in post-conflict and fragile countries when pursuing development goals. Therefore, in order to achieve the MDGs, Fragile States will have a period of transition through the PSGs (Peace building and State building Goals).

The New Deal gives new hope in terms of achieving the MDGs. With the New Deal there is a new focus on sustainable development for these fragile countries, under their ownership and with confidence in new commitments to achieve greater transparency, internal capacity and management to enable better international aid outcomes.

This is also democracy – in the true sense of the word – in action.

As Timor-Leste is Chair of the g7+, I will be distributing copies of the New Deal for all countries in attendance. I would also like to seize this opportunity to urge you all to give us your support, in September 2012, when we will be taking the 5 PSGs to the General Assembly of the United Nations. These 5 PSGs are:

- Legitimate politics
- Security
- Justice
- Economic Foundations
- Revenue and Services

Your Excellency Mr President

Your Excellencies

Ladies and Gentlemen

The world in which we live is seriously threatened.

Signs are emerging of the eminent threat of climate change.

From the fires in Australia, to the floods in Thailand and the rising sea levels threatening the very existence of some Pacific islands, nature is trying to warn humanity that it needs to take urgent measures.

Natural disasters are testing the world's people as we saw with the earthquake and tsunami in Japan, the earthquake in Christchurch, New Zealand and the very recent ones in Turkey.

Unfortunately, for all that has not been done following Kyoto, Copenhagen and Cancun, it seems that Durban is without hope, as noted by the UN Secretary-General yesterday.

Furthermore, the serious threats of terrorism, illegal immigration in frightening numbers, trafficking of persons, drugs and weapons, the global economic crisis, the search for limited food and energy resources, the proliferation of nuclear weapons – among other threats – can lead to conflict and to global insecurity.

Now, more than ever, we need strategic cooperation, dialogue and alliances to undertake intervention. These alliances should not and cannot be constrained by the strategic interests of the major powers. Instead, they must serve the fundamental interests of humanity.

We need new alliances to make peace and not old alliances to wage war. We need a new political and economic world order in which conflicts and discord are replaced with dialogue; in which democracy is used to give voice to the weak and the vulnerable; and in which assistance and solidarity are used correctly to mitigate peoples suffering.

This is the message that must be conveyed to the world's nations, particularly the poorer and weaker ones, so that they can have faith in democracy.

Thank you very much.

IV Constitutional Government

Opening of the Forum on Inclusive Growth

Díli, 6 February 2012

Your Excellencies
Illustrious guests
Ladies and Gentlemen,

It is with great satisfaction that I take part in the opening of the Forum on Inclusive Growth, which is the result of a close partnership between the Ministry of Economy and Development and the United Nations Development Programme, as well as other development partners and donors.

As the Minister of Economy and Development has just stated, this Forum represents a remarkable effort to bring together the cooperative sector, local private sector agents, businesspeople, national legislators, civil society representatives and development partners, enabling a productive exchange of knowledge and experience. This stimulates entrepreneurship and increases productivity, making way for inclusive economic growth.

This Forum has significant international importance and could not have come at a better time, since it coincides with the International Year of Cooperatives. This sector, which has an important role in terms of poverty reduction, employment creation and social integration, is also acknowledged by our Constitution as being vital to the economic organisation of the State, along with the private and public sectors.

I see today representatives from countries as far as Brazil, but also from neighbours such as Malaysia, the Philippines and Indonesia. I see as well representatives from micro, small and medium companies and cooperatives that manage their economic activities according to best practises.

We are very happy to receive you all in our country and to be able to share with you what we have already achieved. We are also looking forward to learning from your experience.

Ladies and Gentlemen,

Last year we presented our *Strategic Development Plan*, which seeks to create a strong and prosperous economy that enables our citizens to continually improve their living situation.

This can only be done if we succeed in involving the entire Timorese community in the development process and if its benefits are shared equally by all. In other words, our Nation's growth must be inclusive.

I do believe we are on the right path!

Our motto '*Goodbye Conflict, Welcome Development*' has been met by an atmosphere of trust and optimism – a result of the 'unprecedented economic growth' in the past four years.

The reforms we introduced, along with an increase in public investment, enabled Timor-Leste to present in 2008 and 2009 the highest economic growth rates not only in the region but in the entire world, at around 12.7% and 12.9% respectively, despite the serious global financial crisis.

2011 has just ended, and as we start 2012 I can say that we have a clear perspective of what we can become in 20 years – a Nation that is strong and prosperous, in accordance with the *Strategic Development Plan*, that belongs to and was accepted by our people.

Ladies and Gentlemen,

The *Strategic Development Plan* provides an accurate picture of the state of the Nation, as well as an objective understanding of the challenges ahead of us in the various areas of the country. As such, I am certain that this Plan is one of the key tools that will enable us to grow. I do believe that today the Timorese Nation meets the basic requirements to build the momentum we require.

We have a credible document to identify challenges, assess priorities and understand the necessary strategies and the consequent actions resulting from the adoption of policies, both at global and sector level.

In the centre of the *Strategic Development Plan* stand the Timorese men and women. It is around them that all our considerations, strategies and actions revolve. The People are the greatest wealth of our Nation, which is why we must invest in them in order for Timor-Leste to move forward. This means that we must provide the People with conditions to evolve in terms of their practises and behaviours, their knowledge and their adaptation to the new technologies needed for their development. Learned and healthy People, with strong principles and ideals, make up a strong and dynamic State and a prosperous and modern Nation.

Ladies and Gentlemen,

Over two days we will be discussing the importance of inclusive growth in other words, the importance of a type of growth that implies the participation by all in the growth process and the participation by all in the sharing of the benefits resulting from that growth.

Chapter 4 of the *Strategic Development Plan* concerns Economic Development and stresses that modernising and diversifying a mostly agriculture-based economy is essential for creating economic opportunities for all the people in Timor-Leste, particularly those residing in rural areas.

There is no doubt that the country must grow economically in order for society to enjoy those benefits. My question then is this: what is the best way for our country to grow without having to deal with the excesses, deviations and constraints felt by other countries?

I believe that the answer to this is focusing on a sustainable development model that is based on inclusive economic growth. This must necessarily entail giving priority to the development of rural areas.

70% of the Timorese population live in rural areas! It is in rural areas that people take the longest to feel the benefits of growth! It is in rural areas that people have the most difficulty in terms of having access to education, drinkable water, basic health care, food and power.

It is also in rural areas that it is the most difficult to implement the Millennium Development Goals, as the wants at several levels are obstacles to development.

However, Timor-Leste has the means to correct this situation!

As is public, the First and Second Development Programmes are already being applied, along with Local Development Programmes focusing on the construction of core infrastructure, on supporting the development of micro, small and medium companies and on the ongoing creation of cooperatives. This has enabled communities to conduct their own business activities, generating employment and vitality within them.

Around $44.3 million were invested in 2011 to fund small infrastructures and to encourage the growth of several construction companies in the districts, sub-districts, sucos and villages of the country, thereby benefiting a significant percentage of the population.

However, sustainable rural development must also take into consideration commercial and subsistence agriculture, continuing to assist farmers with training and extension of new cultivation and treatment techniques, as well as in the rehabilitation and expansion of irrigation systems.

As several studies show, family agriculture is vital to the nutrition of rural communities and is determinant to reduce poverty in the districts.

Ladies and Gentlemen,

It is also necessary to identify agricultural production and forest conservation areas, in parallel with the approval of policies encouraging agricultural exploitation within a commercial perspective. These policies must focus on activities that are adapted to the natural conditions of the district, developing activities that add value and generate employment.

These policies must also promote vocational and specialised training, so as to respond to the needs of our companies represented here today at this forum.

In terms of agricultural production, we conducted an exhaustive survey on the cultivation conditions of staple foods such as rice, corn, cassava, potatoes, beans and vegetables, as well as on the potential of cash crops such as coffee, coconuts, cashew nuts, nutmeg, vanilla, peanuts, etc. We did not neglect Timor-Leste's potential regarding the production of fruit, namely for internal consumption, which will enable us to substitute imports.

This study will serve as a guide for future strategies and actions, both in the identification and expansion of production zones as in what regards systems to support farmers in the use of improve technologies, financial advisory and produce trading assistance.

The sector of livestock has also deserved and continues to deserve due attention. Radical changes are required in terms of breeding habits and training actions are required in order to implement basic animal care and to introduce new practices enabling domestic production of meat and its derivatives, thereby reducing importing needs.

As an island State, Timor-Leste must seize the fishing potential and the wealth provided by the sea. The need to perfect coastal fisheries and the definition of a training and capacity building strategy for offshore fishing will therefore be determinant to nurture the industry, create employment and diversify eating habits.

It is also important to take into account ecological, marine, historical and cultural tourism, as Timor-Leste is one of the most attractive nations of Southeast Asia in terms of enjoying nature untouched by human hands.

In order to have food security, to reduce unemployment and poverty and to achieve harmonious and balanced development in both urban and rural areas it is necessary to involve rural communities in the sectors of agriculture, livestock, fisheries and tourism, where we have great potential.

Involving rural communities is consequently essential for implementing inclusive and sustainable economic development in our Nation.

Ladies and Gentlemen,

The economic growth we want for our country can only be achieved by strengthening micro, small and medium companies and by making our social companies and cooperatives sounder.

The growth we need can only be achieved if we have a sound private sector that complies with the good business practises and that is able to generate wealth outside the structures of the State, thereby nurturing and diversifying the economy and promoting the capacity building of the Timorese citizens.

Consequently the Government has been carrying out several promising activities to support the private sector of the economy. For instance, the National Directorate of Cooperatives, in collaboration with the Institute for Business Support, the Secretariat of State for Professional Training, the Ministry of Agriculture and Fisheries and the Ministry of Tourism, Trade and Industry, has conducted different specialised training, actions to promote and develop the market and diversified business training to micro, small and medium companies.

The microfinance programmes that are vital to the success of any private initiative are becoming increasingly available, not only through credit companies but also through nongovernmental organizations like *Moris Rasik* and *Tuba Rai Metin*, both of which are close to becoming financial agencies.

The former Microfinance Institute of Timor-Leste has recently become the National Commercial Bank of Timor-Leste. This agency is directly dedicated to funding micro, small and medium companies.

In view of all this, I believe that the efforts we have been making in the past few years enable us to look to the future with confidence.

We are sowing seeds! We are watering the land! And very soon we will be collecting the fruits of our labour, which will benefit all Timorese citizens!

I now declare the Forum on Inclusive Growth to be open, trusting that it will give us the opportunity to further learn from the experiences of other countries.

Thank you very much.

Opening of the Conference '10 Years On: The Contribution of Social Programmes to the Construction of the Social State in Timor-Leste'

Díli, 16 February 2012

Your Excellencies
Illustrious Guests
Ladies and Gentlemen,

First and foremost, I must congratulate the Minister of Social Solidarity and her team for their excellent initiative in organising this Conference on the contribution of social programmes to the construction of a Social State. This is a very important topic for Timor-Leste.

It was a relatively short time ago that we gained our National Sovereignty and Independence. It was only twelve years ago that we closed a tragic chapter in our history in which many lives were lost and our society was left with deep scars.

Despite having affirmed the dignity and spirit of the Timorese, the period of war we endured in the recent past left many widows, orphans and disabled, as well as many veterans and elderly people who dedicated their lives to the cause of national liberation. They are disadvantaged today because they didn't have the chance to fight to improve their lives and the lives of their families.

It is exactly because of this that Timor-Leste could never, under any circumstance, create a State other than a Social State!

Ladies and Gentlemen,

In this last decade, and despite the heavy burden we inherited, starting without basic infrastructure, skilled human resources, financial resources of our own, democratic institutions or even any institutional memory, we have succeeded in creating a Democratic State and consolidating the Timorese Nation!

Only ten years on, we can be proud of the considerable progress we have made on many fronts – political, social, economic and diplomatic. Despite some serious failures and setbacks, throughout this Statebuilding phase we never turned down a challenge, we never stopped trying to do more. Little by little, and with great resilience, we have been learning and growing as a Nation.

We have learned from our People that difficult times must be overcome with cohesion, getting all parties – State, Church, NGOs, private sector and Civil Society – involved. Essential to building a Social State in Timor-Leste is democratic participation, so that we may find ways to build social inclusion and protect our most vulnerable citizens.

In pursuing the national development mission, the Government gives priority to social protection policies.

As we grow economically, thanks in part to our natural resource reserves, we must distribute our wealth to those who need it the most.

This is about giving dignity to those who gave us freedom.

This is about protecting Timorese families still living in borderline poverty.

This is about responding to humanitarian emergency situations, as we also have to face the effects of global climate change or, as it unfortunately happened in 2006, having just left behind a post-conflict situation, we had to adopt a policy of recovery on a grand scale.

The social protection programmes implemented by the Ministry of Social Solidarity have been vital in achieving these goals.

In this still early stage of Country building, our social programmes have mitigated extreme poverty for a fragile sector of our population and protected those must vulnerable. In a rather modest way, they have also contributed to nurturing the economy, as supporting households creates possibilities of entrepreneurship which has led to many small businesses being formed throughout the Country.

Your Excellencies

Ladies and Gentlemen,

In order to build a true Social State, we must further strengthen the Government's pro-poor policies. Not only by continuing to provide social support to those most vulnerable, particularly the elderly, women, children at risk, the disabled but also by creating a sound basis for Social Protection, attuned to our demographic, economic and administrative, legal, social and cultural reality.

In order to enable this we are developing a proper legal basis and efficient mechanisms where Timorese citizens are held accountable but where they are also provided with different options. Here we must take into account the sustainability of the system, as we have to foresee medium and long-term impacts.

We believe that building a Social State, a State that values citizenship, is not transforming our society into two classes: one of beggars and another of taxpayers!

The Social State is not a charity State but rather a State that takes action in society, by developing social protection systems to ensure individual protection. At the same time, it creates the necessary conditions for the poorest citizens to free themselves from poverty with dignity.

This requires a thorough joint assessment of the possible solutions for social inequality, as well as direct involvement by people in need, to try and find a way out of poverty. These people must be involved in choosing the paths they will take towards prosperity, with a participative and responsible attitude toward living in society.

The participation and contribution by all against the tragedy of poverty are the cornerstones of a democratic culture. Only with collective accountability and a sense of citizenship can we develop our Country in economic, social and human terms.

I believe that the general principles that Timor-Leste intends to follow are basic and universal:

- Access to social protection by all citizens;
- Equality and non-discrimination;
- Equity, that is ensuring equal treatment in like situations and different treatment in dissimilar situations;
- Balance in policies developed by the State and in actions carried out together with Civil Society;
- And lastly social inclusion, fighting the causes of marginalization and social exclusion and promoting the ability of people to have socially active lives.

As for this last item, we must start paying more attention to our youngsters who, due to a legacy of violence and distrust, may not yet have embraced the genuine values of citizenship. Additionally, because they are already facing the adversities of unemployment and idleness, youngsters may easily become at risk.

This is why I say that the creation of a Social State is a rather complex issue. Social policies must be strategically linked to other sector development policies.

Your Excellencies

Ladies and Gentlemen,

I trust that this Conference will provide us with feasible solutions for creating a Social State. I urge you to reflect on the most adequate ways to arrive at these solutions, as well as to better assess and apply lessons learned and to refrain from repeating errors of the past. This will be important so that we can strengthen existing programmes and draft new ones.

In the 2011-2030 *Strategic Development Plan* we designed some strategies and actions for the future, recognizing that: 'The true wealth of any Nation is the strength of its people. Maximizing the overall health, education and living quality of the Timorese people is essential to have a fair and developed Nation'. This is what I consider to be the definition of a Social State, and this is the vision that I have, and I believe all of you have, for Timor-Leste.

This commitment creates many financial, social and cultural challenges; however, we all know that one aspect of a strong, cohesive and progressive Nation is the ability to protect the rights and interests of its most vulnerable citizens.

To conclude, ladies and gentlemen, I must thank those who have come from afar to take part in this conference and to contribute to the development of a Social Protection System that is fair and adequate for our society.

Regarding international solidarity, we have been fortunate to be able to rely on the selfless assistance of several countries and citizens from around the world. As the recipient of international donations for these past ten years, we have an even greater obligation to implement truly effective systems in Timor-Leste that ensure social protection and support the development of Timorese citizens.

If we fail in providing better living conditions for all Timorese citizens, we will have failed in our Independence ideal.

Thank you very much.

Opening of the Timor 1942 Exhibition at the Anzac Memorial, Hyde Park, Sydney

Sydney, 19 February 2012

New South Wales Minister for Sport and Recreation, Graham Annesley
Barry Grant, President, Commando Association of Australia, NSW
Darren Mitchell, Director Office of Veteran's Affairs
Veterans and their families
It is a pleasure to be here with you today to open this Exhibition.
Thank you Minister Annesley for your words of solidarity.

Yesterday I was in Canberra for a meeting with the Australian Prime Minister and we talked about our countries shared history in the 2nd World War.

It was a defining time in the relationship between the Timorese and Australians – but also a time in which nationality was transcended, and as human beings our people not only suffered deep pain, they also demonstrated acts of great altruism.

Today the Australian Prime Minister is in Darwin to take part in ceremonies commemorating the bombing of Darwin which started just before 10 am, on 19 February, 70 years ago today.

This was the first direct attack on Australian soil and has had a profound effect on the Australian psyche.

While the devastating extent of the bombing was kept secret from most of the Australian population at the time, the stories of despair and survival in Darwin are now embedded in the Australian national story.

What is still less well known, outside of Timor-Leste, is that at 10 o'clock that night 1,000 Japanese troops landed in Dili.

Australian troops had already been on the ground in then neutral Portuguese Timor, for some months. When the Japanese landed, the Australians found themselves fighting a war in difficult conditions, in the hills of our country. They showed great courage and spirit.

They were supported by Timorese people. Many Timorese volunteered to help the soldiers and, at great risk, they carried packs and ammunition, cooked for the troops, and fought alongside them.

This display of solidarity and humanity is a strong foundation for our shared history.

More than 50,000 Timorese lost their lives during World War II. This was a large part of our population and resulted in great hurt to our people. We must not forget this loss.

It has resulted in bonds of friendship and honour that have left an enduring legacy.

The Australian soldiers that fought in Timor during the War have continued to return to our homeland to maintain the friendship with our people, and to support our communities.

One such soldier that we all remember is of course Paddy Kenneally.

Paddy was a great friend of Timor. I was impressed, and touched, by the depth of his connection with Timor, and with his dear friend Rufino Alves Coresia who supported him during the war.

We miss both of these great characters in our shared history.

This connection, forged in war, has also helped the cause of Timor-Leste.

The former soldiers have worked to remind Australians of the support they received from the Timorese in the War, and in doing so have fostered goodwill between us that will last for generations to come.

This Exhibition is a memorial to the acts of goodwill and bravery that bonded humans together.

It showcases exhibits from the 2nd World War – and tells the stories of men and women in times of darkness, and highlight acts of courage and compassion.

In this way, it also acts as a reminder of the great costs of war and of conflict – and, therefore, encourages us to strive for peace.

It is important to remember.

Ladies and Gentlemen,

I trust that this Exhibition that we are opening today will remind us of the deep bonds forged between Australians and the Timorese during the 2nd World War.

Let us continue to honour their bravery and their sacrifice, through building on our shared values and our collective history.

I commend and thank the curators of the exhibition for undertaking this important project.

Thank you very much.

Australia Timor-Leste Business Council Reception

Sydney, 20 February 2012

Thank you Denis Fernandez for your inspiring words and your excellent work as President of the Australia Timor-Leste Business Council.

I'd also like to acknowledge:

H.E Secretary of State, Council of Ministers, H.E. Agio Perreira

H.E. Abel Guterres, Ambassador to Australia and New Zealand

H.E. Miles Armitage, Australia's Ambassador to Timor-Leste

Mr Barry Grant, President of the Commando Association of Australia

H.E. Estela Ferreira, Goodwill Ambassador for Timor-Leste

Representatives from the NSW Government

My very good friend Mr Jerry De Susa

And all the friends of Timor-Leste here with us tonight – thank you for coming.

I would like to thank the Council for organising this event and for its ongoing and strong support of business relationships between our two countries.

I am always pleased to address an Australia Timor-Leste Business Council event.

I did so in 2006 as President and in 2008 as Prime Minister.

Today, I am particularly pleased to be speaking to you.

Not only because it is good to be back in Sydney to meet with many friends who are here today.

But because today I have a brighter story to tell.

Some of you may have heard me speak in December 2006.

It was a terrible time.

In 2006 we tripped and fell. We became caught up in a terrible internal conflict, with widespread civil unrest, that tore at the fabric of our young nation.

At that time I did my best to encourage the business people who had showed faith in our nation.

But the reality was we had just began our process of State building and peace building and our institutions were very fragile.

The business environment in Timor-Leste was poor. We had out-dated and complex business processes, taxation systems and a lack of insurance.

When I spoke at an Australia Timor-Leste Business Council event in 2008 we were in a much better position.

We were making reforms to our State and its administration and we were building peace and security.

At that time I encouraged you all to make the most of the 'first mover advantage' and invest in Timor-Leste.

Looking back, 2008 was a perfect time to invest as Timor-Leste was emerging as a growing economy. Those with the vision and foresight to invest then would have been well rewarded.

And today, I am pleased to say, is an even better time to do business and invest in Timor-Leste.

It has been a long road to get where we are today but we have made much progress and we must not turn back, and we must not gamble with our future.

Ladies and Gentlemen,

In March this year, under the watchful eye of international election observers, we will have the first round of our Presidential elections.

And then in June the Timorese people will go to the polls to elect their next Parliament.

It is critical to our nation's future that we continue on our current path. We must not – and will not – go backwards.

So our fight now is different to our fight for independence, but no less passionate.

We are fortunate that our nation is blessed not only with natural beauty, but with rich natural resources. This includes large reserves of oil and gas.

This petroleum wealth gives us the tools to develop our nation and to invest for our future.

We do not want to be a poor people in a rich country. So we need to use those tools in the right way to develop our nation.

We also recognise that to build a strong nation we need to build a strong private sector.

This is why we are looking to work in partnership with the private sector and to attract foreign investment.

Our sovereign wealth fund, the Petroleum Fund, has a balance of around $10 billion US this is rising every day.

The Petroleum Fund will get a further boost once the Sunrise field is developed and as we look for more natural resources both on-shore and off shore.

We were also the 3rd country in the world, and the first Asia, to be a fully compliant with the international transparency criteria of the Extractive Industries Transparency Initiative.

And so, while we are still a poor country we are positioned well for the future.

Last year, Timor-Leste released its 20 year *Strategic Development Plan*.

The Plan sets out a path to transform Timor-Leste from a low income to an upper middle income country by 2030 in 3 ways:

- Firstly, building our infrastructure
- Secondly developing our economy – with a focus on our petroleum, tourism and agricultural industries; and lastly by
- Improving our human resources.

In line with the Plan, we are starting a major infrastructure program including the building of ports, airports and a national road system.

We will also begin a large investment program to develop our south coast – which faces Australia and is less than an hour's flight from Darwin.

The implementation of the *Strategic Development Plan* will provide investment opportunities across all sectors of the economy.

This will include tourism, hospitality, property development, infrastructure, communications, basic manufacturing and agriculture.

We have invested in power generation and a national grid so that every household in Timor-Leste will have access to electricity.

This is going to transform the lives of our people and stimulate economic growth.

We have introduced one of the world's most attractive tax regimes.

We are already enjoying economic expansion with growth rates averaging 12% since 2007.

In its annual report on Timor-Leste released last month, the International Monetary Fund – the IMF- predicts that our economic growth will continue to be strong over the medium term.

The IMF also found that while access to credit has been poor it has started to grow.

And as credit expands, so will our economy.

That is why we are we are establishing a National Development Bank to help the Timorese private sector to establish international joint ventures.

Happily, our economic growth can be easily witnessed by walking our streets.

We can see new shops, restaurants and businesses opening all the time and there is a building boom in our capital.

Traffic congestion is now, for the first time, a problem! Perhaps people from Sydney don't see that as something to aspire to – but it is an indicator of development none the less.

But most of all, we see our people's growing sense of hope, belief and optimism.

Ladies and Gentlemen,

When we celebrate our 10 year anniversary in May we have good reason to celebrate.

On our half island nation, we have established a free and democratic state, with the rule of law and a safe and secure society.

While, we are a small nation, we have an emerging economy and we have entered the fight to build that economy, pull our people from poverty and consolidate our nation.

It is true that we face large challenges, but also true that we have big dreams for our country.

We look to the future with a strong sense of hope and great optimism – a future including a strong private sector and vibrant foreign investment.

Last Wednesday, we approved a law on Public Private Partnerships to attract foreign investors and international joint ventures.

And so I repeat what I said in 2008, Australian businesses should make the most of the 'first mover advantage'.

I never went to China to spread this message – but the Chinese heard it clearly!

And so I hope, that because of today, more Australian businesses come to Timor-Leste to enjoy the first mover advantage in our country.

Thank you again to the Australia Timor-Leste Business Council for your on-going support and to everyone here tonight for being part of the exciting future of our country.

Thank you very much.

Second Jakarta International Defence Dialogue (JIDD) – 'Military Operations other than War: Regional and National Perspectives'

Jakarta, 21 March 2012

Your Excellency the Minister of Defence of the Republic of Indonesia, Dr Purnomo Yusgiantoro
My dear friend President Fidel Ramos
Your Excellencies
The Ministers of Defence of the various countries in attendance
Illustrious Participants and Heads of Delegations
Dear panel colleagues:
Dr Ng Eng Hen, Minister of Defence of Singapore
Mr Dato Paduka Haji Mustappa Bin Haji Sirat, Deputy Minister of Defence of Brunei Darussalam
Mr Lee Young Geol, Vice Minister of Defence of the Republic of Korea
Professor Dewi Fortuna Anwar, moderator
Ladies and Gentlemen,

It is a great pleasure for me to take part in this Second Jakarta International Defence Dialogue and I trust that it will be as successful as the first one held last year.

Once again, this event, organised by our neighbour Indonesia, was of such significance that it was important that Timor-Leste attended. I would also like to express our appreciation to the Government and People of Indonesia whose efforts enhance the friendly environment between our two countries. Indonesia is at the forefront of encouraging global dialogue on current and pressing topics within the regional and international context, particularly in the areas of defence, security and democracy.

This dialogue and exchange of honest and constructive opinions, within a true spirit of intergovernmental cooperation, could not be held in a more fitting country. In addition to being a gracious host, Indonesia is a stable and successful democracy in our region and provides, as we all know, a leading example of intercultural and religious tolerance.

The issue of tolerance is an excellent starting point for the dialogue on 'Military Operations Other Than War'. We live in times of underlying uncertainty and anxiety, caused by irresponsible acts and feelings of intolerance.

Ladies and Gentlemen,

The First Jakarta International Defence Dialogue strengthened the consensus in relation to the need to build mutual trust and cooperation between countries in order to solve, by ways other than conflict, the differences that may exist in bilateral and multilateral relations.

We have often mentioned the need to strengthen dialogue and develop coordination mechanisms able to ensure peace and harmony in the region and ultimately in the world. An example is R2P, the Responsibility to Protect mentioned earlier by the Secretary General.

This challenge can only be overcome when the policies of 'responsibility for protecting the human rights of the international community' are truly separated from economic interests. The atmosphere of distrust will remain between States while it is the markets – and not the values of the Nations themselves – that dictate if there will be war or peace and that determine the eventual intervention of Peacekeeping Missions, as in the case of Cote d'Ivoire.

Upon reflection I raise a question that for me is essential. It is this:

Since the first JIDD in March last year what have we witnessed taking place in the world?

You may not agree with me but what I see is:
- an Egypt that is socially divided
- a Libya bloodied
- a Yemen experiencing the anxiety of change, a change that we all wish to be peaceful
- and a Syria unable to stop its path to self destruction.

In the Middle East, we have Israel and Palestine who cannot escape their fatal destiny as though condemned by a need to guarantee the integrity of principles and the grandeur of values held in high spheres of decision. We see Iraq destroyed in its entirety as a country, Afghanistan shaken to the core by their differences and disunity and a Pakistan that cannot avoid disconnecting itself from the problem of its neighbours.

And if all this was not enough, we have Iran maintaining a rigid stance whilst an oil embargo that has been imposed, in addition to not resolving the problem, will make the global economic recovery more difficult. By chance there are indications that Saudi Arabia is attempting to reduce the risks of an enormous collapse that would create instability across the globe.

Meanwhile in the African continent the process in Tunisia seems to have developed with maturity, but there are many countries, including some with Peace Keeping Forces deployed, where a solution to conflict and violence in the medium term is not easy.

The economic growth of ASEAN itself, alongside the growth of China and India, and the enduring strengths of Japan and the Republic of Korea, make this, the century of Asia.

Meanwhile, this great region of Asia-Pacific is not immune to the latent and real threats of today's world.

Nowadays interdependence is critical. We are here with the assumption that the States should work together to protect the interests, both national and global.

Could there perhaps also be another venue for us to raise the true causes of other problems that are not merely derived from economic interests?

Asia has become a major buyer of weapons – in an era where multilateralism should guide the acts of States, it seems that we are preparing for an unprecedented war.

The United Nations should offer debates to reorient the policies on intervention in the world. I am glad to hear the UN Secretary General raising this issue earlier. The sending of the highly respected Kofi Annan to Syria was so late that it demonstrates that the community of nations still prefers armed interventions to interventions of a political nature.

The people that are victims of persecution and victims of their own poverty and often unaware of the thin line separating the morality of the international community and the morality of 'national economic security' of the major powers, these people will in the meantime increase the rate of inter-territorial crime and also increase the threat to internal security and the economic and social stability of the community of nations.

I say this because it is said that 'power and influence' follow 'economic trends'.

Within this negative scenario, we must commend the positive developments taking place in Myanmar, both with the political participation of Aung San Suu Kyi and the end of the armed conflict, and we hope these developments will continue on the path to consolidating democracy.

Ladies and Gentlemen,

In terms of security and defence, Timor-Leste, which is located both in Southeast Asia and in the greater Pacific region, is not immune to regional strategic manoeuvrings.

Timor-Leste is part of an archipelago, which is in itself a situation of fragility. We have land borders and sea borders that make us vulnerable to the threats of the modern world: piracy, terrorism, organised crime such as the trafficking of drugs, people, weapons and contraband, as well as illegal immigration.

Located between two major regional powers, Indonesia and Australia, indeed two good friends, we are not immune to the consequences of acts of terrorism carried out in our region. Further, Australia is, of course, also not immune to these threats, as a result of the complex network of international relations.

We were recently presented with the issue of asylum seekers, which ultimately affects Australia but which must be approached within a regional, if not international context. This is yet another example of how we cannot solve conflicts and promote peace in the region, supporting those who flee from domestic crises, without targeting directly the root causes of the problems.

Timor-Leste is a small and young nation and remains vulnerable to frictions affecting our region.

Perhaps because of the recent tensions in the South China Seas, we are witnessing the preparation of defence mechanisms of another major power next to our borders.

Today we understand that the protection of the borders of a country and its maritime territories are not exclusively confined to a country's defence force and is thereby applying a broader concept of defence which obviously has implications for smaller countries like Timor-Leste.

Within the context of regional defence, Timor-Leste, alongside Australia and Indonesia, must not stop searching for a better understanding on maritime security under a trilateral arrangement.

We do not want to risk being considered unfriendly by this country or the other. On the contrary, we want and we seek to have partnerships with everyone, particularly our closest neighbours, so that we can develop our country.

The concept of national security is still a concept in development for our country – as indeed is everything else. We have just begun a profound reflection on the best way to effectively protect our population and our assets, as well as on the best way to ensure territorial integrity and national sovereignty through our security and defence forces and services.

Lately we have been the victim of illegal fishing and destruction of our maritime fauna. We understood that Timorese waters were easy prey to illegal exploitation, in view of our difficulties with patrolling our coastal areas. As you know, we have great wealth in our waters, which is essential for the economic and social development of our people.

On the other hand, we are also vulnerable to natural disasters and calamities that are frequent in our region. The occurrences that took place in different parts of the world made us even more alert to the need to be prepared for these types of adversities.

As such we decided that our Military should be prepared not only to defend our sovereignty, but especially to guarantee the safety of our population and our assets.

It was in this sense that we developed our Naval Component, with a view to our maritime security.

Timor-Leste requires naval capability to respond to the improper use of its national waters for illicit activities. Timor-Leste must be able to carry out monitoring, surveillance, policing and rescue activities in maritime areas under national jurisdiction. These responsibilities will also enable our neighbours to have confidence in our State, which is important in terms of regional stability and to prove that we are serious in our commitment towards collective global security.

Ladies and Gentlemen,

We are seeking ways to be more active in our region and in the world. After overcoming the conflicts in which we lived for over a quarter of a century, including our own internal quarrels, we now want to share our reconciliation experience and to focus our efforts on a more humanist ideal of political and social tolerance to bring dignity and development to everyone.

Since the beginning of this year, a small engineering team from our defence force has been deployed as part of the Portuguese contingent in Lebanon under the UN Mission.

Our participation in international missions will help us to create strong and positive bonds of cooperation with other countries, as well as to put our own experience and our determination for peace at the service of other countries. Our firm willingness to become fully fledged members of ASEAN is also substantiated in this desire to take an active role in the development of peace in the region and to bring our national defence forces more in line with the models held by other countries.

We are aware that many countries cannot or are unable to act as effectively as they would wish in the management of crises and situations of humanitarian emergency. In these times of serious difficulty, combined forces acting under effective international coordination have much better chances of being successful.

Our own experiences teach us that the only way for international peacekeeping operations to be successful is for them to be designed and implemented in an intrinsically transparent manner, without losing sight of the perspectives of the country that receives the assistance.

We know this because we have been living in a long period of peace and stability, supported by the United Nations and the International Stabilisation Forces provided by Australia and New Zealand. During this time we have been adjusting and readjusting internal priorities and needs, without allowing interferences and without disrespecting our own timings and processes.

In conclusion, we can say that we have reasons to be confident. Along with the growth in the Asia-Pacific region, Timor-Leste has also been recording high economic growth rates.

As you have all been following, on the 17th of March we held the Presidential elections and the results indicate that we will go to a second round. The elections ran peacefully and I am confident that the legislative elections in June will be held in a similar manner so as to allow the planned withdrawal of the UN mission and ISF.

And if there is one thing we can say on 'Military Operations Other Than War' is that the security challenges posed to nations leaving behind post-conflict situations are certainly easier to overcome if there is a strong will by the international community to contribute to develop those nations.

I can add that, without first ensuring peace and stability in those fragile States, it will be impossible to enable economic development and to remove the people from misery – which is the worst threat against humanity.

As such, these operations should seek only to promote peace and stability as ends unto themselves. The rest, namely economic and social development and the very consolidation of democracy will follow through naturally from within those societies!

It is not by imposing policies befitting developed countries or by defending economic interests in strategic parts of the world that we can resolve the misery under which the people live. On the contrary, misery that has been ignored by the entire world inevitably turns into tragedy in some part of the globe, to the amazement – if not to the surprise – of all.

Peace or hope for peace, in my view, can only begin where and when there is an end to intolerance.

Promoting peace and reducing poverty in countries that are poor and affected by conflict is therefore the best way to prevent war and to promote world peace.

In April this year, Timor-Leste together with the International Conference of Asian Political Parties, chaired by former speaker of the Philippines Jose de Venecia Jr, will organize an International Conference on Peace and Reconciliation. This is another form of approach to put an end to feelings of intolerance between groups, societies and nations.

This is the contribution that Timor-Leste wants to give to help to reduce the climate of hatred and hostility amongst people.

Thank you very much.

Graduation Ceremony for Senior Students of Universidade Nacional Timor Lorosa'e (UNTL)

Díli, 24 April 2012

Your Excellency the Rector of UNTL, Professor Aurélio Guterres
Your Excellency the Rector of the University of Minho, Professor António Cunha
Distinguished Teachers
Distinguished Guests
Dear students and families,

It is with satisfaction that I return to this University as the Prime Minister of this Country to witness the graduation of 188 students who have studied here, and who have now earned their degrees, as well as the graduation of 12 students who have just earned their Masters.

The courses that these new graduates have studied cover fundamental and indispensible areas for the economic and social development of Timor-Leste, such as law, engineering, science and technology, social science and education, arts and humanities, in addition to the Masters on education and information technologies.

This graduation could not have come at a better time: now more than ever, your Country needs your contribution and dedication to the noble cause of helping to build a democratic and pluralistic State under the rule of law, with which all Timorese can identify and to which they can all feel proud to belong.

We are still at the start of a long path, having taken the first steps precisely ten years ago – we will be celebrating that historical date within a few weeks – and there is much work ahead before we can be content and feel pride in having a State where all agencies work well.

Never forget the sacrifices made by our People, which enable us to live in freedom today. This is the only way to realise that nothing in life is easy and that everything requires sacrifice and much, much dedication.

It is time to look to the future and, with calm and conviction, to concentrate on a new challenge that will undoubtedly be more difficult than the one we faced ten years ago: building a State from scratch. This is a battle that cannot be fought only by a few; on the contrary, it is necessary that all Timorese citizens dedicate themselves fully to this goal, lest we fail and render useless the sacrifice made by our brothers and sisters who gave their lives so that Timor-Leste could be free and independent.

This is the role destined to you who have completed your higher education. We are aware that, unfortunately, Timor-Leste lacks skilled and experienced workers, and that this is something that hinders us and forces us to resort to external assistance for human resources.

The work being done so far by international officers, who have done their best and been indispensable in this first stage of construction of the Timorese State, must be gradually transferred to those of us who were born here and who are willing to spend our lives seeking to develop the Country and to create better living conditions for our People.

The capacity building of our human resources – a task that is given to the University and its various Faculties – is a top priority of the State, which must be assisted by all agents responsible in terms of Education, whether in the public or in the private sector.

I would like, here and now, in the presence of the Rector, Professor Aurélio Guterres, to highlight the importance that the Universidade Nacional Timor Lorosa'e, UNTL, has had in this path we have been walking ever since we were allowed to freely express our desire to be independent. It is because of the UNTL that today we have graduate and skilled young workers performing the most varied tasks in public administration and in the private sector, which is also indispensible in order for Timor-Leste to affirm itself as a sovereign and respected nation among the international community.

Since this will probably be the last time I come here as the Head of the IV Constitutional Government, I would like to make use of this opportunity to acknowledge the extraordinary legacy of the previous Rector, Professor Benjamim Corte-Real, who is undoubtedly the main person responsible for the praiseworthy role that the UNTL rightfully plays in serving our Country.

Thank you, Professor, for everything that you have done and continue to do for Timor-Leste and for the Timorese. Of course this is not a farewell, as your path is not yet over, and we will continue to make use of all your wisdom and care in the many tasks that will be given to you.

I want to urge all young graduates to give it your best in the jobs that await you. The future of the Country is yours, and the feasibility of the affirmation of the Timorese State will depend considerably on your commitment and your ability to carry out the mission that is now given to you.

Please reflect on what I have told you: nothing in life is easy. Do not expect jobs to simply fall into your laps! The State and the private sector are responsible for creating jobs, but these will only go to those who possess the necessary knowledge and who apply it in conditions of transparency and equality.

My generation committed itself to a cause that demanded permanent dedication. No one forced us to fight for the values in which we believed, but we did so because we felt in our hearts it was the right thing to do. We did not expect others to show us the way and we certainly did not expect our battles to be easy.

As such, we had to rely on ourselves and had to set a course and follow it unwaveringly and with determination. This is exactly what we now expect you to do. Do not get comfortable because you have already got a diploma, but, rather, seek the positions that are available and once you obtain the job you crave, work with utmost commitment and dedication.

This is the only way in which Timor-Leste will be able to have its own skilled human resources, so as not to keep relying on foreign labour. Only in this way can we realise our dream of being truly independent.

I trust you will bear in mind that your studies have not ended. In modern societies living in constant change, where what is new today is considered old tomorrow, the only workers who have professional success are the ones who seek to continue improving every day. Knowledge is something that one acquires until the very last day, both through daily experience and through complementary studying.

I further urge you to continue improving your mastery of your Country's official languages. Most of you have had classes in Portuguese, and this language will be very useful to you in the future. It will also be equally important to improve your mastery of Tetum, since in Timor-Leste both languages depend on each other and none can be considered more important than the other.

Finally, I would like to praise all of the teachers in this University, who have worked so hard to provide the best training to all of the students who have now graduated. I would like to highlight the Portuguese teachers from University of Minho, who have travelled to Timor-Leste in order to teach the two Masters courses. Thank you very much, Professor António Cunha, for yet another gesture of solidarity and brotherly friendship.

From the bottom of my heart I wish to all of those who have completed their university education the greatest happiness and professional success. I am sure that you will do our best to help build our State and that you will make the Timorese homeland proud of you.

Thank you very much.

Opening Session of the ICAPP-CAPDI Joint Conference on Peace and Reconciliation in Asia

Díli, 25 April 2012

Your Excellency the President-Elect, Taur Matan Ruak
Your Excellency Jose de Venecia, Founding Chairman of ICAPP and Founding President of CAPDI
Your Excellency Sok An, Deputy Prime Minister of Cambodia, Senior Vice President of CAPDI and Member of the ICAPP Standing Committee
Your Excellency Chung Eui-young, Co-Chairman of the Standing Committee and Secretary General of ICAPP
Your Excellencies
Heads of Delegation
Members of the Diplomatic Corps
Distinguished Members of Parliament
Government Colleagues
Dear Representatives from Civil Society and International Agencies
Ladies and Gentlemen
Dear friends,

First and foremost, on behalf of the Government, I would like to thank all those in attendance for choosing Timor-Leste as the host country for this Conference on such an important subject in the modern world: peace and reconciliation!

Having completed a week ago a two-round presidential election, which took place in accordance with democratic principles, our people salute all of you who have come from so many countries!

It is with great satisfaction that Timor-Leste takes part in the organisation of this ICAPP-CAPDI Joint Conference on Peace and Reconciliation in Asia.

We are all looking for something; we are all trying to assess the needs of modern times and trying to find our true role in this period of great challenges.

Your Excellencies,

For Timor-Leste, which this year is celebrating its 10th Anniversary as an independent country, this is a historical moment.

Allow me to speak for a while on what the Timorese people have endured. Much has already been said and written regarding our struggle for self-determination and independence.

Since 1975, in view of the unique nature of our struggle, being a half island cut off from any external logistical support, it was of the utmost importance to unite the Timorese, who had been divided by a civil war prior to the Indonesian invasion. It was this colossal effort by the people themselves that gave them the ability to reconcile and to forgive.

In this process we gained the support of the undecided and we ensured the return of the people who were in favour of integration within Indonesia, who worked for the Indonesian administration or who were part of the paramilitary and military groups created by the occupying authorities. We had to reconcile and forgive, in order to attain a higher goal – independence.

The struggle was too long for our size and our means; however the Timorese people nurtured the longing to live in peace. And peace meant more than just the end of war.

The Referendum in August 1999 put an end to the occupation struggle, but generated yet more death and destruction.

There was not a single Timorese citizen who did not have at least one traumatic experience. There were still many open wounds that did not have time to heal and many feelings that were hard to let go. However, the greatness of our People's character is in their tolerance and in their deep yearning to live in harmony.

And for the Timorese people, peace meant living free from hatred, revenge and distrust. Peace meant living in harmony with our enemies, and especially with ourselves, both individually and as a whole.

The character of the Timorese People was forged in this desire to live in peace.

Your Excellencies

Ladies and Gentlemen,

This is why the reconciliation processes in Timor-Leste were so successful. We understood from the experiences of other post-conflict countries that if we were to keep hatred and mistrust alive in our society, we would not be able to build our Nation.

We established CAVR (Commission for Reception, Truth and Reconciliation) in order to ascertain the truth regarding the violence by Timorese against Timorese, particularly during the civil war period, as well as to be able to handle that truth.

The reconciliation meetings between Timorese citizens, held in 2000, throughout the border with Indonesia, were truly moving, not only because of the description and acknowledgement of the atrocities committed between perpetrators and victims, but particularly because of the latter's ability to forgive. Consequently, thousands of refugees who had fled to Indonesia and who feared for their acceptance in an independent Timor-Leste, returned and were welcomed by their brothers and sisters.

And this was the first key step in terms of our Nation building!

Our ancestral tradition of reconciliation through dialogue was immensely important in this critical process of rebuilding the country. This process requires the participation by everyone, as well as a common vision concerning the future.

We also let bygones be bygones with our Indonesian neighbours, thereby enabling reconciliation between our peoples. The offences of the past were assessed and, with great courage, particularly by the victims, we began a process of cooperation and friendship between Timor-Leste and Indonesia – a process that has been very important for the development of Timor-Leste.

With the creation of a Commission of Truth and Friendship in Bali, in a joint effort between Timor-Leste and Indonesia, we were able to further strengthen this friendship and to contribute to peace in Southeast Asia. I believe that our common history and the difficult processes we endured and overcame can serve as examples for peace and reconciliation in the region and in the world.

Presently, Indonesia is not only a close and cooperative neighbour, but also an example of stability, democracy and economic growth that Timor-Leste is following and studying closely.

Ladies and Gentlemen,

People develop when they succeed in overcoming their own weaknesses.

And Timor-Leste is no exception. After the exultation of freedom and independence, Timor-Leste was left entangled in a web of internal conflicts. We had disturbances in December 2002, February 2004, March 2006 and February 2008, and it seemed as if we were doomed to a vicious cycle of conflicts every two years.

We had to do some soul-searching and conclude that we had failed in assessing the root causes of problems and that our State's institutions were still very weak. We had had to build our State from scratch.

When my Government entered into office in August 2007, we decided that the priority was to carry out reforms in order to reduce our institutional weaknesses, to restore peace and to ensure, once again, reconciliation among the Timorese.

It is precisely in this spirit of reconciliation and unity that we have been working in order to develop our Nation. In 2009, celebrating the 10th anniversary of the restoration of our freedom, we launched the motto: 'Goodbye Conflict, Welcome Development'.

We also know that without economic growth and without providing education, health and proper living conditions to our people, our mission of living in peace would never be achieved.

The misery in which a great part of the Timorese population still lives does not bring peace of mind to any Timorese citizen. Our struggle for peace is not yet over, and it will not be over while there are people living in poverty in our country. Nevertheless, this struggle will be easier if we all work together towards the common good.

When building a State and Nation there is no room for nurturing past hatreds.

The building process must be shared by all, in dialogue and with mutual understanding. All sovereign bodies, the entire civil society and all citizens must be involved in this process and share in the same spirit.

Further, the commitment by society increases as social and economic conditions present significant improvements in people's lives. We also believe that if stability and safety are ensured the economic and social indicators will be more positive.

Ladies and Gentlemen,

Humankind is living in complex times, where science and technology have evolved tremendously, with catastrophic effects throughout the globe, while the mindsets and actions of human beings are increasingly uncontrollable.

I have participated four times in the Democracy Forum in Bali, a broad initiative of my good friend Dr. Susilo Bambang Yudhoyono, the President of the Republic of Indonesia. Every year there are more countries taking part to have honest discussions in relation to their problems, their pasts, their present, and their future that they aspire to achieve.

In the last month of March I took part in the International Dialogue on Defence, in Jakarta for the second time.

While in Bali the universal values of democracy were discussed in relation to their intrinsic connection to development. In Jakarta, under the perspective of State sovereignty and security, I raised the approach that we need to look at the actual causes of the problems in the world.

The world is living in difficult times. It has become commonplace to say that the world is changing. And these changes concern respect for human rights and respect for free speech.

But what changes can we actually consider at the start of this new millennium?

A few of us here today at this Conference belong to the generation immediately after World War II. In the second half of last century there was also an extraordinary change in the global mapping of countries, from colonised territories to independent countries, putting a more or less permanent end to colonial wars and the consequent extermination of the native populations.

The cold war and the inevitability of ideological and economic control divided the world into two factions, namely socialism and capitalism.

The superpowers exchanged threats of destruction, while protecting and assisting their respective alliances. There was an atmosphere of relative stability throughout the world, despite a few instances of conflict in the struggle for freedom.

Newly independent countries were blessed by their former colonisers if they allowed their wealth to be exploited in exchange for despotic regimes, merely to ensure that communism was kept at bay.

After the reform in the former Soviet Union, what did we see? We saw that the end of the cold war presented a new equation to the world's decision makers.

The international community started waving the banner of human rights, the banner of democracy, the banner of retributive justice.

Former despotic and corrupt allies started to be overthrown one way or another. The world began taking its first steps towards change, although hypocrisy still prevailed in the political chessboard of influences and decisions.

And this political hypocrisy of the Western world led to feelings of dissatisfaction, rebellion, confrontation, hatred and revenge, which were translated into the radical and extremist actions we now call terrorism.

There ceased to be room for dialogue and time to listen and to talk. Today, some countries seek to impose their interest on others that are weaker and more vulnerable. Today there is a prevailing sense of supremacy of values, which are breached in the very countries that impose them onto others. In the Democracy Forum of Bali, the motto was 'every country has its own reality, with its own internal factors' and that there could no longer be a 'one size fits all' policy, as it is highly damaging. Let the peoples decide to have change and help them achieve that change without resorting to violence.

Today they want to make peace by waging wars and imposing democracy by fighting in conflicts, forgetting that armed conflicts only cause disunity within countries, increase people's suffering and pushes people to seek revenge.

After 10 years of war in Iraq, what do we have? We have self-destruction by the Iraqi people. The same is happening in Afghanistan.

The 'Arab Spring' was a successive photocopy of events, where citizens from each country were pushed to kill one another. Arab peoples were led to believe that the power of television can change everything which did not prove true. Fear, hatred and the desire for revenge, both at the personal and group levels, will prevail until such a time when there is full participation by all parts of society. The 'Arab Spring' started in Tunisia, and the atmosphere of stability that enables the intended reforms is evidence of the political maturity of the Tunisian people.

Ladies and Gentlemen,

Timor-Leste is not alone in its desire for reconciliation and peace.

At this time the economic growth of ASEAN together with the growth of China and India and the enduring strength of Japan and the Republic of Korea make this the Asian Century. We see in this region a steadfast desire to preserve peace, despite the perception that in some places there is also the typical defensive position of someone preparing for war, as a result of the real threats of today's world, to which this area of the globe is not immune.

We know that the individual desire of the human being is to live in peace, free from oppression and with respect for the most basic human rights. The international dialogue and the multilateral actions by world leaders must be tireless in seeking to achieve this goal.

Your Excellencies

Ladies and Gentlemen,

Before I conclude I would like to say that Timor-Leste co-chairs the International Dialogue on 'Peacebuilding and Statebuilding'. The first meeting of this body took place in Díli, in 2010, while the second one took place in Monrovia, Liberia, in 2011.

Along with this International Dialogue, the g7+ forum is also a space where fragile States can share experiences and talk to one another. This dialogue has enabled the group to speak as one to the international community, so as to try building States, democracies and peace.

Today the Group covers 19 countries representing over 350 million people, from Africa and Asia to the Pacific. In the Caribbean, Haiti has already stated its willingness to join and to hold a Conference.

For Timor-Leste, the leadership and institutionalisation of the g7+ as a permanent forum is a process we approach with responsibility and pride. As a small and young Nation, being able to take part in the consolidation of this group and to give a voice to States that by themselves would not be heard is to give expression to the desire for peace and democracy in the world. As such, in November 2011 the group took a very important document to Busan, which we called the 'New Deal'. This document is presently being reviewed in the United Nations by the Secretary-General himself.

What is more, ladies and gentlemen, we can never forget our responsibilities in terms of consolidating peace in the world. This is even more so for Timor-Leste, as we received international assistance when building a democratic and pluralistic State, and this has enabled our society to live in peace and freedom.

We can never forget that while we are here talking about peace and reconciliation there are less fortunate people dying in several parts of the world as a result of wars and violence.

We are following the situation in Guinea-Bissau, a member of the g7+, with deep sadness. The group had agreed to hold a Conference in that country, which is so dear to us, on May 24th, but unfortunately we had to cancel it.

We are also rather apprehensive in relation to the conflict between Sudan and Southern Sudan, the latter being a member of the g7+ as well.

It is very important that this meeting produces conclusions that can be used by the community of nations in the search for responses to the conflicts that separate individuals inside their very countries.

Thank you very much.

Timor-Leste and Development Partners Meeting – 'State building 10 Years On: A Reflection on Timor-Leste'

Díli, 15 May 2012

Your Excellencies
Ladies and Gentlemen,

It is with great satisfaction that the Government once more hosts the Timor-Leste Development Partners Meeting.

I salute all those who have travelled from far away and who have honoured this meeting with their presence, which will be the last that will be presided by the IV Constitutional Government. This meeting is also important as is represents the handover of our governance process. Further, it gives us the opportunity to reflect on the progress we have made and on our future challenges and opportunities.

The future of Timor-Leste was determined, in practice, when under the auspices of the international community we restored our sovereignty and assumed, before representatives from many countries, our determination to build the democratic foundation for developing Timorese society and our commitment towards peace.

In this political process of self-determination we once again received representatives from several countries who will be celebrating with us the 10th anniversary of our independence, which will take place this weekend. As such, you will be able to witness that we are now the people who wanted to be free and independent, able to take care of our own destinies.

Despite the obstacles and challenges that characterised these first ten years of State building, I am sure that there is not a single Timorese citizen who thinks or feels inside that the sacrifices they made for their Homeland were in vain, so that today we could stand proudly as one people and one nation.

These first ten years represent, in truth, yet another act of sacrifice and abnegation of our people to build a united nation, tolerant and peaceful.

Ladies and Gentlemen,

Our people had, naturally, many expectations about the future, when in the important ceremony of 20 May 2002 we became masters of our own destinies.

And so we had a demanding society, both individually and collectively, hoping for immediate outcomes that ought to have appeared as the natural consequence of having just won a long and hard battle.

At our starting point we could not escape from a post-conflict context. As such, the first step was to promote reconciliation in order to return to the Timorese that for which they longed the most: to live in peace, to live in harmony, to live reconciled with others and, most of all, with themselves.

In our hearts, we all knew that if hatred and distrust were kept alive in our society we would not have the strength required to face the enormous task of nation building

From the beginning, in addition to seeking to build State agencies from the ashes, we wanted to create a new dynamic that would bring the people together around nation building. If not for the greatness of our people, this would not have been possible.

The reconciliation and capacity building of our communities were key elements for this process.

When I speak of capacity building I am also speaking of understanding the magnitude of this construction task. The implementation of democratic processes and the active participation in the integral development of the nation were completely new concepts for our society, which because of their social and political nature are not, and never will be, a simple application of formulas, providing instant results.

Democracy must be lived and felt every day by the people in solving problems, in implementing programs and in the very ability to think and to act. Essentially, democracy must be adapted to the specific circumstances of each culture and each society.

This is a rather complex and, therefore, requires determination, firmness, patience and time. To demand from People, who always gave their blood and tears in the fight for independence, to sit and reflect on their rights and duties in a responsible manner, placing the whole above the individual at all times, is no simple task. What is more, we must also ask the people not to become passive or to lose their nerve in this new struggle, which is now one of national development.

The genuine participation expected from the Timorese in their own development, which is no more than the exercise of their democratic right, is not easy in a country where most people are poor and psychologically tired of sacrificing so much for the nation.

Our first eight years of sovereign existence were characterised by cycles of violence and crises – occurring almost every two years. This shook the trust and confidence of the people in the institutions of the State and led the international community to wonder if we were on our way to becoming a failed State.

As such, we felt that more than ever we needed to turn this situation around and contain the defeatist spirits that were undermining the morale of the Timorese. For this, we developed efforts to change mentalities, turning our mistakes into important lessons for the future, learning to deal with the weaknesses of the State and most of all handling their root causes responsibly.

Within this context, in the year 2009, on the 10th anniversary of the Referendum, we launched the motto for our Nation: 'Goodbye Conflict, Welcome Development'. And we are now happy to see that during the past three years we have started living in a new atmosphere of security, stability and confidence in the future. We have finally broken the cycle of violence and conflict.

Your Excellencies

Ladies and Gentlemen,

Despite the constraints threatening a smooth transition to development, such as the shortage of skilled human capital, the political inexperience of democratic governance, the lack of core infrastructures and even the lack of financial resources, we looked to the future with determination.

These first 10 years of independence relate the history of this process. The political crisis of 2006 was a reflection of the exasperation of those who, tired of continuing to overcome obstacle after obstacle, lost sight of their duties and focused only on their rights.

We had a climate of insecurity in the country resulting in hundreds of thousands of internally displaced people and as a consequence, countless damages, political and financial, to the State.

Following this crisis we learned our major lesson: we had to be able to deal with the frailty of our State, which resided in the inability to handle the root causes of problems, leading to temporary fixes rather than permanent solutions.

We also had to grow politically, taking good care of our young State and imposing political will so that agencies would cooperate between themselves in the search for solutions, rather than giving political perspectives to situations, which obscures the necessary judgement for handling and solving crises.

Further, we learnt that we had to give priority to restoring collective accountability in terms of rights and duties, so as to grow the desire to build the nation with solidarity, cooperation and tolerance.

We started to realise that the victory of democracy is not an easy one and in the same way that there is no freedom for people who cannot attain it by their own means; there is no true development if it is not a result of the effort made by that same society. The path is always long and difficult to transform the mentality of a society so that they become agents of development and to overcome obstacles together.

The permanent and genuine dialogue and cooperation between all Bodies of Sovereignty and the civil society were vital to break this vicious cycle of conflict.

I take this opportunity to express my gratitude and recognition for the wise leadership of the His Excellency, the President Jose Ramos-Horta.

This Government is proud to have been an active part in this process.

Your Excellencies

Ladies and Gentlemen,

The progress we are celebrating together today is the result of a decade-long process of advances and setbacks; of learning while making errors and corrections; of aligning wills and priorities and, evidently, of growth. It has also been a process of transformation and even adaptation, as circumstances throughout the world have constantly changed and our country, while small and rather young, is not indifferent to these changes.

And it is also important to recognise here that the assistance provided by many countries, most of which are represented here today, has been invaluable in order for us to achieve our goals. It has been and still continues to be!

Since 1999, when we had the first development partners meeting in Tokyo, international aid has come together to contribute to the reconstruction and development of Timor-Leste. It is with emotion and respect that I acknowledge this vital contribution to peace, stability and the construction of our democratic State under the rule of law.

In 2008 we held the first meeting with the development partners in our mandate. The meeting took place in a somewhat troubled atmosphere, as the President of the Republic was still recovering from the attack he had suffered the month before. At that time we were also facing serious problems resulting from the crisis of 2006, such as the thousands of IDPs living in camps in the centre of Díli.

I have a vivid memory of speaking to you at the time on the need to have the courage to implement a reforming program and to set priorities.

In a country where there is a lack of everything, it is common for everyone to demand everything. However, ruling responsibly means making choices. Ruling responsibly means being open to criticisms about the difficult choices that must be made.

And so, we chose to reform that which enables the development of everything else. We decided to start by ensuring stability and security, by reforming public administration and by implementing social justice measures, protecting the most vulnerable groups in our society.

In 2009 we met again, this time with a different mindset in our society. The reforms we had implemented were producing results. Not only had we closed almost all of the IDP camps, we had also started a new stage in the relationship between our police force and our military. We had also given back dignity to our elderly people, combatants, orphans, mothers and women living in precarious conditions, and more importantly we had restored the trust and confidence of the people in State agencies.

Timor-Leste initiated a period of unprecedented peace and harmony.

We continued to receive criticism in a positive way, we continued to make priorities and we continued to make key decisions for the development of the Country.

Around this time we started to create the regulatory frameworks for key agencies in terms of good governance, such as the Civil Service Commission and the Anti-Corruption Commission. We also continued improving public financial management and to build the capacity of our public administration to provide better services throughout the territory.

In addition, we developed an integrated plan concerning core infrastructure essential to the sustainable development and to the wellbeing of the Timorese.

Knowing that the development of infrastructure is the key to creating employment and to ensuring access to knowledge, markets, products and businesses, we considered that investing in infrastructure also meant investing in progress. As such, in 2009 Timor-Leste started on the irreversible path towards progress.

Already in 2010, the atmosphere was so stable that we began to take a more active participation in international dialogues on 'Peace-building and State-building', hosting an international conference on this theme in Díli.

In 2010, and in addition to this International Dialogue in which we became co-chairs, we started to lead a g7+ forum, in which fragile States can share their experiences. This has enabled the group to be heard as one at a global level, in a joint attempt to build States, democracy and peace.

This group has since expanded to 19 countries representing over 350 million people, from Africa to Asia and the Pacific. In the Caribbean, Haiti has already stated its willingness to join and to hold a Conference. For Timor-Leste, the leadership and institutionalisation of the g7+ as a permanent forum is a source of pride, as we are expressing the wish for world peace and democracy.

Our economy has also continued to grow, with Timor-Leste recording one of the fastest growth rates in the world. These growth rates are even more remarkable as they occur at a time when the Government was also managing the impact of the world food price crisis and the Global Financial Crisis.

In 2010 we were already able to announce several successes achieved in little over two years of governance. If the Government did not do everything that was required, we surely did all that was in our power to do.

It was also in that year that we started focusing on two vital aspects for the growth of Timor-Leste, which were yet to be given due attention: the development of our fledgling private sector and rural development.

Timor-Leste has a population of over 1.1 million people, with around 75% residing in rural areas. These people have to deal with serious daily challenges, since in addition to having less access to education, health services and economic and professional training opportunities, they often have to subsist with a severe shortage of food.

Consequently, one of the key targets for this Government was to develop crosscutting reforms in the various areas of governance, so as to enable wider service delivery decentralisation and the creation of opportunities so that communities can lead their own development.

In a completely innovative way, we also started thorough reforms in the private sector, promoting criteria of competence, technical ability and professional honesty.

The Referendum Package, which included the execution of over 800 infrastructure projects, particularly in rural areas, involving over 720 companies, enabled the start of the capacity building and decentralisation of the private sector.

The Decentralized Development Programmes I and II, which followed the Referendum Package, strengthened the economy in the districts and encouraged the creation of local companies, while building and rehabilitating the infrastructure that were so necessary in the districts, sub-districts, *sucos* and villages of the country.

With over 1,100 DDP projects, we also managed to create employment in rural areas and to develop roads, irrigation systems for agriculture, basic sanitation works and public works in education and health, which are vital to communities.

Under the Local Development Programme we supported the *sucos* and villages throughout the Country in relation to their basic needs, namely small public works according to the very plans they presented. We started pilot projects for building the housing specified in the MDG-Sucos Program, in accordance with the Millennium Goals which encompass decent housing, water, sanitation, electricity and access to health, education and markets.

Your Excellencies

Ladies and Gentlemen,

Last year we met in this same venue, and I had the pleasure to launch the *Strategic Development Plan* for 2011-2030.

This plan built on the outcome of the 2010 Census and on a broad consultation throughout every sub-district in the country. It also benefitted from an atmosphere of stability, which is vital for the implementation of the plan.

Before 2011, with the pressing problems we had to solve little by little, and with ever-changing circumstances, it was not possible to plan beyond the next year.

With the *Strategic Development Plan* we are planning the future responsibly, covering three key areas: human capital, infrastructure and economic development.

This Plan was presented within a climate of complete confidence in our future, with an economy almost double the size in late 2011 that it was back in 2006. This growing economy means that more jobs are being created and that there are more economic opportunities for the Timorese.

Also in 2011 we launched the largest-ever infrastructure project in our country. The regular supply of electricity through the National Electrical Grid could not be deferred. It was needed to enable all Timorese, even those living in the most remote areas, to have access to this essential good.

For most of those in attendance here today, this project may mean little, as they probably do not recall or never have had to deal with living without electricity. For the Timorese, this is a very recent reality. In fact, only by the end of the year it should truly be a reality for all.

Also in 2011 we created the Infrastructure Fund and the Human Capital Development Fund for medium to long term multiyear projects.

There could not be a stronger consensus on the need to develop our human resources, particularly in strategic sectors such as natural resources, agriculture, tourism, infrastructure, education and health. We are talking about a significant investment in over 3,800 scholarships, in addition to other professional training programs.

Ladies and Gentlemen,

If you ask me to make a balance of these five years of governance, I must say in all honesty that my balance is a positive one.

Currently our major commitment towards the future is reducing Timor-Leste's dependence on petroleum revenues. Although they have been growing constantly, which results in increasing Petroleum Fund balances, we want to build an economy that is strong and competitive in non-oil sectors.

With the strategies set in the *Strategic Development Plan* for 2011-2030, and with the continuation of the current economy policy direction, Timor-Leste can look forward to a much stronger economy which will result in a prosperous Nation.

Your Excellencies

Ladies and Gentlemen,

Despite all the improvements we have implemented in our Country, I must state that we still have many challenges ahead of us.

The implementation of a *Strategic Development Plan* to develop the country will not be enough to ensure the strong State we need, unless we continue to give priority to the implementation of checks and balances and to well-thought medium and long-term programs. These programs must be clear and provide guarantees of implementation, but also every condition enabling their good performance.

The State must legislate on the transparency of its acts and on the accountability of public accounts, which must be accessible by all. This is the only way for citizens to have confidence in the future of the nation.

For this reason, we have launched in Timor-Leste the Transparency Portal, which enables citizens to monitor Government acts at any time, including public spending execution, procurement processes, project implementation outcomes and even financial aid by donors.

This is an important measure to ensure good governance and to enable civil society to have an overall understanding of the challenges for the country and of the effort made by the State, to encourage a constructive participation in the building process.

Ladies and Gentlemen,

Throughout the world there are 1.5 billion people living in fragile States and States affected by conflict. Over 70% of these fragile States have been living in conflict since 1989.

30% of the Official Development Assistance (ODA) is directed to fragile States, which unfortunately are very far away from meeting the Millennium Development Goals by 2015.

As a result of the international retreat in Juba last October, the g7+ presented the 'New Deal' or the 'New Agreement for Engagement in Fragile States', with 34 countries and international organisations immediately endorsing that New Deal.

The United Nations Secretary-General himself, speaking on the opening session of the Fourth High-Level Forum on Aid Effectiveness in Busan, South Korea, said that international aid is not charity but rather a good investment in security and prosperity.

This is an important landmark in the relationship between fragile States and partner organisations. It is an honest attempt to better understand the challenges inherent to post-conflict and fragile countries in the pursuit of development goals.

Under the New Deal there is new hope for progress in the implementation of MDGs. The New Deal entails a new way to approach sustainable development for these fragile countries, with development being owned and led by the countries themselves, so as to have greater transparency, greater internal capacity and better outcomes.

Your Excellencies

Ladies and Gentlemen,

The presidential elections held last April were peaceful. I believe that the parliamentary elections to be held in July will also go smoothly, which in turn will enable the withdrawal of the United Nations Integrated Mission in Timor-Leste and of the International Stability Forces by the end of the year, as planned.

This also marks the closing of a chapter we have been writing with the international community, as well as another steps towards our consolidation as a stable State deserving of the respect of our society and of the world in general.

In view of the invaluable contribution provided by the international community throughout the past years, we must now respond with our commitment to ensure internal stability and security. We must also continue with our national development, honouring the friendship and solidarity of the countries that are our partners and friends.

Additionally, we must seize the opportunity of being part of a region that is presently the most promising region in the world.

We are witnessing a shift of overall economic and strategic weight towards our region. Asia has been and will continue to be the powerhouse of global economic growth.

Should we be accepted as a fully-fledged member of ASEAN, we will be part of this global geopolitical transition. This is a great challenge that lies ahead for Timor-Leste.

According to the experts, the financial centre of the world will slowly change from New York to Shanghai, from London to Mumbai.

The largest economies in the world are in our region – including China, Japan, India and Indonesia – and will continue to grow and to bring great promise to our Nation.

Timor-Leste must be able to seize these opportunities, benefitting from the huge numbers of new Asian tourists, as well as to build our industries, our fisheries, our agriculture and our markets, in order to meet the demand by the great emerging economies.

Once again, the implementation of the long term Strategic Plan, the pursuit for peace and stability and the assurance of good governance are the conditions we required in order that we not miss out on this unique chance of growth in our Country.

Your Excellencies

Ladies and Gentlemen

Dearest Friends,

I would now like to end by speaking to you about the latest reform implemented by this Government.

For the first time, the IV Constitutional Government will provide an extensive and comprehensive handover to the new government to ensure that there is a smooth transition to a new administration.

By embedding this reform in the processes of government at the end of each mandate, the Government has made sure that the State and the civil service can continue to operate effectively regardless of who forms a government.

The Handover Reports will provide information on the organisational and staffing structure of Ministries, the programs and projects that they are undertaking, budget information, relevant legal frameworks and the capacity to support the program of the incoming government. In this way, the civil service will not have to start from scratch with each new administration but can support any incoming government from day one with the all the information and advice that is required to ensure the effective transition from one government to the next.

Along with this transition we have also drafted a summary of the key reforms implemented by the Government, which will be distributed in this meeting.

These documents represent a significant effort by our staff and public administration and are part of the broader reform to changing the mindsets in our public sector. It is not enough to execute the State budgets approved every year by Parliament; we must also be able to report on and to assume responsibility for the good or bad performance in the execution of public money, which of course belongs to the entire People.

I thank all our Development Partners for their continuous and unconditional support.

Thank you very much.

V Constitutional Government

Swearing-in of the V Constitutional Government

Palácio Lahane, Díli, 8 August 2012

His Excellency, President of the Republic
His Excellency, President of the National Parliament
His Excellency, President of the Court of Appeal
Your Excellencies, Reverend Bishops
His Excellency, the Special Representative of Secretary-General of the United Nations
Members of the National Parliament and Government
Chief of Defence, Armed Forces and the General Commander of the National Police
Distinguished Representatives of the Diplomatic Corps, Ambassadors, Consuls and Heads of Mission
Representatives of State Institutions and Agencies
Representatives of International Agencies
Representatives of Civil Society
Distinguished guests
Ladies and Gentlemen
Timorese People,

On August 8, 2007, and in this same distinguished hall, the IV Constitutional Government was appointed and now ends its mandate.

The socio-political situation then was totally different from today.

Everyone can recall from back then the political insistence, on behalf of 'stability', for the formation of a 'Government of National Unity' in clear disregard of the popular will expressed in the elections of June 30.

All of you recall the attempt, in the name of 'development', to form a 'Government of Great Inclusion', trampling over the Constitution of the Republic.

Exactly five years ago, the AMP received the onerous task of resolving the internal conflict that ravaged the country and that was causing deep wounds in the social fabric of Timor-Leste.

More than 100,000 internally displaced; more than a third of the army who had left the barracks; a PNTL uncontrolled and without command; armed civilians abandoned to their fate and a group of armed rebels loose; all causing greater insecurity and instability – this was the image of a young country, ranked by the international community as a 'failed State' and without prospects.

AMP, with its historical constitution of five parties, represented the union of efforts that answered to the aspirations of our people, for peace and stability and for change, and especially change of attitude and behavior.

Here, and publicly, I want to do justice to the parties of the AMP. Through the harmonisation of the various political commitments, members of the Government and the Parliament, if the AMP did not do what we had undertaken to do, we did everything in our power to reorient the country and break the cycle of violence that, every two years, disturbed the peace of the people.

Timor-Leste currently lives in an environment of security, optimism and confidence in the future, which is the fruit of acquired stability and national security and the result of the first steps for the social and economic development.

AMP, with its potential for action and recognising our weaknesses, broke this skepticism, both domestically and internationally, of many who always have difficulty in recognising the merit of someone else.

With regard to the Failed States Index, a very important point that calls for reflection is the ability of the leadership of a country to assume the responsibility to influence and guide the society to the practice of social ethics and politics that is so necessary to instill an environment of tolerance, mutual respect and solidarity and promote harmony and stability.

The leadership of a country is not only the figures at the top of State institutions, the leadership of a country are those who have a personal responsibility in the different strands of society, from political to religious, from media to civil society from the academic to the professional.

All who feel accountable to groups or organisations, of any nature, have a duty to educate society, have a duty to teach values such as honest policy, responsibility for the best interests of the State and the awareness that Nation is above any individual or group interests.

Our country is young and we have just celebrated its 10th Anniversary. The elections took place peacefully, and we judged as such by the international community. The Timorese people predominately know what democracy brings, not only in terms of human dignity but also in the act of making their decisions. And as a result of democratic choice, expressed on July 7, Your Excellency Mr President swore in today the V Constitutional Government.

Excellency The President
Ladies and Gentlemen

It is with even greater responsibility, once again, that I affirm my commitment, before the Timorese, to lead the country to further strengthen the State and toward establishing the solid foundations of national development.

Timorese society has, to date, looking heavily upon our historical past in an attempt to review the grievances and to measure the sacrifices and pain from the long struggle for liberation.

During our first ten years of peace building and State building, we experiences the frailty of living in a post-conflict nation. Despite the challenges we faced, we can stand up proudly as a determined people and as a sovereign nation.

It is time to build the nation, with eyes fixed on the future. It is time to draw up plans and policies to ensure that there is peace, to ensure that there is work, decent housing and food for all Timorese, for the heroes and victims of the past and the heroes and victims of today.

The V Constitutional Government has a political project of strategic nature, with a mission to inspire confidence and to mobilise the participation of all.

The next five years deserve, therefore, a great collective effort to ensure that the ongoing process of consolidation of internal security and stability will bring progress and welfare to all Timorese.

My Government is committed to be the engine of progress, with an enormous sense of responsibility, dedication, honesty, persistence and courage. We count, however, on the participation and cooperation of all Timorese citizens in this process. United in this common goal, it will be easier to overcome the challenges of development because, together, we have faced more difficult challenges.

Good relations between the organs of State and State authorities and with civil society organisations, the Church and other religious denominations, as well as the positive performance of non-governmental organisations and the private sector will undoubtedly be our barometer. The genuine and frank dialogue between them and the Government is a prerequisite for the success of the nation.

The role reserved for the Opposition, led by the historic FRETILIN party, is crucial in a young democracy like ours. The Opposition has the right and duty to question the Government in its decisions and policy choices, to monitor its actions and proposals in a critical and constructive way, especially considering the experience that the party has acquired working in the best interests of Timor-Leste.

The Opposition is, therefore, an essential element in the composition of our country's democratic formula. A strong Opposition, responsible and enlightened, contributes to a more efficient and transparent government, with the Timorese people being the main beneficiary.

For this same reason, I also appeal to the young people. Each generation has a role to play in the constant challenges facing Timor-Leste. Young people have to embrace this new struggle to develop the country and strengthen peace and democratic values in our society.

I therefore appeal to young people to dare not forget that if you live in a free country today, it is because this country has been handed to them by the sacrifices and tremendous efforts of their parents.

Today, young people can choose which path they wish to follow, they can demand change and better living conditions, and it should happen, however, for the good of all, their actions must be guided by the promotion of a culture of peace, where reconciliation of differences can only be truly achieved through dialogue and peaceful means.

Young people are the future leaders of this nation, they are the ones that will transform our society and our economy. This new Government will strive to create opportunities for young people to develop their skills, their experiences and values, so that they can participate fully in the nation's future.

Excellency, The President of the Republic

Excellencies

Ladies and Gentlemen

The philosophy that guides this Government comes from the IV Constitutional Government and it takes its mission to continue to implement the programs and reforms that have been successfully promoted by the Parliamentary Majority Alliance.

The continuity that we want to imprint on our governance requires continued improvement of the form of action and systems of work and, as becomes obvious, an improvement in the method and workings of administration and management.

We want to continue the reforms introduced in the field of defence and security, which contributed to a more professional and skilled Armed Forces and Police. The Government will continue to ensure that our people enjoy peace in their day-to-day lives, and know that their property will be protected.

Fundamental reforms of financial management and the training of public administrators were implemented to improve service delivery. The V Constitutional Government will continue to promote a culture of ethics, transparency and openness to ensure good governance. For this, we will start a program to ensure consolidation of all State institutions and effectively adopt the system already introduced, and in doing so avoid a bloated bureaucracy and an inefficient public administration.

We all know the difficult conditions experienced by civil servants. My Government will continue to demand greater professionalism, and now promises to pay due attention to this matter to relieve the pressure of the difficulties of their day-to-day working life, thus ensuring better work ethics.

Part of the incentives that the government proposes is the construction of neighborhoods for civil servants, placed in the districts and sub-districts, as a minimum requirement to work hard and free of such undue pressure.

We know that the true wealth of our nation is our people and therefore maximising the health, education, culture and overall quality of life of the Timorese is key to building a just and progressive nation.

The V Constitutional Government will invest in improving services in two key areas, which are health and education.

In the health sector and health institutions we will focus on management, support and resources so that health services operate efficiently. In relation to patients and the general public, health workers must be imbued with a missionary spirit to serve with love, dedication and zeal.

In education, we are committed not only to improve school conditions in terms of rooms, furniture and books, and quality of teachers, but also review the curriculum and quality of teacher-student interaction, which will allow improvement in results, ensure that a reasonable quality of learning is provided and provide better post-primary intellectual development to give our youth more realistic and concrete rewards.

This government will regulate pre-school and basic schools to uphold the principle of inclusiveness and to ensure that no Timorese child is disadvantaged, or provided with inferior opportunities, simply because he or she could not understand in his or her language what is said by the teacher in their first years of schooling.

Priorities for action for my Government will also be in the fair and honest recognition of the Combatants of National Liberation and assistance to the vulnerable.

We will make a revision to the Law on the Status of Combatants of National Liberation, a readjustment of the Commission of Homage activities and resources to a new body that is more effective and responsive, and plan to establish Boards of Combatants from the Districts.

Moreover, because the State is constitutionally obliged to defend a more just society, the Government will embed a process for effective assistance to our elderly, disabled, women and children in vulnerable situations, and it will develop a social security system, which includes financially sustainable pension reform. After the set up an efficient system of payment, the Government will also consider raising, in moderation, the pension for the elderly, widows and the disabled.

Along this line of action, as continuity is given to the construction of houses in organised communities through the MDGs project, the Government will also fulfill the commitment that was made with the National Program for Suco Development, launched in June this year.

Mr President,

When we speak of a more just society, we are also talking about the rightness of our actions. The V Constitutional Government will continue to provide the necessary attention for the improvement of the justice sector. We will continue to develop Timorese human resources, in order to reduce the excessive dependence on international players. We will continue to enhance the capacity of Timorese lawyers, so that they can fully exercise their functions. We will continue to invest in the training of criminal investigators in all specialties necessary to ensure greater credibility to the proceedings that are brought before the justice system. We will also revise the laws that were adopted during an earlier stage of development to ensure that they meet the needs of the socio-economic reality of the country.

We also propose to work towards a more open and more democratic society. To this end, we will strengthen the superstructure of democracy through a free press, which is more enlightened and responsible; with women and the guarantee of the protection of their rights and with equal access to opportunities in cultural spaces which develop critical thinking and the ability to analysis.

We want a society which is freer, more autonomous and more prosperous, and for that we will implement phased decentralisation policies that support local democratic participation and private sector development in rural areas.

We believe that governance should be as close as possible to the people to allow self-determination, dignity and a sense of achievement of immediate needs and aspirations. To this end, we will form new administrative units that are more efficient and representative and that can respond promptly to the challenges of local development.

Mr President of the Republic

Excellencies

Ladies and Gentlemen,

The continuity that this Government intends to achieve also reflects the need to provide form and content to the programs established in the *Strategic Development Plan*, approved by the National Parliament in July last year.

This Plan, necessarily long term, provides a framework to transform the economy of Timor-Leste, with stronger private sector growth. We are planning in a sustained and responsible way to act in three key areas: social capital, infrastructure and economic development.

We know that to build a modern and productive economy and create jobs, we need to build basic and productive infrastructure. The scale and cost of our needs in terms of infrastructure are considerable, and we need to plan and implement our program in an effective and thoughtful way.

We propose to continue to invest in a Plan of integrated infrastructure, which includes the improvement of telecommunications and the connection to the world through a subsea fiber optic capable to provide high speed broadband internet, as well as the development of ports, airports, roads, bridges, sewerage and drainage systems and drinking water supply.

We will also provide regular electricity, 24 hours a day, seven days a week, to all Timorese, with the completion of the construction of the electrical transmission lines which together form a ring around the country.

The development of the south coast and of the oil and gas sector will remain a priority. The establishment of a supply base, a refinery and a pipeline are necessary investments to establish of our own petroleum industry and to generate employment for the Timorese.

The Government is committed to bringing the pipeline from the Greater Sunrise field to the south coast of Timor-Leste. Let's prove to the world that a pipeline to Timor-Leste is a safe and economically viable solution and that our horizon is the development of a petroleum industry able to provide direct economic dividends for our population.

We have been creating a dynamic of progressive growth. Timor-Leste achieving rates of economic growth that were some of the fastest in the world at the same time that the Government was also managing the impact of the international crisis in food prices and the global financial crisis. However, we know that Timor-Leste remains a low-income country with an embryonic private sector, with limited economic diversification and concentration in agricultural production.

The Government will maximise our economic opportunities, which are considerable, using the strategies set out in the *Strategic Development Plan* to become a middle income country with a diversified economy.

And we will do so through a new paradigm of production, productive capacities and opportunities for productive employment. This will include expansion and modernisation of the agricultural sector, creation of a thriving tourist industry and encouragement of private sector activities including the growth of small and micro enterprises.

The Government will establish a permanent relationship with the local private sector, listening to their issues and embracing it as a true partner in development with active participation in the plans and strategies we adopt. The Government will empower the Commercial Bank in supporting small and medium enterprises, and introduce initiatives to foster private sector development, including the establishing a Development Bank.

Although this constitutes a considerable challenge, we have strengths that allow us to restructure of our economy towards our plan. We have the resilience and determination of our people, substantial petroleum revenues, an impressive wealth of marine and mineral resources, as well as our geographical location in the vibrant Asian region, which is currently driving much of world economic growth.

We also have a stunning natural landscape as well as culture, history and a unique heritage, which all offers significant potential for the development of our tourism industry.

In short, with strong investment already started with the development of basic infrastructure and investing in three key areas: agriculture, tourism and petroleum, and supported by a growing private sector, Timor-Leste will diversify its economy building a non-oil economy, so that petroleum revenues can be invested for future generations. However, some of this revenue must be invested now, with courage and determination to allow the development of the country and the current generation.

Excellencies,

It is in with this in mind that the organisational structure of the V Constitutional Government embodies the philosophy of progress to ensure continuity and to achieve our objective of an efficient and effective public administration providing services to the people and undertaking the responsibilities of the State.

The new team of the Government, which takes office today, has a mission to make sure that the spirit of excitement of the past five years does not fade away. Do more and do better is the common platform of understanding in the formation of this new Government.

Our political behavior is guided by the values of civil and human rights, tolerance, peace, dialogue and respect.

Our governing practice is guided by the principles of good governance, inclusion and the principle that everyone should obey the law.

Our vision is a nation in which society is prosperous, healthy, educated and skilled, with widespread access to essential goods and services and with an emerging and productive economy the provides jobs for our people.

Our goal is to create opportunities for everyone in a fair and inclusive way, allowing the growth of a dynamic and innovative economy.

Mr President of the Republic,

We believe that the working relationship between our two institutions will be guided by a spirit of cooperation, trust and solidarity. The current state of the nation demands that the country's leadership assume, without hesitation, its historical responsibility and be courageous in making decisions for a brighter future for the people of Timor-Leste.

Given the complexity of challenges before us to consolidate peace, democracy and eradicate poverty, we must respond firmly, with dedication and courage.

Very soon we will see the withdrawal of the United Nations Integrated Mission and the International Stabilisation Force. This will be bring a new stage in the history of Timor-Leste as we, for the first time, will move on our path without a strong international presence.

Excellencies

Ladies and Gentlemen,

I take this opportunity to thank the contributions of UNMIT, the ISF, the various organisations present in Timor-Leste and the international community.

I am happy as we are able to share the common victory of stability and human dignity in our country.

Our plans for the future are ambitious but I know you will always be available to collaborate on the challenges facing Timor-Leste.

We, moreover, maintain a strong commitment to the international community; not only with our neighboring countries, and with those whom we share common historical ties such as the CPLP countries, but also with those who share the same ideals of peace, tolerance and global development.

The next five years will be decisive for our full membership of ASEAN. This aspiration will bring great advantages to Timor-Leste, but also great challenges.

Being part of this regional forum will give us access to current debates in the context of security, development and economic integration and puts us closer to the centre of global geo-political transition. With the pivot of global strategic and economic weight to Asia, Southeast Asia is the region where we are well placed to be. It is, however, an opportunity which is great for a small country like ours and, therefore, we need to work hard to keep up with these developments.

But Timor-Leste has to grow and no dream of prosperity will be excluded.

I pledge here and now, and on behalf of V Constitutional Government, to govern responsibly, with enthusiasm and vision for the future.

To the Timorese people, old and young, men and women, I address a special message: Today we face a new challenge to develop the nation that we all fought so hard for. With the same principles, values and commitment that were embraced during the long struggle for independence, we must continue to work together to realise our dreams.

It will not be easy, however, I repeat, united we have already faced even greater difficulties.

It is time to put Timor-Leste and the Timorese on the path of development.

Thank you.

g7+ Fragility Assessment Workshop

Díli, 15 August 2012

Secretary-General of the United Nations
Excellencies
Ladies and Gentlemen,

I am delighted to welcome the Secretary-General of the United Nations, His Excellency Ban Ki-moon, and to say a few brief words at this g7+ Fragility Assessment Workshop.

We are honoured to have the Secretary-General attend this g7+ meeting and visit our country again.

With all the important responsibilities of the Secretary-General, he has proved to be a true champion of developing and fragile nations.

We are truly thankful for his personal support – and the support of the United Nations – for Timor-Leste and for the g7+.

In April 2010, the g7+ was born in Díli in the lead up to the International Dialogue on Peacebuilding and Statebuilding hosted by Timor-Leste.

The g7+ formed because we recognised that many fragile States face common issues, and have common concerns, about development assistance – but there was no mechanism to discuss these matters independently of donors and development agencies.

There was also a shared recognition that international responses in the world's poorest and most fragile countries were often inadequate and inappropriate.

In 2010 we came together as brothers and sisters from around the world, in a spirit of solidarity and friendship, with a shared desire to improve the lives of our people.

As an international group that now consists of 17 nations, we want to use our 'voice' in a sophisticated and credible manner to influence the global dialogue on development.

This is why we are pursuing the New Deal.

The New Deal seeks to make sure international development assistance is country owned, and country led, and meets the real needs of our people.

Timor-Leste has lived the philosophy of the New Deal.

At first, we established yearly national priorities to give us the flexibility to address our immediate problems.

Once we had secured stability, we developed a long term plan for our nation, the *Strategic Development Plan 2011-2030*.

That Plan reflects the aspirations of the Timorese people to create a prosperous and strong nation and sets out a pathway to achieve this vision.

Despite all the challenges we faced after our long struggle for independence – having to rebuild our nation's soul, and rebuild our national infrastructure – we have just completed our third round of peaceful democratic elections.

I am proud to say we have moved from conflict and fragility, to peace and stability.

While we still face many hurdles, I am optimistic about our future.

I am also proud that Timor-Leste is now in a position to give something back.

That is why at the Official Lunch today I announced that Timor-Leste will donate $100,000 to the United Nations Civilian Capacity program, CAPMATCH.

It is also why we are dedicated to leading the g7+ and working with other conflict affected nations on the pathway from fragility to resilience.

Ladies and Gentlemen,

The g7+ also hopes to be part of the dialogue to establish globally agreed goals to fight poverty beyond 2015, when the Millennium Development Goals come to an end.

Once again Secretary-General, many thanks for appointing our Finance Minister, Emilia Pires, to the High-level Panel to advise on the global development agenda beyond 2015.

There is already discussion about broadening the goals of the new global development agenda.

However, we ask that it is remembered that while developing countries have made substantial progress – not one low-income fragile or conflict affected country has yet achieved a single Millennium Development Goal.

With one and a half billion people living in areas affected by fragility, organised crime or conflict, addressing insecurity and fragility remains the world's primary development challenge.

We need to learn from the MDG process, to study what worked and what didn't.

What we do know already is that the new global agenda must address global fragility and build the social foundation necessary to address the basic needs of humanity.

We need the whole world working together – governments, civil society, universities, the private sector, trade unions – to ensure humankind has a sustainable future.

Secretary-General,

Thank you again for visiting our nation and for your support to the g7+.

Your presence inspires us to work harder, and to think creatively of new approaches and possibilities for our nation, and the members of the g7+.

Thank you very much.

Presenting the Program for the V Constitutional Government to the National Parliament

National Parliament, Díli, 12 September 2012

Your Excellency, The Speaker of Parliament
Your Excellencies, The Members of Parliament
Fellow Members of Government
Ladies and Gentlemen,

Having being part of the Fourth Constitutional Government myself, it is with sincere humility that, on behalf of the Fifth Constitutional Government, I present our compliments to Your Excellency the Speaker of Parliament and to the honourable Members of Parliament. We sincerely wish every success to the Third Legislature and trust that it will properly serve all Timorese citizens.

Despite the remarkable progress achieved during the last decade, and particularly over the last three years, we are aware of the pressing needs of the nation and of the difficulties that Timorese endure every day.

This year we have been celebrating small victories in our country. We have celebrated the 10th Anniversary of the Restoration of our Independence and the holding of presidential and parliamentary elections that were peaceful, free and democratic. On November 28th we will also be celebrating the 100 year anniversary of the Manufahi revolt.

Importantly, we have also celebrated the visits by international leaders that wanted to see the reality of our country and witness our current atmosphere of peace and stability and hear of our confidence in the future.

Indeed, Timor-Leste is considered to be an international success story. In addition to benefitting from peace and stability, today Timor-Leste also enjoys a strongly growing economy, which has been reflecting in the general improvement in the living conditions of the Timorese people.

The leaders of this country, and of all State agencies, have the moral duty to support and promote the development of Timor-Leste and of striving to improve the living conditions of our people.

This is the overarching commitment of the Fifth Constitutional Government.

Our key goals are to further strengthen the State and to create a solid foundation for national development.

Now that we are already living in peace, we have a plan for the future.

We have concrete objectives and goals to transform Timor-Leste into a medium-high income country, creating opportunities for all in a fair and inclusive manner, and in doing so ensuring the growth of a dynamic economy that creates jobs.

Our vision for the country is the collective vision of the Timorese People expressed in the *Strategic Development Plan 2011-2030* – that is to have a population that is healthy, educated, safe and self-sufficient, with access to justice and to all essential goods and services.

Your Excellency, The Speaker of Parliament

Your Excellencies, The Members of Parliament

Fellow Members of Government

Ladies and Gentlemen,

It is also with a deep sense of responsibility that I come before you, your Honour the Speaker of Parliament and the honourable Members of Government, to present the program of the Fifth Constitutional Government for the next five years.

In line with the Strategic Plan, the program of the Fifth Constitutional Government sets actual plans for what needs to be done in the short term (within the next five years), while also incorporating medium term strategies (5-10 years) and long term considerations (10-20 years).

Eliminating extreme poverty, and enabling our country to succeed, is dependent on our ability to implement the plan that we have set for our national development.

This is why we have come before the National Parliament to present a Program that is built on extensive knowledge of the needs of the people. We are fully open to receiving your contribution, so that the Program of the Fifth Constitutional Government may be the Program of all Timorese citizens.

As such, and prior to presenting the Program, I would like everyone to consider the following:

First – It was not five hundred Timorese who achieved independence, it was the entire people. Consequently it will not be a hundred Timorese, those of us who stand here today, who will put Timor-Leste on an unwavering path towards development – this must be achieved by society as a whole.

We will need civil society, political parties, non-governmental organisations, the Catholic Church and other religious groups, the private sector and all State agencies participating actively to implement the strategic agenda for development.

All Timorese – young, adult, men and women – will be an integral part of the development process. Every Timorese citizen who can do something for this Nation is called upon to contribute with his or her effort and work.

Second – Planning is a difficult task, especially when there are so many priorities. Planning national development involves managing a complex network of challenges.

Although we all know what we want for our country, the challenge is in foreseeing the means and the ways to make our goals more likely to be achieved.

We know that we cannot respond to all priorities at the same time, even more so since our financial, human and logistical resources are still limited.

We cannot distance ourselves from the actual circumstances of our starting point. Our lack of specialised human resources, the stagnation of our productive sectors, the dependency on petroleum revenues – reserves which must be preserved for future generations as well as invested for today – and, often, our very culture and mentality, and particularly our still recent democratic history, are all obstacles to development.

Third – The presentation of the Government Program is the first exercise of the Third Legislature and requires careful and shared reflection. We hope to be able to have an open dialogue with all representatives of the people in this National Parliament, whether they belong to the parliamentary coalition or to the opposition. We are looking forward to a democratic debate on policy options and directions, as well as strong supervision by Parliament and the presentation of alternative proposals in a critical and constructive manner.

We can never lose sight of the fact that there are no winners and losers when we contribute to solving the problems of the country. What we have is over a million Timorese citizens who can benefit from increased freedom, safety, stability and tolerance, as well as from better living conditions.

Plans made in a coherent, sustained and responsible manner are always more likely to succeed, and this is reflected in the Program that we are presenting here today.

Your Excellency, The Speaker of Parliament

Your Excellencies, The Members of Parliament

Fellow Members of Government

Ladies and Gentlemen,

The development of social capital means placing people above all other interests. Valuing the Timorese, which are the true wealth of the Nation, means building a fair and developed Nation.

We vow to improve the quality of – and access to – health, education, professional training, information, social justice and culture.

In the health sector we will be making investments so that health services can be delivered with necessary efficiency, professionalism and promptness. This will include improving the institutional structures, management, support and resources.

The Government will be introducing new legislation in the sector and will focus on the agencies that can provide quality care, including the private health sector which will be an integral part of the national health system, as well the provision of essential medication and blood supply diagnosis systems.

We will also strengthen the national health sector through capacity building, effective control over pharmacies and other retail stores and domiciliary health care programs as well as the efficient provision of ambulances and quality communication systems.

Improving the health sector requires large investments in human resources, including doctors, nurses, midwives and laboratory technicians, as well as on health infrastructure, including the rehabilitation and construction of health posts throughout the country, the rehabilitation of community health centres and the expansion of the National Hospital and of the five referral hospitals.

The Government's strategic agenda also includes other initiatives related with the promotion of general health, including nutrition programs, particularly for children and mothers, immunisation programs, access to drinking water and basic sanitation and access to preventative health education.

Maternal and child health, including reducing the child mortality rate, will still be a priority. Significant progress will achieved through developing a broad child health policy, improving preventive and integrated care, including the expansion of immunisation services especially for polio, measles, tuberculosis, diphtheria and hepatitis B, in accordance with the Millennium Development Goals.

In education, we vow to improve school conditions including the state of classrooms, furniture, and education materials, as well as improve the quality of teachers through investing heavily in the teacher training.

We will review the curricula and teaching methods so that we may improve school and student performance. We will provide for mandatory schooling and an increase in learning ability to improve the intellectual growth of our children. This will enable the country to have young people who are better prepared, and able to take part, in the development of the nation.

This Government will regulate pre-school and basic education, guided by the principle of inclusiveness, so that no Timorese child is at a disadvantage, or has fewer opportunities, because she or he cannot understand what is said by the teacher during the first years of schooling because her or his maternal language is not used.

Secondary education will be divided into general secondary schools, directed to preparing students to move up to higher studies, and technical secondary schools, which will prepare students to enter the work force or to have access to higher technical education.

The Government will also promote an efficient polytechnic and university system to create opportunities for the children of the nation. The goal will be to progressively regulate standards and criteria that ensure quality higher education, through the National Agency for Academic Evaluation and Accreditation, as well as to develop partnerships with higher education institutions in order to improve the management and coordination of universities. The Government will continue to encourage private higher education institutions including the improvement in their teaching quality and will look to providing the necessary support so that they can meet the required standards.

Over the next five years the Government will begin establishing polytechnic institutes in strategic sectors, such as the Engineering Polytechnic in Suai, the Tourism and Hospitality Services Polytechnic in Lospalos, the Agriculture Polytechnic on the south coast and a Fishing Academy on the north coast.

One of the key strategies of the Government in the medium term is to expand the National University of Timor-Leste, a vital institution for developing our human capital, into seven faculties. The Faculties of Agriculture, Engineering, Science and Technology, Medicine and Health Sciences, Economics and Management, Education, Arts and Humanities and Law and Social Sciences will consolidate a national quality higher education system, with internationally recognised quality standards.

Supporting human capital development goes beyond formal education and training. The Government will continue to promote recurrent education and lifelong learning, as well as contribute to the eradication of illiteracy through the continuation of successful programs and the establishment of 65 Community Learning Centres.

We will implement the National Training Commitment in order to ensure that our young people have access to accredited and funded training programs. The creation and delivery of a national traineeship program will qualify young people to enter the work force or motivate them to start their own business.

With our professional training and employment policies, we will be investing to train young people in areas important to our strategic development such as the petroleum, agriculture, tourism and construction sectors. This strategy will include the training of trainers, the building of practical teaching and learning infrastructure and facilities and establishing a stronger connection between training centres and the private sector.

Ladies and Gentlemen,

A national development policy that is fair must respond to our most vulnerable citizens. The Government will continue to support our children, our women at risk of abuse, poor families, the elderly and, of course, our veterans.

For this purpose we will revise the Law on Veterans and establish Veteran Councils in the districts, so as to safeguard the credibility of the verification and validation of registrations and to complete appealed and contested cases.

We will also continue to provide financial support to the veterans and to provide scholarships to their children and to the children of the Martyrs, giving priority to the most underprivileged among them.

In compliance with the State's constitutional obligation to defend a fairer society that provides everyone with opportunities for personal fulfilment, the Government will establish effective mechanisms for supporting our elderly, our disabled and women and children at risk. To do this we will implement of a permanent social security system, that includes retirement pensions, that is economically sustainable for the State.

The Government will consider increasing the pensions for the elderly, widows and the disabled. As soon as the social security regime is established in a universal and contributory manner, the Government will also seek to ensure that all workers, either in the public or private sector, are entitled to pensions in case of retirement, disability or death.

A strong society is a vital cornerstone of an economically developed society. The Government will strengthen its commitment to ensuring that women have the same rights and opportunities as men in all areas of family, cultural, social, economic and political life. This approach will be adopted across Government, ensuring a gender sensitive administration in all activities of the State.

We will also promote a Zero Tolerance Policy regarding violence against women and children. This policy will be promoted in the context of children having a constitutional entitlement of special protection, particularly against all forms of abandonment, discrimination, violence, oppression, abuse and neglect.

We will implement the Child Protection Policy through awareness and education programs, as well as proactive measures such as efficient monitoring and evaluation systems for protecting children and the creation of a 24-hours a day, 7 days a week 'child line', enabling people to report situations of child abuse by telephone.

We will also protect young people and encourage them to participate in their own development, providing them with greater access to education and professional training and to programs and initiatives that raise their potential, including participation in sporting, cultural, artistic or other activities that promote the values of ethics, tolerance and dialogue. We will do this to develop the intellectual capacity of our young people, so that they can become the true agents of the change we all want to see in the country.

Finally, and still in relation to the development of social capital, I must mention two key issues: access to knowledge, which is increasingly important in this 21st century, and the sustainable management of our environment, which is absolutely vital for the Timorese People.

The Government will promote the diversity and independence of the media and ensure access to information, freedom of speech and freedom of the press. These are vital requirements for consolidating our democracy and for us to move towards a developed, prosperous and civilised Nation.

We must also protect our natural habitat, which means that we must conserve our marine and land biodiversity, effectively control pollution and mitigate, to the extent that we are able, the impacts of climate change.

Your Excellency, The Speaker of Parliament

Your Excellencies, The Members of Parliament

Fellow Members of Government

Ladies and Gentlemen,

Infrastructure development is the driving force of national development. Basic infrastructure will enable us to develop social capital and a dynamic and productive economy that can create jobs and consolidate a strong and organised institutional framework throughout our nation.

We vow to invest in the development of infrastructure, in a planned and staged manner, and recognising the needs in terms of finance, technical expertise and skilled labour.

Over the next five years we will undertake a large investment program to update, repair, improve or build key infrastructure to enable access to health, schools, markets, industries and businesses.

We will invest in the following:

- The full reconstruction of all national, district and rural roads, including the connections between Díli, Manatuto and Baucau; the connection between Manatuto and Natarbora; the road project linking Díli, Liquiçá and Bobonaro; and we will begin the road project linking Díli, Aileu, Maubisse, Aituto, Ainaro and Cassa.
- The design of a national motorway ring road.
- Begin the reconstruction and maintenance of over 450 bridges in the country, both large and small.
- Installation of at least 400 drinking water systems providing for around 25,000 rural homes, the construction of community latrines, the provision of technical expertise and the recruitment of 88 water and sanitation facilitators.
- The development of a District Centre Master Plan, in order to gradually restore water and sanitation infrastructure, including piping, so as to provide clean water to the people.
- The implementation of the Díli Drainage and Sanitation Master Plan to dramatically reduce drainage, address floods risks and improve sanitation and community health.
- Expansion of the power network to provide reliable electricity throughout the country with the use of renewable energies including solar and wind power projects.

- Construction of a new multi-purpose national port in Tibar able to receive commercial and passenger vessels.
- Establishment of a logistics base for the petroleum sector in Suai, where a new port will be a key development.
- Design and deliver a regional port-building program in order to build, repair and expand facilities in Laga, Lautém, Ataúro, Kairabela, Oecussi and Manatuto.
- Expansion of President Nicolau Lobato International Airport, in Díli, and develop of an aviation plan for the districts to rehabilitate runways in the districts of Suai, Oecussi, Lospalos, Maliana, Viqueque, Ataúro and Same.
- Developing the Baucau airport so that it can cater for cargo and military uses.
- Connecting Timor-Leste to the world through a sub-sea fibre optic cable to provide high speed broadband services and significantly improve telecommunications in the country.

In view of the vital importance of these projects, and of the need to ensure cost effectiveness and quality technical implementation, the National Procurement Commission will supervise procurement processes, with support from a specialised international procurement firm, so as to guarantee transparency and professionalism in the implementation of complex and large projects.

Your Excellency, The Speaker of Parliament
Your Excellencies, The Members of Parliament
Fellow Members of Government
Ladies and Gentlemen,

To realise the full potential of Timorese people we need economic development and job creation. We believe that investing in economic development is a policy and social principle that promotes freedom, safety and national stability.

We vow to build a modern and diversified economy, based on agriculture, tourism and the petroleum industry, with a growing private sector and the creation of opportunities for all Timorese citizens.

We want to replace subsistence agriculture with commercial agriculture, so as to achieve food self-sufficiency in the medium term and, later, to export.

As such, we will continue supporting improved agricultural practices in order to achieve higher yields of rice and maize and to promote the growth of staple crops such as coffee, vanilla, nutmeg and coconut oil. This goal can only be achieved if we invest in the rehabilitation of irrigation systems and in the improvement of water supplies, including through the use of dams.

We will also promote improved farming skills and the provision of technical assistance, as well as increase the number of agricultural extension officers and while building more Agriculture Service Centres in the districts.

Over the next five years the Government also vows to improve the Integrated Animal Husbandry Plan, promoting basic animal health care, including free inoculation. We will also expand fishing and aquaculture activities by implementing deep sea commercial fishing strategies and the National Aquaculture Development Strategy, which will contribute to the food and nutritional security of the Timorese.

Along with environmental protection and nature preservation, the Government will develop a sustainable forestry industry and prepare a Forest Management Plan that promotes reforestation and sustainable land use. This policy will include study on the use of local wood, including the commercialisation of bamboo, and the development of community nurseries. Starting in 2015, we will also plant 1 million trees every year.

Ladies and Gentlemen,

The petroleum sector will be a cornerstone of the development of the country, making the most of our natural wealth and multiplying its dividends so as to benefit every Timorese citizen.

Within his context, and along with the capacity building of our National Petroleum Company – Timor GAP EP., we will ensure that:
- Petroleum revenues continue to be fully transparent and used for the economic and social development of the country;
- The petroleum sector is developed with maximum participation by Timorese citizens and companies;
- The necessary human resources for exploring this sector are improved and developed, including by way of training Timorese citizens in geology, chemical and petroleum engineering, and petroleum finance and management; and that
- The south coast is developed with proper infrastructure, in order to support the expansion of our petroleum industry.

The Tasi-Mane Project is a multiyear development of three industrial clusters: the supply base of Suai, the petrochemical refinery and industry in Betano; and the liquefied natural gas facility in Beaço.

With our nation's natural beauty, unique history and culture the tourism sector also offers great potential for our economic development. As such, the Government will focus on developing the tourism industry, which includes professional training, the refurbishing of buildings relevant to the sector and tourist promotion at home and abroad which will include participation in the 2015 Milan World Expo.

The program's strategy to develop tourism highlights the following areas of the country:
- The eastern tourist area, with pristine beaches, mountain landscapes and adventure activities. We will properly develop both ecological and cultural tourism in National Park Nino Konia Santana and historical and adventure tourism in Mount Matebian.
- The central tourist area, particularly the island of Ataúro and the region of Maubisse, which will be the starting point for treks to Mount Ramelau. We will also promote the existing cultural institutions in Díli.
- The western tourist area, which in addition to its beaches also provides access to historic sites at Balibo, to the hot springs of Marobo and to the coffee lands in Ermera, where we will develop local hospitality and ecological tourism.

By expanding agriculture, the petroleum industry and tourism and by implementing the infrastructure programme, the Government will create direct employment in the public sector, as well as private sector jobs and the attraction of foreign investors and building of the Timorese private sector.

Your Excellency, The Speaker of Parliament
Your Excellencies, The Members of Parliament
Fellow Members of Government
Ladies and Gentlemen,

In order for it to be successful, this strategy must be supported by effective economic policies. This includes the development of credit agencies, business regulations and the capacity building of the private sector.

Consequently we would like to highlight the following priorities, to which the Government will give its full attention:
- Improvement of the business environment, including a new investment law, the improvement and simplification of the business registration process and the strengthening of the Chamber of Commerce and Industry;
- Establishing an effective Investment Promotion Agency and producing a comprehensive information package for potential investors;
- Development of Public-Private Partnerships;
- Establishment of a National Development Bank and consolidation of the National Commercial Bank of Timor-Leste;
- Establishment of Special Economic Zones, with a clear regulatory and tax environment, so as to attract foreign investment and international companies; and

- Land tenure legislation, implementing fair and equitable rules that protect land ownership and transfer, including the registration of properties and the issuing of land titles.

Lastly, I must stress that in order for development to be fair and inclusive it must include rural areas.

To ensure that this is the case we will be creating the National Planning Framework, which will identify development opportunities based on the specific characteristics of certain regions, so as to reduce regional asymmetries and the gap between urban and rural areas.

The Business Development Support Institute has Business Development Centres set up in Baucau, Díli, Maliana, Maubisse, Suai, Lospalos, Ermera, Viqueque and Oecussi, which will provide training in every district. We are also planning to expand these Business Development Centres to every district and to broaden the range of services that they provide.

Through the Government's decentralisation policies we will support the development of the private sector in rural areas and increase local democratic participation. This will be guided by a belief that governance should be as close to the people as possible, in order to promote self-determination and dignity.

The Government will introduce a new level of municipal government, seeking to establish three to five municipalities by the end of its mandate. For this purpose we will be creating the Municipality Preparatory Committees in all thirteen districts and undertaking an ongoing review on whether they meet the minimum requirements for creating municipalities, so that we may introduce electoral procedures.

The Government will also continue to support the Millennium Development Goals Program for the Sucos, building an additional 55,000 houses as we review community development across the 2,225 villages. These houses will include solar power, water supply and basic sanitation.

We want to improve living conditions in rural areas and to introduce a community spirit of mutual assistance and solidarity among neighbours. In this way, people may assist in building houses for their more vulnerable neighbours. In line with this, we will also start the National Programme for Developing the Sucos, which will last 8 years.

Finally, in order to achieve economic development the Government will be investing in agribusinesses and in the cooperative sector, by providing = support to the cooperatives, including credits for purchasing equipment and tools and for setting up markets. The Government will also improve infrastructure such as cooperative head offices.

Your Excellency, The Speaker of Parliament
Your Excellencies, The Members of Parliament

Fellow Members of Government
Ladies and Gentlemen,

The consolidation of the institutional framework is essential to sustain our development ambitions. Without a strong public sector, without internal security and national stability, and without a credible justice system that safeguards the rights and guarantees of the Timorese, we cannot consider ourselves a modern and democratic State and we cannot defend a foreign policy that encourages the international community to believe in the progress of Timor-Leste.

We vow to promote good governance and to develop a public sector that is professional, respectable, responsible and efficient. The public sector is presently the main driving force of economic growth, which means that we must continue investing strongly in this sector.

We will be continuing reforms to public administration, including the strict control over public expenditure, the improvement of financial management systems, the capacity building of civil servants and the accountability and transparency of the information provided to the public, including through the Transparency Portals, which will be duly updated.

We will also draft and apply a Code of Conduct for the members of Government. This code will provide strict rules and duties in relation to matters such as conflicts of interest and commercial activities.

We will create an electronic platform that will provide useful information to the public on the activities of the Government, strengthening the current Government Portal and increasing the services available to the Timorese citizens through a new 'e-government' initiative.

By defending a fairer society, the Fifth Constitutional Government could not neglect the improvement of the justice sector. We will continue to capacity-build Timorese human resources and to improve national advocacy ability.

We will also be investing in the training of criminal investigators in all necessary specialities, so as to ensure greater credibility in the cases that go to court. We vow to review the legislation already approved and to draft new legislation that reflects the country's development level and that is adjusted to our social and economic reality.

Finally, we will continue the reforms we introduced in the sector of defence and security, enabling a more professional and efficient Armed Forces and Police. This Government will always give priority to ensuring safety and stability.

In relation to our foreign policy, we will continue investing in the development of cooperation and friendly relations with all the countries in the world, with special attention to our closest neighbours, to our brothers and sisters of the CPLP, and to our strategic partners in Asia, particularly the ASEAN countries. And we will look to becoming an effective member of ASEAN very soon.

We must never forget that Timor-Leste is in a highly strategic geographic location, which means that our security and the protection of our natural resources are dependent upon a responsible and diplomatic foreign policy.

Our strong involvement with the CPLP countries will be demonstrated when we shall preside over this community of Portuguese-speaking countries in 2014. The Government will also continue to lead the g7+, supporting this group of fragile nations to help them secure peace, stability and prosperity, as Timor-Leste has done.

Your Excellency, The Speaker of Parliament

Your Excellencies, The Members of Parliament

Fellow Members of Government

Ladies and Gentlemen,

The Program of the Fifth Government may be considered ambitious, but it is feasible. It is bold, but carefully thought through. It is expensive, but absolutely necessary.

Most of all, it is a program that is based on the will to ensure the continuity of the progress achieved so far, leading public administration towards goals of efficiency and effectiveness, so as to improve service delivery to our People.

It is a program that will be implemented by a government team that wants to do more and to do better for the country, with the conviction that the public interest, the interest of the Timorese people, is above any individual interest.

Our development has never been constrained by a lack of quality of our people, but simply, by a lack of opportunities!

The Government Program seeks to change this situation, knowing that the challenges are enormous but that the will to overcome them is even greater.

As it was in the past, the will of the Timorese people is the most decisive factor for success in implementing this strategic agenda.

I thank you in advance, honourable Members of Government, for your valuable input so that together we may develop our beloved Nation.

Celebration of the 1st Anniversary of the Central Bank of Timor-Leste

Hotel Timor, Díli, 13 September 2012

Your Excellency, the Speaker of Parliament
Your Excellencies, Members of Parliament and fellow Government Members
Your Excellencies, Representatives of Civil Society
Your Excellency, the Governor of the Central Bank of Timor-Leste
Your Excellencies, the Members of the Administration Board
Honourable guests,
Ladies and Gentlemen,

Today we are celebrating not only the first anniversary of the Central Bank of Timor-Leste, but also the consolidation of a sound and independent institution that has been serving the Timorese people well.

It was precisely one year ago that the Banking and Payments Authority was transformed into a Central Bank. Indeed, the Constitution required the State to create a national Central Bank, which would share the responsibility for drafting and executing monetary and financial policies.

However, this institution has already been regulating and supervising our banking sector for over ten years, through the Banking and Payments Authority, having successfully introduced the US dollar as the official currency and maintaining the proper quantities of bills and coins to be used by the citizens and businesspeople of the country.

Additionally, this institution has been managing the Petroleum Fund remarkably well since 2005. This is acknowledged internationally, particularly when we consider Timor-Leste's lack of experience in terms of financial management.

In this way, the path of the Central Bank mirrors in many ways the process that the country has been undergoing since its independence in relation to the tasks, responsibilities and roles it has performed. These have been growing both in terms of quantity and complexity, so as to meet the needs of our young Nation.

In addition to being the people's banker, the Central Bank also has a mandate concerning insurance companies and the regular publication of economic and financial statistics, including the Nation's balance of payments. In this way it contributes to improved economic planning and consequently to the development of the country.

As any other central bank in the world, our Central Bank, which is now fully established, is responsible for pursuing policies to achieve and maintain domestic price stability, including the liquidity and solvency of the banking and financial systems, drafting exchange rate policies and promoting a safe, sound and efficient system of payments.

Ladies and Gentlemen,

The Central Bank of Timor-Leste also has a vital role in supporting the general economic policies of the Government. This means that the Government and the Central Bank will collaborate in the drafting of the national economic policy.

As you are aware, yesterday the Fifth Constitutional Government presented its Government Program to Parliament.

The key message of the Program is quite clear and represents the main mission of our governance: to strengthen the State and to provide a sound foundation for the national development of the country.

We have a plan for the future. We have actual goals and objectives to transform Timor-Leste into a medium-high income country, creating opportunities for all in a fair and inclusive manner, so as to enable the growth of a dynamic and job-creating economy.

This is the collective vision of the Timorese People, expressed in the *Strategic Development Plan 2011-2030*. We want to have a population that is healthy, educated, safe and self-sufficient, with access to justice and all essential goods and services.

This requires economic development and job creation. The private sector is therefore a strategic partner of the Government.

We vow to build a modern and diversified economy based on agriculture, tourism and the petroleum industry, with a strong and emerging private sector that supports the creation of opportunities for all Timorese citizens.

This is a vital strategy for breaking the dependence on our petroleum revenues.

Our Petroleum Fund continues to grow, standing currently at US$ 11 billion. This is remarkable when we recall that in September 2005, when the Petroleum Fund started to operate, it stood at US$ 250 million.

Although we have improved the management of the Fund during the last few years – and here we must credit mainly the Central Bank team – the Government intends to invest in the diversification of the economy, so that we do not continue to depend excessively from the Petroleum Fund and that we can ensure alternative financial resources for future generations.

Ladies and Gentlemen,

In view of this, the Government wants to:

First – focus on a commercial agriculture that goes beyond food self-sufficiency, enabling the development of agricultural exports.

Second – focus on the petroleum industry, developing the south coast with proper infrastructure, through the Tasi-Mane project. This includes the multi-year investment in the development of three industrial clusters: the Suai supply base, the Betano refinery and petrochemical industry and the Beaço liquefied natural gas plant.

Third – focus on the tourism sector and associated industries, maximising Timor-Leste's potential in terms of supply, benefiting from the fact that we have great natural beauty, unique history and culture, tropical beaches that are rich in marine life and mountain ranges that will prove a draw card for tourists.

In this way, and by expanding agriculture, the petroleum industry and tourism, which will be fully supported by comprehensive infrastructure and human capital development programs, as well as by promoting the capacity building and training of Timorese citizens at all levels, the Government will create opportunities for the development of the private sector.

Ladies and Gentlemen,

In order for this strategy to succeed, it must be supported by effective economic policies. This includes the development of credit agencies, business regulation and the capacity building of the private sector.

As such, we highlight the following priorities, which will receive the Government's full attention:

- Improve the business environment, including the increasing the capacity for obtaining finance, improve contract enforcement, simplify the business registration procedure, reinforce land titles and property registration and provide effective mechanisms for the settlement of business disputes.
- Introduce a new investment law containing general tax provisions for business investment.
- Support the strengthening of the Chamber of Commerce and Industry.
- Promote the creation of an effective and responsive Investment Promotion Agency that is able to provide information and advice to national and international investors.
- Develop Public-Private Partnerships.
- Establish the National Development Bank of Timor-Leste to enable access by the private sector to long term funding.
- Support the establishment of the Timor-Leste Investment Company to support companies, that operates in a commercial manner in accordance with clear and strict investment guidelines and independent management.
- Consolidate the National Commercial Bank of Timor-Leste, in order to support the expansion of small companies be providing credit.
- Establish Special Economic Zones, with a clear and simple regulatory and tax environment, enabling Timor-Leste to attract foreign investment and

international companies, in addition to creating development opportunities for the national private sector, with the establishment of industrial, commercial and service zones.
- Expand the IADE Business Development Centres to every district and expand the array of services they provide, including the 'Business Incubator' concept. This will promote the renting and purchasing of machinery, as well as access to services such as transportation, storage and marketing.
- Approve and implement legislation on land tenure.

The Government's decentralisation policies will also support the development of the private sector in rural areas. In addition to this, we will invest in agribusinesses and in the cooperative sector, through direct support to cooperatives, including credit grants for equipment and tools, the establishment of markets and for improving infrastructure, such as cooperative headquarters.

Ladies and Gentlemen,

Although the Central Bank has specific responsibilities in terms of supporting the development of the financial sector, we are also expecting it to provide valuable contributions to progress in other sectors of the economy and in doing so contribute to the sustainable development of the nation.

The role that the Central Bank will play in supervising the banking sector, which will grow as a result of the new economic policies that we will implement, is in itself a key undertaking for achieving our development goals.

Further, the regulation of and supervision of insurance companies, one of which has already been granted a licence, and the efforts made to prevent and fight money laundering, are also clear ways in which the Central Bank is supporting the economic policies set out in the *Strategic Development Plan* and in the Government Program.

Therefore, it is with great satisfaction that I congratulate the Central Bank on its first anniversary and on its performance towards the sustainable development of the country. I would also like to seize this opportunity to call upon the entire private sector, and all economic and financial institutions in attendance here today, to take an active part in the development of our beloved nation.

Thank you very much.

67th Session of The United Nations General Assembly

New York, 25 September 2012

Excellency, the President of the General Assembly
Excellency, the Secretary General of the United Nations
Excellencies, the Heads of State and Government
Ladies and Gentlemen

It is a great pleasure for me to address this great General Assembly of the United Nations for the second year in a row.

Last September, I tried to convey to you a message of progress and hope. Today I bring from the People of Timor-Leste a message of both joy and thankfulness.

The United Nations has been in Timor-Leste since the difficult times of our emancipation, having led the Popular Consultation of 1999.

Since then, it has been an enormous challenge to build from scratch the foundations of a new State under the rule of law, based on democratic governance and respect for human rights. As such, after UNAMET we have had missions like UNTAET, UNMISET, UNOTIL and UNMIT accompanying us in this crucial journey of Statebuilding, as well as in the creation of an atmosphere of reconciliation and harmony, in view of enabling peace and stability.

In our still short existence as a State, we have been trying to learn from the errors of the past. Today I can say that we have decidedly moved away from the difficult circumstances that characterize post-conflict countries or, in other words, countries with recent histories of conflict and violence.

We have come to understand (along with several countries) that peace and stability are essential prerequisites for State building. The current year, 2012, therefore marks not exactly the end of a chapter in our history of peace building – but, more particularly, the start of a new one – a chapter of ongoing institutional strengthening, seeking to boost national development.

After two rounds of presidential elections, which took place in March and April, our People elected as the 3rd President of the Republic, Major-General Taur Matan Ruak, a historical figure of the Struggle for Liberation, who has been serving the motherland since 1975. Taur Matan Ruak has led the Armed Resistance and became Chief of Defence Force in 1999.

In May, we had the pleasure of hosting five Heads of State and many delegations from friendly countries to celebrate with us the 10th Anniversary of the Restoration of our Independence. This took place within an atmosphere of peace, stability and confidence in the future.

The landmark moment of the celebrations was the constitutional transfer of power from the then President of the Republic, Dr José Ramos-Horta, to the new Head of State, in a highly dignified manner for our young democracy.

On 7th July, the Timorese People were called to vote, once again, and on the 30th of the same month, the new Parliament entered into office.

As a result of those elections, three parties were chosen to ensure the governance of Timor-Leste from 2012 to 2017. Consequently, on 8 August the Fifth Constitutional Government was sworn-in and given the mission of continuing to consolidate the vital institutions of a peaceful and democratic Nation. In this way, we will also be continuing the work done by the previous Government, which consisted of a 5-party coalition, and had undoubtedly sown the seeds for national peace and stability, in addition to boosting our economy.

During this year we have also been honoured with visits by several personalities, from which I would highlight two high level dignitaries:

In August, the Secretary General of the United Nations, His Excellency Ban Ki-moon, decided to see by himself the changes that had taken place in our country since his last visit 5 years ago. The visit of the Secretary General was a magnificent gesture of support by a man with a broad vision on peace and development – a vision that is shared by the Timorese people. The Secretary General acknowledged the progress made and left words of encouragement regarding the strengthening of the cooperation ties between the United Nations and Timor-Leste in an area that is no less important, which is 'Education First' – in his Global Education Initiative.

More recently, we have also had the pleasure of hosting the U.S. Secretary of State, Madam Hillary Clinton. This was the first time that a senior representative from the US Government visited our young country. Mrs Clinton also conveyed an important message of confidence and solidarity, praising the strong commitment by Timor-Leste in relation to the values and principles of democracy and good governance.

These events are even more important as UNMIT (United Nations Integrated Mission in Timor-Leste) and ISF (International Stabilization Force) will withdraw by the end of the present year. This will mark the end of peacekeeping operations in Timor-Leste.

All of this has instilled in the hearts of the Timorese a very special feeling of accomplishment and national pride.

As such, I would like to convey this feeling of joy and thankfulness to all United Nations member countries and to the various international Organizations that have provided us with ongoing support in terms of consolidating peace, democracy and human rights.

The President of the Republic, Taur Matan Ruak, has asked me to make public that, on 20 May 2013, the Timorese State will be honouring, with the highest insignia of Timor-Leste, all countries that have taken part in missions in Timor-Leste, starting with the United Nations General Assembly and the Security Council.

For our people, these will be an act of profound recognition, wishing that from now on the United Nations could pay more attention to our fellow brothers and sisters in need.

The success of Timor-Leste belongs to everyone – to the international community, for their dedicated support and solidarity, and to the Timorese people, for the courage to acknowledge their mistakes and their firmness and determination to correct them.

Throughout the last four years our people have clearly said 'no' to conflict, in order to fully embrace the aspirations of their own development.

The Timorese people were also able to display a high degree of political maturity by expressing, in a peaceful and constructive manner, renewed confidence in the elected leaders and in the State institutions. All of this is essential for reaffirming here today that, more than ever, we are ready to continue leading the national development process, including the full establishment of our democratic State under the rule of law and the gradual implementation of the *Strategic Development Plan 2011-2030*.

However, we want to maintain strong ties with the United Nations and other partners under a new cooperation framework, taking as a starting point the current and actual needs of the country either in the area of institutional strengthening or in development sectors.

Based on the principles of the New Deal, which are advocated by the g7+, we hope to see relationships of cooperation being established in an innovative, dynamic and effective manner.

Mr President

Mr Secretary General

Excellencies

Ladies and Gentlemen,

After overcoming the main obstacles in terms of State building, Timor-Leste is now looking to the future with optimism. Consequently, the Government's programme for the 2012-2017 mandate, which has already been endorsed by Parliament, establishes short term (5 years) activities, lists sectors where activities can be started to have impacts in the medium term (5-10 years) and includes long term (10-20 years) objectives, implemented according to priorities and execution time.

We will continue to invest in social capital with the aim to build the capacity and to dignify the Timorese citizens by maximising the quality of and access to health, education, professional training, information, social justice and culture.

We will invest in basic infrastructures, which will be the driving force of the country's development.

We will develop the economic sector to make better use of our potential and to create employment. We will encourage the growth of the private sector, for both local and foreign.

We will continue our efforts to consolidate the institutional framework to improve the function, management and implementation of programmes. This includes a strong public sector, good governance and a credible system of justice.

Meanwhile, we will improve our social programmes that cater to our most vulnerable citizens, including the disabled, the elderly, and women and children at risk, in order to ensure that no Timorese citizen is marginalized or socially left out. We will also continue to dignify our veterans.

Today we have a plan, a vision, a goal – to transform Timor-Leste from a low income country to a medium-high income country by 2030. We want to be a prosperous and safe Nation, with a healthy and educated population with skilled employment for all.

However, in the short term, by 2015, Timor-Leste will not meet the Millennium Development Goals. The current major challenge for Timor-Leste is the fight against poverty – a challenge that we share with over one billion people in our planet.

Regrettably, around 20% of the world's population live in conditions of extreme poverty. Hunger and the lack of access to water sources will remain insurmountable challenges. Mothers and children throughout the world will continue to die tragically due to lack of access to the most basic needs.

Unfortunately, these are the current projections for 2015.

As such, it was very timely of the United Nations Secretary General to create a High Level Panel to help establish new guidelines for beyond 2015. Here, I must confess, that we were proud to see a Timorese woman, our Minister of Finance, Emília Pires, been deservingly chosen as a Panel member.

Timor-Leste wants to contribute, in a clear and constructive manner, to the debate on this issue. It is urgent to address the structural factors that have hindered the efforts that so many good willed people have made without obtaining tangible results.

We have a historical opportunity to try to change things. We can learn from the lessons of the Millennium Development Goals process, analysing what worked and what did not, so that we can do better in the future.

Strengthening the role of the United Nations is essential; however it will require the courage to break with the old way of handling things. We need new action paradigms and new coordination mechanisms, so that programmes may truly benefit the people of the more affected countries.

The g7+ was created in April 2010 in Díli, during the preparation for the International Dialogue on Peacebuilding and Statebuilding, which took place in Timor-Leste.

Prior to the creation of the g7+, there was no mechanism where fragile States with common concerns in terms of peace and development, could discuss these matters in a less subservient way in their relationships with donors and development agencies.

It is quite common for the recipient countries to consider that the international assistance was not the most appropriate to meet their real needs. Countries complain of the lack of an accountability system in relation to the money that is actually spent on the poor, in comparison with the amounts spent to improve the wellbeing of those who manage the projects and those who manage the reports on the projects, in long documents that are irrelevant because they are out of touch with the reality on the ground.

Thus, within a true spirit of openness and sharing, with a common desire to improve the living conditions of their people, as well as to contribute to sustainable peace and development, fragile countries created this international group to be able to speak with one voice. Yes, we say one voice! Speaking as one, we will be able to demand responsibility from the leaders of beneficiary countries and also accountability to the taxpayers of the donor countries.

This is also the reason why we are advocating the New Deal, which seeks to ensure better coordination and ownership of international assistance by recipient countries. We want to make actual impacts on the people and to correspond better to the true needs of the beneficiary populations.

Timor-Leste is fully committed to leading the g7+, the same way it was committed when moving from a situation of conflict and fragility to a situation of social and political peace and stability. We want to contribute in a way that is sound and based on actual experiences from the g7+ itself. We are a small country that is still fragile in some aspects, but we share the same huge concerns of the 17 Nations that make up our group, with a total population of more than 300 million people.

Mr President

Mr Secretary General

Excellencies

Ladies and Gentlemen,

We have seen how intolerance causes irreparable destruction in several parts of the world, particularly in the daily lives of innocent people. The brunt of the impact is borne by women, mothers, children and the elderly, making them even more vulnerable.

Intolerance breeds hatred and the desire for vengeance. The world is not changing as much as it is destroying itself.

Consolidating the gains of the Arab Spring is proving to be difficult. Syria is a terrible example of internal conflict. Iraq and Afghanistan do not present better perspectives of being able to solve their internal differences that are becoming deeper.

My good friend, Dr Susilo Bambang Yudhiono, the President of the Republic of Indonesia, has been hosting the Bali Democracy Forum, which has been registering greater interest each year, along with an increasing number of participating countries. We have always defended in that forum that democracy cannot be imposed upon the people, the same way as we cannot impose solar panels on homes without food, and therefore, without any perspectives of sustainability.

Democracy must be an internal process. This process is sometimes long, but it is vital for a lasting solution. The most recent, dynamic and inspirational example comes from Myanmar. Here I would like to commend Aung San Suu Kyi, a woman with an unshakable character, a born leader, a resolute democrat, defender of peaceful solutions and who is today, an advocate for internal reconciliation.

I would also like to commend the leaders of Myanmar for their courage to make changes in the country.

On behalf of the people of Timor-Leste, I would like to salute the people of Myanmar and wish them prosperity with an appeal for dialogue, reconciliation and tolerance.

Today's world faces very serious problems and is sliding over to an increasingly dangerous lack of control.

In addition to a recent atmosphere of regional instabilities, environmental threats continue to grow and hinder the legitimate perspectives of emerging and developing countries in relation to their natural resources. In the Pacific region, some Island States see their very natural survival at risk.

Food security is also coming to the foreground as also a result of climate changes, requiring careful thought, undelayable and broad strategy. In several parts of the world we see an immoral increase in inequality, with a rich and powerful elite dominating the globe with impunity, while the poor become even poorer and eternally dependent on wasteful assistance. What is more, it is difficult to know from where this assistance will come.

In order to meet these challenges, we need a strong and efficient United Nations that cooperates more effectively with International and Regional Organizations, and that operates with great respect for the sovereignty of each State.

The United Nations, which consists of all of us here today, has a duty to humanity. We should all acknowledge that we are the privileged agents of the necessary collective change into a better and safer world. Our collective efforts to preserve peace, security and human dignity must be translated from the altruistic idealism plan to a more interventive one, which in turn means replacing a reactive agenda with a proactive one.

It also means reducing the dominance of political and economic interests in favour of social and humanitarian interests. This requires the mobilization of the public opinion in the entire world concerning the values of peace and harmony between civilizations and cultures, mutual respect between societies and tolerance between groups, through dialogue.

It can also start with the reform of the Security Council, which should be more representative. There is an imperative need to renew mindsets, by the incorporation of new members, so as to energise new commitments and new responsibilities that reflect the current situations of today's world.

Timor-Leste has been walking the corridors of the United Nations for 38 years. In the beginning we wanted to mobilize public opinion in favour of our cause and to warn the world that our fundamental rights were being violated. Today, we have been informing the international community of our setbacks and our achievements in the construction of a sovereign State.

While as guerrilla fighters in the mountains, we heard about a new world order. Today, many people are still oppressed because they suffer in one way or another. We are here to speak in favour of dialogue and fair decision-making. Human dignity must be at the core of decisions on problems affecting our planet. We must have an overall sense of the existence, the fears, the suffering, the despair and the fight for survival of men and women around the world.

Today we are here to ask for honest, constructive and incessant dialogue to solve the problems that trouble the world – for the small and large problems, for small and large conflicts, and for small and large Nations.

Thank you very much.

High Level Event on 'Peacebuilding: A Way Towards Sustainable Peace and Security'

New York, 25 September 2012

His Excellency, Ban Ki-moon, Secretary General of the United Nations
The Honourable, Sheikh Hasina, Prime Minister of the People's Republic of Bangladesh
The Honourable, Julia Gillard, Prime Minister of Australia
Excellencies
Ladies and Gentlemen,

It is a great pleasure to speak at this High Level Event on peace building, and ways towards sustainable peace and security.

I commend the People's Republic of Bangladesh for hosting this event and for their efforts and leadership in chairing the United Nations Peacebuilding Commission, and its mission to address the root causes of conflict and enable the fulfillment of lasting peace and the promotion of development.

Let me also take this opportunity to highlight the contribution of peacekeepers from Bangladesh to the peace and stability of Timor-Leste, and as they are a large contributor of peacekeepers, to many other countries as well.

I have been invited to share my country's experiences of peace building with you today.

In May this year, Timor-Leste celebrated the 10 year anniversary of the restoration of our independence, after the Popular Consultation in August 1999.

We also celebrated the fact that Timor-Leste now enjoys stability and security, better living conditions, and some of the highest economic growth rates in the world.

But our path to peace has not been an easy one.

Until 2008, there were times when we were fearful that violence and civil unrest would undo our dream, which sustained us during the 24 year long struggle, of a peaceful and safe nation.

Around every two years, since independence, Timor-Leste experienced trouble. It was as if we were trapped in a vicious cycle of conflict.

The worst outbreak of civil unrest was in 2006 in which people were killed and which resulted in around 150,000 internally displaced people.

And so, as a government and as a people, we set about addressing our fragility.

We undertook a genuine inclusive dialogue, between State institutions, as well as with civil society.

We recognised that we were fragile because we were unable to leave behind the traumatized past of conflict and because our institutions were still weak – so we understood that peace building and state building go hand in hand.

We also recognised that we had to address the root causes of our problems to achieve permanent solutions.

Despite being told that we would need ten years to fix all these problems we were facing, by raising a collective accountability and building cooperation and tolerance, we worked hard and could resolve the issues by 2008.

In 2009, we launched a national motto 'Goodbye Conflict, Welcome Development'.

For this to be effective, there needed to be local ownership and leadership, to make sure everyone became an agent of our peace and development.

While we started critical reforms in the security sector, we established new institutions, including an independent Civil Service Commission and an Anti-Corruption Commission and reinforced the justice sector, to promote good governance and the rule of law.

In 2011, we set up a 20 year *Strategic Development Plan*, aiming to turn a low income country into a medium high income by 2030, with a safe and democratic nation. And from there, we started to get our economy working to create more jobs for our young people.

Ladies and Gentlemen,

Our initiatives had strong local ownership and the support of our development partners.

Part of our success was our long term partnership with the UN, our neighbours, and the international community.

With this support, our success also became the success of our international partners. At the end of this year, we will put an end to the UN peace operation mission and to the International Stabilisation Forces as well.

Now we look forward to establishing a new framework of cooperation with the UN and our development partners.

Ladies and Gentlemen,

One and a half billion people live in areas affected by fragility, organised crime or conflict.

Not one low income fragile country will achieve the Millennium Development Goals by 2015.

This is why addressing fragility is the world's primary development challenge.

This Event, and the UN Peacebuilding Commission, will help address this challenge.

The g7+ group of 17 fragile nations, with more than 300 million people, is also working to build sustainable peace in its member countries.

This group seeks to improve international understanding and shape global dialogue and action to ensure it is relevant to the experiences and priorities of fragile nations.

Tomorrow morning, the g7+ is hosting a High Level Event and I invite you all to attend.

Thank you for allowing me to speak today about Timor-Leste's peace building experience.

I have hope that by working together, and learning from each other, all nations can achieve peace and stability, and start to embrace the commitment to the well-being of their people and the sustainable development of their country.

Thank you very much.

Reception to Launch The United Nations Secretary General's Education First Initiative

New York, 26 September 2012

The Right Honourable Gordon Brown, Special Envoy for Education
Excellencies
Ladies and Gentlemen,

It is a great pleasure to be here for the official launch of the 'Education First Initiative'.

Just last month, Timor-Leste had the honour of hosting a visit from the Secretary General, His Excellency, Ban Ki-moon, his Special Envoy for Education, the Right Honourable Gordon Brown and the Director General of UNESCO, Mrs. Irina Borkova.

During their visit, the Education First initiative was first publicly announced.

The initiative aims to improve the quality of education, ensure every child has equal access to learning.

It provides a simple, targeted and effective framework to improve education across the globe; and to support the achievement of the Millennium Challenge Goals.

Education not only changes the lives of people – it drives the future of nations.

East Asia is becoming the world's economic powerhouse, largely because countries such as China, South Korea, Singapore and Australia have focused on education.

Regrettably, in the Least Developed Nations, and in particular in fragile and conflict affected nations, many children have no access to education.

Children in conflict-affected poor countries make up 42% of children out of school.

This inequality puts at risk social cohesion – making it is more important than ever that every child gets the benefit of a quality education.

Fortunately, this is exactly what Education First aims to achieve.

Ladies and Gentlemen,

Timor-Leste has successfully emerged from conflict. We have secured peace, and are now focused on building a strong economy to provide a future for our people.

But while our country is full of promise, we still face many challenges.

Many of our people still live in extreme poverty. Unemployment is high, and our infrastructure, our roads, schools and hospitals require major investment.

Timor-Leste is also a young country with a young population. Over half of our population is under the age of 19. This means that more than 500,000 are under the age of 19.

When I was a child, less than 4000 Timorese went to school each year. And I could only complete secondary school. Today, Timor-Leste already has a few institutions of higher education. And today 90 per cent of children enter primary school. This is a great improvement but we need to see 100 per cent of children in primary school, given that regrettably more than 50 per cent drop out.

We need to build more classrooms, especially in remote and marginalised areas, so we can provide all children with a safe and happy learning environment.

It is not good enough that many have to walk hours each day, to an overcrowded class room, without appropriate books and curriculum.

And in some schools, students do not understand the language being spoken by the teachers.

We are working hard to address these challenges.

We are training more teachers, and providing more books and learning materials.

We are focusing on equality of opportunity to make sure that our girls get a fair go.

And we are looking to make sure young children are taught in a language they can understand so that language is not a barrier to education.

We are determined to give our young people the chance of a better future.

We are installing fibre optic network across the country, which at an opportune time will help us to introduce early education, facilitating a more productive and quality education.

We are also hoping to organize an 'Education First' Mini-Summit in Díli in November, with a view to learning from the experiences of nations such as Finland, South Korea and Cambodia, in achieving significant and rapid progress in education systems, quality and equality.

Ladies and Gentlemen,

I would like to give thanks to His Excellency, the Secretary General of the United Nations, Ban Ki-moon, for promoting the Education First initiative.

Timor-Leste looks forward to working in partnership with the United Nations to give our children the opportunity, the hope, and the promise provided by a quality education.

Thank you very much.

g7+ High Level Side Event of The United Nations General Assembly

New York, 26 September 2012

Excellencies

Ladies and Gentlemen,

Looking at this high level participation, I must say that today marks an important step for the g7+ New Deal.

Since its first meeting in Díli, in early 2010, the g7+ has grown to become an influential advocate for the people of fragile and conflict-affected countries.

The g7+ was established because we recognised that fragile States require tailored policy responses that address the reality of our situations.

The g7+ also provided an opportunity for fragile nations to meet, independently of our development partners, and to have a collective voice in the global development dialogue.

We all know – everyone in this room knows – that one and a half billion people live in areas affected by fragility, organised crime or conflict.

This is why, addressing insecurity and fragility, should be the primary development challenge for the Least Developed Countries.

At the great hall of the General-Assembly, listening to all the distinguished speakers, from yesterday to this morning, we can say, this is the real problem of today's world.

We know we cannot address this challenge alone. While fragile nations can learn from, and support each other – we also need help. But I remind you all of this profound thought from South Sudan, the youngest post conflict country:

'NOTHING ABOUT US, WITHOUT US'

Ladies and Gentlemen,

This is why we are pursuing the New Deal.

The New Deal seeks to ensure that, international development assistance is country owned, and country led, and meets the real needs of our people. It seeks, therefore, to make sure aid is effective.

As everyone knows, Timor-Leste is located between two big neighbours. We are pleased to have here the Honorable Julia Gillard. I have to thank Australia for pushing Timor-Leste to this process, by encouraging us to participate in the Accra Conference on Aid Effectiveness in 2008.

Timor-Leste has lived the philosophy of the New Deal.

When we were very fragile, we began with short term priorities, to give us flexibility to address our urgent problems.

Our focus was on peace building.

Once we secured peace and stability, we could already develop a long term plan, our *Strategic Development Plan 2011-2030*. And now, we are at the implementation stage.

Ladies and Gentlemen,

As a new nation, as a post-conflict country that fought against Indonesia, our progress would not have been possible without our reconciliation, cooperation and deep friendship with Jakarta.

And for this, I would like to acknowledge the contribution of one of the world's great statesmen, His Excellency, President Susilo Bambang Yudhoyono.

And I have to remind you, it was not only with Indonesia, because the post-conflict situation was visible within our own society. Therefore, ours was not an easy path and we met many challenges along the way. But we succeeded, through dialogue and a community rooted reconciliation process!

We are making progress and celebrated our ten year anniversary of independence in May this year.

While we have achieved stability, there are still risks ahead.

We know that we are not fragile because we are poor; we are fragile because our institutions are weak. And so, we must continue to build our State.

And while our stability has encouraged strong economic growth, we now have to ensure that our prosperity is shared.

Rising inequality is an emerging risk for social division, and so it is critical that we improve the lives of all the people across our country.

We have to work to eradicate poverty, and to create jobs, particularly in the rural areas.

Like many g7+ nations, we are rich in natural resources and know that this provides a solid foundation to build our future.

We made sure that we carefully manage the income from our petroleum resources, so we could start building schools and hospitals and other essential infrastructure, while saving most of the revenue for future generations.

Timor-Leste was the third nation in the world to be fully compliant with the Extractive Industries Transparency Initiative.

Ladies and Gentlemen,

Before I finish, I would like to urge the g7+ to be a part of the global dialogue, to set goals to fight poverty beyond 2015, when the MDGs come to an end.

And we must remember that while developing countries have made substantial progress – not one low-income fragile or conflict affected country, has yet achieved a single Millennium Development Goal.

The new global goals will help define how people approach development. They will shape views as to what development looks like.

And in this dialogue, we need to be wary of grand narratives, which seek to provide a one size fits all solution, but do not respond to the needs or reality of fragile nations.

That is why the new global agenda must address fragility and security.

It must recognise that peace, and a legitimate and strong State, are needed before sustainable steps can be taken to eradicate poverty. And, from stability, by strengthening the rule of law, good governance, reconciliation and social harmony, the national Leaders, together with their people, can improve the lives of the population and march towards a sustainable development.

Ladies and Gentlemen,

It is a great pleasure to see such strong support for the g7+.

It gives us hope that by working together, all nations can achieve the common goals. As I said last night in the General Assembly, human dignity must be at the core of decisions on problems affecting our planet. We must have an overall sense of humankind existence, the aspirations and fears, the dreams and suffering, the will and despair, all the drama in the fight for survival of women and men around the world.

Thank you very much.

Ceremony Marking the end of the Operational Activity of the ISF and UNPOL

Government Palace, Díli, 31 October 2012

Excellency, President of the Republic,
Excellency, President of the National Parliament,
Excellency, President of the Court of Appeal
Excellency, Prosecutor-General of the Republic
Excellency, Acting Special Representative of the Secretary-General of the United Nations
Excellency, Commander of UNPOL
Excellency, Commander of ISF
Excellencies, Members of Parliament
Excellencies, Members of Government
Excellency, Chief of the Defence Force
Excellency, Commander-General of PNTL
Excellencies, Representatives of the Diplomatic Corps accredited in Díli,
Distinguished Guests,

The building of a State involves a process that cannot be free from error. This is even more the case when the task begins following a conflict resulting from a struggle for liberation. In fact, there has been no part of the world in which a State has been built in a short period of time.

In light of this, our first decade of sovereignty did not bring us only happiness. We faced many of the difficulties that are common to those who take the first steps in leading a young Nation.

We all knew that one of the most demanding challenges would be to transform a guerrilla force into modern and professional armed forces, along with creating from scratch a police force able to secure by itself internal security and peace among our people.

In hindsight, we must acknowledge that there were key gaps, which included the quality of basic training of the police officers that were recruited for the PNTL. This contributed to PNTL growing with serious weaknesses, which became evident when the institution failed to maintain public order in 2006 at a time when our nation needed it most. Instead, the PNTL almost ceased to operate.

And as a result of internal problems, the F-FDTL experienced nearly a third of its personnel leaving their ranks. Many of these then went on to challenge the authority of the State, which led to serious conflict throughout the country and in particular in Díli.

In 2006, recognising that we were unable to restore public order by ourselves, and with the survival of our democratic and independent State operating under the rule of law in jeopardy, we were forced to call for international assistance. This decision was shared by our bodies of sovereignty.

We were fortunate to be able to rely on the great solidarity and the operational readiness of four friendly countries, Australia, New Zealand, Malaysia and Portugal, which did not hesitate to send military and security forces to Timor-Leste. Step by step, these forces helped us to return to normality.

Meanwhile the United Nations Security Council also responded to our request and sent a mission to become the sole institution responsible for internal security in Timor-Leste. This force was UNPOL.

Over the past six years, the Timorese State was not in a position to exert its exclusive competence for providing security for people and their property. We must recognise, however, that this was necessary to allow us to mend the errors of the past, which included addressing the quality of the training of the various units of the PNTL, and especially those dedicated to handling more complex criminal matters.

At the same time, and working together with UNPOL, we undertook thorough reform of the PNTL, correcting its deficiencies and organising its operation.

It was with persistence and determination that we managed to solve problems caused by the crisis, which threatened the stability and wellbeing of the people, such as the IDPs and the issue of the petitioners.

In 2008, following attacks against the heads of bodies of sovereignty, Operation Halibur became an opportunity to demonstrate the ability of soldiers and police officers to work in close coordination and cooperation towards a common goal. This operation was a significant success in terms of peace, stability and security in the country, and gave the Defence and Security Forces a desire to work harder in order to succeed in their missions.

We started the gradual process of handing over to PNTL the responsibility for police operations in the various districts of the country. This process was completed on 27 March 2011, with the handing over of the General Command.

We witnessed with satisfaction how the Defence and Security Forces proved, in an increasingly confident and effective way, to be able to ensure internal security and the defence of the people. Nevertheless, we continued to rely on the generous support of the ISF and UNPOL.

Since the F-FDTL and PNTL proved to be able to perform the tasks given to them by the Constitution with professionalism and competence, it was clear that they could not continue to receive foreign assistance indefinitely. We all agreed, therefore, that by the end of this year the United Nations would permanently end their mission in Timor-Leste and that ISF would withdraw their troops from our national territory.

As such, today signals a landmark for the recent but wonderful history of our homeland. It is a cause for joy and pride for all Timorese, but not because the police officers and soldiers who generously volunteered to assist us are now leaving Timor-Leste. Instead, it is because their assistance enabled us to correct our errors and to improve our technical and professional skills.

This is precisely the reason we are here today at this ceremony that seeks first to acknowledge the important role that UNPOL and the ISF played in making Timorese society safer and more just. The awarding of the Order of Timor-Leste to both these institutions represents our genuine gratitude to all those who, for the past six years, have served UNPOL and the ISF, and consequently, Timor-Leste and its people.

In my name, and on behalf of the Government that I lead, I thank and congratulate the Commanders of UNPOL and the ISF for their good work in Timor-Leste. I also want to thank the United Nations, represented by the Acting Special Representative of the Secretary-General, as well as the Governments of Australia and New Zealand, for providing the assistance that comes to an end today.

We are aware that there will be new challenges in the future. Having rebuilt our security forces, we must now strive to train their members, so that the recent past is never repeated and that our police force is always up to the task.

The future cooperation with police forces from friendly countries, with models similar to that of PNTL, will now be undertaken bilaterally. This will also be the model by which we will undertake international military cooperation.

I thank all the international police officers and soldiers and wish you all the best in the future. I hope that your trip back home is a pleasant one.

Thank you very much.

Bali Democracy Forum V – 'Advancing Democracy Principles at the Global Setting'

Bali, 8 November 2012

Your Excellency, the President of the Republic of Indonesia, Dr Susilo Bambang Yudhoyono
Your Excellencies the Co-Chairs,
Your Majesty,
Excellencies, Heads of State and Government
Excellencies, Heads of Delegations
Ladies and Gentlemen,

It is with great satisfaction that, for the fifth consecutive year, I take part in this important annual meeting.

I am pleased to see a growing number of participants every year, which reflects the importance of our common agenda of Peace and Democracy and which is the central theme of the Bali Democracy Forum.

Once again, I must commend my dear friend, and President of the Republic of Indonesia, Dr Susilo Yudhoyono, for his initiative in starting this Forum in December 2008. Since its inception, the President has been steadfastly dedicated to giving this event energy and leadership, which has ensured that people from many countries around the region, and around the world, come together in an inclusive way to work on a project of dignity, of democracy and of development.

This is the true spirit of the Asian Century which has been fostered right here by this great nation of Indonesia.

Indonesia is not only the third largest democracy in the world; it is also an example of pluralism and tolerance.

Indonesia inspires us to work towards a model of sustainable development that does not neglect the aspirations of the people or the importance of cooperation and friendship with other countries in the region.

As an emerging power, Indonesia has undergone a dynamic transition which has been so important to this region of which Timor-Leste is a part. This change occurred in a manner which respected the culture and the tradition of the people of Indonesia and which has enabled the transformation of the Indonesian economy. Most importantly, it has promoted peace and national stability.

Ladies and Gentlemen,

We cannot meet this year, on this island, without remembering the terrible events of ten years ago that had a devastating impact on Bali. The terrorist attacks of 12 October had a deep impact on Indonesia as well as the countries of the region – having brought home to us the shocking cruelty of indiscriminate violence – and around the world.

Ten years later, however, Bali continues to be a prime tourism destination and the best place for international events. This is not only because of its rich natural beauty and its culture but because of the strength of its people who have shown great courage and compassion in the face of terrible setbacks.

We continue to condemn, with all our hearts, attacks of terror that have harmed so many people around the world, causing generalised fear and mistrust and hindering our liberty and our human dignity. Ultimately, these attacks represent attempts to destroy the tradition of religious tolerance and cultural freedom.

However, the damaging association often made between Islam and terrorism, should also be firmly rejected.

The Muslim community has contributed so much to develop humanity itself, living side-by-side with other religions and sharing its knowledge and wisdom in an open and constructive manner.

Indonesia, the country with the largest Muslim community in the world, has been a shining example of this reality.

Ladies and Gentlemen,

The world is facing serious problems and is sliding over to an increasingly dangerous lack of control.

One and a half billion people now live in areas affected by fragility, organised crime or conflict.

In some regions, we see many people expressing their despair at being subject to autocracies that have no regard for human rights or common decency.

Europeans are also experiencing an uncertain future, within a setting of growing unemployment, economic crisis and the setback of the welfare state.

In other countries, those who have always been poor continue to live in miserable conditions, striving to survive everlasting hunger while continuing to depend on charitable aid to deal with drought or torrential rains.

Across the world, we have witnessed devastating natural disasters that have taken so many lives and caused incalculable damage.

In the Pacific region, for instance, the very survival of some countries is at risk because of climate change, including the paradisiacal Maldives in the Indian Ocean.

But the problem is that the climate change also threatens global food security, which requires an urgent and united world strategy.

In view of this, responding to the situations of fragility that multiply around the world should be the main challenge of current democracies.

Democracy – with its principles and universal values – continues to be a safe haven as well as a starting point to address the challenges that are ahead for humankind.

This Forum, which assembles the representatives of democracies from around the world, in all their different forms, will contribute to addressing these global challenges.

Ladies and Gentlemen,

As we have been discussing at the Bali Democracy Forum for the last several years, democracy cannot be imposed on a country, ignoring its entire historical, cultural and economic context. Instead, it is a process that must be nurtured continuously, and which must respect the timings and the idiosyncrasies of each society.

Dialogue is the essence of democracy. Dialogue enables us to move forward as a community of nations, as a nation, as a people and as citizens.

Removing the component of dialogue and the stages and processes that are inherent to the very concept of democracy is to deny its substance and to lose faith in humankind.

As such, we are sad to see that world leaders are not working harder to replace intransigent political positions with mechanisms of dialogue, to look for solutions to the world's economic, environmental and security problems.

In addition to this, we cannot accept being misled when noble democratic ideals are used thoughtlessly to feed and reinforce dominant political and economic interests, while disguised as social and humanitarian concerns.

By using this Forum to discuss sector-crossing issues such as the promotion of international peace, security and stability, along with the promotion of human rights, good governance and the fight against poverty, we can promote democracy and ensure it serves us well in transforming our societies.

Your Excellencies

Ladies and Gentlemen,

The people of Timor-Leste have had intense experience of the various nuances of the democratic process, with some successes as well as some setbacks.

In our still short existence as a State, we have made several mistakes and endured cyclical periods of instability. Notwithstanding our setbacks, as apprentices of a true democratic experience, we have tried to learn from the errors of our past and move forward from the difficult circumstances that will always face a post-conflict country, or more particularly, a country with a recent and long past of conflict and violence.

This year, living already in an atmosphere of peace and stability, we held two rounds of presidential elections, in the months of March and April. Both election rounds were judged to be free and fair by the international community.

On 7 July this year the Timorese People were once again called to vote in elections for our legislature, and our new Parliament was sworn in on 30 July.

As a result of this election, three parties were chosen to lead Timor-Leste from 2012 to 2017. Consequently, the new Constitutional Government was sworn in and given the task to consolidate the key institutions of a peaceful and democratic nation and to ensure the continuation of our economic growth.

Today, we face a new stage in the history of Timor-Leste, in which we become the sole masters of our fate. By the end of the year both UNMIT (United Nations Integrated Mission in Timor-Leste) and the ISF (International Stabilisation Forces) will have withdrawn from our nation, thereby ending peacekeeping operations in Timor-Leste.

We could not be more grateful for the solidarity and readiness of four friendly countries, Australia, New Zealand, Malaysia and Portugal, which did not hesitate in sending their military and security forces to Timor-Leste when we were going through the hardest of difficulties, as well as the international community through the UN Security Council.

I wish to take this opportunity to congratulate Prime Minister Julia Gillard on Australia's membership to the UN Security Council, and I hope that it will not only bring 'an Australian accent' to this important body but could also add a Pacific and Asian flavour to it.

Last September at the UN General Assembly, I defended the need to reform the Security Council to enable better representation so as to allow for more democratic resolutions.

Now, more than ever, we are ready to continue to ensure the ownership of the national development process, by implementing our *Strategic Development Plan 2011-2030*.

For this, we will continue to invest in the development of social capital, so as to build the capacity and skills of the Timorese and to maximise access to health, education, professional training, information, social justice and culture.

We will be investing in basic infrastructure and developing our economy to create employment. And we will nurture our potential and encourage both national and international private sector investment in Timor-Leste.

Today we have a plan, a vision, a goal – to transform Timor-Leste from a low income country into a medium-high income country by 2030. We want to become a prosperous and safe Nation, with a healthy and educated population, with skilled employment for everyone.

Your Excellencies

Ladies and Gentlemen,

At a time when we are witnessing a historic shift in global economic and strategic weight to Asia, and in which Asia continues to drive economic growth despite the global downturn, it is up to Timor-Leste to make sure that it benefits from its place in this region.

We are seeing the rise in Asia of future dominant economies of the world, including China, India, South Korea and Indonesia as well as the enduring strength of Japan.

It is expected that this growth will allow countries in the region to lift millions of people from poverty in coming years.

On the other hand, taking into account a possible strategic change in terms of decision making regarding politics, economy and even defence and security in this corner of the world, it is now more important than ever to build trust, dialogue and cooperation between the countries in the region.

This transition must also not neglect the development of the smallest and poorest countries. They must also benefit from this progress, which in turn will contribute to stability in the region.

Timor-Leste is on the verge of joining the Association of Southeast Asian Nations, which entails both challenges and opportunities. Once we are accepted as a fully fledged member of ASEAN, we will become a closer part of this global economic transition and be able to engage more actively in the strategic agenda of regional development.

Timor-Leste is committed to seizing the opportunities of the Asian Century which will see increased economic demand in the region. We will do this by developing our industries, our fisheries and our agriculture, by expanding our markets and by developing our tourism sector.

The fight against poverty in our country is a pressing priority, a challenge we share with over one billion people in the world.

By 2015, Timor-Leste will not meet the Millennium Development Goals and around 20% of the world population still live in conditions of extreme poverty.

As such, we have been focusing increasingly on participating in regional and international bodies, contributing with our experience to debates on constructive solutions for building peace and development.

We feel a mix of pride and responsibility that our Minister of Finance, Emília Pires, has been chosen to be part of the United Nations High-Level Panel which will draft the post-2015 sustainable development agenda.

We believe that progress that we have been making over the last several years in peace building and stability, along with economic growth, has made us more capable of contributing to this agenda.

Our active leadership of the g7+ also reflects our internal strength and enthusiasm to pursue sustainable development for our nation. But this contribution is part of a larger movement to leverage all fragile States who face similar obstacles but, based on democratic principles, know they can overcome the trap of poverty and instability.

This is also why we are advocating for the New Deal, which seeks to ensure that international assistance is better coordinated and owned by recipient countries, so that it may truly have an impact on the people that need it the most.

The New Deal gives new hope to the sustainable development of fragile countries and to the actual fulfilment of democratic principles.

Next week, and in addition to an Official Visit, I will be participating in the g7+ Ministerial Retreat, which will take place in Port-au-Prince. Haiti has been particularly affected by devastating natural disasters that have hit the region of Central America and the Caribbean.

While the repercussions of the earthquake of January 2010 still impact the daily lives of the Haitians, despite the large amount of aid, the recent passing of Hurricane Sandy again devastated the country, with direct and terrible implications for its infrastructure, housing, health and the food security of families.

My visit to Haiti will also serve to express the heartfelt sympathy and friendship of the Timorese people towards the Haitian people, who have displayed remarkable survival skills in the face of disaster.

This is consistent with the common sense of solidarity and mutual support within the g7+, as well as with the true democratic spirit.

Your Excellencies

Ladies and Gentlemen,

Besides the recent climate of regional instability, environmental threats continue to be on the rise, hindering the legitimate perspectives of emerging and developing countries concerning the use of their own natural resources.

The destructive impact of Hurricane Sandy in the United States of America is a perfect example of how developed countries are also affected by natural disasters. We express solidarity and distress with the American people who also suffered greatly. We also know that the United States needs to make significant changes in their response to environmental problems.

The truth is that developed economies cannot continue to ignore their responsibility for environmental degradation when even their own societies are clearly suffering from the tragic impact of this degradation.

Taking the opportunity to congratulate President Barack Obama for his outstanding election victory as well as to commend the American people for their unshakable commitment to democracy, we trust that climate change will be a key agenda item for the new administration, which in turn may encourage other developed countries to pay more attention to this matter.

The United States of America is a great democracy that has inspired many countries all over the world. We know that they will overcome this tragedy with dignity and renewed energy to create new mechanisms of prevention and response to such crisis. In this and in other humanitarian crisis, the intervention of developed countries, with their experience, capabilities, human and financial resources, is crucial.

In the universalism of the democratic spirit, the vision of progress belongs to all people, not only to those with more resources to overcome crisis.

Further, the problems of poverty and instability are not exclusive to the countries that experience them, because their consequences are threats for their close neighbours, for the region, and have an impact on the whole world.

That is why, ladies and gentlemen, in a scenario of challenges that know no borders, responses must also be global.

The dialogue between world leaders and the permanent collaboration in search of integrated solutions to protect our people should focus on enhanced adaptability and on a changing of mindsets.

In the face of today's uncertainty, democracy is what will enable us to move beyond the rigidity of unilateral decisions and to find joint, connected and creative responses for the challenges that we face together.

Thank you very much!

g7+ Haiti Ministerial Retreat

Port-au-Prince, Haiti, 13 November 2012

Excellency, Prime Minister Lamothe
Excellencies, Madam Ministers of Finance
Excellencies
Ladies and Gentlemen,

It is a great pleasure to be here in Haiti, for this g7+ Ministerial Retreat.

I thank the Government, and the people of Haiti, for hosting this meeting, and for their hospitality during this very difficult time.

It is testimony to the resilience and strength of the people of Haiti that we are able to meet here today, in the wake of the terrible loss of life and destruction caused by Hurricane Sandy.

We extend our deepest condolences, and affirm that the thoughts of people from around the world, including from our small, half island nation of Timor-Leste in the crossroad between Pacific and South East Asia, are with Haiti and its people.

The courage and dignity the people of Haiti have shown, in the face of devastating natural disasters, give us all faith in the promise of the human spirit.

Hurricane Sandy comes almost three years after the tragic earthquake that devastated Haiti.

These natural disasters also reinforce the need for a better and more effective international cooperation.

Ladies and Gentlemen,

It is with great satisfaction to meet again with the g7+ family.

This retreat follows the first Ministerial Retreat in Juba, very soon after the birth of South Sudan as a nation, where we did enjoy the warm hospitality of our South Sudanese brothers and sisters.

The Juba Ministerial Retreat was a great success. It brought us together around the New Deal, and enabled us to develop the strategy to take to the Fourth High Level Forum on Aid Effectiveness in Busan, South Korea.

Thanks to that Retreat, and our hard work in Busan, we have enjoyed widespread international recognition for the g7+ and its agenda, as well as broad endorsement of the New Deal.

And we must celebrate our wins.

This Retreat in Haiti also follows the g7+ High Level Side Event, that was held in New York, during the recent United Nations General Assembly.

That event, attended by many of us here today, as well as other world leaders, provided added momentum and promoted international understanding of the agenda of the g7+.

And so, I am pleased to offer my congratulations for the hard and determined work of the g7+, and to Haiti for hosting this important Ministerial Retreat.

Ladies and Gentlemen,

The reason, we are here today, is because we are determined to make sure that our people have the ownership of the future of their respective nations. It means that it is our people who understand best the challenges that our nations face; it is our people who recognize what is needed to make progress; and it is our people who know best how to go about securing our future.

And that is why we say that development assistance must be 'country owned and country led'.

This is the core principle of the New Deal.

Meeting in Haiti provides the g7+ with inspiration. The people of Haiti have a proud history of fighting for freedom and for self determination.

The people of Haiti, who dared to overthrow slave masters and became independent in 1804, has used its independence and membership of the United Nations to strongly support decolonization and the independence of African nations.

Being colonized for more than 450 years, on the 28 of this month, we will be celebrating 100 years of the last rebellion against the Portuguese rule. Yesterday, we celebrated the 21st anniversary of a massacre, perpetrated by Indonesian occupiers, against a peaceful youth demonstration demanding the end of the war.

It is with this same spirit of solidarity and resolve that we aspire to make progress in the g7+ agenda.

In 2000, we entered into the new millennium with great hope for a future, free of the mistakes and conflicts of the past – a future that reflects the better side of humanity and which recognizes that we all have a common cause in protecting our planet and its people.

We are here, at the time the international community recognizes its failure to accomplish Millennium Development Goals in 2015. Now that the United Nations is committed to review the action plan for the post-2015, we must all be part of this process.

I just came from Indonesia, after participating for the fifth consecutive year, in the Bali Democracy Forum promoted by President Susilo Bambang Yudhoyono. In that Conference, we tried to raise cross-cutting issues, such as democracy, peace and stability, human rights and development.

And so, as the world decides on the development agenda beyond 2015, we must make sure that addressing fragility is at the forefront of discussions so that our countries can succeed.

As we all know here today, achieving national stability, peace and resilience is not easy.

We can see from international historical experience that national stability has not been the natural order of things.

And the world should start by focusing on the fragile nations of the world, including the nations represented by the g7+.

We all watched in disbelief as billions and billions of dollars were poured into bailouts for western countries that spent beyond their means.

And as billions of dollars were given to bail out the global financial industry – the same industry that was responsible for plunging the world into recession.

And yet, the people of many of our nations continue to face extreme poverty and deprivation.

We are doing our best for our countries, working hard to provide hope and promise for our people.

But more needs to be done, and the international development agenda must align with the real needs of the world's poor and vulnerable.

Later today Professor Paul Collier will address this Ministerial Retreat.

He has looked in detail at the terrible costs of fragility, and of extreme poverty, not only in the countries where the so called 'bottom billion' live, but also in surrounding nations and the world as a whole.

And he makes a strong case that by focusing on conflict affected, and post-conflict States, and making a strong concerted effort, we can break the cycle of fragility.

Importantly, and I think we all agree, he argues that international efforts should be concentrated in the most difficult environments – environments where it may not be easy, but where help is most needed.

Ladies and Gentlemen,

According to the World Bank, around one and a half billion people now live in areas affected by fragility, organised crime or conflict.

And from our own experience, it is obvious that you cannot achieve development, improve health and education and alleviate poverty, when you are living in a state of conflict.

This is why not one low-income fragile or conflict affected country has yet achieved a single Millennium Development Goal.

And in facing this challenge, the people of fragile nations must be at the forefront of this effort.

No one else can speak for us.

No one else can better understand the dreams our people have for their future.

The world has learnt the hard way that peace and stability cannot be imposed upon a country; and that to make progress in fragile nations there must be true local ownership and leadership.

But it can be difficult for a fragile nation to stand alone to fight for its interests in the global development agenda.

That is why we need the g7+.

We need a strong, collective voice so that we are heard when decisions are being made that affect our nations.

We can also learn from each other, and support each other as we move from fragility to resilience.

The experience and the expertise in finding solutions to national fragility reside not in London, or in Brussels, or in New York, but in Port-au-Prince, and in Juba and in the Solomon Islands.

And together, we can bring this experience and expertise.

Ladies and Gentlemen,

I look forward to working together with you over the next day and a half.

Before I finish, I would like to make some comments on the issues that we have to grapple with during the Retreat.

We must work to reinforce our agenda, and the fact that the foundation of the New Deal is the interconnected approaches set out in the Peacebuilding and Statebuilding Goals, as the FOCUS and TRUST principles.

As we trial our fragility assessments, we must also recognise that it is more important to get our processes right, and get our indicators right, than to rush implementation and risk losing our voice.

As my friend Minister Kosti from South Sudan put it so well, the assessments cannot be 'about us, without us'.

We must not be afraid of writing in our own voice, and in our own language, and from our own perspective.

We must also make sure that we get right our indicators on peace building and State building.

This will ensure that it is first necessary to address peace and stability before broader development goals can be achieved.

And we must continue to make our voice heard. We must make up for the fact that we had no voice for too long. And we must continue to participate in global forums and raise global recognition of our needs.

I hope that we can produce a collective statement at this Ministerial Retreat so that we can take the results of our discussions forward.

Ladies and Gentlemen,

This Retreat gives us all the chance to meet again, as friends, to form new bonds across nations and to make sure that our people get a fair go from the global development agenda.

I would like to again thank our generous hosts for their support and for their hospitality.

Thank you very much.

End of Mission of the International Stabilisation Force

Ministry of Defence, Díli, 21 November 2012

Your Excellency, Chief of the Defence Force of Australia
Your Excellency, the Commander of the International Stabilisation Force
Your Excellencies, Members of Parliament
Your Excellencies, Members of Government
Your Excellency, the Chief of the Defence Force of Timor-Leste
Your Excellencies, the Representatives of the Diplomatic Corps
Distinguished Guests,

It is a great pleasure to speak today at this landmark ceremony marking the end of mission of the International Stabilisation Force in Timor-Leste.

This is an important occasion for Timor-Leste, as well as for our friends and partners, Australia and New Zealand.

Following a request made by Timor-Leste in May 2006, the ISF was deployed to our nation to help maintain and restore public order.

At that time, Timor-Leste was experiencing widespread unrest and violence. In the immense and difficult task of building our State, we had stumbled, and we knew that we needed international help to get back on track.

We were fortunate to be able to rely on the great solidarity, as well as the operational readiness, of both Australia and New Zealand.

The arrival of the ISF was welcomed by our people, and the soldiers played an important role in the restoration of normality in our country.

Timor-Leste has now enjoyed many years of peace and security, which has provided a foundation for our country to grow, and from which we can work to build our nation and tackle poverty.

It is thanks to this foundation of security that Timor-Leste was able to move beyond dealing with short term crises, and engage in long term planning to prepare and implement our *Strategic Development Plan 2011-2030*.

On behalf of the Government and the People of Timor-Leste I give thanks to Australia and New Zealand, and the brave soldiers that served with the ISF, for helping us achieve stability.

As a result we now look to the future with optimism and hope.

The Australian and New Zealand soldiers of the ISF have served our country well. They deserve their reputation as some of the most professional and dedicated soldiers in the world.

The soldiers of the ISF have provided a model for the professional development of the F-FDTL and I am pleased that the Defence Cooperation Program will continue to support the development our armed forces.

Ladies and Gentlemen,

The departure of the ISF also represents a new stage for our nation in which we must take responsibility for our own security and for the future of our country.

We are pleased to witness the increasing effectiveness of the F-FDTL, which has proved to be able to perform the tasks assigned under the Constitution, and to defend our people with professionalism and competence.

As such, today is another proud landmark for our people in the history of our nation.

This ceremony, therefore, it not only a thank you to the generous military support provided by Australia and New Zealand – it also marks an important step for Timor-Leste.

We know that we have many challenges to face, but we can now move forward with dignity, belief and confidence.

Finally, I would like to give a special thanks to all the ISF soldiers that will be leaving our nation.

In recognition of your service and dedication to our country, Timor-Leste is pleased to award you with the Medal of Solidarity.

We trust that you will remember your time in our country, just as our people will always remember the contribution that you have made.

I hope that your return home is a good one and wish you all the best in the future.

Thank you very much.

Graduation Ceremony for the Finalist Students of UNTL

Díli, 26 November 2012

Illustrious Rector, Prof. Dr. Aurélio Guterres
Minister of Health
Minister of Education
Distinguished Members of Parliament
Members of the Government
Distinguished Faculty Members
Ambassador of Cuba
Distinguished Guests
Dear graduates and families,

Today's ceremony, that marks the graduation of 450 students of medicine, represents more than an academic formality. It is, above all, an historical mark in the development of Timor-Leste that should be celebrated with joy.

The graduation of a so many sons and daughters of this land, in the health sector that is so essential for our people, is reason for great jubilation and renewed hope for the future.

It is, therefore, with immense satisfaction, that I participate in this ceremony to express my profound admiration for these young people who, despite the difficulties that were certainly felt throughout these years, never gave up!

Your efforts in contributing to the building of our social State honour the sacrifices of our people to liberate the country and allow for a future of hope for our children.

Your dedication demonstrates the true fibre of our people, our fighting and persistent spirit. Hence, just like the veterans and martyrs of the past, you now belong to the list of new heroes of the present!

Ambassador of Cuba,

I cannot forget to mention to you how grateful we are for Cuba having generously accepted these hundreds of young people, enriching them with knowledge and technical training to allow them to perform their obligations to their people, in the area of medicine.

I ask you, Mr Ambassador, that you convey to my dear and most respected friend Commandant Fidel Castro, to President Raul Castro, to the Cuban Government and people, not only my personal gratitude but also that of all Timorese, who will never forget who are their true friends.

Excellencies

Ladies and Gentlemen,

This year, as you know, we commemorate important dates that symbolise our still most recent process of 'State Building and Nation Building'.

It is fundamental that the young people here present, above all consider that they are part of the new Timorese intellectual elite, who understand well the process and know well our history.

Always keep in your minds that our independence, of which the 10th anniversary we celebrated on 20 May, was achieved with much suffering.

That you never forget that during our short existence as a State, we committed various errors and experienced cyclical periods of instability; we stumbled in the gigantic and difficult task of building and we had to appeal for international assistance to help us restore and maintain public order.

But in the actual rhythm of building the State and the Nation, we have been looking to learn from our mistakes and have been distancing ourselves from difficult circumstances that enfold a country with a recent past of conflict and violence.

These last few years have, fortunately, been years of peace and security, allowing us to build the foundation to make our nation grow, to build our nation and direct our efforts to combat poverty.

Still in this year of 2012, in a frank climate of peace and stability, two rounds of presidential elections were conducted and were considered free and fair by the international community and in July, the Timorese people returned to the polls to elect the V Constitutional Government.

This new Government was invested with the mission to proceed with the consolidation of fundamental institutions of a peaceful and democratic nation and to guarantee the continuation of the growth of our economy.

We have been witnessing the gradual withdrawal of UNMIT (United Nations Integrated Mission in Timor-Leste) and of the ISF (International Stabilisation Force), thus ending the peacekeeping operations in Timor-Leste.

This is a new phase in our history, where we assume, exclusively, the reins of our destiny. It is up to all of us Timorese, especially the young people of this nation, to assume now the responsibility to contribute to ensure that there is no regression in this period of consolidating the gains achieved in terms of peace and stability.

It is in this spirit that we close the celebrations of this year, on the 28th November in Same, celebrating the 37th Anniversary of the Proclamation of Independence and

100 years since the last rebellion against Portuguese rule, which became known as the Revolt of Manufahi.

We hope that these dates, celebrated in this year of 2012, link us to the more recent past of the struggle for independence and the older roots that made us unique in the regional and world context, and also serve to affirm our sovereign Nation of peace, tolerance and development.

Excellencies

Ladies and Gentlemen

Dear graduates,

Our objectives for State institutional building legitimise a strong investment in the development of our human resources and generally, in the social capital of the nation.

The *Strategic Development Plan* places great emphasis on the human dignity that should be above any other interest.

The State has the obligation to meet the necessary conditions so that the Timorese, who are the true wealth of the nation, are healthier, more learned and have greater access to justice, information and culture.

This is a premise to building a just and developed Nation.

Presently, Timor-Leste has 13 medical specialists, 139 general practitioners, 1271 nurses and assistant nurses, 427 midwives and 416 health technicians.

To these numbers, we add today's graduates.

Despite not yet being possible for Timor-Leste to be able to rely merely on its own cadre, and having to continue to seek qualified external labour, we are little by little working to achieve this goal for the near future.

As such, it is important that you not forget that your studies do not end today. Today's ceremony does not represent the closing of a book but the beginning of a new chapter.

The career you have chosen is very demanding and in today's global world, where we are witnessing constant changes, only those who continue to increase their knowledge, those who with an open spirit seek to be continually updated are professionally successful and can participate better in the development of society.

Dear graduates,

The challenges that you will face in your profession are the challenges that the nation itself faces.

My appeal to you is that you concentrate with determination in carrying out your mission, so that our country appreciates the new generation of intellectuals and professionals. The people will be very sad if you start demanding more in terms of your rights and forgetting your duties to serve the sick who need your help with care and devotion.

Around half of the population live in conditions of extreme poverty, with difficulties of guaranteeing their own food security and precarious basic infrastructure, which obviously has direct implications on the people's general state of health.

The infant mortality rate is 44 deaths out of 1000 live births. The mortality rate of children under 5 years of age is 64 deaths in every 1,000 children, with 53% suffering from chronic malnutrition and 49% of malnutrition. The incidence of tuberculosis and malaria is still excessively high, with 133 for every 100,000 people and 104.2 in every 1000 people.

Only 64% of the population have access to potable water and 43% to basic sanitation.

These are the challenges that we have to resolve in a whole of government form, where the shortage of qualified human resources is still our major obstacle.

This is the image of Timor-Leste with 10 years of independence.

In September 1999, I participated in the Millennium Assembly in New York where the United Nations established the Millennium Development Goals, known as MDGs, to be achieved by 2015. Only in 2002 was Timor-Leste able to commit to the MDGs.

As you all know, the Secretary-General Ban Ki-moon recently established a High Level Panel to look at the problem and outline an agenda for after 2015 because not one developing country is able to fulfil a single MDG.

Everyone knows as well that Timor-Leste has a person on the High Level Panel, based on her own merit and for the leadership that Minister Emília Pires is assuming of the group of fragile nations, known as g7+.

The Government is working in preparation to host a meeting in February 2013, where specialists from various parts of the world will gather and discuss here in Díli, how to present concrete proposals to the High Level Panel that is advising the UN Secretary-General.

The Government in the next five years will continue to invest in the development of the health sector at various levels:

At the institutional and legislative level, covering management, support and resources so that the health service delivery is carried out with efficiency, professionalism and celerity. We are looking at private health services that will be an integral part of the national health system and on the provision of essential medications, on diagnostic systems and supply of blood.

At the health infrastructure level, from the refurbishment and construction of Health Posts across the country, to the refurbishment of health community centres and the expansion of the National Hospital and the five referral hospitals.

At the general health level, from nutritional programs, above all for children and mothers, to vaccination programs, access to potable water and basic sanitation and education on the prevention of illnesses. Maternal and infant health, particularly in terms of reducing the infant mortality rate, will continue to be a priority.

And we will continue to invest heavily in human resources development until we achieve the objective of having at least one doctor, two nurses, two midwives and one laboratory technician in each Suco of the Country (with at least 2,000 habitants).

This is the vision of sustainable development that we have for the country. Timor-Leste can only truly be free when the day comes when it has the capacity to provide the essential services to its people and when these services are delivered by the sons and daughters of these same people.

Today, with your graduation, we are a little closer to this goal.

Congratulations and every success!

V Constitutional Government

Presentation of the Draft Budget Law for 2013

National Parliament, Díli, 4 February 2013

Your Excellency, the President of Parliament
Your Excellencies, the Vice Presidents of Parliament
Your Excellencies, the Members of Parliament
Fellow Government members
Ladies and Gentlemen,

It is a great privilege and honour to address Your Excellency, the Speaker of Parliament, and all the honourable Members of Parliament in this Great House, to present the 2013 State Budget.

Last September I had the opportunity of presenting here, at this Great House, the Program of the Fifth Constitutional Government. At that time I underlined the fact that today we have a vision, and a plan to implement, to transform Timor-Leste from the poor country it is today into an upper-middle income country by 2030, with a safe, healthy, educated and productive population.

In these ten years as an independent and sovereign State we have had setbacks, due to our situation as a post-conflict country. However, and more so than in other countries, the consistent political will shown by Timorese leaders, and the participation of all parts of our society, enabled us to overcome this post-conflict situation with courage and clarity.

In this decade-long process of State building (from scratch) and consolidating, we were aware that we were part of the LDC (Least Developed Countries) group.

There were long studies made by experts on how LDCs develop, within perspectives of sustainability and without losing sight of the Millennium Development Goals.

These theories and experiences by agencies that were familiar dealing with the entrenched poverty of others helped us to lead the dialogue of the g7+, which consists of 18 countries representing over 350 million people. We have insisted with the international community regarding the need to adopt new mechanisms to replace the old ones, which have been used for dozens of years and have proven to be completely ineffective.

The New Deal launched in Busan, South Korea, and debated in the hallways of the UN, basically reflects the need for developing countries to know their own (social, political and economic) reality, their weaknesses and their potential, so that they can own the process and choose the best path to steady and sound development, in order to ensure stability.

Another guiding principle of the Group is to take into account the macro principles and the universal micro doctrines, but only to guide annual and medium and long term policies. These policies must in turn reflect the current and actual needs of each country, so as to prevent governments from becoming too theoretical and too subjective in their action plans.

The macroeconomic theories have failed to solve the great global financial crisis. Today's world requires a more humane doctrine to free itself from the mathematic calculations of profits and money that defines the statistic GDP of nations, as an instrument for separating rich and poor, with the latter being subject to the speculations of the markets. These speculations and markets show that in the US and in the European Union, the rich and powerful transfer every year $1.7 trillion and $1.3 trillion respectively, to avoid paying taxes.

The world has already realised that the current system is not merely sick but rotten inside. The world has also realised that 99% of humanity is at the mercy of the rich and powerful, whose experts, working in their comfortable offices and earning huge salaries, draft doctrines to be followed by the poor.

Just in 2004, Timor-Leste signed the UN's global anti-poverty programme, known as the Millennium Development Goals. Despite the short time we had, we have achieved some small success (reducing child mortality, improving the fight against tuberculosis, etc.), better than some countries that have been independent for over half a century. Nevertheless, we keep our feet on the ground and do not forget that what we are achieving is very relative, since we are a small country with only 1 million people. We cannot compare ourselves with nations that already have very sound economies and where classic macroeconomic concepts (such as employment and unemployment, imports and exports, expenditure and revenues) would be easier to apply, even though they are not.

This is the current challenge of the modern and globalised world, in which the poor absorb or consume concepts and theories without realising that these concepts and theories only serve the large decision-making centres and the ones that have the money and keep the weak and the poor down with tricks and threats.

Your Excellencies,

While the *Strategic Development Plan* sets the rules for the next 20 years, the Fifth Constitutional Government presented its 5-year political program, setting the goals to be achieved by the end of its mandate. It is with particular satisfaction that I now present to the honourable members of Parliament the 2013 SGB, which responds to the program of the first year of our mandate.

I would like to remind the honourable members of Parliament and all the People that the 5-year plan is, in practice, the program for the first five years of the SDP.

This Government must necessarily look to the future, lest it become too busy with immediate day to day problems. The Government is aware that unless it adopts a broad vision or a Road Map to start and continue a steady and consistent development process we will lose ourselves in small reviews and become confused in our efforts.

A social and economic process, particularly at the start as is the case in Timor-Leste, is always complex requiring thorough review of priorities with medium term impact and of the connection between activities covered.

As such, national projects must take into account the goals they seek to achieve in the medium and long term. The policies to be developed must also be staged in consideration of impacts and benefits, which cannot be immediate, since the immediate is always temporary.

Consequently, the projects concerning the National Power Grid and Tasi Mane must also be seen as a whole, taking into consideration the impact and the benefits that they will stimulate and produce in the medium and long term.

The Government has adopted the idea of a new development benchmark. The fight against poverty is the eternal slogan of the international community, with the United Nations, the World Bank, the IMF and OECD being at the forefront of the fight against poverty. The results are plain to see, particularly in Africa. Billions and billions of dollars are invested and much of the world population continues to go without food, shelter, health, education or safety.

Some curious person found out that in Timor-Leste, between the end of 1999 and 2007, the international community invested over 8 billion dollars and yet we, the Timorese, were responsible when the number of poor people increased by 5% in 2007.

We Timorese must avoid following the trend of simple statistical and mathematical calculations regarding the outcome of our actions only to justify the investments we want to make. When millions of Americans fear to lose their homes because they cannot continue to pay their mortgages, when millions of Europeans cannot afford a single meal a day, do we say that they are poor or simply that they are unemployed? In Timor-Leste we have adopted the international standard that considers as poor someone who 'lives with under $1 every day'.

I ask these questions so that we do not lose sight of our reality and can look to the medium and long term.

The First Constitutional Government set the goal of 'Fighting poverty' as a 'National Cause', and we continue committed to eradicating poverty in our country.

The Program of the Fifth Constitutional Government, in line with the *Strategic Development Plan*, creates and promotes the Special Economic Zones. The Constitution of the RDTL grants special regimes to Oecussi and Ataúro, however it is necessary to carry out proper and thorough studies before both these territories may acquire their special status.

Timor-Leste has been the leading player in various international initiatives, at least in regard to the EITI (Extractive Industries Transparency Initiative), being the 3rd country in the world and the 1st in Asia to be granted full compliance status and having already provided support to several countries that want to become more familiar with our practice in order to replicate it. Timor-Leste is also leading the g7+.

We Timorese will star in another initiative under the new development benchmark to try convincing the world that it is effective in the sustainable fight against poverty.

Making use of the legal and conceptual bases available to us, the Government has decided to start a Special Economic Zone pilot project in Oecussi, to be called, under the new benchmark, a 'Social and Market Special Economic Zone'.

Being a member of the CPLP and part of the Economic Forum of Macau, as well as close to entering ASEAN, which is debating the subjects of 'common market' and 'market chain', the Special Economic Zone of Oecussi should be a trade and industrial centre directed to the market but also with social concerns regarding the 'atoni' population and consequently the whole of Timor-Leste.

With the agreement of the President of the Republic, the Government has decided to appoint Dr Mari Alkatiri as the representative of the State in this initiative of studies, reviews and contacts with the CPLP countries and – why not? – the ASEAN and Pacific countries. This strategically relevant program will then be expanded to Ataúro and other parts of the country.

Your Excellencies,

The philosophy that guides this Government is the same that guided the Fourth Government. In other words, this Government has received the mission to continue implementing the successful programs and reforms. Continuity implies the ongoing correction of operating mechanisms and working systems, as well as the fine-tuning of methodologies and of administration and management.

The budget I present today to Parliament takes into consideration the macroeconomic policy goals and is the financial expression of what we want to do in the short term in order to eradicate poverty in Timor-Leste in the medium and long term.

This is a complex challenge requiring strong economic growth, better infrastructure and a skilled labour. Achieving these goals will require significant public investment.

The economic miracles in the 2nd half of the 20th century, many without the help of natural resources, show a consistent focus on public investment, in the creation of basic conditions for generating other types of wealth, in maintaining a double-digit growth rate and in dealing with a double-digit inflation rate. The question put to them when seeking proper solutions in each of their programs' period of implementation was how low it should be and how high it can be. However the real dilemma was whether they should stop development programs in order to focus on inflation or whether they should merely strive not to let inflation run wild while continuing with the development programs that were requiring significant public investment.

The 2013 Budget invests in new policies, based on the Program of the Fifth Government and on the *Strategic Development Plan*, while strengthening investment in policies started in previous years, which have led the country to greater stability, better management of State affairs and economic growth.

Timor-Leste has enormous wealth in natural resources, namely oil and gas. We all know that these resources are not renewable, which is why I have already stated before this Parliament that they must be used so that in a not so distant future we may have an economy that is not dependent on the petroleum sector.

Since the First Government we have made a commitment to the Timorese People to use the money from petroleum revenues in a sustainable manner, so as to protect future generations. That was why Parliament authorised the diversification of Petroleum Fund investments.

Financially, this means that there is a perspective that overall public spending will be reduced in the future. It also means that we must start immediately to limit the growth of current expenditure. This is a challenge for the entire public administration, and here we must bear in mind that our State agencies are also growing. This Government is committed to improving service delivery to the people and to correcting management irregularities, so as to achieve the budget stabilisation of current expenses.

Only by thinking of 'building and consolidating' can we generate domestic revenue for funding a larger percentage of State expenditure and attract investments in productive sectors in order to benefit the Timorese People.

The 2013 State Budget enables the achievement of this goal in a prudent manner.

The 2013 State Budget sets priorities properly.

The 2013 State Budget is a balanced budget.

Your Excellency, the President of Parliament

Your Excellencies, the Members of Parliament,

The debate on the 2013 SGB, which we are starting today, must take into account the successes and achievements of the previous Government's policies and budgets.

As we turn the page on our first decade as an independent Nation, we must acknowledge that, despite the obstacles, we have managed to build a sound political and institutional architecture that has brought us social stability.

In 2013, Timor-Leste finds itself in a different and special situation. Last year we had two landmark moments in our experience as a sovereign Nation: we had presidential and parliamentary elections, strengthening the soundness of our democracy, and we witnessed the withdrawal of the United Nations Mission and of the International Stabilisation Force, confirming that we are ready to become the masters of our fate.

Our commitment to ensuring an atmosphere of peace and security has not been for nothing, since presently Timor-Leste is a promise of development.

Development progress can be measured in many ways. One way is through economic growth, which in our nation has been an average of 11.9% since 2007!

In the international press, the renowned Economist magazine recently stated that Timor-Leste was the sixth fastest growing economy in the world. This recognition fills us with confidence and resilience to meet the future ahead. The Economist does not say we are the world's sixth largest economy, it merely says we are growing well and that we are doing so in a very difficult time for the entire world.

This economic growth means that there is greater economic activity in the country. It reflects the existence of an emerging private sector, the creation of more employment, the increase of commercial and tourist activities, greater production levels (including agricultural production) and a larger percentage of tax revenues to support State services. In short, it means generation of wealth.

Progress in development can also be measured by looking at health and education. Here Timor-Leste is also making strong progress. From 2010 to 2011 the total number of children enrolled increased by 5%, 8% and 17% in basic, general secondary and secondary technical education respectively. Child mortality rates have also seen a sharp decline from 83 to 64 per thousand live births between 2003 and 2009/2010. Life expectancy at birth has also increased from 59.5 in 2006 to 64.64 in 2011.

Your Excellencies, the Members of Parliament,

For the good of the future generations, it is up to us to use the available resources in a way that is balanced and responsible, but also ambitious. As such, the Fifth Constitutional Government has set very clear priorities for the country, and will continue to focus on four key aspects:

- Development of social capital, particularly investment in the capacity building of our human resources and in the education and health of the Timorese;
- Development of the basic infrastructure;

- Development of the economy, particularly agriculture, tourism and the petroleum industry;
- Consolidation of the institutional framework, continuing to promote good governance and starting the decentralisation process.

Economic growth may only be considered a favourable indicator of national development if it observes two fundamental principles: inclusiveness and equity.

This means that every Timorese citizen should, directly or indirectly, be able to experience the benefits and opportunities of this economic growth. It does not matter whether they are men or women, young or old, whether they live in Fatumean or Tutuala, Nítibe or Laklubar, Alas or Ataúro, or whether they are farmers, fishers, carpenters, traders or teachers.

Since the First Government we have been working to establish administrative decentralisation and to implement Local Power. In 2013 we will be creating the establishment framework for the municipalities. We will also be promoting a broad public consultation, to be started in April, so that we may choose together the model best suited to the needs of the Timorese. After this we will start creating the Municipal Installation Committees in each of the 13 districts.

The creation of the Municipalities will bring citizens and the public administration closer and, along with a more effective local democratic participation, will promote the supply of public services able to drive social and economic growth, nurture the development of the private sector in rural areas, ensure environmental sustainability and promote gender equality. Furthermore, it will enable us to mobilise more efficiently the collective effort for implementing the *Strategic Development Plan*.

The Local Development Program, the Suco Development Plan and the Decentralised Development Program (which started in 2010), have enabled local and district administrations to become familiar with systems and actions in terms of planning, management and execution of projects, making our country better prepared for this unique process of greater democratisation and development. There are still aspects to be corrected, however we now have greater confidence and certainty in terms of improving implementation.

Based on previous experiences, the District Integrated Development Plan (PDID) established a budget planning and implementation system at district and sub-district level, preparing the Districts before the creation of the Municipalities.

The Government will continue to improve the management of the two main funds – the Infrastructure Fund and the Human Capital Development Fund. These funds will receive special attention this year, since their impact is expected to cover the entire society. These two pillars are essential for a balanced and sustainable economic development project and are a source of opportunities for men and women of all ages throughout the country.

As such, the number of scholarships provided by this Fund will be increased. We awarded 3,256 scholarships in 2012 and this year we intend to continue awarding scholarships in areas that are very important for the development of the country. Nevertheless, in 2013 the Government wants to carry out a study in order to improve the application of the HCDF, including a plan on more specialised training in strategic areas to meet the needs the country will have in 7-15 years.

We will also be providing professional training to an average of 2,500 young people a year, ensuring that access to capacity building will be the same in the capital as it is in the Districts. In view of this, we will be acknowledging 20 new community professional training centres a year.

The supply of basic education and health services is a priority in 2013.

We will continue to build health posts in order to ensure that every Suco has access to essential care, giving particular attention to those located in remote areas. In the next few years we will also start to improve considerably the services of the National Hospital and to expand the care provided.

In the area of education, we are planning to build 250 new pre-schools and, as a priority, 5 new technical and vocational schools and 4 Polytechnic Institutes. There is a pressing need to build the capacity of young people in order to obtain professional employment without forcing everyone to go to higher education facilities in Díli. Therefore we will be giving young people alternatives to acquire know-how that will prepare them to find productive employment.

In 2013 we want to generate wealth by creating more employment. This will be done by investing in the economic sectors.

Poverty reduction is also closely connected with the direct improvement of the living situation of the Timorese. The 2013 SGB foresees that drinkable water systems will start to be installed in 25,000 rural households. Additionally, the MDG Sucos project will continue, building 55,000 houses in several community clusters throughout the country within the next few years.

The traditional economic sectors such as agriculture and fisheries will be nurtured in parallel with areas where Timor-Leste may become extremely competitive, such as tourism.

This year we are planning the construction of a Training Centre of Tourism and Hospitality and we will be establishing two new Tourist Information Centres, one in Batugade and the other in Díli. We will prepare, through an implementation unit, the establishment of the Academy of Arts, Culture and Creative Industries of Timor-Leste, complete one of six new Regional Cultural Centres and move forward with the establishment of the Library, Museum and Cultural Centre of Díli, for which land has already been allocated. We will also be continuing the work in terms of identifying the Timorese cultural legacy.

While the Government has a key role to play in making major investments in these essential areas, it is also a priority to strengthen the private sector so that it may take on a greater role in the development of Timor-Leste in the medium term. The inclusion of a Secretary of State for the Support and Promotion of the Private Sector in the Organic Structure of the Fifth Constitutional Government is both necessary and timely.

However, infrastructure must also respond to the needs of the country's economic characteristics, which requires a strong effort in terms of building the national roads. The Government is also focusing on the South Coast, building a set of refinery and petrochemical infrastructure as well as roads, so as to ensure that the economic potential of this cluster is not wasted.

The Government foresees that by the end of the mandate it will establish 7 Public-Private Partnerships that will contribute to the national development goals.

This year there are two Public-Private Partnership projects that will begin construction works: the expansion of Airport President Nicolau Lobato and the Tibar Port. The current Díli port can no longer deal with the flow of commodities and this has contributed to price increases in consumable goods, since in the present conditions it is inevitable to have mooring delays. For instance, a few weeks before Christmas we had 24 freighters in the Díli territorial waters and some of them are yet to unload their cargo.

Only by improving the country's administrative and financial management can we ensure good governance.

As such, the Government will focus its attention in assisting State agencies so that they become characterised by their effectiveness, transparency and accountability. The Secretary of State for Institutional Strengthening will implement a performance and verification audit in every line ministry, thereby promoting the operational capacity building of public administration.

The Ministry of Finance will also continue to promote training in the areas of procurement, contract management and legal and administrative procedures, as well as to report to the public the policy decisions of the Government, including in the areas of Budget, Assistance, Procurement and Outcomes, by way of the Transparency Portal.

The Government defends the ongoing correction of systems and processes and even policies that prove to be inefficient or weak. This implies permanent oversight, which is why we will establish a Commission to review the Government's policy and expenditure options and to suggest corrections.

The work of this Commission will include the drafting of spending reports and reviews, namely on the Infrastructure Fund, the Decentralised Development Programs I and II and other topics suggested by Parliament, in view of the long term sustainability of social policies and other economical impact studies.

The Government continues to be fully committed to good governance. Performance by State agencies in this area has been acknowledged by the Corruption Perceptions Index of Transparency International in 2012, with Timor-Leste climbing up 30 places in the ranking – a significant improvement that must not make us think that we can stop working hard in this area.

Your Excellencies

Ladies and Gentlemen,

The Government is aware that strong economic growth has been accompanied by high inflation. Year on year inflation in Timor-Leste peaked at 15.4% in December 2011 but then dropped and stabilised at around 11%.

We know that increases in prices of goods, particularly food, reduce the purchasing power of our citizens. We also recognise that high inflation increases the costs of materials and causes problems for businesses in Timor-Leste, affecting the quality of works in their relation with the profits to which businesses are entitled. We further recognise that inflation increases the costs of Goods and Services and Minor Capital acquired by the State.

It is for these reasons that the Government is seriously committed to reducing inflation. As such, we have been carefully recording, monitoring and analysing inflation.

Nevertheless, the causes of inflation are complex and vary over time. Due to the global recession and its effects so far, the American dollar has decreased in value compared to the currencies of our trading partners, such as Indonesia and Australia, which led to imports becoming more expensive. Increases in international food and commodity prices have also contributed to inflation in the past. These causes, along with the rise in the price of oil, either due to war or economic sanctions, are outside of the Government's control.

Another cause of inflation in Timor-Leste is the balance between the amount of money and goods produced. In our fledgling economy there must be a persistent and ongoing effort to produce goods in the country. There is no other magical solution.

As such, Timor-Leste needs to produce more. The current budget gives priority to agriculture. A greater (public and private) investment in agriculture, livestock and fisheries should contribute to a production increase in the short and medium term.

The Government proposes to facilitate the establishment of new companies by creating business incubators and a 'one-stop shop' to simplify their registration and reduce the time necessary for establishing companies. This will also provide support to micro and small companies, cooperatives and industrial and commercial groups, in order to nurture employment creation and stimulate various productive sectors.

Increasing productivity, skilled labour and business competitiveness is the only way to support strong economic growth in the long term and to reduce and stabilise inflation. The Government will do everything it can to reduce inflation below 8%, in accordance with the priorities set in the 2013 State Budget.

Your Excellency, the President of Parliament
Your Excellencies, the Vice Presidents of Parliament
Your Excellencies, the Members of Parliament
Ladies and Gentlemen,

In 2013 we will be investing a total of $1,797.52 million to meet the needs of the country, giving priority to Infrastructures, Agriculture, Health and Education.

In comparison with the previous year, we have increased the investment in agriculture by 28%, in education by 12% and in health by 15%.

The 2013 State Budget is set to invest $892 million in development capital, including $753 million for large multi-year projects in the Infrastructure Fund.

The three largest programmes in the Infrastructure Fund are:

Power ($173.9 million)

In 2013 we will be finalising the works in Betano and thus completing the construction of the National Transmission and Distribution Grid. Improving power generation and supply should support strong economic growth in both micro and small companies in the districts and future medium and large industries.

One key error in these ten years of State building was the absence of a maintenance culture. In order to rectify this situation, we have allocated $10 million in the category of Goods and Services of the respective Ministry to ensure the operation and maintenance of the Hera Power Plant and of the substations. The increase in electricity production due to the completion of the Hera and Betano power plants will boost industry and require higher fuel consumption. To pay for this, we have allocated $117.8 million.

Roads ($116 million)

The Government is determined to build high quality roads throughout the country, in order to facilitate the transport of people and commodities and to reduce the costs of manufactured goods.

In addition to building the roads set out in the Infrastructure Fund, the Government is also building the Díli–Manatuto–Baucau road and the Díli–Liquiçá–Tibar–Ermera road. These works will be paid for by borrowing from JICA and the Asian Development Bank, respectively.

The Government will be investing around $44 million in this loan program to fund projects with high rates of economic return. The rate of interest on both of these loans is significantly lower than the estimated yield on Petroleum Fund investments. We, alongside financial agencies and other countries, are continuing to study the feasibility of other loans concerning major projects such as the Aileu–Ainaro–Maubisse road and the Manatuto–Natarbora road.

Tasi Mane ($139 million)

The creation of the National Company TIMOR GAP resulted in a boost for starting works in the South Coast, including on the petrochemical projects and the Supply Base. Just last February 1st a Memorandum of Understanding was signed between TIMOR GAP and Thailand's PTT.

Another $139 million included in the category of capital development of the Consolidated Fund for Timor-Leste will fund the development of small infrastructure, namely the construction of education and health facilities and of water supply, sanitation and irrigation systems, in accordance with local needs. These projects shall be awarded to Timorese construction companies, thereby nurturing local development and keeping profits in Timor-Leste.

The investment of $68.2 million, through the PDID, seeks to continue promoting the construction of infrastructure throughout the country, so as to meet the basic needs of the population in a fair and inclusive manner that relies on the active participation by local citizens and leaders.

I would like to inform the illustrious Members of Parliament that the 2013 State General Budget only considered as eligible the capital development projects that met the following criteria:

Certification by the Directorate of Land and Property regarding land use;

Approval of design and BoQ's by ADN; and

Approval by the Policy Budget Review Committee.

In this way, we want to ensure better execution rates for infrastructure projects.

Your Excellencies

Ladies and Gentlemen,

The Government is determined to boost agricultural production. Better agricultural production is essential to reduce imports and improve food security. We are also conducting a thorough study on malnutrition that takes into account the calories that exist in Timorese produce, as well as encouraging a new food diet in our society.

The 2013 State Budget allocates $3 million to the Goods and Services budget in the Ministry of Agriculture for buying seeds. This should boost the volume and value of farm production. The Infrastructure Fund also includes nearly $10 million of expenditure on agriculture projects. Much of this expenditure is for the construction and supervision of irrigation schemes which the Government believes will increase agricultural productivity.

Three areas of health spending have received increased budgets.

First, we have increased expenditure with Salaries and Wages to $21 million, in order to implement the new career regime for health professionals. This regime will increase the pay of health professionals with appropriate qualifications. The Government will be stricter in ensuring that health professionals respond to these incentives by displaying enthusiasm, dedication and empathy in the performance of their duties. The Government will also employ and adequately compensate recently qualified health professionals from Cuba. Better qualified and more motivated staff should improve the quality of healthcare in Timor-Leste in the short term.

Second, the Ministry of Health's budget for the purchase of medicines and drugs has been increased to $7 million. This will contribute to better health care and outcomes.

Third, $5 million has been allocated to purchase medical equipment in the Ministry of Health. This money will be used to purchase operation theatre equipment, anaesthesia machines, heart monitoring machines, a defibrillator and other medical equipment.

Education is another key factor in the development of a nation. The Government will pay due attention to the 'Education for All' Program, as this is related to the 'Education First' initiative by the Secretary General of the United Nations. I believe that all children should receive a decent education and that an educated workforce is a productive work force. Some progress has already been made and going forward we are determined to further improve education in Timor-Leste.

The quality of teaching is an important determinant of education outcomes. As such, the Government will continue to strive to ensure quality education in every school level. The Government is aware that no one should be pleased with the quantity of graduates every year given that the quality of education continues to be below expectations. Furthermore, education costs the parents of the students a lot of money. These parents are making sacrifices to try and provide better futures for their children.

The 2013 State Budget includes measures to raise the salaries of key groups of educators. More specifically, the UNTL's salary and wage budget has been increased to $7.6 million, due to the new career regime for higher education professionals. We will also be paying salaries to teachers who had previously worked as volunteers.

Additionally, the $42 million allocated to the Human Capital Development Fund, which includes the Scholarship Program, the Professional Training Program, the Technical Training Program and other types of training in key sectors, will train and build the capacity of our human resources to become the leading actors of national development.

In 2013 we will continue to invest in social policies seeking to improve the living situation of the Timorese. Investing in the people, particularly the most vulnerable

ones, is a moral obligation of the State. For this purpose we have allocated $236.5 million in the category of Public Transfers, namely:
- $84.8 million for personal benefits to Veterans.
- $38.2 million for our elderly and to those with demonstrated disabilities.
- $18 million for supporting Non-government Organisations and Religious Organisations promoting cultural and religious activities, thereby contributing to the social, cultural and spiritual wellbeing of the Timorese.
- $10.5 million for funding SEFOPE's 'cash for work' programme, thereby contributing to lower unemployment.
- $8 million for funding the Suco National Development Program, directly involving communities in their own development.
- $3.7 million for paying pensions to civil servants, in accordance with the approved Law.
- $3 million for land-related compensation.
- $5 million for funding the 'Ita Nia Rai' Program.

Finally, the Government will continue to invest in key sectors contributing to the consolidation of our democratic State under the rule of law.

We want to increase the PNTL's Salary and Wage budget to $13.6 million, thus ensuring the recruitment of more police officers to ensure safety in the country. We will also increase the F-FDTL's Salary and Wage budget to $7.9 million, so as to strengthen the capability of the Armed Forces.

Associated with this investment we have a **$1.3 million** grant for acquiring furniture for the houses of soldiers and police officers throughout the country, as well as $1.2 million for purchasing vehicles and equipment in order to help improve security at the airport.

We cannot neglect our foreign policy, particularly at a stage where Asia continues to be the fastest growing region in the world, boosting the growth of emerging and developing economies. As such, Timor-Leste is located in a region that presently offers strategic advantages.

This year, in addition to establishing two new Embassies, namely one in the United Kingdom and one in New Zealand, as well as consulates in Darwin and Atambua, which resulted in an increase of **$9.1 million** in the Ministry of Foreign Affairs and Cooperation's salary and wage budget, we will be investing in other key aspects:

Establish a Unit that will carry out the preparatory work in order for Timor-Leste to assume the presidency of CPLP in 2014-2016. This is even more important because it will test our organisation capabilities before becoming full-fledged members of ASEAN.

Prepare the establishment of the Diplomatic Study Centre in order to train and build the capacity of Timorese diplomats.

Intensify the process on the demarcation of land and maritime borders.

Continue to preside over the g7+ and to promote fragile States in terms of their collective development goals.

Participate in the High Level Panel on the Post-2015 Development Agenda, represented by the Minister of Finance.

These regional and international diplomacy and integration efforts will, in the medium and long term, result in immeasurable benefits for the future generations of Timorese citizens. In today's globalised world, no country can overcome the obstacles to development by working alone and isolated from the dynamics of international relations.

Your Excellency, the President of Parliament
Your Excellencies, the Vice Presidents of Parliament
Your Excellencies, the Members of Parliament
Ladies and Gentlemen,

In the 2013 State Budget this Government clearly explains how all expenditures will be paid for. Domestic revenue receipts are forecasted at $146 million for 2013. This represents a 9% increase compared to 2012.

Our goal is to lower steadily the percentage of the budget effort that is paid by the Petroleum Fund. For this purpose we will draft a broad reform in order to expand the tax base and to increase State revenue receipts. During the mandate period, it is estimated that this reform will allow us to increase domestic State revenue receipts from $134 million in 2012 to $218.4 million in 2017.

The difference between domestic revenue and expenditure is approximately $1,651 million. This is paid for by withdraws from the petroleum fund, the use of funds held in the Government's accounts and borrowing.

The 2013 State Budget includes $1,198 million of withdraws from the Petroleum Fund. This represents a sharp fall compared to the $1,495 million withdrawn in 2012. The decrease in the amount of money withdrawn from the petroleum fund shows the Government's commitment to fiscal prudence and sustainability.

Additionally, budget execution rates have been increasing since 2007. In 2012, and although we are not yet ready to present final figures as the accounts are yet to be audited, we estimate that the Consolidated Fund for Timor-Leste will have a 'cash' budget execution of approximately 88%.

If we take into account the execution of the Special Funds, the overall cash execution rate is estimated at 66%.

We recognise that the execution rate of the Special Funds, particularly the Infrastructure Fund, has not corresponded to the initial estimates, due to the persistent weakness in terms of implementing physical projects and other factors outside the Government's control. Nevertheless, the ongoing correction of the system and the introduction of new policies give us confidence that we will overcome this challenge in 2013.

In conclusion

> Your Excellencies,
>
> Ladies and Gentlemen
>
> People of Timor-Leste,

Today, more than ever, we are responsible for the path we want our country to follow!

Our ambition in terms of development, or better still our moral duty to reduce poverty among our People, requires coordinated sustainable policies, a plan and responsibility.

The Government I have the duty of leading is committed to being successful in this path towards development.

However, this will take time! We must walk this journey step by step, looking back to see how far we have come, correcting our stride whenever necessary and constantly reassessing the path still ahead of us.

In this collective effort, no one should be left behind. More importantly still, we cannot 'cheat' our travelling companions.

Consequently, the 2013 State General Budget is another important step in this journey. As such, I look forward to having a constructive debate on this budget that will determine the development of our country and our nation in the short, medium and long term.

Thank you very much.

2013 World Summit on 'Peace, Security and Human Development'

Seoul, 23 February 2013

Your Excellencies the Heads of State and Government
Your Excellencies the Heads of Delegations
Your Excellencies, First Ladies
Distinguished leaders of the UPF
Mr Tajeldin Hamad
Ladies and Gentlemen,

It is a great privilege to be here representing my country and I feel honoured to be invited to participate in this World Summit, side by side with so many important dignitaries.

Taking into consideration the participation of the Women for Peace forum, I would like to congratulate Madam Park Geun-hye, President-elect of the Republic of Korea, which validates the importance of women in this noble cause and, consequently, of the leaders of the whole world.

I pay my respect to Father Moon and Mother Moon and congratulate the Universal Peace Federation for their effort, which is dedicated to the cause of peace in the world, and I would like to give thanks for the magnificent hospitality given to me and the delegation of Timor-Leste.

Timor-Leste became independent on 20 May 2002 after 24 years of a difficult struggle for freedom. As a country recently emerging from a prolonged conflict, with Indonesia, and between ourselves, we decided to give real value to our struggle in order to avoid being subjugated by the memories of the sacrifices of the past.

We understood that peace was not just the absence of war, but the calmness in the mind of each Timorese and the harmony between our communities and the relations of friendship with other people.

We forged a reconciliation process with Indonesia, and today the two countries enjoy as neighbours the strong ties of friendship and cooperation. We also proceeded with the proper mechanisms to slowly heal our internal wounds, even if we were unable to avoid entering into a violent crisis in 2006.

We reflected deeply about our post-conflict situation and, in 2009, on the 10th anniversary of the Popular Consultation of 1999, which concluded with the uncontrollable destruction of our country, we launched an appeal to the people, who went forward with the motto 'Good-bye Conflict, Welcome Development'.

Since then, the people of Timor-Leste have lived in a climate of peace and stability.

In 2010, we had the honour to organise an international conference for fragile and post-conflict countries, with the theme 'peace building and State building', to define a clear road map for the countries with difficulties in shaking the state of inertia that subjugated them.

We realised that without democracy there can be no inclusive and integrated development, but that without stability there can be no development, and that true peace can only be achieved if democracy walks together with it in firm steps and in a continuous process. For this to happen, democracy needs to be an internal process for each country, undertaken conscientiously by the people.

Democratisation processes that are imposed from outside are bound to be unsustainable, because it promotes deep internal divisions that will take too long to heal and, in the end, will cause great suffering to innocent civilians.

As a young State, we have been searching to learn from the errors and setbacks that we were making. And, in a permanent dialogue with all public institutions and civil society, we have been overcoming the challenges inherent to State building. Fortunately, we are now at the beginning of a new chapter of our history, which includes the ongoing strengthening of our State agencies, economic growth and sustainable development.

Today, we have a *Strategic Development Plan* for a period of 20 years, within which, we will seek to transform our country from a low income nation to a country with upper-middle income levels by 2030, with a population that is educated, healthy, secure and prosperous.

The process of peace requires continuity and it must include giving the dividends of peace to each home, and to each family. It must include providing better conditions to every man and every woman so that they are able to live with full security in a broader dimension: political, social, economic, cultural and environmental.

Excellencies

Ladies and Gentlemen,

Nowadays, we are witnessing an increase in regional and international forums debating constructive solutions, towards peace and/or development of human beings. We have lived the experiences, and considered the theories, of prestigious institutions that permanently deal with the poverty of people and both have failed in their application to the realities of each country by using the standard approach of one size fits all.

In this last decade Timor-Leste was also a recipient of international assistance, which we are very grateful for. However, with this partnership, there were successes and failures, which do not justify the amount of money spent.

And so, Timor-Leste started to lead the g7+ dialogues, a group comprised of 18 countries representing a total of more than 350 million people. We have been insisting, with the international community, about the need to adopt new mechanisms of cooperation because the old ones, which have been used for decades, have proved inefficient.

It is also for this reason, that we are defending the New Deal, which was launched right here in South Korea, in the city of Busan, which reflects the need for developing countries to know their own reality (social, political and economic), their weaknesses and their potential, in the way to conduct their own development process in a credible, responsible and gradual way.

The New Deal brings a new hope for the sustainable development of fragile States, enabling better leadership by the recipient countries and better coordination of international assistance. This new approach focusing on the realities, that are inherent to the beneficiaries, and their needs, will have greater impact on their people.

This new approach is not only necessary, it is urgent. Around 1.5 billion people across the world live in areas affected by fragility, organised crime and conflict.

In this regard, in three days coming, we will be hosting in Díli the leaders of the Governments of the g7+ countries, and of the close neighbours of Timor-Leste from the Pacific, as well as Australia and Indonesia, to hold an International Conference on the post-2015 Development Agenda. The theme of this conference is 'Development for All – We will not leave 1.5 billion people behind'.

It is our intention, through this joint reflection, to be able to contribute, with pertinent recommendations, to be included in the United Nations High Level Panel Report, which our Minister of Finance is part of.

Excellencies

Ladies and Gentlemen,

As I said before, there is a need for a new approach to lift 1.5 billion people from conditions of misery and suffering. Now, let me speak about another new approach to building peace in the world.

Last January, my Government decided to support the realisation of a Conference in Díli, which is planned for this year, to be organised by the Asian Peace and Reconciliation Council. The APRC was established in September last year in Bangkok.

I am particularly satisfied with the presence of the ICAPP here which, almost a year ago, held a conference in Díli. My good friend, the Honourable Jose de Venecia, is also a founding member of the Asian Peace and Reconciliation Council, along with other distinguished individuals in East Asia, including our former President of the Republic, Dr Jose Ramos-Horta, today the SRSG in Guinea-Bissau.

On the 8th of this month, we inaugurated in front of the building of our National Parliament the statue of Sri Chinmoy – a replica of the one inaugurated for the London Olympics.

The meditation sessions, which the dreamer of World Peace Sri Chinmoy promoted in the United Nations headquarters, should have had a more positive result on the DPKO interventions and in the United Nations Security Council decisions.

The problem is this – that the Arab Spring, 'Inshya Allah', will not become the Arab hell!

Iraq and Afghanistan suffered profound ruptures in their social fabric and any prospect of bringing an end to these situations will not guarantee the end of conflict and of internal violence. Africa is wounded from the inside. Asia is agitated with nerves and each country faces their own problems, both internal and with their neighbours.

In the world of today, democracies cannot be built with violence; in the world of today, wars don't bring peace!

The phenomenon of war has undergone deep changes, which have resulted in more and more civilian populations being affected and which have required further aid assistance to humanitarian organisations but, in the end, it is unsustainable over the time and places. War today goes beyond borders and disguises ongoing acts of violence with unacceptable motivations, which makes more complex the process of their resolution.

It is time for all of us to reflect if these failures, of the so called good will of these international organisations, political and military, are not associated with the eternal primacy of economic interests, that act against the genuine will of a nation and its people.

While international interventions are often motivated by interests that are not truly the political needs of each process, this effort will continue to be counterproductive.

The need for a courageous changing of attitudes, from world leaders, is urgent. Also urgent is the need for a structural change of minds, which focuses on the root causes of problems and not just their consequences. It is urgent that world powers, and their international organisations, recognise the need to apply a new diplomacy that opens a space for more dialogue, and more contact.

Dialogue and contact between civilisations and between religions, guided by the principle of respect, can produce a common understanding about the crucial problems of humanity.

In this millennium, there should be no more space for the exercise of power, and for attitudes of intolerance, or behaviours of economic, cultural, political and social supremacy.

Excellencies

Ladies and Gentlemen,

This Summit could not be held in a more appropriate setting than in South Korea. We are witnessing a unique historical moment, considering the new leadership in nations that are central to regional stability and development such as China, Japan, South Korea and North Korea.

This is an opportunity to overcome the lingering tensions in this region, mainly the latent threats on the Korean Peninsula.

The Republic of Korea, China and Japan are very good friends of Timor-Leste and have been providing great support to our development. I am confident that, with the new leadership of these countries, the stability of the region will be reinforced through the strengthening of dialogue and the searching for creative and peaceful solutions, that may even lead to the denuclearisation of the region.

As my dear friend the President of Brazil, Dilma Rousseff, stated at the United Nations General Assembly 'More than ever, the fate of the world is in the hands of its leaders – all of them, without exception. We can either unite and together emerge victorious; or we can emerge defeated'.

Opening of the International Conference on the Post-2015 Development Agenda

Díli, 27 February 2013

Excellency, Anote Tong, President of the Republic of Kiribati
Excellency, Gordon Darcy Lilo, Prime Minister of the Solomon Islands
Excellency, Minister Emilia Pires, Member of the High Level Panel
Dr. Kuntoro Mangkusubroto, Special Envoy of H.E. President of the Republic of Indonesia
Dr. Oluremi Gabriel Sogunro, Advisor to H.E. President of the Republic of Liberia
Dr. David Hallam, on behalf of the Office of the Prime Minister of the United Kingdom of Great Britain and Northern Ireland
Honourable Ministers of the g7+ and the Pacific Nations and PALOPs
Excellency, Dr. Noeleen Heyzer, Under-Secretary-General of the United Nations and Executive Secretary of ESCAP
Distinguished Members of Parliament and Government
Ambassadors
Representatives of the Church, Civil Society and the Private Sector
Distinguished guests
Ladies and Gentlemen,

It is an honour to welcome you all, on behalf of the Government and the People of Timor-Leste, to this International Conference. I would like to give a special welcome to our 227 international guests, who have travelled from all over the world to participate in this conference.

It is a privilege to have such a distinguished group of international leaders, development experts, academics, representatives of civil society and the private sector, here with us, in Timor-Leste.

I believe we come together with common goals – to eradicate poverty and to contribute to world peace. Speaking of peace, I returned yesterday from South Korea where I participated in a World Summit on 'Peace, Security and Human Development'. There, in Seoul, I informed the plenary that we would be gathered here today to discuss the post-2015 Development Agenda.

The Millennium Development Goals, which were launched in 2000, have helped us on the path to development, but some countries – many of the world's poorest countries – have been left behind.

This is why, over the next two days, we have to speak. We have to be prepared to listen to what is good and what is bad, what was successful and what provoked stagnation or failure, in each one of our countries and in the larger family of the Least Developed Countries (LDCs).

As we approach 2015, there is not one LDC (fragile or conflict affected nation) in the world that has achieved even a single Millennium Development Goal. We are all here in the spirit of learning, from each other and to support each other, to change the course of events, in each one of our countries and in our relations with the international community.

Over 1.5 billion people live in fragility and conflict affected nations. This is almost twenty per cent of humanity.

What we have learnt in Timor-Leste, from experience, is that development cannot be achieved without security, without peace.

We had to stop fighting among ourselves and learn to reconcile our differences peacefully, before we could even begin to properly address the Millennium Development Goals.

That is why we believe that addressing global fragility is one of the most pressing development challenges of our time.

Together, we must change the mindsets of development policies.

We must work out why, with all the efforts and aid, from donor countries and international organisations, there is still so much poverty in the world.

And we must explore how – in this modern and globalised world – mainstream economic theories are imposed on, or absorbed by, the poor and the weak when these theories cause such harm and only serve the interest of the strong and powerful.

But, firstly, we have the obligation to look at ourselves, to the errors that we have committed, to the setbacks that we may have caused in our own processes. Only in this way, will we be able to guide our future plans, with a realistic roadmap of practical actions.

Ladies and Gentlemen,

With the MDGs soon to expire, the world community has the opportunity to set new priorities, and a new vision, for years beyond 2015.

We embark upon this task at a time of global uncertainty.

Along with conflict and fragility, the world is experiencing increasing inequality.

We are seeing global wealth concentrated in the hands of a few, while many remain in extreme poverty.

And too often the poverty – and the conflict – of powerless nations benefit the powerful nations. And so, poor people continue to suffer. And unemployment around the world continues to rise. And with lack of jobs comes criminality and conflict.

We must not continue to pretend that inequality and conflict are unrelated. That is why, Timor-Leste is so committed to the g7+ group of fragile and conflict affected nations.

This group of 18 nations works in solidarity, and speaks with one voice, to build peace and strengthen our States. But now, we need more than 18 countries working together, we need the whole global community focused on achieving agreed goals.

Yesterday, our brothers and sisters from the Pacific Islands came together to make their voice heard. We will hear their message today.

They are 13 and adding the voices of five PALOPs nations, with the development partners, we have here a total of 48 nations, one quarter of UN Member States.

Together, we can have a powerful voice.

Ladies and Gentlemen,

We must now not only look at the future, we must shape the future.

Now is the time for discussion about what has been working in the past and what we should do to secure our shared future.

As you know, the UN Secretary-General has established a High Level Panel.

Two days ago, I participated in the inauguration ceremony of the President of South Korea, Mrs. Park Geun-hye and I could see the pride in the Korean people's eyes.

We too are proud of having a Timorese woman on the UN High Level Panel. We trust in her, because we know how much she is doing to reform our system, how much she gives to the g7+ to change bad practices of development aid and how strong she has been in the process of State building.

Ladies and Gentlemen

The results of our discussions at this Conference will feed into the UN High Level Panel Report to the Secretary General.

And so, I urge you all to participate, to share your views and work together.

This is why the agenda of the Conference is so interactive. It has break-out sessions designed to allow everyone to participate and to allow everyone to be heard.

We must remember that great ideas can come from the most unexpected of places.

They can come from the youngest person or from the smallest nation.

And while many of you are from places where your voices are rarely heard on the global stage, they are places that the world must listen to for the post-2015 development agenda to have a real meaning. That is why the theme of the Conference is 'Development for All'.

And so, while we must be practical in our contributions, this does not mean we cannot be ambitious.

We must not forget that peace building and State building are critical to establishing a foundation, on which to eradicate poverty and achieve our development goals.

Excellencies

Ladies and Gentlemen

Thank you for attending this Conference.

I would like to give a special thanks to our generous supporters who have made this conference possible, the Pacific Institute of Public Policy, the United Nations Economic and Social Commission for Asia and the Pacific, AusAID and the g7+.

Here, we are all among friends, among brothers and sisters. I hope that the ideas discussed, and the conversations we take part in, will inspire us all and will unite us.

I look forward to joining with you over the next two days and trust that this will be an important and productive conference, in shaping the global vision post-2015.

I wish you all very participatory discussions!

Public Private Partnership Investor Conference

Ministry of Foreign Affairs, Díli, 7 March 2013

Minister for Finance, H.E. Emilia Pires
Minister for Transport and Communications, H.E. Pedro Lay
International guests
Representatives of the business community
Ambassadors
Milissa Day, Resident Representative of the International Finance Corporation
Excellencies
Ladies and Gentlemen,

It is a pleasure to speak today at this Investor Conference to discuss the development of two of our major infrastructure projects in Timor-Leste.

I am also pleased to welcome so many senior business leaders and international guests to this Conference and to Timor-Leste.

It was only last week that Timor-Leste hosted a major international conference on the post-2015 global development agenda. At that conference, we had over 200 international guests and representatives from over 50 countries from all across the world.

The successful hosting of international conferences is just one small measure of the progress of our country – but it is a significant one.

Excellencies
Ladies and Gentlemen,

It is important to understand that reality, and the context, of our country.

The people of Timor-Leste have struggled through a difficult history and have sacrificed much for their independence, and for their sovereignty.

While we have experienced stumbles on our road to peace, we have now emerged from conflict. The Timorese people have decided to give real value to their struggle so as not to become trapped by the memories of the past.

We reflected deeply, and in 2009 on the 10th Anniversary of our vote for independence, we embraced the motto 'Goodbye conflict, Welcome development'.

While the process of peace building never stops, we are now focused on State building.

State building is a complex process that involves institution building, the development of human resources, the changing of mentalities, ongoing dialogue between the people, as well as building physical infrastructure.

To guide the process of State building, Timor-Leste has a long term plan – our *Strategic Development Plan 2011-2030*. I urge you to read our Plan as it provides a framework for us to achieve our dream of moving from a low income country, to an upper middle income country; with a healthy, well educated and safe population.

The Strategic Development Plan sets out actions in three key areas to transform our nation. They are:
- Improving human resources and human capital
- Building core infrastructure; and
- Developing our economy – with a focus on our petroleum, tourism and agriculture.

We must have a focus on infrastructure because it is needed to build our nation, to underpin balanced economic growth, and to create jobs and support the critical development of our private sector.

Ladies and Gentlemen,

We need a sea port and an airport that have the capacity to service and support the building of our nation.

With all the goodwill in the world we will not be able to develop our tourism industry if people cannot fly to our country; and we will not be able to build our petroleum industry if we do not have a port to bring in the critical goods and heavy equipment that are needed.

We have completed the first stage of our infrastructure program which was building our national electricity generation and distribution network.

In this mandate of the new Government, we are committed to building a national port, a national airport and major roads.

This is an important part of the process of State building and it will drive our economic growth and our development.

Ladies and Gentlemen,

Timor-Leste needs a new national port. We are currently dependent on Díli port for our general cargo imports and exports. The average growth in container handling of Díli port over the last 7 years has been almost 20% and the port is struggling to cope.

Limited port capacity already means that there can be a long berthing backlog and we often see many ships waiting in Díli harbour – and, as you know, waiting time costs money and causes inflation in our country. It also means that both cargo and passenger ships pass our country by.

If nothing is done, Díli port will be severely congested by 2015 which would come at a large economic cost to our people and result in a serious economic bottleneck. There is no room to expand the Díli port.

And so, we need a new national port. We will be building this port at Tibar Bay, a short distance from Díli.

Our plans are for a wharf that is capable of servicing large, modern ships including cruise ships. A benefit of building the Port at Tibar is that we will have scope to expand its capacity as our economy grows.

The Tibar port will require extensive dredging and the building of port facilities including a container yard, terminal buildings and mobile cranes. A new road project, supported by the Asian Development Bank, will also be built with sufficient capacity to cope with new port traffic.

I am pleased that today we have at this conference some of the world's top port operators as well as regional and national business leaders. I look forward to working together with you to build our national port.

Excellencies

Ladies and Gentlemen,

We also need to undertake major development of our airport because it does not have the capacity to meet the future demands of passengers, aircraft and safety.

Timor-Leste has identified tourism as a strategic industry to create jobs and grow our economy. Our tourist visa numbers have been growing strongly every year and we expect this growth to continue as the East Asian tourist industry expands rapidly.

We also have growing domestic demand for air travel as well as expected increasing demand as we develop our petroleum industry.

As Timor-Leste works towards full membership of ASEAN we also need an airport that can allow direct flights to ASEAN capitals and we need terminals and facilities which are appropriate for ASEAN delegates.

We are examining carefully our airport development options and needs which may include new terminal buildings, a car park precinct, freight and ground services, commercial spaces for retail, a longer runway, a sea wall and a bridge over Comoro River.

The airport development will be an important project for our nation and we are encouraged by the strong interest from domestic and international businesses and investors to partner with us.

Ladies and Gentlemen,

I am pleased that we have such senior representatives from global and regional firms with extensive experience of Public Private Partnerships.

There are, of course, different ways to finance and manage major infrastructure projects.

Public Private Partnerships will allow the Government to control projects while securing the benefits of private sector involvement. It will bring private sector expertise to build and operate while creating job opportunities for our people.

A Public Private Partnership will also transfer risks away from the Government to the private sector which will help to control building and operation costs as well as manage timing and delivery risks. This will help the Government to minimise its financial contributions while providing access to the technical and managerial skills of the private sector.

And we expect that international firms will partner with local business to create jobs and build our private sector.

And so, we will be conducting an open, transparent and competitive process to ensure that we obtain value for money and private partners that can deliver the best long term benefit for the Timorese people.

We welcome foreign investors to Timor-Leste and I know that the Minister for Finance, Emilia Pires, will soon outline our bright economic future.

We are a high growth emerging nation, with low tax rates and around $12 billion in our Petroleum Fund which is growing every day. We are also fortunate to be in East Asia and to be able to leverage off the Asian powerhouses that are supporting the global economy.

I encourage you all to learn about our infrastructure plans and our proposed process during this conference. I also urge you to attend the site visits tomorrow of our airport as well as Tibar port to gain a greater understanding of what the projects involve.

I would like thank the International Finance Cooperation for working with the Government to organise this Investor Conference and for its support for the airport and Tibar port projects.

The Government is pleased that there is such strong interest in our infrastructure projects and our nation's development.

I look forward to working together with many of you in the future to build a better Timor-Leste.

Thank you very much.

Third Jakarta International Defence Dialogue: 'Defence and Diplomacy in the Asia-Pacific Region'

Jakarta, 20 March 2013

Your Excellency Dr Susilo Bambang Yudhoyono, President of the Republic of Indonesia
Your Excellency Mr Purnomo Yusgiantoro, Minister of Defence of Indonesia
Your Excellency Mr Terje Rod-Larsen, President of the International Peace Institute
Your Excellencies
Ministers of the various countries in attendance
Distinguished Participants and Heads of Delegations
Ladies and Gentlemen,

It is with the same pleasure and enthusiasm that I take part in this Third Jakarta International Defence Dialogue as I did the two before it.

It is an honour for me to address the JIDD again as it plays such an important role in the promotion of peace, democracy, security and development in our region and beyond.

I would like to thank the Indonesian Government, particularly my dear friend President Susilo Bambang Yudhoyono, for the warmth and hospitality shown to me and to the delegation of Timor-Leste.

Mr President, I cannot overstate my gratitude to the Indonesian Government, and to the Indonesian People, for the support given to Timor-Leste. The ties of friendship and cooperation between our two countries are strong and have contributed to the growth of our small nation.

We Timorese feel very much at home in this vibrant city that is the heart of your great nation.

I would also like to thank the International Peace Institute for its tireless efforts for world peace, as well as for supporting this Dialogue.

Excellencies

Ladies and Gentlemen,

I congratulate the Government of Indonesia for being able to bring together experts from various fields and key government figures of the region to this third JIDD.

The first JIDD brought to attention the need for transparency of actions, by States and international organisations, while the second JIDD last year asked us all to consider perspectives on 'military operations other than war'.

I understood that my previous interventions were too philosophical in tone, committing the error of failing to suggest concrete actions.

The third JIDD asks us all, as those responsible for the defence of our respective countries, to consider more dynamic strategies to positively influence political decisions to ensure that they are in sufficient accord with diplomatic efforts.

There have been many debates and today we understand the spectrum of possible threats and the great array of challenges that are presented to us, both now and in the future, ranging from 'economic shocks, rapid socio-economic changes, demographic shifts, climate change, resources scarcity, environmental degradation, terrorism, transnational organised crime to piracy and the ongoing and emerging conflicts.'

Lately, we have been witnessing a huge increase in the establishment of important forums, alongside the holding of successive conferences, covering crucial themes such as 'peace, reconciliation, justice and human rights', and which demonstrate a collective concern for issues of regional and global significance.

The world, in reality, is facing unprecedented serious problems, unimaginable even in the Cold War period.

This new millennium brought with it a lot of hope based on the commitment to a rapid, appropriate and comprehensive response to reduce the misery that ravaged a large part of humanity.

The Millennium Development Goals were acclaimed, in the silence of the desperation of millions of families, across the four corners of the globe. However, today, the international community has understood that not one Millennium Development Goal will be achieved by the poor who are living and wasting away in the painful drama of poverty and isolation and enduring the pressure of violence and conflict.

To make matters worse, the world recession that has come to affect the old continent, and even the United States of America itself, almost puts the world on a path without a way out, where a rapid solution cannot be found. The irony of it all is that developing or under-developed countries are always judged by malpractices of governance and management, while developed countries commit more serious actions of irresponsibility, with highly damaging effects that are prejudicial to the lives of their own citizens and the survival of hundreds of millions of people subjugated by misery, hunger and illness and that, in many cases, are highly offensive to the integrity and sovereignty of weak and poor countries.

The Arab Spring will continue to be a complex and long process to heal wounds, and make way for a mentality of true democracy. The circumstances in Iraq and Afghanistan are proving to result from the unacceptable errors of analysis by the great centres of power, who thought that they could impose peace and establish democracy through war while helping to create disharmony in the social fabric of the people. Africa continues to be wounded on the inside, in both mind and body, and here in Asia we face all the problems that the third JIDD asks 'to be addressed'.

The Asia-Pacific region is spoken of by the big and the powerful, the politicians and the economists, the diplomats and the military, and in financial and entrepreneurial circles.

Never has the future looked so promising for the Asia-Pacific region, which in part is captured by an expression, too beautiful to become a reality to all – that this is to be the 'Asian Century'.

In the history of the world, civilisation began in the Middle East, which is today shaken by the demands of the global and standardised world in which we live and is being destroyed from the inside.

The Asian century will not give more value to the over thousand-year old culture of China or Japan and or even India, because it will continue to present, in a daily menu, the challenges that the JIDD organisers have so intelligently known to put to the participants.

These challenges should merit careful attention, above all from political actors, so that decisions are made respecting the interests of all and not merely the interests of the rich, the big and the powerful.

It is time that relations between States and peoples are based on the principle of equality and on the principle of honesty, a vital condition to create and deepen the ties of cooperation, founded on mutual trust and mutual respect.

There can be no more room for the benefits of advanced technology being enjoyed by the few, and worse still, for profit to be made from the weakness and inexperience of other countries, with deceptive practices being used to extract advantage and achieve domination through robbery and fraud, pushing small and under developed countries to a dependency, that is established in an immoral and unacceptable form in today's times.

The world needs a new paradigm because the laws of the market are excessively subject to speculation and the calculations of profits and the fraud of the financial industry that has pushed humanity towards the abyss of disgrace and led hundreds of millions of people to despair.

Today's world needs a new paradigm because the established system – rooted in a superficial analysis that is influencing how decisions are made to reduce the suffering of humanity and guarantee a small piece of dignity to all and any human being – has already proven, in accordance with my wretched interpretation, to be unhealthy and incapable of guaranteeing long term sustainable solutions.

Excellencies

Ladies and Gentlemen,

The common project of peaceful cooperation and development in the Asia-Pacific region, however, continues to be an issue. We should recognise that peace in this region, which is associated with persistent global challenges, continues to be vulnerable.

It is absolutely necessary to act with a more effective inter-dependence, for a more viable integration of efforts by every State in the world. States must work together to protect regional and global interests, and as a result, to protect their own national interests.

The emerging global challenges in this century, in addition to those mentioned previously, including above all climate change and the emerging security challenges in the area of energy, food and humankind's most valuable resource: water.

As global environmental threats continue to increase, the legitimate interests of emerging and developing countries in controlling and utilising their national resources is put into question. And in the Pacific the very survival of some islands States is itself in question, as they run the risk of slowly sinking into the vastness of the ocean, as is the case with Kiribati, the Marshall Islands and Tuvalu.

I wish to take this opportunity to launch a message, an appeal and a challenge to the highly developed countries that are the principal causes of the tragedy of climate change. These countries should, through moral and political obligation, assume responsibility and indemnify, in compensation, the countries that are irretrievably condemned to disappear. And the decision has to be made now. We should now put aside the famous 'carbon credit' aid which is so irrelevant and which is even conditional on poor countries not producing emissions.

Despite the prevailing strength and optimism, sustainable growth in our region will be dependent on a culture of cooperation and dialogue that approaches the challenges in a serious and responsible manner and that does not leave behind the around 20 percent of humanity that live in fragile and conflict-affected nations.

Dialogue, the asset of diplomacy, is the only weapon that can respond to the problems of today.

We must safeguard a future, free of conflicts in the search for scarce resources, which would make poor countries even poorer and rich countries even needier for resources.

The Pacific is enormous and I believe, rich in natural resources, which include magnificent maritime fauna and flora and reserves of petroleum and natural gas. Regrettably, this can provoke a tendency, which has become national policy in some countries, for unfairness and dishonesty in relations of cooperation.

At this precise moment when we are witnessing the shift of economic, political and military power to the Asia-Pacific region, it becomes increasingly prudent, particularly within the context of regional defence, to seek understandings in relation to the sea, and to develop concerted mechanisms of cooperation that give priority not only to maritime security but, above all, to the security of people and of States that are involved or interested, regardless of how small, weak or poor they may be.

For this reason, sharing the security challenges in our region will contribute to improved strategic trust among the countries of the region. China and the United States of America are two giants that are vital to the prosperous and safe development of the Asia-Pacific region this century. Given this, a positive relationship of cooperation between these two great powers is not only in their own interests but is also a duty on behalf of the development of all nations in the region. As the former Secretary of State Hillary Clinton said during her visit to Díli last year, the Asia-Pacific region is big enough to receive all those who want to contribute to the development of peace, cooperation and economy.

In these strategic matters, and in order to deal with the maritime challenges in the region, peaceful coexistence and the overcoming of differences requires a shared effort of cooperation in which the defence of the interests of one party does not mean the obstruction, in the minimum, of the very legitimate development expectations of other parties. Diplomacy – along with measured defence capabilities – is vital for the preservation of peace and stability, grounded in cooperation between States defending the rightful interests of their people and not the economic interests of the countries and their rulers.

Excellencies

Ladies and Gentlemen,

Goodwill and effort should be directed so that in Asia, as the economies of countries grow, military spending and the modernisation of armed forces focuses on national defence and that it does not replace dialogue. I hope that the new leaderships in the region, including importantly China, Japan, South Korea and North Korea, may lead to a 'new diplomacy' that makes way for more negotiation and more contact, especially in regard to the Korean Peninsula, while not forgetting the latent tensions in the South China Sea or disputes over small islands and maritime borders that impact other nations in the region.

It is urgent for world leaders to have the courage to change their attitudes. It is also urgent to pursue structural changes that, as I have said before, will address the root causes of problems rather than just their consequences, both within each State and at the global level.

The strengthening of dialogue and contact between nations, and between religions, on the fundamental principles that bring people of the world closer, or that may tear them apart, may also lead to common understandings on the key problems of humankind. The election of the new Pope brings new hope and new confidence for a positive dialogue between two of the world's largest faiths – Islam and Christianity; and to promote world peace and tolerance.

The strategic partnerships for promoting peace and stability can, and should, go beyond States. We must try to break the reactive attitude of only being prepared to intervene in places and regions of conflict with expensive apparatus of war and to give way to consensus and pragmatic understandings, without offending the dignity of the people and national sovereignty.

A new concept of global defence that favours the promotion of peace should be instilled with a spirit of diplomacy that covers both the leaders and every person active in representing the interests of the peoples of the world and able to contribute to dialogue and to the strengthening of inclusive cooperation.

In today's world, building trust between countries is a more important and safer investment than preparing for war. This should be the cornerstone for new strategic alliances, especially as we know from experience that wars do not build peace!

Excellencies

Ladies and Gentlemen,

Before I conclude, I would like to speak briefly about the role that Timor-Leste wants to play in ASEAN, as this year I plan to visit a majority of these nations.

In this geo-strategic chessboard that is the South East Asian region, every piece counts. This includes even the smallest pieces, with small economies and populations. They count not because of their military power, or their defensive capabilities, but rather because of the stability that they can provide to the region. Indeed, as we know, the primary agents of non-conventional threats today are non-State actors from countries where poverty and inequalities prevail.

Within this broad framework of security, development and democracy, having Timor-Leste join ASEAN will enable our country to benefit from the regional stability provided by this organisation, as well as allow us to make an active contribution.

Regional stability would not have been possible without the formation of economic partnerships as well as partnerships in defence and security, in which diplomacy was used as an art towards supporting shared development. Although fragile, regional stability has allowed for a common vision of peace and security that has fuelled unprecedented growth in these last decades.

Several regional organisations and forums of discussion, in which dialogue is the common denominator, have become increasingly strong and institutionalised. They are now not only reflecting on the future but are shaping the future. ASEAN, APEC, the ARF, and more recently the Bali Democracy Forum and the JIDD are good examples of this.

Timor-Leste is following this progress closely and whilst we are the youngest nation in the region, we already feel a strong sense of regional identity and have been adopting public policies that fit this local development framework, starting firstly by giving priority to policies of reconciliation and the promotion of internal security and national stability.

At the same time, we have been consolidating our democratic processes as we know this is necessary to achieve our goal of integrated and inclusive development. We believe that consolidating democracy must be an internal process for every country, undertaken consciously by the people of each country, under a process that must be continuous and that respects the timings and pace dictated by local context.

The progress we have made within this last decade is not spectacular because of its size or scope, but rather because of the short amount of time in which it was achieved. This is particularly impressive for a country where most people are poor and that has only recently emerged from a post-conflict situation.

We have reason to celebrate our achievements, which include one of the highest economic growth rates in the world, and progress in terms of human development, as well as the consolidation of peace, stability and friendly relations with virtually every country in the world, under our foreign policy of zero enemies. Our relations with our giant neighbours are excellent. Through the Community of Portuguese-Speaking Countries we also have special ties of friendship with countries in Africa, Europe and Latin America, as well as a strong relationship with the European Union.

With the 2013 Human Development Report released by the United Nations Development Programme last Thursday, Timor-Leste has now moved up five places in the Human Development Index since 2007. In fact, Timor-Leste has had the largest annual average index growth of all East Asian and Pacific Countries from 2000 to 2012.

Over the last three years we have also been committed to leading a new cause to give voice to fragile and post-conflict States throughout the world, and sharing the experiences and challenges of peace building and State building, so as to develop a secure roadmap for countries having difficulty overcoming the inertia in which they find themselves. We also wanted to rewrite our own development story, rather than continue to have it written by others that did not actually live or experience the problems we face.

The Agencies for International Support and the United Nations continue to hold on to the idea that they should dictate the destiny of peoples and do not accept our assertions when we tell them that they are wrong in the 'assumptions' they make of our countries. We continue to have difficulties in reaching a common understanding with those experts on the poverty of others, who have yet to prove that the large amount of money they have expended has reduced misery in even some part of the world.

This cause includes the process of changing the poor practices of development assistance and is led by a group of 18 nations called the g7+. This group is also proud to have a Timorese woman on the UN High Level Panel contributing to the post-2015 Development Agenda. Further, last month we held a meeting in Díli with the theme 'Development for All', where 48 nations participated, including the g7+ countries, the Portuguese-speaking African countries, around 13 Pacific countries and our development partners.

Finally, in 2013, we will be supporting the holding of a Conference in Díli, to be organised by the Asian Peace and Reconciliation Council. The APRC was established in September 2012 in Bangkok, and its founding members are distinguished states people from Asia, including my friend José de Venecia, the former Vice President of Indonesia, Jusuf Kalla, and our former President of the Republic, Dr José Ramos-Horta, who is currently the SRSG in Guinea-Bissau.

Cooperation towards peace and development, mutual understanding and negotiation by way of dialogue and diplomacy are the best strategies of defence for the nations of the world.

Thank you.

69th Session of the Economic and Social Commission for Asia and the Pacific

UNESCAP, Bangkok, 29 April 2013

H.E. Mr Thein Sein, President of Myanmar
H.E. Mr Gordon Darcy Lilo, Prime Minister of the Solomon Islands
H.E. Mr Plodprasop Suraswadi, Deputy Prime Minister of Thailand
H.E. Mr Jan Eliasson, Deputy Secretary-General of the United Nations
H.E. Ms. Noeleen Heyzer, Under-Secretary-General of the United Nations and Executive Secretary of ESCAP.
Excellencies
Distinguished Delegates
Ladies and Gentlemen,

I thank you all for the confidence placed in me and the great honour that you have bestowed on my country and on me.

I am aware of the great responsibility of serving as the Chairperson of our Commission, and I am very thankful I will have the benefit of the expert leadership of the Executive Secretary of ESCAP, Dr. Noeleen Heyzer.

The annual Commission session is the highest intergovernmental forum for policy dialogue on development issues in the Asian and Pacific region. The Commission session is the most inclusive regional platform for our 62 Governments, to forge Asia-Pacific perspectives on economic and social development challenges.

Please allow me to say a few additional words.

Distinguished delegates
Ladies and Gentlemen,

Sixty-six years ago, the great and visionary Nehru made a call to countries to stand-up together and to face the challenges of that time, and the Economic and Social Commission for Asia and Far East was formed.

I have to say, in 1947, I was 1 year old and my people were trying to dry out the tears of the devastation of the Second World War.

In 1974, while the organization changed its name to the Economic and Social Commission for Asia and the Pacific, my people were involved, in a violent way, in breaking 500 years of colonial rule, having unilaterally declared our independence on 28 November 1975.

Nine days later, Timor-Leste was invaded and occupied for 24 years, which forced us into a long and difficult struggle.

So it is a great honour and indeed, recognition of the fighting spirit and resilience of my people, to chair this Commission Session today.

This Commission session aims to achieve inclusive and sustainable economic and social development for our region.

As much of the world faces austerity, the Asia-Pacific region is making remarkable progress and is home to emerging economies that are driving global growth and lifting millions from poverty. We should all feel proud to be part of this region, which is becoming a centre of global economic and strategic weight.

While our region does face growing tensions we all trust that international leaders will move beyond statements made in good faith and will take constructive actions – and participate in real dialogue and active engagement – so that we can move beyond these concerns to focus on the needs of our people.

The economic success in our region has already helped so many people out of poverty and has been an inspiration to the LDCs. And it seems that we are all enlightened by the big picture of the Asian Century.

Regrettably, some of the economic growth in our region has often not being balanced and inequality is rising, and we are still home to nearly two–thirds of the world's poor people.

The real problem in today's world is the need for economic growth versus social exclusion and inequality or, in another words, is GDP growth versus poverty.

In our region, we can draw a map of countries in, at least, 3 levels of economic and social development (developed, emerging economies and LDCs).

And when we read the analyses from the macroeconomic experts, we get the impression of a colossal and difficult task, that we can call 'Mission Impossible'.

I have to recognise and value all the hard work that presents us with a very detailed examination of each country and their challenges ahead, which also allows us to have a more global understanding of the need to work together and of the need to change our way of thinking!

Distinguished delegates,

The interdependency of today's economy is a factor that can help one push ahead one's own policy but, at the same time, can create obstacles to others. The fundamental problem is the imbalance among countries.

Some countries, and perhaps countries within a region, are not able to run the economic marathon race together with, we can call, professional runners, in terms of trade policy, imports and exports, inflation, together with investment and core infrastructure. The LDCs are simply disqualified before the start.

Besides this, all the LDCs are not able to address their own priorities from the long list of needs, underscored with equal importance, such as:
- Stability
- Political environment
- Gender issues
- Unemployment
- Education
- Impoverished rural areas
- Human rights
- Health
- Water, Sanitation and Energy
- Food security
- Environment
- And natural disasters among others.

This is the reason I'm here accepting the responsibility to chair this session.

With the support of my colleagues, the Honourable Vice Chairpersons, and the ESCAP Secretariat, I promise to discharge the responsibilities of serving as your Chairperson to help bring about more inclusive, sustainable economic and social development in our region.

And I'm here to make a different call – we have to work together to draw a road map, in a joint approach with a regional and sub-regional integrated development plan.

Isolated efforts will not succeed if we all are committed to lift the 1.5 billion people from poverty, hunger, disease, exclusion and neglect.

Therefore, all the social and economic issues can be addressed together, their barriers and their potential, reducing the difficulties each country faces alone and improving the capabilities for a sustainable growth for all!

Economic growth can only be sustainable if we put emphasis on the improvement in the social well being of the people.

We have to change the too strict and unhelpful macroeconomic policy standards that only benefit the rich countries, in detriment of the poor.

Excellencies

Distinguished delegates

Ladies and Gentlemen,

Later today, this forum will be considering Sustainable Development and the Development Agenda Beyond 2015. And so, I want to draw your attention to an important new collaboration between many of the worlds' fragile nations known as the g7+ group.

The group was formed in 2010 to provide a united voice for fragile countries and to advocate for change in global development policies. The g7+ knows from bitter experience that without peace and stability there can be no development. Not one fragile or conflict affected nation has achieved even one Millennium Development Goal.

This means that it will not be possible to eradicate poverty in the world without first addressing the issues of fragile and conflict affected countries. That is why the g7+ nations are working together to ensure that the post-2015 development agenda addresses the need for peace and stability, and that the perspectives of fragile States are central to the global dialogue.

Ladies and Gentlemen,

In February, with the support of ESCAP, Timor-Leste hosted an international conference with the theme 'Development for All'. The Conference brought together participants from around the world, including Africa, Asia and the Pacific, and it agreed on the 'Díli Consensus' that set out our priorities, and hopes, for the post–2015 development agenda.

We recognised that standard approaches to development were failing to acknowledge that the challenges we face in the mountains of Timor-Leste for example, are not the same as those faced by families struggling to survive a drought in Pakistan, or living in a world that is slowly sinking into the vastness of the ocean, like Kiribati.

Next time we have to focus not just on goals and targets – but on means of implementation.

Importantly, it must be recognised that development cannot be achieved when countries are fragile – we must address fragility directly.

And while hunger persists, we cannot speak of democracy and freedom and so we must achieve food security for the sake of our common humanity.

And so, we must make sure that there is local ownership of the development process – we must make sure there is not only 'development for all', but 'development by all'.

I look forward to working with you towards peace, social development and progress. I know that together, and acting with determination and courage, a brighter future belongs to us all.

Thank you very much.

International Conference on Decentralization and Local Government

Díli, 28 May 2013

Your Excellency, the Speaker of Parliament
Your Excellencies, the Members of Parliament
Your Excellency, Mrs Isabel Ferreira, First Lady of Timor-Leste
Fellow Government Members
Distinguished guests, Ladies and Gentlemen,

First and foremost, I would like to congratulate Commission A of the National Parliament, along with the Ministry of State Administration, for organizing this International Conference that will enable us to learn from other countries regarding this debate that is so important to the strengthening of our Governance.

I would like to thank those in attendance, namely the distinguished guests from Portugal, Cape Verde, Australia and Indonesia, who are here today to share with us their experiences on local government. We are very pleased to host you in this new meeting gathering Nations from these two regions – CPLP and Asia-Pacific – between which Timor-Leste is proud to establish bridges of dialogue and cooperation.

Learning from your experiences will enable us to choose carefully the model of local government that we want for our country. The most important aspect for this model is to be adequate to the Timorese reality, our ancient traditions, our history and our communities. However, learning about your decentralization experiences will surely make our decision-making process more informed and consequently more effective.

I must also extend my very personal gratitude to the Portuguese mayors that have provided unconditional support to our effort. I would like to make a special reference to my friend Mr António Rodrigues, the Mayor of Torres Novas, who has just issued a book on this subject.

Following the support by the Portuguese mayors, we had the idea to establish a special status of fraternity between Portuguese cities and some Timorese villages. Cooperation ties were established between some of those, through the process of twinning. For instance, Díli is twinned with Coimbra, which is a landmark of Portuguese history, culture and academics. Being twinned cities, they have been establishing ties of solidarity and friendship that bridge the oceans and continents that separate us, made even stronger by our mutual language and history.

In order to strengthen the special relationship with Portuguese cities, on 21 March 2013, in Lisbon, we signed a Protocol of Cooperation with 26 Portuguese municipalities, which vowed, in pairs, to support the creation of each of the 13 Municipalities of Timor-Leste. As such, I would like to give a special salute to the representative of the National Association of Portuguese Municipalities, without which this Protocol would not have been possible.

Lastly, I would like to address the multilateral development partners in attendance here today, who want to accompany Timor-Leste in yet another step towards democratic consolidation.

I welcome you all to this debate which is so important for the future of Timor-Leste.

We know where we want to be within a few decades. We know the country we want to become. The *Strategic Development Plan 2011-2030* has a clear vision for Timor-Leste. It sets a path that will transform us into a medium-high income country within 20 years, with a society that is more prosperous, socially and politically stable, educated and healthy. We want poverty reduction, through the diversification of the economy and the capacity building of our professionals, to transform the profile of Timor-Leste. We want this transformation to reach every Suco, every Village, every family.

Only then will we be able to say that our State rebuilding process is truly consolidated. Only then will we know that we have fully disseminated the peace dividends to every Timorese citizen who fought for 24 years so that Timor-Leste could become democratic and independent.

During these eleven years as an independent Nation, which we have just completed this May, we have made remarkable achievements. There have been obstacles in our path, but we have managed to overcome every one of them and become stronger as a Nation in the process.

Today we are living in a time of political stability and peace, which would not have been possible without a spirit of reconciliation and understanding. We have a fully functional Democratic State under the Rule of Law, with independent, strong and efficient Sovereignty Bodies. The vital foundations of our Democracy are sound. Since 1999 the Timorese people have displayed a unique democratic enthusiasm, with an extraordinary level of electoral participation.

Democracy cannot be limited to the right to vote, although the right to vote is a cornerstone principle of democracy. Elections are fundamental moments for democratic States, and in 2012 – with the Presidential and Parliamentary Elections – we saw how they strengthen the very basis of democratic architecture. However, the participation by citizens cannot be limited to polling. There has to be a more daily participation, so that every Timorese citizen may have a say regarding the actual decisions that influence their lives.

During these last few weeks of popular consultation in the Districts, I saw that this willingness to be responsible for the direction their country takes is deeply imbedded in the spirit of the Timorese people. The involvement by the Timorese in this consultation shows us that we are on the right path and that we must extend the political debate to every citizen in every part of the country. We must create institutional mechanisms that bring the Government closer to its population, particularly in the more remote rural areas.

Reducing the distance that still exists today will make it easier for the Timorese to be heard and for the State to perform its duties efficiently, namely as a provider of public services, since these services will be better suited to the specific needs of each community.

If decentralization will enable the State to be closer to the Timorese, then reflecting on aspects of how and when will be essential.

We know that if we want to have an efficient governance apparatus the model that we choose must be functional and not too costly or bureaucratic. It should prevent overlapping between local government and national government, setting clear boundaries between the responsible and competences of each type of government.

We must find an adequate model of local government that is compatible with our community traditions, since these are the cornerstone of our living as a Nation.

It was in order to answer these questions that we started the discussion with the popular consultation. As you know, the process is still ongoing. During this mandate we want to establish the 13 Municipality Installation Committees. Furthermore, by 2017 we want to create 3 out of the 5 Municipalities.

I would like to remind that this commitment towards administrative decentralization was also a concern of the previous governments. This was not something that started with the Fifth Constitutional Government or even with its predecessor. This debate had started before and sought, like today, to honour the Constitution.

The Local Development Programme, started in 2004, was a first approximation to the local government models, experimenting administrative decentralization levels in each district of Timor-Leste. That Programme created 25 local assemblies, provided with administrative support and seeking to develop some small infrastructure projects.

As such, today we are better prepared to resume this reflection, since we can build on what has been done before and learn important lessons from it.

I also believe that this Conference will improve our debate, since we will be taking a look at the decentralization experiences in countries so different as Portugal and Indonesia, and Cape Verde and Australia. In every country, the selected model had to take into account the historical and traditional features in existence.

Your Excellencies,

The people of Timor-Leste know their country well. We are very familiar with our mountains, our coastline and the Sea that bathes us.

Approximately three quarters of our population reside in rural areas, often in remote locations where access is difficult. As you know, during this mandate we want to make a significant investment in the national road network and improve transports and communications. Nevertheless, we know that this is not enough to change our country's cartography. Like Minister Jorge Teme, I think about Ataúro and Oecussi, for instance, which have additional difficulties in terms of access to Díli. In the case of Oecussi, Dr Mari Alkatiri was appointed by the State to prepare the process that will transform the enclave into a Special Social and Market Economic Zone.

All these conditions have direct implications on the political participation by the Timorese and on the development of governance. Only an open debate can lead us to a consensus on a more inclusive governance model that can provide faster and more effective responses to the specific needs of our People.

Reducing the distance between the Government and its citizens through local government hubs is therefore a vital step for our Democracy and for creating a society that is more regionally balanced and consequently more cohesive as a Nation.

Thank you very much.

Twelfth International Institute for Strategic Studies Asia Security Summit. The Shangri-la Dialogue, Second Plenary Session: 'Defending National Interest, Preventing Conflict'

Singapore, 1 June 2013

Dr. John Chipman, Director-General and Chief Executive, IISS
Itsunori Onodera, Minister of Defence of Japan
Catherine Ashton, High Representative of the EU for Foreign Affairs and Security Policy
Excellencies
Distinguished Participants and Heads of Delegations
Ladies and Gentlemen,

It is an honour for me to take part in this already important forum, so instrumental for promoting peace, security and cooperation, both within our region and at the global level.

As I am about to undertake an Official Visit to Singapore, and since I am also the Minister of Defense and Security, I could not let the opportunity pass to be here at the Shangri-La Dialogue. The excellent organisation of this Dialogue is a tribute to the efficiency and generosity of the Government of Singapore.

I must also congratulate this initiative by the IISS which, for the last 12 years, has been bringing together speakers from all over the world in the area of defence, to analyse and debate fundamental themes which often go beyond defence in its strictest sense.

Today, investment in strategic cooperation in the areas of defence and security would mean building solid foundations for peace and development.

Therefore, it is gratifying to see that, in recent times, there has been a growing collective concern regarding regional and global matters. Many debates have been held seeking to better understand the spectrum of possible threats and the variety of challenges that we have in common.

As Ms Ashton said before me, the threats and challenges range from economic shocks to socio-economic distortions, from demographic trends to climate change, from the lack of essential resources to environmental degradation, from terrorism to transnational crime and from piracy to latent and emerging conflicts.

Meanwhile, it is necessary to remember that around 1.5 billion people are living in areas affected by fragility, organised crime or conflict. Around 20% of the world's population face extreme situations of poverty, hunger, disease, exclusion and abandonment every day, while peacekeeping operations have been, at best, extremely expensive.

The fragility and the poverty of people and of their respective nations are at the end of the day, constant threats to the overall security of humanity.

Even with only eleven years as a State, Timor-Leste knows well these challenges, not only because we are one of the poorest countries in Southeast Asia, but also because our recent history registered periods of war and conflict, which undoubtedly shape the way in which we view challenges of security and of development.

What we learned in Timor-Leste, from our own experience, is that development cannot be achieved and universal democratic principles and values cannot be assumed, without security and internal peace.

We had to stop fighting among ourselves, and to learn to conciliate our differences peacefully, before we could even begin to properly address the Millennium Development Goals, which gave hope to Timor-Leste, and to many fragile States throughout the world, at the beginning of this new millennium. And we soon realised that not a single MDG will be reached in 2015 by any fragile State.

Fundamental issues such as development policies, and approaches to security and defence, require a radical change of mind-set in the decision-making centres of the globalised world.

The world needs a new paradigm, where international leaders have the courage to decide on options for intervention when really motivated by the genuine needs of each nation and their people, and respond to the true political needs of each peace process, rather than being obliged by economic interests.

There is a crying need to correct the policy of labelling people, organisations and States as 'enemies', which leads to inflexible and radicalised positions. Because, instead of searching for solutions, it fosters exclusion and isolation and feeds hatred and vengeance. The world, as a result, is experiencing an uncontrollable crisis of violent confrontation between civilisations, cultures and religions, surpassing, in nature and character, the open conflict of the anti-colonial era and the Cold War.

Therefore, it is necessary that States acknowledge the need to apply a 'new diplomacy' that will give more space for dialogue and for more contacts, which requires perseverance. Strategic partnerships for the promotion of peace and stability must go beyond States, focusing more directly on the true causes of conflict. The option taken by international institutions through reactive interventions in places and regions of conflict, usually involving expensive war apparatus, has been proven that it cannot bring a solution by itself. Room must be given for a greater effort for prevention, through consensus and pragmatic understandings without losing sight of the dignity of the people and national sovereignty.

And speaking of dignity of people and of national sovereignty, I would now like to touch on the concept of 'defending national interests'. Humanity lives in extremely complex times, where this concept of defending national interests of a nation, when disassociated from a real global perspective, can instead of preventing conflict provoke new centres of tension.

What may appear to be defending legitimate national interests can, from another angle, involve irreversible adversities for others. And these, ladies and gentlemen, end up contributing to a spiral of threats in the form of acts of provocation, or demonstrations of force, or surges of crime, acts of terrorism, influxes of illegal immigration, among other things, which reach innocent victims in various parts of the globe.

A new concept of global defence that favours promoting peace should be instilled in a spirit of diplomacy that goes beyond leaders, so as to cover all active stakeholders that represent the interests of the peoples of the world and who can contribute to dialogue and to the strengthening of inclusive cooperation.

As such, building trust between countries is a more important and safer investment, than preparing for war, and should be the base of new strategic alliances that must not exclude any State – whether small or large – regardless of culture, religion or ideology.

Due to the interdependency between States in today's globalised world, it is imperative that they work together towards a common goal. This is so rare with today's global decisions where more emphasis is placed on the primacy of the economic order, already perverted as the crisis that is affecting the world is showing.

Excellencies

Ladies and Gentlemen,

Despite the austerity faced by the majority of countries in the world, the Asia-Pacific region has achieved notable progress, allowing for various emerging economies to grow and lifting millions of people out of poverty.

For those who live in this region, which is becoming more and more the centre of global economic and strategic weight, there should be a sense of pride but also a sense of responsibility to the lesser developed nations of the world.

What inspires us in the Asian Century, or if we prefer the Asia-Pacific Century, can (or should), in the architecture of geo-strategic relations, place new contours on the course of global order (or to put it better, correct the course of actual global disorder), so that we can all be capable of facing the new security challenges with a common vision less belligerent for the good of all humanity.

Despite growing tensions in our region, we must trust that international leaders will turn the words spoken in good faith into constructive action – under the auspices of true dialogue, by building the strategic trust, as the Prime Minister of Vietnam outlined in his speech last night – so that we may leave these concerns behind and focus on the needs of the people.

In Timor-Leste we have been adopting public policies that have allowed for a sustainable development framework.

We have achieved some successes, including high economic growth rates, progress in human development, consolidation of peace and stability, and above all the strengthening of the relationships of friendship and partnership that we have with many countries in the world, especially those within our region.

Our defence and security challenges are common to every country. We believe that Timor-Leste has a strong role to play on the geo-strategic scene, not because of any military and defence capability, but towards contributing with an environment of stability in the region.

It is also in this sense that we are so committed to becoming a fully-fledged member of ASEAN. An effective response to the challenges ahead for the countries in this community requires a collective approach and close cooperation between the neighbours in the region.

I repeat here the appeal I made at the Third Jakarta International Defence Dialogue in March this year about the real situation facing Kiribati, the Marshall Islands and Tuvalu that are drowning day after day as they disappear into the vastness of the ocean. The developed countries, who are the main contributors to climate change, must, by moral obligation, think of a Marshall Plan of financial compensation that will allow these countries to save their dignity as States and as Peoples.

Ladies and Gentlemen,

Today, defending national interests with the view to prevent presumed conflicts, can nurture an environment of hostility and distrust, if frankness and honesty are not the basis of dialogue between nations.

The defence of a country's borders and its maritime area is not exclusively confined to the defence forces that it has at its disposal. This is instilled in a broader concept of security, with implications for those smaller countries that, for obvious reasons, are still developing their own concept of national security, naturally giving priority to the security of the population and its wealth.

Small and defenceless countries, such as Timor-Leste, are concerned with the movements of big powers, that are strategically positioning their forces as though preparing for a future of military confrontation. Between who? This is a question that can only be answered by the analysts and decision-makers of the world.

The challenge for us is to find out whether this is to discourage us, when we address matters of sovereignty concerning our resources, with the logic that results from the conflicts created by the powerful to defend so-called national interests.

Many internal instabilities, in various countries, were provoked to promote fragility in these nations so as to protect multi-national interests. In this case, the possible enemy has no face.

In today's time, when defence is fed by so many technological advances and when in other regions we see war being waged with faceless technologies, in our region it should be different by giving a human face to this debate.

It should be different by reinforcing that peace is made by, and for, people.

It should be different by investing in dialogue and strategic cooperation and by recognising and benefiting from our similarities and our inequalities.

It should be different by presenting to the world a region that embraces different historical experiences as the ones of Timor-Leste and Singapore, or, with a difficult common past as with the case of the now excellent relations between Timor-Leste and Indonesia, so that our community of nations may inspire a safer and more prosperous world for all peoples and all humanity.

Lecture on Timor-Leste's Role and Future in a Rising Asia-Pacific – The S. Rajaratnam School of International Studies

Singapore, 4 June 2013

Mr Barry Desker, Dean, S. Rajaratnam School of International Studies
Excellencies
Ladies and Gentlemen,

It is a great pleasure to be here today to speak at the S. Rajaratnam School of International Studies.

The RSIS is a leading educational institution and makes a valuable contribution to strategic thinking on national security, defence, diplomacy and international affairs in the Asia-Pacific. Indeed, it is an honour to give a lecture for such as prestigious School.

The importance of critical thinking and discussion on these issues cannot be overstated in this uncertain and changing world. We were reminded of this, over the weekend, during the Shangri-La Dialogue, at which I was pleased to be a participant. This Dialogue presents another important international forum, for discussing regional security challenges and international cooperation.

At the Dialogue, I intervened on the topic 'defending national interest and defence'. Today, I have been asked to speak about a topic closer to home: Timor-Leste's role and future, in a rising Asia-Pacific.

Last month we celebrated the 11-year anniversary of the Restoration of our Independence and our nation is now moving towards greater international engagement, as we look beyond our shores to how we can contribute to the global community. However, before discussing our nation's future, I will speak briefly of our country's past and our current context. In this way, we can all consider the best course for Timor-Leste to chart, as we engage with the Asia-Pacific and beyond.

Ladies and Gentlemen,

I became aware that the motto of the RSIS is 'Ponder the Improbable.' This is a clever motto, as the path of human history is marked by unexpected twists and turns.

The dramatic fall of the Soviet Union, the Asian Financial Crisis, the development of the internet, the September 11 attacks, the Global Financial Crisis and even the Arab Spring – these were all events that both dramatically changed the world and were unexpected by most.

Another recent example is in Southeast Asia, where few predicted the remarkable pace of reform and progress that we are witnessing in Myanmar.

But even after these events occurred, their consequences were not fully known and we saw how they played out in unpredictable ways. The Asian Financial Crisis, in the late 90s, led to the establishment of democracy in the world's largest Muslim nation. The Global Financial Crisis denounced the unfairness of the practices of financial institutions, affecting world commerce and gave rise to the sovereign debt crisis, which is causing havoc across the European Union. And we have seen the hopes and dreams of the Arab Spring turn into a nightmare for the people of Syria.

I see many young students in the audience today and we can all ponder the dramatic turns in history that you will experience in your life. The RSIS does us all a service by engaging us in thinking about the international scenarios we may face. This allows us to undertake strategic planning and preparation. And it reminds us that the future belongs to those that are ready for it.

Ladies and Gentlemen,

Today I want to start by talking about another event that was considered improbable by most – a free Timor-Leste.

The path of our history led us into a guerrilla war with a regional giant, with most of the world giving us little chance of success.

In fact, our past is similar to that of many Southeast Asian nations, which experienced a long history of European colonialism, followed by a difficult transition to independence, after the Second World War.

Along the centuries of Portuguese colonial rule, our people attempted, unsuccessfully, various revolts and also resisted in the period of occupation during the Second World War. And then, in 1974, a revolution in Portugal changed the system, by granting the right to self-determination to its colonies.

This was at a time of high international political tension in Southeast Asia. The war in Vietnam was raising western fears of the spread of communism and a year later, in April 1975, Saigon fell and communist governments came to power in Vietnam, Cambodia and Laos.

It was against this political backdrop, that we decided to take control of our destiny and, on 28 November 1975, we made an unilateral declaration of independence. Nine days later we were invaded.

Thanks to the courage and leadership of Foreign Minister S. Rajaratnam, Singapore was one of the very few nations to immediately denounce the invasion. I am, of course, grateful that His Excellency was on the right side of history.

But our people were forsaken by the major western powers that remained silent or supported our annexation. For 24 years, we fought a war without any external military support, while developed nations supplied weapons, tanks, aircraft and training to the occupying forces to destroy the resistance of the small Timorese guerrilla army. We were so small, and so ill equipped, and we were fighting a giant and its allies.

But we had a dream as our ancestors had a dream that inspired us to persist in the guerrilla campaign in the mountains and valleys of Timor, as we never gave up in the diplomatic campaign at the United Nations and around the globe.

And finally, in 1999, our people were allowed to vote in a referendum on independence, supervised by the United Nations. On 30 August 1999, our people bravely voted for independence in the Referendum – but the vote brought more violence which left much of our country destroyed.

We did, however, achieve what most thought was improbable, if not impossible – the independence of our people and the establishment of a sovereign and democratic State of Timor-Leste.

I tell this story to you today, not only to share some of the background of Timor-Leste's place in the Asia-Pacific. I also tell it, as a case study so that we can all ponder the improbable path that history can take.

Ladies and Gentlemen,

For almost three years the United Nations administered our country, until our Restoration of Independence on 20 May 2002. After that, other missions remained in Timor-Leste to support our development. At the end of last year, we said good-bye to the last one, the United Nations Integrated Mission in East Timor. We are thankful for the international community support, through the UN, but now we walk on our own two feet as a nation.

Our early years of nationhood were not easy. Our legacy of colonialism and occupation left us with very limited human resources and almost no infrastructure. And we had no money. This meant that we had great challenges in building the foundations of our new nation.

Further, we were still, socially and psychologically, exposed to the trauma of the past, incapable of avoiding its consequences. We suffered setbacks and came through a cycle of violence, commonly experienced by post-conflict nations around the world.

The worst incidence of unrest occurred in 2006, through 2007, when we feared our country would be torn apart. Lingering disputes and conflict, between our police and military, led to widespread violence and burning houses. As a result, around 150,000 Timorese left their homes and became Internally Displaced People.

Those terrible events shocked us all and, as a nation, we realised that we had to come together, conciliate our differences and deeply reflect about the destructive way we were paving our future.

And so, we began a dialogue with all Timorese people, and started to address the root causes of the problems. It was only then that we were able to work through the issues facing our country and secure a lasting peace.

Our difficult process of dialogue took all the year of 2008 but was successful and, since 2009, we have enjoyed stability and we have a growing sense of hope and confidence in our future.

Timor-Leste is a small but emerging economy, with open and free markets. Since 2008, we have enjoyed average rates of economic growth above 10%, our sovereign wealth fund, the Petroleum Fund, has grown to over $13 billion and we have some of the world's most competitive tax rates.

We still face many challenges as a nation. We need to radically improve our human resources, build core national infrastructure and eliminate extreme poverty.

But after building peace, we are now embarked on the process of State building. Having overcome a period of crisis, in which we had no option but to focus on resolving issues of the short term, we can look now to the future, which we want to be a bright one for our country.

After an extensive period of nation consultation, we released a long-term plan for the future: our *Strategic Development Plan 2011-2030*. This Plan provides a framework to move our country from a low-income country to an upper middle income country, with a healthy, well educated and safe population by 2030.

To implement this Plan, we are asking our people to demonstrate the same dedication and commitment to building the nation, as they did to the struggle for self-determination. Where once we dreamt of independence, we now dream of development.

Ladies and Gentlemen,

Being part of Southeast Asia, and the broader Asian Pacific region, gives us reason for confidence in our future.

At a time of global economic weakness, the Asian region continues to make incredible progress. It is home to emerging economies that are driving world growth, lifting millions from poverty and shifting international economic and strategic weight to our region.

And Southeast Asia is a central part of this remarkable Asian transformation. The ASEAN group of nations together have a larger economy than India, Singapore has consolidated its place as a global financial centre and Indonesia is one of the great emerging economies of the world.

Improved governance, investment in human and physical development, along with its access to foreign and domestic capital, has helped power this incredible rise of Asia.

Singapore is the perfect example of this transformation. As a global centre of both knowledge and capital, and with its good governance, Singapore provides a model of success.

However, in this Asian Century, our region is still not without its challenges. Some of our economic growth has not been balanced and extreme poverty remains. Inequality is also rising which presents risks to our social fabric and progress. While the Asia-Pacific region is home to many of the world's great economic powers, it is also home to nearly two-thirds of the world's poor. We are also seeing a worrying rise in gender inequality and violence against women and girls.

There are also growing regional strategic tensions, many of which are fuelled by a number of complex competing territorial claims. These tensions are rising, at the same time as the region's growing prosperity allows nations to modernise and expand their defence forces.

Now, as much as ever, we need to step up our defence and security dialogue. And we need institutions like the RSIS to help us navigate our future towards cooperation and stability.

This is because the continued growth of our region depends on its security. We need stable relations between nations and a focus on building positive relationships of respect and friendship.

We need to see international leaders moving beyond words of good faith to taking constructive actions – and participating in real dialogue and active engagement – in the best interests of our common security. Part of the solution to calm some regional tensions will also involve reconciling a past of conflict and building upon our shared interests.

This brings to mind North East Asia where we see a need to improve relationships between key players in the rise of Asia. We are in a historic period in which we have new leaders in China, Japan, the Republic of Korea and North Korea.

At the Shangri-la Dialogue, the Japanese Defence Minister, publicly expressed the apology of the Japanese Government and People to all the nations that suffered under Japanese occupation in World War Two. This was a sincere and courageous political gesture.

This should help provide an opportunity for progress and we all hope that this moment is seized.

And so, while the Asia-Pacific has made tremendous progress, there remain challenges, that no nation can address alone.

Ladies and Gentlemen,

This brings me to speak directly about Timor-Leste's role and future in the Asia Pacific.

We may be a small nation, but we are part of our interconnected region. Our nation shares an island with Indonesia. We are part of the fabric of Southeast Asia. And we are on the cross road of Asia and the Pacific.

We want to participate in the growing prosperity and success of the region, as well as contribute together to addressing our common challenges. Timor-Leste also knows that our future depends on our regional integration.

To develop our country, we need to invest in our people and our economy. And so, we have established a Human Capital Development Fund and are spreading our students throughout Asia, to learn the skills that are necessary for building our State. Timor-Leste is also open to foreign capital and investment, with some of the world's lowest tax rates, which are helping to power our positive economic growth.

Timor-Leste is also committed to greater political integration in the region. Closer to home, Timor-Leste has forged the most positive of relations with Indonesia. Many would have thought this too would be improbable.

In a model of reconciliation, and with a firm commitment to focus on the future, we have built a strong relationship of trust and friendship. Rather than being enslaved by the trauma of our history, we are instead honouring our struggle by working towards a better future for our people. We know that Indonesia and Timor-Leste not only share an island, we share a future.

We have also begun to hold trilateral meetings between the leaders of Australia, Indonesia and Timor-Leste. Last November, we held the first trilateral meeting with the President of Indonesia and the Prime Minister of Australia. Last weekend, the Ministers of Defence of the three countries held their first trilateral meeting, agreeing to meet on an annual basis for consultation and cooperation.

Again, if just over a decade ago someone had suggested that the three of us would be meeting in such a trilateral arrangement it would have been dismissed as more than improbable.

And as you know, Timor-Leste has made an application to join ASEAN. ASEAN has been a global success story in establishing a region of peace, cooperation and development. It should provide a model, and an aspiration, for so many regions of the world.

As Timor-Leste is part of Southeast Asia, we also want to be part of ASEAN and, together, contribute to regional growth, social progress and cultural development in a spirit of partnership. We feel like an integral part of our neighbourhood and have a strong sense of regionalism and solidarity with our Southeast Asian Nations – we are one of you.

We also know we must work together on regional issues, including the management of cross border security threats and cooperate on humanitarian assistance, disaster relief, environmental management and the tackling of climate change.

Timor–Leste can also offer ASEAN the benefits of our special historical and ongoing ties and relationships across the globe. This includes with the Community of Portuguese-Speaking Countries, from Africa to Brazil.

Timor-Leste knows that it has to build its human resources to enable us to contribute fully to ASEAN. That is why we are training our people so that they can join the organisation, as a key part of our future role in Asia.

To progress our ascension to ASEAN, and to build Timor-Leste's relationship with the South East Asian region, this year I will be visiting most ASEAN nations. Singapore is the second ASEAN country I have been to, on this program of Official Visits, and I am very grateful to the Government of Singapore for being so enthusiastic and supportive of this visit.

In April this year, Timor-Leste was honoured to take over the Chair of the 69th session of the United Nations Economic and Social Commission for the Asia-Pacific. And so I have the privilege to Chair this session over the next year and work with ESCAP, and the nations of the Asia-Pacific, to make further progress and improve human development. Again, this contribution is an important part of Timor-Leste stepping out, to be a part of not only the Asian region, but the Asia-Pacific.

And we must not forget that an important part of the Asia-Pacific is the great island nations of the Pacific. At times, Timor-Leste feels like a bridge between Southeast Asia and the Pacific Islands. We share so many of the challenges and the opportunities that the Pacific Islands face and we contribute strongly as an observer to the annual Pacific Islands Forum, which Timor-Leste always attends.

Our solidarity with the Pacific Islands runs deep. We will be ever thankful for the unwavering support of Vanuatu in our struggle for independence. We are working together with our close friend, the Solomon Islands, on tackling the shared fragility of our countries. And we are in solidarity with the Republic of Kiribati, the Marshall Islands and Tuvalu that are slowly sinking into the vastness of the ocean, because of the perils of climate change.

Ladies and Gentlemen,

The people of Timor-Leste want to contribute solutions to some of the human development challenges facing the Asia-Pacific. We know that, to do so, involves not only local and regional responses but also global commitments and action.

I have already mentioned some of the development challenges that the Asia-Pacific faces. This includes widespread poverty, rising inequality and violence against women. Regrettably, these are development challenges that are common through much of the world. They are also the challenges that the Millennium Development Goals were designed to address.

As you know, the world is now in a dialogue to develop the post-2015 development agenda, on the expiry of the MDGs. Timor-Leste is proud of having our

Finance Minister, Emilia Pires, as a member of the High Level Panel. I can inform that the Minister has just returned from New York in that role, having the Panel finalised the report to the Secretary General. This report will be presented to the United Nations General Assembly in September.

We are determined to ensure that the United Nations is aware that not one fragile or conflict affected nation has achieved even one Millennium Development Goal.

That is why in 2010, Timor-Leste hosted an international conference with the theme 'peace building and State building'. A significant outcome of the conference was the formation of the g7+, an international forum that provides a united voice for fragile countries to advocate for change in global development policies.

The g7+ countries know, from bitter experience, that it is not possible to eradicate poverty without peace and stability. That is why the g7+ nations are working together to ensure that the post-2015 development agenda addresses the need for peace and stability, and that the perspectives of fragile States are central to the global dialogue.

This message was repeated loudly and clearly, when the g7+ nations, and some of our neighbours from Asia and the Pacific Islands and also from Africa and Middle East, met in Díli, in February of this year, at an international conference, hosted by my Government with the theme 'Development for All'. The Conference agreed on the 'Díli Consensus', that set out our priorities, and hopes, for the post-2015 development agenda.

The 'Díli Consensus' recognised that the standard approaches to development have failed to acknowledge that the challenges we face vary depending upon local context. That means the problems and solutions to achieving human development will differ from a Southeast Asian nation, compared to one of the Pacific island nations and that it will not be possible to eradicate poverty in the Asia-Pacific, and across the world, without first addressing the issues of fragile and conflict affected countries.

Ladies and Gentlemen,

Timor-Leste is not only a small country; we are also the youngest nation in the Asia-Pacific. Precisely because we are small, and because we are young, it is important that we work together with our neighbours to improve the lives of our people and the human development of our region.

I have covered a lot of ground today, setting out the history of Timor-Leste in the context of the rise of the Asia-Pacific and charting a course for our nation's international engagement. I know in doing so, I have touched on many issues and I hope that, in at least a small way, this provokes some of you to ponder the future, and importantly, to ponder the improbable.

Thank you very much.

Lecture at the Lee Kuan Yew School of Public Policy at the National University of Singapore: 'Peace Building and State Building: From Fragility to Resilience'

Singapore, 4 June 2013

Professor Jeffrey Straussman, Vice Dean, Lee Kuan Yew School of Public Policy
Excellencies
Ladies and Gentlemen,

Today I would like to share with you a reflection on the Timorese experience – our difficult but successful transition from conflict to development, from fragility to resilience.

But first, I want to thank you for coming today, and I want to thank the Lee Kuan Yew School of Public Policy for organising this event.

It is a great honour to address such a distinguished audience, at such a prestigious university – the National University of Singapore.

Ladies and Gentlemen,

The Timorese people's struggle for self-determination and freedom has left the pages of our history marked with bloodshed; but they are also coloured by heroic deeds and humbling acts of sacrifice, and the final chapter tells of success as we achieved our dream of independence.

Other countries throughout the world have similar histories. We know we are not the only nation to work on peace building and Statebuilding, after emerging from a long period of conflict.

For example, Timor-Leste is just one of forty-nine countries the United Nations labels 'Least Developed Countries'.

We are one of the thirty countries labeled by the World Bank as 'Fragile States'.

We are also one of eighteen countries that have come together to form a group – known as the g7+ – to monitor, report and draw attention to the specific challenges faced by fragile states.

And we know that, around the world, there are still some 1.5 billion people living in extreme poverty.

So we are not alone but, we also know, our story is unique, as in a different way, Singapore's story is also unique.

As I share our story of struggle, of triumph, of transition and growth, I ask you to listen with an open mind, and understand that I am not advocating any kind of a model, that can be considered as the recipe to successful processes.

Development programs must be adapted to the cultural, social and economic context of each society as, I always say, the democratic process must also take into account the context of each reality. They must meet the needs and aspirations of the local population, and be accepted by them. The programs must be 'country owned, and country led'.

Ignoring local realities is often the reason why international assistance, to Least Developed Countries undergoing transition, fails.

Ladies and Gentlemen,

That is why I would like to briefly share Timor-Leste's journey. It was a long and difficult journey from colonial times and occupation to peace building and State building: from fragility to resilience.

Timor-Leste is half of an island, with the other half belonging to Indonesia. For over four centuries, we were administered as a colony of Portugal. On 28 November 1975, a year after the Portuguese Carnation Revolution, we made a unilateral declaration of independence. Nine days later we were invaded.

Singapore was one of the very few nations with the courage to immediately denounce the invasion. It was support like this that inspired us and gave us the necessary strength.

For 24 years, we persisted in a guerrilla resistance to the military occupation. Our people suffered and endured all kinds of sacrifice, but we held on to our dream of freedom. When we were granted a referendum on 30 August 1999, despite the climate of violence, our people decided and overwhelmingly voted for independence– but the result brought more killings and spread destruction all over the country.

Ladies and Gentlemen,

From late1999, we were under the administration of the United Nations, which, with the support of the international community, helped us to build from scratch the foundations for the democratic institutions of the new State.

Finally, on 20 May 2002, we became the masters of our fate, and the Democratic Republic of Timor-Leste was reborn as an independent and sovereign nation.

While we had achieved our independence, we did not have the apparatus of a State.

We had no experience running a government and we lacked human resources and finance. We also lacked the basic infrastructure needed to run a productive economy or serve the essential needs of our people.

But our people had high expectations. Many believed that our freedom would end our suffering. After so much struggle, our people wanted a new life and better living conditions – and they wanted those things immediately.

For a family that struggles both in times of war and of peace, that lives in basic conditions with no access to health, education and other services, democracy could only be an abstract concept, and they demand the right answer to concrete needs.

The truth is that there are no shortcuts for consolidating democracy and development. It is necessary to walk a long and difficult path, in order to change the mindset of society and to give meaning to our values to change the experiences of every citizen, taking into account a people scarred by a long conflict.

In our early years, the challenges we faced were enormous and the expectations so high, that we struggled with political and social intolerance.

Our beloved country was gripped by a cycle of violence, which saw conflict erupt every two years. And then, in 2006, we had a serious political crisis that led to confrontations between the police and the military, opening the way to hundreds of thousands of internally displaced people.

But we pulled together and, from this crisis, we learned our first major lesson: we urgently needed to deal with the fragility of our State, and address the root causes of our problems.

We had to encourage State institutions to cooperate and work together to find solutions, rather than focusing on old rivalries and on the political dimensions of every situation.

We focused our efforts on establishing peace and stability, as well as solving the most critical problems of the country, knowing that, without addressing the problem of stability and internal security, any development effort would be in vain.

It was through constant dialogue and genuine cooperation between all bodies of the State and civil society, together with the introduction of social justice measures and government reform that we managed to break the cycle of conflict.

And so, we embarked on a new process – of peacebuilding to Statebuilding.

Income started to flow from oil reserves in the Timor Sea and we made sure we had systems in place, to be able to provide for the urgent needs of today, while protecting income for future generations. We established a Petroleum Fund that has grown from $1.8 billion in 2007 (the year of instability) to over $13 billion today.

We were the first in Asia, and third in the world, to be compliant with the EITI (Extractive Industry Transparency Initiative), so that every dollar that comes in, from petroleum revenue, is publicly disclosed and matched with the records of the resource companies.

We established a National Petroleum Authority that employs some of Timor-Leste's most educated women and men, to manage and regulate petroleum activities in Timor-Leste's exclusive jurisdictional areas, and in the Joint Petroleum Development Area with Australia.

We are creating a highly transparent financial system, where anyone in the world eventually will be able to track the budget being executed in real time, track aid expenditure, track procurement and most importantly, track results.

We invested in capacity building in the security sector to improve professionalism in the Police and in the Military, bringing about a new stage of cooperation and solidarity among the two institutions.

We provided pensions to our veterans, the elderly, the disabled, widows and orphans and introduced similar social justice measures for other vulnerable groups such as women, children and youth.

Most importantly, we reflected deeply on our recent experience and realised that, without peace and internal reconciliation, there can be no inclusive development.

And so, together as a nation, we forged peace. After breaking our cycle of conflict and enjoying many years of peace, we were able to move to a new stage focused on long term planning and State building.

We said goodbye to conflict, and we welcomed development.

Ladies and Gentlemen,

Having established a foundation of peace and security, we could begin long term planning and enter a new phase of our development.

In 2011, we released the *Timor-Leste Strategic Development Plan 2011-2030* that provides a comprehensive framework to transform our country from a low income nation to a country with upper-middle income levels by 2030, with a population that is secure, educated and healthy.

We have begun to implement our Plan and we are already achieving some outstanding results.

Our progress can be measured in many ways. One way is through economic growth, and Timor-Leste has been growing at an average of 11.9%, since 2007 as the year of reference, and the International Monetary Fund predicts that this level of growth will continue into the future.

But we also know that growth must be balanced and the benefits shared in an inclusive way. We have adopted local development programs to create jobs and improve living conditions of the population in the rural areas, especially with assistance in health, power supply, water and sanitation and access to education and to markets. In addition to this, we have started to build community neighbourhoods in various locations.

That is why we are implementing large programs to build infrastructure projects in every village in the nation.

Our economic growth also means an expanding private sector that is creating more jobs for our people and paying more taxes to fund the provision of basic public services.

Our progress can also be measured by looking at health and education.

Child mortality rates have also seen a sharp decline from 83 to 64 per thousand live births, between 2003 and 2009/2010. Life expectancy at birth has also increased from 59.5 in 2006 to 64.6 in 2011.

In the other sector, from 2010 to 2011, the total number of children enrolled in school, increased by 5%, 8% and 17% in basic, general secondary and secondary technical education respectively.

We have completed the largest infrastructure project in our people's history, by building a national electricity grid with generation and distribution across the country.

And we are embarking on an infrastructure program to provide a basis for a nation's sustainable economic future, which will include a new national port, a major airport upgrade, a national road network and the extensive development of our south coast to become a sub-regional centre for the petroleum industry.

We have established a Human Capital Development Fund to build the human resources of our nation and already our students are spread out around Asia and the world to learn the skills necessary for State building.

We are heading in the right direction as a nation and we are building our State.

In recognition of our progress, last year the last United Nation's Mission left Timor-Leste. We now stand firmly on our own two feet.

We are pleased that the withdrawal of the United Nation's Mission has not impacted the momentum of our progress or the security of our country.

Our transition from fragility to resilience has been possible because we took control and ownership of our future.

We know that we still face many challenges and that the process of State building is ongoing. But we have a plan and we have the same commitment to developing our nation as we did to freeing it.

Ladies and Gentlemen,

Our transition from fragility to resilience has also given us the space to look beyond our own shores and allowed us to enhance our international engagement.

Just as the international community has done so much to support our people, now we want to be able to contribute something in return.

Part of our international focus is on supporting and working with other fragile countries around the world. An important part of this is working with the g7+, which is an important new collaboration between 18 fragile States.

The group was formed in 2010 to provide a united voice for fragile countries and to advocate for change in global development policies. The g7+ knows, from bitter experience, that without peace and stability there can be no development. Not one fragile or conflict affected nation has achieved even one Millennium Development Goal.

This means that it will not be possible to eradicate poverty in the world, without first addressing the issues of fragile and conflict affected countries. That is why the g7+ nations have worked together to ensure that the post-2015 development agenda addresses the need for peace and stability, and that the perspectives of fragile States are central to the global dialogue.

As you know, the world is finalising its dialogue on the post-2015 development agenda on the expiry of the MDGs. Timor-Leste is proud of our Finance Minister, Emilia Pires, being a member of the High Level Panel that advised the United Nations Secretary General on this agenda.

To assist this work, in February this year, Díli hosted the leaders from around the world, including from the Asia-Pacific and Africa, at an International Conference on the post-2015 Development Agenda.

As a result of our discussions and deliberations, we formulated the 'Díli Consensus' – a document that set out our priorities, and hopes, for the post 2015 development agenda. Importantly, it stated that we must set out a credible, responsible and realistic pathway to development.

Timor-Leste has also made an application to join ASEAN. ASEAN has been an international success story in establishing a region of peace, cooperation and development. As Timor-Leste is part of Southeast Asia we also want to be part of ASEAN and together contribute to regional growth, social progress and cultural development.

We also know we must work together on regional issues, including the management of cross border security threats and cooperate on humanitarian assistance, disaster relief, environmental management and the tackling of climate change.

And in April this year, Timor-Leste was honoured to take over the Chair of the 69th session of the United Nations Economic and Social Commission for the Asia-Pacific. And so I have the privilege to Chair this session over the next year and work with ESCAP, and the nations of the Asia-Pacific, to make further progress and improve human development.

In the meantime, Timor-Leste is supporting the APRC (the Asian Peace and Reconciliation Council), established last year, in Bangkok, which comprises former Heads of State, former members of Government from across Asia and academics. The Council aims to help facilitate dialogue within societies and between nations, in order to put an end to frictions or prevent confrontations. Timor-Leste values this noble ideal and mission, to help nurture a culture of peace in our region.

Again, all of these contributions are also part of Timor-Leste's progress towards resilience, as we take our place in the international community.

Ladies and Gentlemen,

Last May, we celebrated eleven years of independence.

It has been a long road for our people, and we still have a long way to go, but we are travelling in the right direction and the future looks promising.

I urge you to continue to follow our progress and to visit our beautiful country to see for yourself the achievements of our people.

Thank you for listening.

Address at the Thomson Reuters Asia Petroleum Lunch

Singapore, 5 June 2013

Mr Alfred Loo, Thomson Reuters
Excellencies
Ladies and Gentlemen

It is a pleasure to be here today to talk about the progress of Timor-Leste and the developments in our oil and gas industry.

Thank you to Thomson Reuters for giving me this opportunity and for organising and hosting this event.

I would also like to thank everyone here in this distinguished audience, for coming today and for your interest in our young country.

I would like to take this opportunity to again thank the State of Singapore for its wonderful hospitality and for making our visit such a success.

For many developing nations, including Timor-Leste, Singapore is an inspirational model of what can be achieved with a clear vision, commitment to education and strong public leadership.

In Timor-Leste, we have great admiration for Singapore's remarkable transformation, and study your experience for lessons to inform our own development.

As you know, Timor-Leste has been through some difficult times on our road to development. We achieved our Independence in 2002 following almost three years of United Nations administration.

From the beginning our task was daunting. Most of our infrastructure had been destroyed in the aftermath of our vote for independence, we lacked the human resources to build a nation and our people carried scars of the trauma of our struggle for independence.

But as our fight for independence demonstrated, our people have great courage and resilience. Now we are harnessing this same determination to develop our nation.

Ladies and Gentlemen,

Like Singapore, in Timor-Leste, we proved that our true strength was our people.

Last month we celebrated the 11th anniversary of our Restoration of Independence and we had much to celebrate.

After a difficult beginning, we have now enjoyed many years of peace and security. In recognition of our progress, last year we said goodbye to the United Nations Mission and I am pleased to say that its withdrawal has not impacted the momentum of our progress or the security of our country.

One of the areas of our success has been our economic management. Timor-Leste is a small but emerging economy with open and free markets and some of the lowest tax rates in the world.

Since my Government was elected in 2007 we have enjoyed average rates of economic growth of 11.9% and the International Monetary Fund predicts high growth will continue. This is creating jobs and opportunities for our people.

Our sovereign wealth fund, the Petroleum Fund, has grown from $1.8 billion in 2007 to over $13.6 billion today. Since January this year, the fund has increased on average by $324 million each month.

Now that we have built a firm foundation of security and stability there is a strong sense of hope and confidence in Timor-Leste. This has also allowed us to plan for the long-term future.

And so, in 2011 we released our comprehensive Timor-Leste *Strategic Development Plan 2011-2030* to transform our country from a low income nation to a country with upper-middle income levels by 2030, with a population that is secure, educated and healthy.

An important part of this Plan is our economic progress and the development of industries, which will drive our prosperity. The *Strategic Development Plan 2011-2030* designates three strategic industries, which will be the key to our future. They are agriculture, tourism and petroleum.

Ladies and Gentlemen,

Our petroleum industry is critical to our economic growth and our capacity to build our nation and support our people. Unlike Singapore, we have the advantage of being able to fund our development from oil and gas revenue. Income from our petroleum sector funds much of our budget, our infrastructure spending and delivery of education and health services.

Because of the importance of our petroleum revenue, which belongs to our people, we are totally committed to transparency. We are proud that Timor-Leste was the first country in Asia, and third country in the world, to comply with the Extractive Industry Transparency Initiative.

This means that every dollar earned from our oil and gas resources is accounted for and audited so that the funds are managed transparently for the benefit of our people.

To make sure that we make the most of our oil and gas resources we have some of the best minds in our nation, and from around the world, to work out how we can grow our petroleum sector to ensure the benefits flow to all the Timorese people.

Currently, Timor-Leste has two fields producing in the Joint Petroleum Development Area – a petroleum rich zone of the Timor Sea defined in the Timor Sea Treaty signed by Timor-Leste and Australia in 2002.

They are the Bayu Undan project, operated by Conoco Phillips, and the KITAN project, operated by Eni. These two fields are currently producing on average 6 million barrels of oil equivalent each month.

In the Joint Petroleum Development Area, Bayu Undan and Greater Sunrise are the two biggest fields discovered to date. The Bayu Undan field contains recoverable reserves of 500 million barrels of liquids and 4 trillion cubic feet of gas, while the Greater Sunrise field contains recoverable reserves of 7.67 trillion cubic feet of gas and 298 million barrels of condensate.

Exploration activities, in both the JPDA and in our exclusive offshore areas in the Timor Sea, including seismic surveys and drilling, indicate there is an active petroleum system in the area with a number of prospects, which will attract further exploration in the future.

As many resource-based developing countries have done, Timor-Leste has adopted the Petroleum Sharing Contract regime as a means to engage international and national petroleum exploration and production companies to invest in petroleum exploration.

Timor-Leste is also fortunate to have resources both offshore and on shore. In addition to petroleum resources, we also have substantial mineral resources. Preliminary data and information indicates that this includes gold, copper, manganese, marble, phosphate, gypsum and iron ore. The exploration of these resources can be undertaken once our draft Mining Law, which is currently subject to public consultation, is signed into law.

Ladies and Gentlemen,

As part of making sure that we make the most of our resources, we have established a National Petroleum Company, TIMOR GAP, E.P, which stands for the Timor Gas and Petroleum, Empresa Pública or public company. TIMOR GAP, E.P. is leading the development of our industry through direct participation, ownership and investment in the petroleum sector.

TIMOR GAP's mandate covers all aspects of the oil and gas industry, both upstream and downstream and including services to the industry. It is responsible for creating business and employment opportunities for the people of Timor-Leste, and ensuring skills and technological transfer, while upholding good health, safety and environment standards. TIMOR GAP, E.P. may form joint ventures with international companies to carry out business activities.

TIMOR GAP, E.P. gives us a direct stake in the expansion of our industry and allows us to improve our human resources and capital infrastructure to build a sustainable and long term industry for our nation.

Ladies and Gentlemen,

Another responsibility entrusted to TIMOR GAP, E.P. is the management of the Tasi Mane Project. The Tasi Mane Project will develop our south coast as a sub-regional centre for the petroleum industry, bringing petroleum development to our shores. It will also provide a direct economic dividend from our petroleum industry activities.

The Tasi Mane Project involves three operation clusters along 155 kilometres of Timor-Leste's south coast facing the Timor Sea, which is home to the Timor-Leste Exclusive Area as well as the Joint Petroleum Development Area – both promising oil and gas exploration zones. It will include building a Supply Base in Suai, where logistics and service works will be undertaken and sourced for the petroleum industry. At Suai, major port facilities will be built in phases as multi-purpose and multi-user facilities and the local airport will be rehabilitated.

Further east along the coast, a refinery and a petrochemical industry will be established at the town of Betano. The Betano refinery will consist of an industrial park where refinery and petrochemical industries will be located along with a petroleum industry administration city. The refinery will provide domestic fuel needs such as diesel, gasoline, jet-fuel and asphalts.

At the end of the corridor, and further east at Beaço, the Government has designated a sizeable area for the development of Liquified Natural Gas projects. Several gas fields have been discovered in the nearby Timor Sea, including the Greater Sunrise field, and the Beaço LNG Facility will be the location at which the natural gas pipeline reaches Timor-Leste.

To link the clusters the government is planning to construct a highway from Suai to Beaço, a distance of 156 km.

Over the past 5 years the Government has invested heavily in studies to prove the technical and commercial viabilities of Tasi Mane Projects and the projects are at different stages of planning and development.

The Tasi Mane Project will establish a dynamic and integrated petroleum industry along our south coast bringing development, jobs and industry to our country. We look forward to working with the private sector on this project, which is so central to our nation's progress.

Ladies and Gentlemen,

Before I conclude, I know that some of you may be interested in the CMATS arbitration process, which will clarify the validity of the CMATS Treaty.

This is a matter that Timor-Leste takes very seriously. As the issues are currently subject to a formal arbitration it would not be appropriate for me to make an argument in public or to comment further but we hope the matter is resolved quickly for the benefit of all parties.

I would like to reinforce, however, that Timor-Leste and Australia enjoy a very mature and positive bilateral relationship. We are steadfast friends and Australia has contributed so much, and continues to contribute, to our national development. We are confident that the arbitration will not impact on our greater friendship with Australia.

Ladies and Gentlemen,

Thank you again for coming today and thank you to Thomson Reuters for hosting this event.

I hope you have learnt more about our nation and our petroleum industry. I urge you to talk to our Ministers, and the members of our government, during this lunch. Our Minister for Petroleum and Mineral Resources, Alfredo Pires, is here today, along with Francisco Monteiro, the President and CEO of TIMOR GAP, EP, and Gualdino da Silva, the President of the National Petroleum Authority of Timor-Leste. They will all be pleased to discuss in more detail the plans we have for our future.

Together, working with the petroleum industry, Timor-Leste looks forward to building a better future for our people.

Thank you very much.

Address at the UP College of Law, University of the Philippines – 'Peace and Reconciliation: The Timorese Experience'

Manila, 7 June 2013

Excellency, Alfredo E. Pascual, President of the University of the Philippines,
Representatives of the Diplomatic Corps
Excellencies
Ladies and Gentlemen,

It is a great honour and pleasure for me to be here today in this century-old institution of higher education, which is one of the most prestigious in the region, and a traditional source of leaders and other senior officers of your great country.

I want to thank the UP College of Law for inviting me to speak here today and for hosting this event. As I have never attended university, like you all here today, I feel truly privileged to be able to address you.

This place, as the Dean and Fernando Peña reminded us, holds special meaning for the Timorese struggle, as it was here that the Asia-Pacific Coalition for East Timor, better known as APCET was born. APCET was for many years and continues to be a strong advocate for the rights of the Timorese and I am delighted to have caught up with my good friend and long-time freedom fighter of the Timorese cause, Gus Miclat. I still remember when my special representative at the time, José Ramos-Horta came to Manila to attend an APCET meeting and he read my message from Cipinang prison. I was called in by the Indonesian military intelligence and was subjected to a difficult interrogation. But I was glad to know that we had friends on the outside that cared enough to speak out about our cause.

Today's world faces serious problems, problems that could not have been imagined even during the period of the Cold War.

The global recession that is affecting the old continent, as well as the United States of America, is now hindering the development efforts of the poorest countries, at the same time it sends millions of people in the developed countries into unemployment.

The demonstrations, disturbances and acts of violence in these countries, which are finding out the hard way that they cannot hold on to their welfare State, express the feelings of anger in those societies that previously were such vocal advocates of world peace.

The irony here is, of course, that the underdeveloped countries were always viewed as having poor governance practices, while in fact it is the developed countries that have committed such terrible acts of irresponsibility, seriously damaging the lives of their own citizens and jeopardising the survival of hundreds of millions of people, around the world, while at the same time often offending the integrity and sovereignty of weak and poor nations.

The dreams of the Arab Spring have become a nightmare for the region, particularly for the people of Syria. The cries for freedom and democracy, which at once surprised and thrilled the world, have now been stifled by distant echoes of massacred populations, and forgotten by foreign powers for which dialogue and diplomacy do not satisfy their need to defend their geo-strategic interests.

The circumstances in Iraq and Afghanistan demonstrate that peace and democracy cannot be imposed through war, and that reconciliation and harmony in the social fabric of the countries in crisis are key factors for peace. As well, Africa continues to bleed internally, in both body and mind.

At the same time, the Asia-Pacific region and its successes are discussed by the large and the powerful, the politicians and the economists, the diplomats and the military, and within financial and business circles. I just came from the Shangri-la Dialogue where US-China relations and emerging threats dominated discussions. It is said that this is the 'Asian Century', with the nations of the region coming to dominate global geopolitics and where big powers are fighting for their interests in the region.

However, we all know the challenges we face, from regional tensions to territorial disputes, from nuclear threats to even latent conflicts that may arise with competition for the increasingly needed resources.

It is in this context, in this world turned upside down, that we are talking about Peace and Reconciliation.

It is undoubtedly easier to wage war than to build peace. It is easier to breed mistrust than to show tolerance and mutual understanding between nations, and this is because it has proved easier to safeguard the interests of the powerful few than the wellbeing of the many.

The principles of equality and honesty must be at the forefront of State relations, as they are indispensible in creating and strengthening ties of cooperation based on mutual trust and mutual respect.

We cannot postpone a new world paradigm, since the current system – based on a superficial analysis that is influencing the way in which decisions are made for reducing the suffering of humanity and ensuring a small piece of dignity to each and every human being – has already proven, in my humble opinion, to be unhealthy and unable to secure sustainable long term solutions.

Excellencies

Ladies and Gentlemen,

Timor-Leste, a half island, located in a corner of Southeast Asia where thousands of islands, both large and small, make up Indonesia, and farther south, Australia and the Pacific Islands, also felt the consequences of 20th century world history, including the influence of the Cold War.

We were under centuries of Portuguese colonial rule that experienced various revolts. Between 1941 and 1945, despite being short, the Japanese occupation covered the entire territory, causing more than 60,000 deaths.

If you want to believe the researchers, on the history of that time, the Timorese people would not have suffered much if the Australian troops did not come to Timor-Leste, with the objective to stop the invasion of Australia, by the Japanese based in our soil.

Also, according to the researchers, it was already in 1963 that, in Washington, the US, UK, Australia and New Zealand secretly agreed with the integration of Timor-Leste to Indonesia, as the best solution for world peace.

After 400 years of European colonialism, and one year after the Carnation Revolution in Portugal, on 28 November 1975 we unilaterally declared our independence.

However, we Timorese entered into a brief civil war, caused by ideological differences that in part were instigated by foreign interests to annex Timor-Leste. Tragically, nine days later, we were brutally invaded by Indonesia, with the US having given the green light.

Moreover, the terrible 24 year long military occupation would not have lasted so long, had the US, UK, France and Germany not supplied weapons, tanks and aircrafts and training to Indonesian military to improve their combat capabilities, with the aim to exterminate the small guerrilla resistance force.

On the other hand, our neighbour, Australia, was at the time, the only Western country to recognise the annexation. But, worst indeed, Australia signed an agreement with Indonesia to share the resources of the Timor Sea, in 1989.

And it happened at the time when hundreds of thousands of Timorese perished. For more than two decades, the Timorese people suffered and fought alone, without any military support from outside. Timorese families, above all our women and children, experienced deprivations and indescribable abuses.

In many places of Timor-Leste, thousands of my countrymen were killed in systematic wipe-out operations, while hunger, exhaustion and disease slowly took a toll on the survivors.

From our side, it took us some years, and much destruction, before we recognised that we needed to unite the Timorese people around the common ideal of independence, and this required us to reconcile our differences. Although we always sought peace with our occupiers, we were faithful to our motto of 'independence or death' and we knew that if we resisted together we would win in the end.

This recognition came from the people themselves, and it is this greatness of spirit, of being able to forgive and reconcile, that has been enabling us to achieve our dreams.

Meanwhile, the Referendum finally took place on 30 August 1999 and the results lead once again to uncontrollable violence by those who could not accept the democratic choice of the majority.

Despite the moral, psychological and political burden, and despite the violence and physical destruction of the already impoverished country, the desire of our people to live in peace did not diminish.

Tolerance overcame vengeance. Forgiveness overcame hatred.

We knew that independence, and the sacrifices of our people, would have no value, and that we could not achieve social harmony, if the hearts of the Timorese were filled with hatred and the desire for revenge.

Peace is more than the end of war! Peace also requires the healing of wounds through pragmatic decisions and policies that end hatred, vengeance and mistrust. Living in peace means being free from these corrosive feelings; it means living reconciled with our enemies, and especially with ourselves, both individually and as a whole.

And so, our people forgave the Timorese sisters and brothers, that fled to Indonesia, asking them to return, even those who had defended and fought for integration, so that together we could build our country. And importantly, the Timorese people vowed to establish a relationship of openness and solidarity with the Indonesian people, so that both Timorese and Indonesian could prosper.

We also understood, through the experiences of other post-conflict countries, that we would be unable to build our Nation if the seeds of hatred and mistrust were planted in our society.

Reconciliation is a prerequisite for national stability, which in turn is a requirement for development.

We created the CAVR (Commission for Reception, Truth and Reconciliation), the first reconciliation commission in Asia. We were pioneers in the promotion of human rights, creating a model that determined the truth concerning acts of violence committed in the past and that helped people to deal with that truth.

The reconciliation meetings between the Timorese in 2000, along the Indonesian border, were profound and touched the heart. Not only did the perpetrators acknowledge what they had done, but the victims also forgave them. As a result, thousands of refugees who had fled to Indonesia and feared about their acceptance in an independent Timor-Leste were able to return and were well received by their brothers and sisters.

This was the first decisive step for building our Nation!

In this critical process, we were fortunate to be able to rely on our ancestral tradition of reconciliation, which we call 'badame'. 'Ba dame' literally means 'to opt for peace' and is a tradition of public apology in Timor-Leste, with the perpetrator confessing their crimes publicly to the victim, before the elders and the members of the community.

This type of public apology is an indispensible condition for the perpetrator's reinstatement in the community and for restoring the reputation of the victim, by way of dialogue and with the participation of the entire community.

The reconciliation of each individual with the 'other' and with society is largely dependent on their capacity to reconcile with themselves. This is the most difficult part of the reconciliation process, since any bad feelings, any desire for confrontation starts within an individual, not between individuals.

Excellencies

Ladies and Gentlemen,

We have also put the past of our Indonesian occupation behind so that we could reconcile between our two peoples. The crimes were reviewed with great courage, particularly on the part of the victims, and a process of cooperation and friendship was started between both countries. This process has been contributing a great deal to the development of Timor-Leste.

Currently, Indonesia represents more than a close and friendly neighbour. It is also an example of stability, democracy and economic growth that inspires Timor-Leste.

With the establishment of a Commission of Truth and Friendship in Bali, in a joint effort between Timor-Leste and Indonesia, we were able to strengthen this friendship even further and to contribute to peace in Southeast Asia. I believe that our common history, and the difficult process we have endured and overcome, may serve as an example in our region and in the world, as a lesson of peace and reconciliation.

We are now proud to have built relationships of friendship with so many countries in the world, having a foreign policy of 'zero enemies'. Our relations with our neighbours, Australia and Indonesia, are excellent and we have privileged ties of friendship in Africa, Europe and Latin and South America, as well as, of course, countries of the Asia-Pacific.

Excellencies

Ladies and Gentlemen,

People develop when they manage to overcome their own weaknesses.

This is a complex process that takes time. A country taking its first steps on the path towards development, and carrying on its back the heavy burden of a conflicted past, will make mistakes and suffer setbacks.

Indeed, after our independence we entered a vicious cycle of conflict that arose every two years, as if to remind us that peace is a very delicate treasure that requires extreme care.

In Timor-Leste, leaders had to often be reminded that the people, those who sacrificed so that Timor-Leste could become independent, are not yet enjoying the fruits of freedom. Only by being close to the people and understanding their aspirations can we ensure stability and develop the nation.

We needed to secure political will at an institutional level to ensure cooperation in the search for solutions, as otherwise we would lack the realistic judgement to face and solve crises.

It is not easy to learn to live in democracy. The same way that there can be no freedom for people who cannot attain it by themselves, there can be no development if it is not achieved as a result of the effort of a society itself.

In order to break the vicious cycles of conflict we needed permanent and genuine dialogue, as well as cooperation between all Bodies of Sovereignty as well as civil society.

In addition to reconciliation, which was essential, the capacity building of our communities was also a key element necessary for maintaining peace in the country.

It is difficult to ask people to put collective interests ahead of their individual needs, and to take on a new fight with relish – the fight for national development. This, again, requires sacrifice and enormous patience.

This was why in 2009, on the 10th anniversary of the Referendum, we launched a new motto for our Nation: 'Goodbye Conflict, Welcome Development'.

Since then, we have been fortunate to live in a new atmosphere of security, stability and confidence in the future. We are implementing our *Strategic Development Plan*, our economic growth rates are among the highest in the world, and we are getting closer to our goal of becoming a full-fledged member of ASEAN.

Ladies and Gentlemen,

Each nation has its own context, its own history, its own culture. Independence is always achieved in a unique manner and each development process has its own reality and its own internal factors.

However, I believe that all people yearn for the same thing: to live in peace and harmony.

This is why I believe that dialogue is so important – dialogue within every nation and international dialogue respecting the sovereignty of each country, where the powerful do not seek to impose their interests on the weak and more vulnerable, as if their values are in some way superior, as if their rights are superior.

World peace will never be achieved while political hypocrisy prevails in the background of the western world, creating hatred, conflict, mistrust, desire for revenge and generalised feelings of dissatisfaction. At the Shangri-la Dialogue, I made an appeal to Western countries not to label people, organisations as 'enemies' as it does not help to resolve problems. Instead it promotes exclusion, isolation and fears.

We have to move from hostility and mistrust to mutual understanding, reconciliation and cooperation. International dialogue and multilateral deeds by world leaders must be tireless in seeking this goal.

Excellencies

Ladies and Gentlemen,

Timor-Leste does not forget its responsibilities in regard to consolidating world peace. After we survived through the most difficult pages in our history we were fortunate to receive international assistance, which has enabled us to build our nation and to live in peace and freedom.

Our cause was helped not only by the development partners of Timor-Leste, but also by citizens from all over the world, including the Filipinos and APCET, working alongside us so that peace could reach to every Timorese family, so our dream could become a reality. I would like to take this opportunity to thank Jaime de los Santos and Rodolfo Tor who played an important role in our nation building.

This history must not be ignored. Every individual counts. The history of humankind is not only that of the deeds of leaders; instead, we must also acknowledge those anonymous individuals who dedicate their lives to serving others.

Peace, ladies and gentlemen, begins and ends with each one of us.

Before I conclude, I would like to call your attention to a new and important collaboration between many of the fragile nations of the world – the so-called g7+.

This group was created in 2010 to give a united voice to fragile countries and to seek changes to global development policies. The g7+ knows from bitter experience that without peace and stability it is impossible to achieve development. Not one fragile or conflict-affected nation in the world has achieved a single Millennium Development Goal.

This means that it will not be possible to eradicate poverty in the world without first addressing the circumstances of fragile and conflict-affected countries. This is why the g7+ group of nations are working together to ensure that the post-2015 development agenda responds to the need for peace and stability and that the perspectives of fragile States will be seen as central to world dialogue.

Timor-Leste has the honour of leading this group and putting its experience to the service of all fragile and conflict-affected nations, promoting peace and reconciliation as the means and the ultimate goal of development.

And in 2013 we will support the holding of a Conference in Díli, organised by the Asian Peace and Reconciliation Council. The APRC was established last September in Bangkok and its founding members are distinguished individuals from Asia, including my friend José de Venecia, the former Vice President of Indonesia, Jusuf Kalla, and our former President of the Republic, Dr José Ramos-Horta, who is currently the SRSG in Guinea-Bissau.

I have been following with interest the latest developments in the Philippines. The Government and the people of the Philippines have been great supporters of the development of Timor-Leste, and we are lucky to have a large Filipino community in our country helping to build our nation. Indeed, I would like to take this opportunity to thank you personally, and on behalf of the Timorese people, for this support and solidarity.

Last, I would like to pay homage to the Government of the Philippines and to the Moro National Liberation Front for their efforts to find a peaceful, broad and lasting solution to the issues that separate them.

I hope that both will remain steadfast in taking the path of dialogue, since this is the only weapon that can put an end to insurgencies and overcome differences.

I have no doubt that the majority of Christians and Muslim alike desire peace. Maybe the time has come for the peaceful silent majorities to give a hand to the minorities. As I have said before, it is harder to fill a heart with peace than it is to fill it with hatred!

However, by building confidence and promoting tolerance, dialogue and reconciliation, it is possible to achieve a world of peace.

Thank you very much.

Opening Session of the 2013 Timor-Leste Development Partners Meeting – 'State Building for the Next Decade: A Reflection on Timor-Leste's Experiences and Expectations in State Building'

Díli, 19 June 2013

H.E. President Taur Matan Ruak
Excellencies Vice Presidents of National Parliament
H.E. President of Tribunal de Recurso, Dr. Claudio Ximenes
Members of Parliament
H.E. Francisco Almeida Leite, Secretary of State for Foreign Affairs and Cooperation, Portugal
Dr. Noeleen Heyzer, UNSG Under Secretary, Executive Secretary of ESCAP and Special Advisor for Timor-Leste
Mr Bert Hofman, Chief Economist for East Asia and the Pacific, the World Bank
Ambassadors, Heads of Agencies, Heads of Delegations
Civil Society and Private Sector Representatives
Ladies and Gentlemen and Distinguished Guests,

It is with great honour and pleasure that Timor-Leste welcomes once again the meeting of our development partners. This annual meeting is now part of Timor-Leste's history and provides an overview of the path we have taken since achieving our independence.

Once again partners and friends from different parts of the world have come to discuss and evaluate with us our challenges, our plans and our vision for the future.

I am also delighted to welcome Dr Heyzer who has been appointed by the United Nations Secretary General as the non-resident Special Adviser to Timor-Leste and who will support our country in its efforts towards peace building and State building and sustainable development.

I am also pleased to be able to work with Dr Heyzer in chairing the 69th session of the United Nations Economic and Social Commission for the Asia-Pacific.

During this year in this role we have the the privilege of working with ESCAP, and the nations of the Asia-Pacific, to make further regional progress and improve human development.

Thank you very much to all of you for being here and particularly for your dedication to the development of Timor-Leste.

I would like to invite you to reflect on 'State building'. Timor-Leste persists with the concept of 'State building' because, even if still young, we understand that throughout the world there are States with over half a century of existence that are also considered to be fragile States.

We are still witnessing major social and political shocks that put into question the legitimacy of States, such as in the Middle East (Iraq, Afghanistan and now Syria) and in North Africa (Tunisia, Libya and Egypt).

Everyone knows that Timor-Leste is one of 49 least development countries, and also one of 35 fragile and conflict affected.

What is the difference between those fragile States, some of which are even considered to be failed States, and States (like Iraq, Afghanistan and Syria) where international interventions to support democratisation and human rights has contributed, or is contributing to, the destruction of these countries, in their social fabric, their infrastructure and even their viability as a State.

The news from the G8 Summit in Northern Ireland, that concluded yesterday, brought some hope that world leaders are finally trying to find solutions through dialogue and with the involvement of all sides.

But, how are we to look at the major social (and political) problems in countries such as Portugal, Spain, Cyprus and perhaps even France and Italy?

Is Greece a failed State, since even the public broadcaster has been closed? Is Turkey now a candidate to become a fragile State within the European Community?

In many parts of the world some countries, with enormous reserves of natural resources (exploited by multinationals), face serious problems of fragility and insecurity, when their resources could make them viable and economically sustainable.

It is a pity that after so many dozens of years, the international community has still not managed to resolve the root problems of those countries and instead maintains their fragility.

It is regrettable that the decision making centres of the world were not able to clearly analyse the consequences of their actions so that we might have prevented the incongruence of the appeal, by the United Nations High Commissioner for Refugees, for $5 billion to assist Syrian refugees. We are relieved to hear British Prime Minister David Cameron announce that the G8 will donate $1.5 billion for humanitarian aid to the Syrian refugees.

And all of this takes place, ladies and gentlemen, while more than 1.5 billion people in the underdeveloped world go hungry and suffer from disease, exclusion, violence and social conflicts!

With the increase of violence, which is accepted and consented to in the defence of democracy and human rights, we are not able to foresee a successful outcome for the Post-2015 Development Agenda, which appear to correct the errors of the Millennium Development Goals set in 2000. The major global financial crisis does not allow us to have great hopes that the Post-2015 Development Agenda will become a reality, in the medium term!

I ask these questions so that we, the Timorese, can understand that the process of State building is not an easy task. I ask these questions so that we, the Timorese, can also understand that the governance of States, that are developed over centuries of existence, have their own internal problems which are, socially and economically, very serious – as we can see throughout Europe.

It was precisely to answer our own question of 'why... all of this?', happening in the globalised world, and in this world of enormous technological breakthroughs that, in April 2010, we promoted an International Conference on 'Peacebuilding and Statebuilding', out of which emerged the g7+, advocating a 'New Deal' for engaging with the development partners.

As a young member of the United Nations, we felt that we also had the duty to contribute to the correction of the mechanisms used to deal with poor and weak countries.

This correction must necessarily entail these countries taking responsibility for examining themselves, and through this analysis, to understand their weaknesses, their flaws and the errors they have made, in order to firmly enable the correction of these flaws and errors through a process of ongoing programs.

However, this process must belong to the countries themselves, which must follow the principles of 'ownership and leadership'.

It was guided by this perspective of 'ownership and leadership' that, during the difficult circumstances of 2008, we decided to ask UNMIT/UNPOL and the ISF to remain quiet in their barracks, so that the F-FDTL and the PNTL might take on full responsibility for solving the problems brought by the crisis that belonged to us, the Timorese. Immediately afterwards, we gave back to these international organisations their competencies, thus beginning the reform process of our two security institutions.

At the time, the first goal was to 'step away from fragility' in terms of political and social instability, which reflected itself in the insecurity of our population and their assets. And we did it.

When we celebrated our first ten years as a sovereign State, we were able to convey to our people a new sense of security, allowing a new confidence in the future of this nation. The withdrawal of UNMIT and the ISF, at the end of 2012, was a confirmation of this success, in which UNMIT and the ISF played an active role.

The second goal was to consolidate the core institutions of the State, seeking to provide gradual capacity and ongoing training to staff, so that in the medium to long term they will surely be able to respond by themselves to the problems and challenges faced by the nation.

After leaving behind the crisis of 2006-2008, (the same crisis that some experts, with considerable experience in handling crises in several countries, said we would only solve after 2018) we initiated a long process in order to prepare our future as a State and as a Nation. We became aware that we could no longer guide ourselves only by Annual Action Plans.

Therefore, in 2011, after an extensive consultation throughout the country, we approved a *Strategic Development Plan* for the next 20 years.

Additionally, an important guiding principle is that we must always take into account the social, cultural, economic and political reality of Timor-Leste.

Only this clear conscience of our own reality can liberate ourselves from the 'sense of guilt', if indeed it exists, for not agreeing with assessments that did not reflect these specific characteristics of our process, since they would require us to wear shoes that are too big for our feet. Or, as can happen every year, we can refuse partners assistance when it is not integrated in our own annual programs.

I am reading the Report by the 'International Crisis Group' and my first impression is that the ICG experts continue to have reviewing parameters that would be more appropriate for countries like Iraq, Afghanistan, Syria, Guinea-Bissau or Mali, for example.

Excellencies

During these first ten years of existence as a sovereign State we made fighting poverty a National Cause, and will continue to do so until it is eradicated from Timor-Leste. As such, we are focusing on social and economic policies to reduce social inequities in terms of education, health and job creation.

We are aware of the great challenges ahead of us before we can achieve the Millennium Development Goals.

Accordingly, the Fifth Constitutional Government drafted the guidelines for carrying out the *Strategic Development Plan* during the five years of its mandate. This will drive the carrying out of activities to gradually reduce poverty, seeking to eradicate it in the medium term.

As a complementary instrument we have the 2010 Census which provides us with an objective snapshot of the actual living conditions of each household. This will enable us to measure progress, periodically, to determine the advancement which has been achieved.

Excellencies

Although the *Strategic Development Plan* concerns the period from 2011 to 2030, and while we started with research and studies in good time, 2012 was a year full of electoral activities, preventing us from continuing major projects in the manner that we would have liked.

The Fifth Constitutional Government entered into office on 8 August 2012 and its 5-year Program was approved on 12 September of that same year. In a way, I should say, the Program of the Fifth Constitutional Government is the program for the first five years of the *Strategic Development Plan*.

When presenting this Program to the National Parliament I reminded the lawmakers and all Timorese that planning is not an easy task, particularly when there are so many different and competing priorities. Planning national development is like managing a complex network of challenges, since it is not possible to cover all priorities at the same time. We must also take into account our limitations in terms of specialised human resources, as well as the stagnation of our productive sectors.

For these 5 years, the Government has given special attention to the development of Social Capital, recognising that the true wealth of any nation is in its people. And so, the Government is committed to maximising service delivery in the health and education sectors and to improve the overall living quality of the Timorese as a condition for a fair and progressive society.

In the same way, the Government is aware that to develop the nation, build a modern and productive economy and create jobs it is necessary to build core infrastructure. And so, the Government has a broad infrastructure program covering roads and bridges, water and sanitation, ports and airports.

On the other hand, the Government considered the stage of the national private sector and the fact that there is little economic diversification, with excessive concentration in agricultural production which, even so, lacks major expansion and productivity gains. The Government intends to explore the strong economic potential in the areas of agriculture, livestock, fisheries and tourism.

The Government seeks to encourage the creation of cooperatives and the development of agro-industries, while implementing the National Development Plan for Sucos, so as to continue and strengthen the quality of the Decentralised Development Programs.

In order to be able to achieve all these goals there is an absolute need to improve the country's administrative and financial management, since this is a requirement for good governance. As such, the Government will provide assistance to State institutions, promoting the operational capacity of public administration, so that institutions may carry out their tasks with a sense of rigour, transparency and accountability.

The Government is also aware of the need to bring public administration closer to the citizens, in order to provide better service delivery and to enable more effective local democratic participation. We have held public debates in the 13 districts so that every Timorese citizen knows that creating a municipality means more than just establishing a structure that may result in additional expenses for the State. It is necessary to carry out training and capacity building programs so that the structures to be created may actually respond to the problems and challenges that every municipality will necessarily face.

We embraced the idea of a new development paradigm. We, the Timorese, want to get away from simplistic mathematical and statistical calculations of our actions to justify our proposed investments.

And to make it possible to establish a new paradigm of action in the efficient and sustainable fight against poverty, Dr Mari Alktiri is leading the transformation of Oe-Kusse into a Special Zone of Economic and Social Markets.

Excellencies

We know the country we want to be ten years from now. We want to have a healthy and educated population with more opportunities to develop professional activities and that can protect the people's wellbeing in a politically and socially stable and safe environment.

Ten years from now, we want to have a health service able to provide specialised care, with primary services provided by health clinics in an adequate ratio across the territory.

We want investment in education across all levels and all social sectors, including specific attention to the more fragile and socially marginalised groups. We want investment in education to include technical and professional capacity building, since we want young Timorese students to have sound education alternatives within the national territory, namely a higher education sector integrated and articulated with the business sector, so as to provide a first working experience.

One fundamental pillar is the substantial improvement of our infrastructure, which is our primary foundation for our economic growth and for improving the living conditions of all Timorese. Improving our roads to international standards will enable the movement of people, goods and services throughout the country, which is essential for the growth of Timor-Leste. There will be public water supply and sanitation covering every home, in accordance with a vital effort to improve national health.

The development of infrastructure will also comply with the principle of energy efficiency, focusing on renewable energy alternatives so that at least half of the needs in the sector are met through renewable sources.

Also in the infrastructure sector, ten years from now we will have established in several parts of the country the ports and airports we need so that Timor-Leste can have integrated growth. More particularly, we want to transform the south coast into a primary development area of our country, thereby making the best use of the petroleum sector. This means that, ten years from now, we will have the Suai Supply Base operational and the Betano Refinery project in an advanced stage of construction.

Ten years from now, the investment made in sectors such as petroleum and other national resources will enable the diversification of the economy by strengthening other traditional sectors like agriculture, livestock and fisheries. Ten years from now, our sectors of livestock and fisheries should be oriented towards exports, with food production increasing in such a way as to enable supply to exceed demand.

Timor-Leste also possesses unique wealth, such as the beauty of our mountains and our coast and the depth of our culture and traditions. This legacy has an enormous potential as the basis for the sustainable growth of our tourism sector. Ten years from now we want to be able to receive visitors throughout the national territory, aided by an improved infrastructure network and efficient local companies.

Indeed, the multiplication of local companies is one of the key goals in the Program of the Fifth Constitutional Government. We know that for balanced growth across the country we need to stimulate a dynamic and entrepreneurial private sector, with a sound structure that enables the creation of employment and sustainable livelihoods for all Timorese. Ten years from now, we want that structure to include several pillars, such as an Development Bank, an Investment Agency, a strong Commercial Bank and an efficient legal framework in terms of property rights, land rights and labour law.

In order to boost the private sector and to transform Timor-Leste into a high middle income country, we know that one of our priorities must continue to be the strengthening of the institutional framework. This has been a cornerstone in our democratic evolution, which is why during the next decade we want to continue strengthening our institutions. This way we will give the Timorese, foreign investors and our development partners the necessary confidence to build this country together.

In regard to governance, we want the management of public assets to be characterised by transparency and a culture of accountability. Ten years from now, we also want Municipalities in each district to be fully operational administrations, so as to make governance more efficient throughout the country, correcting imbalances between urban and rural areas.

The justice sector will also receive special attention. Ten years from now, we want every Timorese citizen to have real access to efficient and effective legal services, so that they may feel that justice is impartial, because justice upholds equality in its judgments.

We also want Timor-Leste to become a country that complies in full with commitments to human rights and gender equality at every level of society.

This is the vision of a country that wants to modernise in every aspect, with general access to information technology supported by fibre optic cables around the country.

We also believe that ascension to ASEAN will enable Timor-Leste to play a different role in the world, by making use of the special ties we have with our neighbours in Asia and in the Pacific, as well as by establishing bridges with our friends in the CPLP group. By opening diplomatic representations in other regions, Timor-Leste will be able to open new channels of dialogue that may also promote foreign investment in our country.

We want to invest in a new participation by our country in the international system, namely by entering other multilateral debates and decision-making spheres. We also want to make an active contribution to improving international policies regarding aid and conflict resolution, through forums of dialogue such as the g7+, which we are proud to lead.

Excellencies,

In general terms, our principle is to take into account the macro and micro doctrines that are supposed to be universal but only as a guideline to our annual and long term policies. The fundamental reason is that these policies have to reflect the current and real needs of our country.

These macro economic theories were not capable of solving the global financial crisis. The world today needs a more human doctrine to free itself from the mathematical calculations of money that define the GDP of nations as an instrument to evaluate and separate the rich from the poor all living at the cost of the speculations of the market.

In February I asked this question at our National Parliament and today the group of the 8 more developed countries is discussing the issue of tax evasion of trillions of dollars a year in the US and the European Union.

We know that inflation will be a constant challenge for our economic growth that will demand considerable public investment.

The economic miracles in the 2nd half of the 20th century, many without the help of natural resources, show a consistent focus on public investment, in the creation of basic conditions for generating other types of wealth, in maintaining a double digit growth rates and in dealing with a double digit inflation. The question put to them when seeking proper solutions in each of their programs' period of implementation was how low it should be and how high it can be.

However the dilemma is choosing between stopping the programs of development to deal with inflation or whether they should merely strive not to let inflation run wild without the necessary control. We are conscious of the various factors, external and internal, that produce inflation in our country and for that reason we will create the necessary conditions and instruments capable of minimising it.

Timor-Leste has enormous wealth in terms of natural resources, namely in oil and gas. We know that they are not renewable resources. However, it is absolutely necessary to utilise these resources to develop our country and the reason is so that in the future we are able to be a non-petroleum dependent economy. We assumed since the First Constitutional Government a commitment to the people of using the money of the petroleum revenues in a sustainable way to ensure the prosperity of future generations. Today, we are studying the best way to diversify the investment in our petroleum fund.

Timor-Leste subscribed to the requirements of the Extractive Industries Transparency Initiative (EITI) being the third country in the world and the first in Asia to do so and we have already supported several countries that want to understand better our practices.

Excellencies,

We strongly believe in this project. We believe in the vision that we have for Timor-Leste, especially because we know our country from one end to the other, and we know the determination of our future when they know the future ahead.

We know that the challenges we must face are immense and that the only way that they can be overcome is through an integrated and sustainable development.

I hope that the development partners in attendance today will accept this challenge and join us in believing in this vision and in this project. It was precisely the combination of national determination and firm support from the international community that brought us this far. We believe that if we continue walking this path together, today as we did yesterday, we may continue to transform Timor-Leste into the country that we all want it to be.

Thank you very much.

Closing of the Timor-Leste and Development Partners Meeting

Díli, 20 June 2013

Your Excellencies
Ladies and Gentlemen,

At the closing of this meeting with our Development Partners, I have to thank you again for joining us and for your valuable contributions. Together we are guided by the *Strategic Development Plan* and working to fight poverty and provide better living conditions for every Timorese citizen.

After the last two and a half days of work, we can conclude that we have enormous challenges ahead of us, but that these challenges also entail important opportunities for growing and developing Timor-Leste.

The various speeches delivered here can be summarised in an important message for our country: the problems Timor-Leste still faces are now viewed as challenges; the obstacles to our development can be overcome if we work together with responsibility and commitment.

The Government and other State institutions, our civil society, the private sector and our development partners have achieved an important landmark at this meeting. From now on, there is a strong and shared commitment to implementing the *Strategic Development Plan*.

We have never known the real circumstances of the country as thoroughly as we do today.

After overcoming initial difficulties in the State building process, including regular crises that threatened our national project, we have finally managed to find the path towards peace and stability, which are essential prerequisites for development.

The last few years have been characterised by structural reforms and while they may not have led to easily quantifiable outcomes they have set the foundation that allows us to be here today discussing the steps to be taken to provide the tangible results for our people for which they have waited so long.

I believe that we all considered this TLDPM to be different. We did not need to debate the policies required to put Timor-Leste on the right track, as it is clear that we already share a common vision.

Instead, we reflected together on how to do it well and in good time!

Timor-Leste took responsibility for analysing the state of the Nation. This exercise was undertaken and the results were set out in the *Strategic Development Plan*.

We have now taken another step, by establishing a mechanism that will enable the effective implementation of the *Strategic Development Plan*. The Development Policy Coordination Mechanism seeks to facilitate coordination among ministries, enable better communication with the development partners and improve the systems for monitoring and evaluating the impact of development policies.

In short, we now possess the instrument that will allow us to implement our collective vision.

We want to make our vision a reality through a staged and operational program because we understand that to build a united and fair Nation requires small acts of change to be taken every single day.

And to do this, we must also have confidence!

This project requires the participation of all parts of our society, which is why I would like to acknowledge the active and conscientious role played by civil society organisations, which are promoting a culture of accountability and which are strengthening our decision making processes.

Concerns that have been raised have already been addressed in our work agenda. This includes the critical need to empower women in our society, the need to protect our most vulnerable, the promotion of a culture of transparency and accountability in public management, the need to give priority to health and education, the importance of regional balance, the modernisation of agriculture, the importance of inclusive development and the need to promote justice.

All these legitimate expectations are, and must be, addressed with an integrated and whole of government approach. Indeed, the priorities listed in the planning process are but part of an interdependent whole, like the strands in a tais.

As such, this project requires us to work with the determination that we have always shown, knowing that it is by everyone and for everyone!

And so, I ask you not to limit yourself to a superficial or limited understanding of each individual goal and appreciate that they all contribute to realising our total vision.

We know that the task ahead of us is immense and that there are no shortcuts that we can take. Even so, while we have a long way ahead of us, we believe that we are on the right track.

And we know that Timor-Leste is not the only country to have experienced an eventful last few years. The world itself has changed, raising new concerns about the development framework. We will need to be able to respond to these concerns.

Some of our major partners are themselves facing difficulties as a result of world economic conditions. I hope that this fact will make us even more responsible in pursuing our goals.

Your Excellencies

Ladies and Gentlemen

Dear friends,

I am pleased that this meeting has come to an agreed compact on the implementation of the *Strategic Development Plan*. This compact has four important components. First we will be benchmarking progress on a quarterly basis linking the *Strategic Development Plan* with the New Deal and the Millennium Development Goals. Second, we are committed to strengthening coordination of the four sectors which are economic, social, infrastructure development and governance and institution building. Third, in 2014 we will establish a joint review mechanism. And the last commitment is to undertake a 2015 mid-term progress review, informed by the joint review mechanism, to hold ourselves accountable and report on our achievements.

After approving the consolidated matrices for putting the *Strategic Development Plan* into practice, we have reached another key moment for Timor-Leste, a new stage in which we need to work hard to achieve effective results.

Once again, and in conclusion, we know that we are not alone. Indeed, it would be arrogant of us to believe that we could deliver everything we are setting out to achieve without the ongoing assistance of our partners.

Our relationship is already a long one and becomes stronger with each step we take together in our nation building process. Let us honour the commitment we have made here together, so that we may ensure a brighter future for the Timorese people.

Thank you very much.

Forum for Economic and Trade Cooperation between China and Portuguese Speaking Countries: 'A New Investment Paradigm in Timor-Leste'

Díli, 1 July 2013

Excellencies
Dear Business leaders
Ladies and Gentlemen,

It is with great pleasure that Timor-Leste hosts, for the first time, the ninth meeting of the Forum for Economic and Trade Cooperation between China and Portuguese Speaking Countries which is like closing the cycle of the 8 CPLP countries plus China.

I would like to thank all of you for being here today, especially those who have come from far away. I hope that with this short stay in our country you have the opportunity to make contacts with the national private sector and with our relevant institutions as well as enjoy the moments of pleasure knowing a little of our people and our country.

All of you know our history of struggle and sacrifice and I believe that you understand the challenges we had to overcome in order to become a sovereign State and the masters of our own fate.

All of you also know as well that our starting point was not an easy one considering that in 2000 we needed to start from nothing in terms of administration and infrastructure of which more than 70% was destroyed and also our lack of our own financial resources.

However, after a difficult start to our process of State building, after eleven years as a sovereign State, we can now say that our people enjoy an environment of peace, security and stability which resulted from a process of structural reform within our public institutions and which also contributed to the establishment of the foundations to kick start our economic development.

Today, although we face our own difficulties, we have institutions of the State operating with confidence and with gradual and continuous improvement. Today, having in mind that our private sector is still in an emerging stage we know that we need to continue to give all the support needed, including financial support, with urgent establishment of banks providing credit to motivate the spirit of entrepreneurship.

Ladies and Gentlemen,

I would also like to commend the topic selected for this Forum. 'The new Paradigm of Investment in Timor-Leste' reflects the strategic goals of this Government and the importance that we look to give to the economic sector as a driving force for the overall development of Timor-Leste.

Timor-Leste is a small but emerging economy, with free and open markets, which welcomes foreign investment and enjoys some of the lowest tax rates in the world. With our fiscal policy we look to attract investment, which side by side with our private sector, can boost the economy.

Additionally, we have also been recording high economic growth rates. Our average growth since 2007 is 11.9%, with the International Monetary Fund estimating that Timor-Leste's grow will continue at these levels.

This growth can only be a result of increasing economic activity in the country. However, we are conscious that this growth is primarily a result of the enormous investment of the public sector. And that is why it is important, and urgent, that this strong feeling of trust and confidence in the future of Timor-Leste is shared with the business sector.

The key goals are the generation of more wealth, the creation of more jobs, an increase in commercial activities and an increase in production.

However, we know that economic growth can only be considered as a positive indicator of national development when it meets two fundamental principles: inclusiveness and equity.

These principles are the substance, the core of the new paradigm for investment in Timor-Leste. We want to grow, but we want to grow well – with the distribution of the dividends among all people and across the national territory.

Our privileged economic and trade partners will be the ones that share this strategic vision, which is not just of the Government but also of all the Timorese people.

Ladies and Gentlemen,

I am sure that everyone here has already had the opportunity to take a look at our *Strategic Development Plan 2011-2030*.

Recently, from 19-20 June, in the TLDPM we agreed on a matrix compact to drive the execution of our programs to execute the Strategic development Plan.

The obstacles to Timor-Leste's development were identified with the view to addressing our challenges in the short and medium term.

Investors arriving in our country can find many opportunities, that is, a broad range of potential areas that are promising and advantageous for all parties. In other words, we are looking for partners for the implementation of our *Strategic Development Plan*.

This Plan establishes the necessary path to transform Timor-Leste from a low income country to a medium-high income country, by focusing on three key areas:
- Capacity building and specialisation of human resources;
- Building core infrastructure; and
- Developing our economy – particularly petroleum, tourism and agriculture.

To start, we want to multiply the benefits resulting from the petroleum sector. Currently, Timor-Leste has two fields producing in the Joint Petroleum Development Area: the Bayu Undan project, operated by Conoco Phillips, and the KITAN project, operated by Eni.

Seismic surveys and drilling, in both the JPDA and in our exclusive offshore areas, indicate that as well as Greater Sunrise, there is an active petroleum system in the area with great potential.

Without wanting to making comparisons of any kind, I should inform you that our petroleum fund has grown from $1.8 billion in 2007 to over $13.6 billion today. In 2013, the Fund has grown an average of $324 million every month.

We are proud of the fact that Timor-Leste is the first country in Asia and the third in the entire world to comply with the Extractive Industries Transparency Initiative.

We are developing a project of great national significance on the south coast for the petroleum industry, which is named Tasi Mane, with a supply base in the western part, with a refinery and a petrochemical industry in the centre, and with Liquefied Natural Gas projects in the east. Along the 155 kilometres a highway will connect these three industrial clusters.

Over the past 5 years the Government has invested heavily in studies to assess the technical and commercial viabilities of the Tasi Mane Projects, which are at different stages of planning and development.

The establishment of a dynamic and integrated petroleum industry along our south coast will undoubtedly contribute to development, employment and industrial growth in our country.

In addition to petroleum resources, we also have substantial mineral resources. Preliminary data and information indicates that this includes gold, copper, manganese, marble, phosphate, gypsum and iron ore.

With the conclusion of the first stage of national power plan for the generation and distribution of electricity we made an important step for the gradual modernisation of our economy and for improving the lives of our people.

Other important parts of our plan include the construction of ports, airports and a road network to an international level. We are studying the viability of using PPP approaches for the construction and operation of these projects, even if it is just to be in one or another.

As such, we are confident that the pursuit of new forms of cooperation and partnership with the private sector will be advantageous to Timor-Leste, the achievement of our social and economic development goals, as well as to our partners.

Your Excellencies

Ladies and Gentlemen,

We believe that focusing on sectors such as petroleum and other natural resources will allow us to diversify our economy and to strengthen our traditional sectors such as agriculture, livestock and fisheries, and in doing so increase national productivity and create added value for certain products in the international market.

Timor-Leste is also other wealthy in other ways. There is the beauty of our mountains, stunning beaches and rich maritime resources, along with our unique history, tradition and culture.

And so, we have enormous potential for sustainable growth in our tourism sector. Having improved infrastructure and developed local service companies, we will be able to offer eco tourism to sports tourism, and even adventure tourism, from religious tourism to historic tourism.

Further, the Strategic Plan includes a new approach to sustainable development by promoting Special Economic Zones. Dr Mari Alkatiri is currently leading work to transform Oecussi into

As a pilot project in Oecussi, that can be extended to other parts of the country, that we call a Special Economic and Social Zone, because it will have a deep social approach to the problematic the effects humanity which is the sustainable fight against poverty.

However, this economy will be directed to the market with the desire the Oecussi will become an industrial and commercial platform facing the markets in the region.

We are in the process of accession to ASEAN and we have good relations with the Pacific Forum as well as being part of the Macau Economic Forum.

Timor-Leste is also a member of CPLP – in fact, we will assume the presidency from 2014 to 2016 – and we want to more active contribution to boost this Community, and giving it a more visibility.

We are strategically located between the CPLP countries and Asian countries, China and the Pacific Islands. In the world of today, with disturbances agitating the global economy, the central theme of debates are the 'common market' and the 'market chain'. Being in the most promising region of the world in terms of economic growth, Timor-Leste cannot put aside this factor and must take advantage of its location in coordination with the potential partners that here you represent.

Excellencies

Ladies and Gentlemen,

I would like to take full advantage of the presence here today of business leaders from countries that are friends of Timor-Leste to emphasise that your experiences and knowledge are vital for stimulating and guiding the development of our business sector.

The strengthening of local Timorese companies is a key issue for us, and is the only way to create sustainable wealth, employment and competitiveness in our country. Although Timorese business people require know-how, they already understand that they must produce and find opportunities and exploit market niches where they may produce competitive products.

I hope that the experiences our friends in other countries may also inspire Timorese business people in new business opportunities. This will surely be discussed during the two days of this conference, as the opportunities cover areas as diverse as bamboo trading, hotel management, transportation, small industries and other service companies.

The Timorese State will support these efforts, creating conditions to facilitate investment and stimulating the business environment in order to produce goods that can be sold and exported.

As a said earlier, the establishment of an investment agency and a development bank, side by side with the existing commercial bank that will need to be operationally stronger, will be part of our priorities. And along with fiscal reforms, there is also a need to establish an efficient legal framework including with regard to land law and labour law.

I would like to, once again, emphasise the strategic opportunities that can arise from public private partnerships with the ones that are represented here.

Dear Businesspeople

Ladies and Gentlemen,

China is one of the world's biggest economies and is a strong development partner for African countries. President Obama is visiting Africa and he said, two days ago in Pretoria, that Africa is big enough to accommodate the United States and China and other countries that have an interest.

Timor-Leste is strategically located in Southeast Asia. The former secretary of state, in her visit to Dli last year, also affirmed that the Asia-Pacific is big enough to accommodate investments from China to the United States, from Russia to the European Community.

I believe that Portuguese speaking countries and China, with a strategic platform in Macau, strengthening their economic and commercial relations even further and develop together especially now as we face the challenges of the Global Financial Crisis and the imperative of economic growth of our respective countries.

Before I conclude, I would like to thank all those who made it possible for this meeting to be held here in Timor-Leste, particularly TradeInvest and the Chamber of Commerce and Industry of Timor-Leste, the Investment Promotion Institute of Macau and the China Council for the Promotion of International Trade.

I hope that this meeting will result in better reciprocal knowledge and in the strengthening of economic and commercial partnerships between our companies.

May you take home to your countries the knowledge of profitable and safe investment in Timor-Leste and, once there, may you work on those projects stimulated by the best coffee in the world, our coffee!

Thank you very much.

Reflecting on the State of the Nation

National Parliament, Díli, 12 July 2013

Your Excellency the President of Parliament
Your Excellencies the Vice Presidents
Distinguished Members of Parliament
Fellow Government Members
Distinguished Guests
Ladies and Gentlemen
People of Timor-Leste,

Coming here to this great house to speak about the State of the Nation is both a privilege and a duty I am pleased to perform.

It is also a great honour, being the first time Parliament has held a session dedicated exclusively to this subject, with the solemnity it deserves and in accordance with the Constitution of the Republic.

I believe that everyone in attendance here today recognises that our Country is on the right path and that we have made great progress as a Nation.

I say this because, looking across the world, I can find no other country that has achieved so much in such a short period of time.

In order to better understand the state of our Nation, it is vital that we look at what is happening in Europe, at the situation in America, at the problems in the Middle East and at what is happening around us, in Asia.

The world of today is experiencing much more conflict than at the time of the Cold War, when open conflicts involved struggles of liberation against colonialism.

The new world order, which came about after the fall of the Soviet Union, turned out to be an absence of order, ruled by those who hold the power.

This is the world in which we live, ladies and gentlemen, where for the great democracies of the world elections are an end unto themselves, rather than a means. We can see the results of this in the major social and political turmoil in Egypt, which is entering a turbulent transition...from a springtime democracy to a summertime democracy.

This is the world in which we live, ladies and gentlemen, where imposing democracy is, for the great decision making centres, an end that justifies every means. We can see the results of this in the decade-long wars in Iraq and Afghanistan and in the complete self-destruction of Syria.

World news has also been more exciting since the start of the Global Financial Crisis, because now it also include scandals. In addition to the scandals in the world financial systems, with banks devoid of money, deceiving society, we now have the scandal of billionaires and of million-dollar companies transferring trillions of dollars into offshore paradises, in order to avoid paying taxes, while Governments struggle with a lack of money to support their countries. Further, in addition to the scandal started by the Australian Julian Assange with his Wikileaks, we have now learned of the spying scandal directed at allies and the European Commission, disclosed by the American, Edward Snowden. This in turn led to another scandal, which was the deviation of the airplane of the President of Bolivia.

The economic war, the war for strategic influence, the war for control over the resources of other countries and the war in the search of new markets for the products of the great economic powers are the setting for what I would call the Second Cold War.

And still it is we, the developing or underdeveloped countries, which in accordance with the International Conventions we have signed, must draft annual reports on Human Rights and Democracy, on Poverty and Malnutrition, on Money Laundering and Corruption, on Transparency and Civic Rights.

This very week the Pope spoke about the 'globalisation of indifference', however I would prefer the globalisation of hypocrisy.

By hypocrisy I am referring to the great democratic centres of power that 'impose' so-called universal standards on others, while breaching them with the impunity recommended by so-called 'national interests' and defended by the so-called 'security' of their States.

I – Introduction

President of the Parliament
Vice Presidents
Leaders of the Parliamentary Benches
Distinguished Members of Parliament
Ladies and Gentlemen,
Firstly, I believe that today I must start by paying homage to the Timorese People.

If today Timor-Leste is a feasible State in a sound period of construction and consolidation, we owe it essentially to our People, who are once again taking part in this process with the same dignity as before, in order to make this country a peaceful, tolerant and united Nation.

This act of complete dedication to a noble mission is already part of the character of the Timorese People. The past has proven that our People can rise from adversity and gain new energy.

Eleven years have now passed since that historical day of 20 May 2002. This was a day of jubilation for a body tired of waiting, a day of jubilation hiding a mind that was traumatised by a long conflict, a day of jubilation nurturing a new spirit that was full of dreams. However, these dreams and hopes were too much for the fledgling State to meet, and so they created a society that was too demanding for immediate results.

As such, the start was extraordinarily complex.

The State will never forget, since it is part of our memories, that we began practically from nothing in every aspect, from our inexperience in governance to the lack of human and financial resources, from the absence of laws to the lack of experience living in a democracy, from the lack of infrastructure to the need to rebuild, from the lack of institutions to the inability to respond to the needs of the country.

On the part of every Timorese, our society confused duty with right, confused democracy with freedom to do whatever one pleased. Society lost sight of the long process that was the liberation of the country and began to assume, wrongly, the need to demand immediate responses to their requests. Additionally, there were individuals and groups reclaiming compensation for past services.

As citizens, we have absorbed universal values and principles that were conveyed to us by others. We swallowed them in one go, causing social cramps and political indigestion.

This resulted in a cycle of crises which emerged at the end of 2002 (the very year of independence), December 2004, April 2005 and April 2006 to February 2008.

Once again we smelled fire, we saw blood spilled on the ground of our homeland and we revisited the recesses of hatred, vengeance and violence.

This led our People to stop trusting the institutions of the State. It also led international experts to rush to the conclusion that Timor-Leste was fast becoming a failed State.

In 2000, a study that was not drafted by us, revealed that 41% of our population lived below the poverty line. In 2007, further research showed that the number of poor people in our Country had increased to 49.7%. This scientific data sought to prove the failure of democracy and the rule of law in Timor-Leste, suggesting that the Timorese were unable to be the masters of their fate.

Further research, this one more independent, mentioned that from 2000 to 2007 over $8 billion was spent in one way or another on Timor-Leste. This led us to try finding any positive outcome that this money had had on the poor in our country, which had even increased in number during the period.

The last major crises of 2006-2008 even led some international experts, very experienced in solving crises all over Africa, the Middle East and Asia, to estimate that we would not be able to solve our problems before 2018. They further stated that in order to do this, we Timorese would need to understand the concepts of 'crisis management sustainability' and the existence of 'actual long term and staged plans' for ensuring 'respect for human rights' and enable a 'participative democracy'. With all these inputs, we would still have 5 years of work ahead of us before 2018!

Ladies and Gentlemen,

We need to reflect thoroughly on our 'post-conflict' situation. Timor-Leste is part of the group of 49 least developed countries, as well as of the group of 30 fragile countries.

In the history of the resistance, the Timorese People showed unquestionable ability to think critically about their own responsibilities and correct the political deviations making them explosive, intolerant and aggressive. The Timorese People managed to change their attitude, overcome differences and bring people together, thus strengthening the struggle.

As such, in 2009, on the 10th Anniversary of the Popular Consultation, our People embraced the motto 'Goodbye Conflict, Welcome Development'. Since then, we have been living in peace and stability.

It was also on this path that, in 2010, we organised the First International Conference for fragile and post-conflict countries, under the theme 'Peace-building and State-building', enabling us to better understand the difficulties and challenges that other countries were facing in their efforts to remove the label of 'fragile State' or even 'failed State.'

It was important for us Timorese to realise that the 'State-building' process is no easy task. It is also important for us Timorese to realise that the issues of governing States, even those that have existed for centuries, are conditioned by internal problems that are intrinsic to each country, from political to social and economic problems, as we are seeing throughout Europe. The scale of these problems is influencing a new vision of the globalised world of today.

This is why that Conference in April 2010, in Díli, resulted in the creation of the g7+ group, seeking to advocate a 'New Deal' in the relationship between fragile countries and their development partners.

As a young member of the United Nations, we also felt that it was our duty to contribute to correcting the mechanisms used to deal with poor and weak countries.

This correction must necessarily entail the ownership, by those very countries, of the responsibility to examine themselves critically, as we Timorese have been doing, in order to start establishing ongoing programs to gradually correct the flaws, gaps and errors made.

We all understand that democracy is a universal value, but we also understand that most of all it involves a specific process for each country, assumed and worked on by the people of each country, without exact formulas that can be copied from other societies. This is essential so that there can be 'ownership' and 'leadership' by each country in relation to its democratic process.

It was under this perspective of ownership and leadership that in February 2008 we decided that the ISF and UNMIT/UNPOL should return to their barracks so that F-FDTL and PNTL could take on full responsibility for handling the problems resulting from the crisis... which were ours and no one else's! That was also the time when we began the reformation of both institutions, starting by changing mindsets and behaviours.

I must say that being a young State we strived to learn from our errors and setbacks, and here the dialogue within State agencies and between State Agencies and Civil Society proved to be invaluable. I believe that all of you will agree that this ongoing and genuine dialogue, as well as the cooperation between every Body of Sovereignty and Civil Society, were the key to our success.

Ladies and Gentlemen,

Unlike many countries, Timor-Leste started with many political parties running for the Constituent Assembly and becoming a part of the First Legislature. In the Second Parliament there was a clear reduction in the number of political parties with seats in Parliament. This reduction continued in the Third Parliament, in which only four political parties now sit in Parliament.

Democracy is not limited to elections and the representation of parties in the legislative body of the State, which is the Parliament. Our democracy is forged in the active participation of society in general, through public and broad consultations, through the interaction of the different parts of society and through dialogue.

Today, Timor-Leste is living in an innovative and dynamic environment. The State has established a mechanism of structured dialogue reflecting the spirit of applicable democratic rules, to which everyone is subjected.

Therefore, in this new decade of State building, in this new chapter of our history, we are all more engaged in the strengthening of our institutions, more committed to the plans for economic growth and better prepared to sustainably develop the Nation.

It is important to say that we are all aware that national interests are the general interests of our country and the long term interests of our people.

II – State Building

Institutional reforms
Distinguished Members of Parliament
Ladies and Gentlemen,
From the start, the State has strived to build the society and the Nation.

Since 2000, we have been carrying out an intense and thorough process of internal reconciliation, along with an effort to provide civic education to our society, seeking to convey the due balance between rights and duties in this construction process, and the fundamental obligations by the State to the People and to the Nation.

We all remember the difficulties that our guerrilla fighters endured in the barracks of Aileu, without conditions to give them the proper dignity as Armed Forces of National Liberation. We all witnessed the lengthy process of transforming guerrilla forces into conventional forces.

We all remember the initial difficulties we had creating a Timorese Police that would accompany the activities of the UN Police. We all recall the enormous difficulties that our police officers endured in terms of learning and adaptation, since each country involved in that good intention of assisting Timor-Leste provided a different type of training.

Believing that there cannot be development without security and stability, we undertook crucial reforms in the defence and security sector, seeking to build capacity and to professionalise the Defence Forces and the National Police.

These reforms may not please everyone, but the fact is that each institution now has a more efficient legal and administrative framework, in addition to a policy framework of solidarity and cooperation in joint activities, which have been producing positive outcomes.

Meanwhile, the Defence Forces are guiding their vision towards a more effective participation in international missions in the areas of peacekeeping and natural disaster response. The Defence Forces also seek to improve their readiness to ensure security in our south seas, including with surveillance and rescue missions.

Further, the National Police, in addition to investing in conflict prevention policy through community based policing, is preparing for activities outside Timor-Leste, taking into account our future membership of ASEAN and a more effective cooperation within the establishment of an integrated development region with the neighbouring islands of Indonesia, including the Northern Territory of Australia. The National Police must be better prepared in order to be able to deal with transnational crime, which currently concerns every State, particularly small and still weak States such as Timor-Leste.

Ladies and Gentlemen,

The Government has also made broad reforms in terms of State management and administration, working to develop a more professional, competent and independent public sector. Timor-Leste has taken large steps towards good governance and transparency in the public sector, including through:

- The establishment of the Civil Service Commission;
- The establishment of the Anti-Corruption Commission;
- The strengthening of the competences of the Inspector General of the State;

- The creation of the Audit Chamber, to carry out audits independently from the Government;
- The launching of the Timor-Leste Transparency Model, including the Budget Transparency Portal, the eProcurement Portal, the Aid Transparency Portal and the Government Results Portal – in order to bring services closer to the public and to enable the public to monitor the execution of expenditure, State procurement projects and the outcomes of financial execution and contracts;
- The improvement of public financial management, with greater decentralisation, increased efficiency and better service delivery to the People.

Following these reforms, in 2012 Timor-Leste climbed 30 places in the Corruption Perceptions Index world ranking by Transparency International, which was an acknowledgement of the significant efforts made by State agencies in this area.

The 2013 Resource Management Index report by the Revenue Watch Institute stated that Timor-Leste 'adopted transparent and accountable systems for managing its petroleum wealth'. Timor-Leste was ranked 13th among 58 countries, being placed above some of our developed neighbours in terms of safeguards and quality control.

Further regarding the reform of public financial management and administration, Timor-Leste implemented important good governance policies, such as:
- The establishment of the National Procurement Commission, for assessing large projects, with the support of an international procurement company, assuring quality, cost-efficiency and a high level of transparency, professionalism and integrity in key infrastructure projects;
- The establishment of the National Development Agency, responsible for assessing the main infrastructure bids and monitoring and reporting on the execution of infrastructure projects;
- The operation of a financial system called FreeBalance in order to manage, control and monitor the budget, government finances and payments by the State.

The improvement of the functions of the Treasury, enabling Full Reconciliation of Accounts and the establishment of a Single Account Treasury System in the Government, providing greater scrutiny over operations in all bank accounts held by the Treasury.

The dramatic improvement of budget execution rates, by way of improving public finance and building the capacity of civil servants.

The establishment of an Infrastructure Fund and a Human Capital Development Fund, allowing multiyear projects and ensuring the continuity of large investment projects in infrastructure and in the development of Timorese human resources in strategic sectors.

The establishment of a quarterly reporting system to Parliament, with the main activities of each line ministry set out and in accordance with budget execution.

Ladies and Gentlemen,

The Constitution of the Republic requires the State to recognise all those who gave their best so that Timor-Leste could become independent, as well as to protect the citizens that need the most protection.

Under this mandate there is a broad program of recognition and homage to our national heroes and veterans. In addition to providing subsidies and pensions, the State has built Monuments and Memorial Houses throughout the country. The 2nd Veteran Demobilisation Ceremony will take place in Betano on 20 August 2013.

In line with its goals, the State has decided that it could not postpone measures promoting social justice and protecting our society's most marginalised citizens. As such, the State is operating a program for providing assistance to the elderly, the disabled and other vulnerable groups.

The State is also preparing for the establishment of a universal and contributory welfare regime, ensuring that every worker, both in the public and private sectors, will receive a pension on retirement, disability or death.

Here I must underline that every reform and policy enabling the development of other sectors and high economic growth would not have been possible without strong institutional cooperation, preserving the checks and balances befitting a democratic State, as set in our Constitution.

Consequently, our People are living today in an atmosphere of safety and stability, our Nation is more attractive to foreign investment and our society has acquired greater confidence in a bright future for its beloved homeland.

Economic Growth

Your Excellency the President of Parliament
Your Excellencies the Vice Presidents
Distinguished Members of Parliament
Ladies and Gentlemen,

The evolution of a society or a people is based on the economy. When the economy has clear goals and moves forward, the society and the people progress.

Building a nation has never been an easy task in any part of the world. Building a nation requires firstly a vision for the future, a realistic perception of what may be and an objective assessment of all strengths and weaknesses.

At the start of any progress there are countless priorities and the desire is always larger than the ability to provide proper responses. The ability to provide responses is the ability to make a decision on options – the right options.

And that is what we have done, what the Timorese have done. The *Strategic Development Plan* lists the policies to be made at every step and at every stage – policies based on the strong potential of Timor-Leste.

We want to become a high middle income country within 20 years, with a healthy, safe and educated population.

This philosophy reflects the current situation of poverty in the country and the misery that our people still face. Since the First Government, we have all assumed the Fight against Poverty as a National Cause.

Ironically, while there are still 1.5 billion people living in misery throughout the world, dying of disease, hunger and exclusion, the great centres of power in the world prefer to feed hatred, vengeance and violence through wars and conflicts that they cause or provoke, under the slogan of defending the national interests of their countries.

As such, in Timor-Leste we must only consider the growth of our economy to be a favourable indicator of national development if it observes two key principles: inclusiveness and equity.

We will develop what and we need to develop, but we want to develop well, distributing the dividends of the growth of the economy across the entire population, from Tutuala to Pássabe, from Fatu Mean to Laklubar, from Ataúro to Hato Builiko.

As you know, it was the First Government that began efforts to establish administrative decentralisation and to implement Local Government.

Recently we have been creating the framework for the municipalities. This year we have started the popular consultation to establish the 13 Municipality Installation Committees and to create 3-5 Municipalities within the next few years.

In addition to the decentralisation process, which is vital for stimulating entrepreneurship, the State is also creating conditions for facilitating investment and nurturing the business environment, in order for it to produce goods that can be traded and exported, and in doing so, make our economy more competitive.

Timor-Leste is a small but emerging economy, with a free and open market.

By implementing tax reform, with some of the lowest tax rates in the world, we have become more attractive to national and foreign investment. This reform was further strengthened by the approval of the Private Investment Law in 2011, granting exemptions of up to 100% for investors that obtain investor certificates.

Since 2008, we have been recording high rates of economic growth. Our average growth rate since 2007 has been 11.9%, with the International Monetary Fund estimating that Timor-Leste's growth will continue at these levels.

This growth means that there is greater economic activity in the country, as anyone can plainly see, and reflects the existence of a private sector that, while emerging, is beginning to affirm itself and contribute to overall development.

It also means a steady generation of wealth, with the creation of more employment, an increase in trade and tourism activities, both in Díli and in the districts, and greater production, including agricultural production.

Ladies and Gentlemen,

In order to achieve the principles of inclusiveness and equity we have been having greater budget balance in terms of the distribution of wealth in projects throughout the territory since 2008.

In 2009, we launched the Referendum Package. This was an innovative measure that, among other things, enabled the creation of local companies, so that entrepreneurship would no longer be centralised in Díli.

With the Referendum Package we also managed to build local leaders who were aware of the need to take part in the decision making process on projects, in order to ensure greater local ownership and control and to increase social accountability.

In 2010, we established the Decentralisation Programs, seeking to decentralise administration to the district level. In 2012 we established a planning, implementation and funding system to ensure that the State Budget is invested in areas that the District and Sub-Districts define as priorities. This was called the Integrated District Development Planning (PDID).

In 2013, we will be implementing the National Program for Suco Development (PNDS), initially in 30 sucos. This plan harmonises both the SDP and the LDPs.

We have learned practical lessons from the Referendum Package and from PDD I and PDD II. As such, we can now say that these measures have enabled the development of the private sector, benefitting populations in several parts of the country through the construction of small infrastructure works.

Distinguished Members of Parliament

Ladies and Gentlemen,

We know that the private sector, rather than the State, should be the main driving force of the economy, including in regard to generating wealth and creating employment throughout the country.

The creation of the Chamber of Commerce and Industry was timely, since it represents and defends the interests of the Timorese private sector and works alongside the State on developing opportunities and in the search for solutions. However, there is still much to be done in order to clarify responsibilities.

We believe that it is crucial to create an Investment Agency and a Development Bank to work alongside our Commercial Bank. As such, these two agencies are considered to be priorities for the country. The greatest weakness of our business environment is the lack of financial capacity; therefore, there is an urgent need for access to credit. This is why, that in addition to tax reforms, the State is establishing an efficient legal framework for property law, land law and labour law.

The creation of a 'single counter – SERVE' in June 2013 will simplify and reduce the time for registering companies. This, together with the support being given to small and medium sized companies and to industrial and commercial cooperatives and groups, will boost the diversified productive sectors.

The State is aware that strong economic growth has been accompanied by high inflation, putting pressure on the purchasing power of the Timorese. We have been recording, monitoring and assessing inflation carefully, as the Timorese State is committed to lowering it.

The State is also aware of the various external and internal factors that cause inflation in our country, which is why we will create the necessary instruments to minimise them. We will not stop investing in development programs – we will just ensure that inflation does not shoot out of control.

Ladies and Gentlemen,

Our natural resources are essential for developing the country in a diversified manner, so that in the relatively near future we may have an economy that is not oil-dependent.

Since the first moment we have assumed a commitment before the people to use the money from the petroleum wealth in a sustainable manner, so as to provide for future generations. Consequently we continue studying the best way to diversify the investment of our Petroleum Fund, which will require investment in specialised Timorese human resources.

Timor-Leste, despite being independent for only a decade, has developed a world class revenue management system and was the first country in Asia and the third in the entire world to be granted compliance status with the Extractive Industry Transparency Initiative.

Part of the reason why this was possible was that the First Government established the proper system for receiving revenues from the oil reserves in the Timor Sea, in order to benefit both current and future generations. This system is the Petroleum Fund, which currently has a balance of over $13 billion.

In 2008 we established the National Petroleum Authority, responsible for managing and regulating petroleum activities in the areas of exclusive jurisdiction of Timor-Leste, as well as in the Joint Petroleum Development Area with Australia.

Currently, we have two fields producing in the Joint Petroleum Development Area: the Bayu Undan project, operated by Conoco Phillips, and the KITAN project, operated by ENI.

Exploration activities, in both the JPDA and in our exclusive offshore areas in the Timor Sea, including seismic surveys and drilling, indicate there is an active petroleum system in the area with a number of prospects which will attract further exploration in the future.

Timor-Leste has adopted the Petroleum Sharing Contract regime as a means to engage international and national petroleum exploration and production companies to invest in petroleum exploration.

Consequently, the National Petroleum Company of Timor-Leste, Timor-GAP E.P, created in 2011, signed its first petroleum sharing contract in 2013, enabling Timor-Leste to participate directly in a partnership for exploring and developing our resources in the Timor Sea. Our share is 24%, which is a starting point for testing our capacity.

The establishment of a dynamic and integrated petroleum industry along our southern coast will undoubtedly contribute to the development and start of the industrial sector, as well as for creating jobs.

As you know, in addition to petroleum resources, we also have substantial mineral resources. Preliminary data and information indicates that this includes gold, copper, manganese, marble, phosphate, gypsum and iron ore.

We believe that focusing on sectors such as oil and natural resources will lead to the diversification of the economy by strengthening traditional sectors such as agriculture, livestock and fisheries, increasing national productivity in order to create added value in certain products that can be sold in the international market.

Your Excellencies

Ladies and Gentlemen,

Investing in improved basic infrastructure and liberalising the telecommunications sector will make an enormous contribution to our already strong economic growth.

With the completion of the first stage of our national electricity generation and distribution network, we have taken an important step towards modernising our economy and improving the living situation of the people. On 20 August of this year we will be inaugurating the Betano Power Plant.

Only by building a road network to an international standard can we have integrated development in all sectors, including health and education.

We have already planned to build national roads from Díli to Baucau, Díli to Ermera, Díli to Motain and Díli to Ainaro, with loans from JICA, ADB and the World Bank.

The State has also approved the mechanisms for establishing Public-Private Partnerships, which will make use of specialised knowledge in construction and / or operation. As such, the International Financial Cooperation is currently working with the Timorese State on studies concerning the feasibility of the PPP program in relation to the Port of Tibar and to the Nicolau Lobato International Airport.

This year we signed a Memorandum of Understanding to kick-off the feasibility, economic, and technical studies for the construction of a fibre optic underwater cable from Darwin to Suai, which will significantly improve data communications in Timor-Leste.

We are committed to investing in diversity and innovation, so that Timor-Leste can transform its economic profile. However, this effort will only make sense if it is accompanied by a drastic improvement in the more immediate quality of living of our population.

Ladies and Gentlemen,

When we speak about the actual quality of living of our population, we are speaking about inclusiveness and equity.

In addition to the PNDS and PDID decentralised programs, the Infrastructure Fund currently features 18 development programs that will significantly improve several sectors, by building or repairing agriculture irrigation systems, roads and bridges throughout the country, new schools in various districts, police stations, defence buildings and public health buildings.

The existence of clean water supply, basic sanitation and sewers is essential, since it will contribute to improved public health. We are investing in this in rural, regional and urban areas, while implementing the Sanitation and Drainage Master Plan in Díli.

We are also carrying out the necessary engineering studies to provide solutions to local communities about drainage problems. The maintenance of the existing drainage pipes is a key part of these solutions.

Over the past few years several agricultural initiatives have been implemented to improve productivity, using more and better infrastructure, irrigation systems, seeds, fertilisers and equipment and machinery.

As such, we have increased agricultural production in some staple crops. The production levels of rice and maize in 2012 were much higher than in 2011. The total production in staple crops increased from little more than 100,000 tonnes in 2012 to almost 200,000 tonnes in 2012.

This achievement is confirmed by the statistics related to rice imports. In 2011 we imported around 100,000 tonnes of rice, while in 2012 we imported less than 40,000 tonnes.

The continuous rains have caused much damage to the tilled plains and affected the production of maize. As such, the State now considers it necessary to increase the stock of food in order to ensure that there is no shortage in Timor-Leste until March 2014.

The sectors of fisheries and livestock have also been continuously supported by the State, through technical training, vaccination of around 80% of the animals across the entire country, creation of fish hatcheries and distribution of fishing boats and equipment.

In April 2013 we established a Development Policy Coordination Mechanism, which was presented recently at the Development Partners' Meeting, seeking to ensure an ongoing and effective monitoring of our ability to implement the *Strategic Development Plan*.

This mechanism will ensure the implementation of policies required for economic growth and sustainable development, as well as the inclusion of the participation of representatives from the civil society, the private sector and the development partners.

The *Strategic Development Plan* also sets out a new action approach to sustainable development and the fight against poverty through promoting the establishment of Special Economic Zones. Currently, Dr. Mari Alkatiri is leading the development of Oecussi, which as you all know will become a Special Zone of Social and Market Economy.

The Oecussi pilot project, which may be extended to other parts of the country, is called a Special Zone of Social and Market Economy because it will be part of the State's sustained fight against poverty.

The SZSME should have an impact on the living situation of the entire population of Oecussi and should boost local productivity and entrepreneurship.

In the future, depending on the enthusiasm of the 'atoni' population, Oecussi may become a commercial and industrial centre focusing on market opportunities in the region.

There have already been preparations in relation to this project, from the legal framework of financial regulations to the staging of its implementation. We have also considered the possibility of allowing the participation by the Timorese private sector and by the local population itself in this process.

I must say that the project is innovative and exciting. Nevertheless, the Government continues to weigh the possible risks, since the investment to be made is considerable. The Government is sure that a Memorandum of Understanding can facilitate greater trust and stimulate more productive debates.

Human Development

Your Excellency the President of Parliament,
Distinguished Members of Parliament,

The main goal of the Timorese State is to continue improving the living situation of Timorese citizens and their development as people.

Timor-Leste has moved up five places in the Human Development Index since 2007, according to the 2013 report by the United Nations Development Programme.

This is the greatest annual average growth in the index between 2000 and 2012 by a Nation in East Asia and the Pacific.

In 1980, the living expectancy of the average Timorese citizen at birth was 35 years. This increased to 56 years in 2000 and to 63 years in 2012.

Timor-Leste has a Human Development Index of 0.576, being ranked in the 134th place among 187 countries and territories, which places us in the category of medium human development.

Between 2000 and 2012 our classification in the Human Development Index increased 38%, from 0.418 to 0.576. Timor-Leste's per capita GNP also increased 356% from 2000 to 2012.

We can also measure our progress by looking at the health and education sector.

Child mortality rates have dropped considerably, from 83 deaths in every 1,000 live births in 2003 to 43 deaths in every 1,000 live births in 2009/2010. Life expectancy at birth also increased from 59.5 years in 2006 to 64.6 years in 2011.

In October 2012, Timor-Leste had 13 specialised doctors, 139 general practitioners, 1,271 nurses and assistant nurses, 427 midwives and 416 health professionals, in addition to the 400 new doctors that recently graduated from UNTL.

By 2016 we should have over 1,000 Timorese medical graduates working as fully-fledged doctors in Timor-Leste. The successful integration of these doctors in the health system of Timor-Leste is a key priority for the State.

In the education sector, the overall number of enrolled children increased 5% in basic education, 8% in general secondary education and 17% in the technical secondary education between 2010 and 2011.

We have established a Human Capital Development Fund in order to develop human resources in our Nation. We are also sending students to countries throughout Asia and the world, so that they can acquire the necessary qualifications for building our State.

In 2012 the State issued 1,564 scholarships in strategic areas under this Fund. The State also funded the participation by 884 Timorese citizens in technical and professional development courses.

Ladies and Gentlemen,

Timor-Leste recognised that the Millennium Development Goals in the areas of poverty, malnutrition, health, gender equality and environmental sustainability would form a basis for improving the living situation of the population. The areas which have provided particularly difficult, however, include poverty, underweight children, maternal mortality and sanitation.

Nevertheless, Timor-Leste is making significant progress in relation to two MDGs: achieving universal primary education and promoting gender equality and empowering women.

In regard to gender equality, 38% of all Members of Parliament are women following the 2012 elections. This is the highest percentage of women elected for a Parliament in all of Asia.

This outcome was due in good part to the change of the Parliamentary Election Law in 2011, seeking to increase the quota of women in candidate lists to one woman for every three candidates. After we create the municipalities we will also strive to encourage women candidates to run in municipal elections.

The Law against Domestic Violence is in operation and the 2012-2014 National Action Plan on Gender-Based Violence is being implemented in order to reduce domestic violence and gender-based violence.

Ladies and Gentlemen,

In the last few years we have also made considerable progress in the area of justice, and we now want to consolidate this progress.

Here I can highlight the improvement in terms of generalised access to justice, including the rehabilitation of infrastructure and the strengthening of the legal framework.

The State will continue to strengthen the independence of magistrates, the autonomy of the Public Prosecution and the professionalism of legal professionals.

The State vows to increasingly adopt legislation that uses simple and plain language and to hold regular dialogue with civil society and the public concerning the drafting of laws. The State is also working to make justice services available in the districts, by deploying more magistrates, prosecutors and public defenders throughout the country.

Important steps are being taken to regulate and promote alternative ways of solving disputes, such as mediation and conciliation, particularly in regards to labour disputes, family disputes or disputes regarding the possession of land.

The State is giving priority to technical and human capacity building in the areas of criminal investigation and other forensic sciences, in order to be able to respond to complex crimes such as organised crime, corruption and money laundering, as well as to domestic and sexual crimes.

International Relations

In this debate on the State of the Nation, it is also important to understand our place in the world. The internal effort for consolidating our institutions and our economy will also enable us to change the image that our international partners have of Timor-Leste. Indeed, this image is changing already.

International confidence in a strong Nation has enabled Timor-Leste to move from a transition where it mostly received aid to a new era where we attract investment and place ourselves in an advantageous position in order to have our voice heard.

In the area of international and multilateral relations, Timor-Leste has developed a foreign policy of having good international relationships, respect for the sovereignty and integrity of Nations and cooperation with mutual benefit.

Our relationships with our large neighbours are excellent.

A High Level Trilateral Meeting was organised for the first time between the Heads of State and Government of Indonesia, Australia and Timor-Leste. In addition to the trilateral meetings between the Ministers of Foreign Affairs, which usually take place in New York, we have also had the first trilateral meeting of Defence Ministers.

We also have privileged ties of friendship with the CPLP, the presidency of which we will hold for the period from 2014 to 2016. The preparatory work is currently being undertaken. Taking into account the difficulties faced by some countries in the CPLP, Timor-Leste wants to make a more active contribution towards the enhancement of this community, modernising relations between the members and shining light on economic issues.

We are on our way to becoming full-fledged members of ASEAN and we believe that, within the broad framework of security, development and democracy, this membership will not only benefit Timor-Leste in terms of stability and development, but also benefit the community by way of the small contributions that we can make.

Timor-Leste also has excellent relations with the Pacific Islands Forum. We will continue to strengthen these relations and explore further areas of cooperation.

We are determined to be part of the various regional forums of debate, including the Bali Democracy Forum, the Jakarta International Defence Forum, the Shangri-La Dialogue, the Pacific Islands Forum and others, so as to reflect on the future and to better understand the array of possible threats and the great variety of challenges ahead.

We know that strategic thinking for a country is increasingly inseparable from a complex framework of interconnected threats. Consequently, no Nation can presume to set a strategy for solving its internal problems – in terms of development, democracy, peace, security and even safeguarding human rights – without taking into consideration the challenges faced by the world.

These threats are increasingly unexpected, or even random, requiring greater adaptability and joint responses through dialogue, tolerance and mutual understanding between nations. This requires flexibility and respect for the specific needs of each nation and its people.

Timor-Leste was not alone in undergoing deep changes these last few years. The world itself has changed considerably, bringing new concerns to the international agenda.

The imminent global challenges of the 21st century are increasingly diverse, as are climate changes and the challenges resulting from security in terms of power, food and humankind's most precious resource: water. The world must also deal with economic shocks, rapid social and economic changes, demographic transitions, terrorism, transnational organised crime, piracy and latent and emerging conflicts.

In truth, the world is facing serious problems that could not have been imagined even during the period of the Cold War.

This is why a new paradigm is imperative. Market laws are too susceptible to speculation, profit calculation and fraud by the financial industry. Indeed, these realities have driven hundreds of millions of people to despair.

In this topsy-turvy world, global priorities are still disorganised. International policies should focus on people as an end rather than as a means to achieve less dignified goals.

This is the lesson that we learned at our expense during the last few years, and which we want to share internationally, as our contribution to a new vision on development.

Timor-Leste believes in the common project of peaceful cooperation and development and wants to take a more active part in the resolution of regional problems, including the management of transnational security threats, as well as to cooperate in the areas of humanitarian assistance, disaster relief, environmental management and response to climate changes.

III – Timor-Leste and the Change of the Old Paradigm

Your Excellency the President of Parliament
Your Excellencies the Vice Presidents
Distinguished Members of Parliament
Ladies and Gentlemen,

I believe that we Timorese may start another initiative, a new development paradigm, in order to try to convince the world in relation to the effective and sustained fight against poverty.

Timor-Leste is considered by the international community to be one of the forty-nine countries that the United Nations calls the 'Least Developed Countries'.

We are also considered one of the thirty countries that the World Bank calls 'Fragile States'.

However, we are also one of the eighteen countries that came together to create the g7+, which seeks to monitor, report and call attention to the specific challenges faced by fragile States that, up until now, lacked the voice to be heard properly.

It was in this process of making our voice heard that we came to realise we needed a new development paradigm.

The international community, the United Nations, the World Bank, the IMF and OECD have been the great promoters in the fight against poverty. However, the results of this fight are plain to see, particularly in Africa.

We have noticed that, although billions and billions of dollars are invested every year, much of the world population remains without food, shelter, health, education and safety.

Throughout the world there are around 1.5 billion people living in extreme poverty.

We often see how internal instability is caused in many countries in order to promote fragility in those nations and to protect multinational interests.

We have learned at our expense that the need to change this paradigm is strategic as well as ethical. We have learned that governments must lead their policies, not only because that is morally correct but also because policies invariably fail where there is no ownership.

This is why the g7+ nations have been working together to ensure that the post-2015 development agenda will provide an actual response to their needs in terms of peace and stability, as well as to hold the perspectives of fragile States as central to global dialogue.

It is urgent to focus more in action for underdeveloped countries, instead of insisting on empty slogans that are merely words to sell to others.

As you know, the world is currently finalising the dialogue in order to develop the post-2015 development agenda, which will cover the period after the MDGs. The Minister of Finance of Timor-Leste, Emília Pires, is a member of the High Level Panel that has advised the Secretary General of the United Nations in relation to this agenda.

I would even say to the People of Timor-Leste what I have already said abroad: that the UN itself needs an urgent reform. This heavy organisation is like a turtle with a hard and heavy shell, trying to overcome the tides in order to get to the beach. This is so because going to the beach is precisely what some peacekeeping officers do in the countries where they are deployed. Later on they receive medals for the great sacrifice of not having been able to solve the problems that those countries had.

In order to help change these mechanisms, in February Timor-Leste received in Díli leaders from several countries throughout the world, including the Asia-Pacific and Africa, hosting an International Conference on the Post-2015 Development Agenda. This was the largest international conference ever held in Timor-Leste.

One of the outcomes of our discussions and deliberations was the 'Díli Consensus', which establishes our priorities and hopes for the post-2015 development agenda. A key aspect of this document states that we must set a credible, responsible and realistic path towards development.

In April 2013, Timor-Leste had the honour of assuming the presidency of the United Nation's 69th Session of the Economic and Social Commission for Asia and the Pacific. As such I will have the privilege of presiding over this session during the next year, as well as working with ESCAP and with the nations of Asia and the Pacific in order to achieve progress and improve human development.

Meanwhile, Timor-Leste is also supporting the APRC Council (Asian Peace and Reconciliation Council), established last year in Bangkok, which includes former Heads of State, former members of Asian Governments and scholars. The Council wants to facilitate dialogue within societies and between nations, so as to end frictions and prevent conflicts.

Timor-Leste looks favourably on this noble ideal and on this worthy mission of helping to nurture a culture of peace in our region.

During the past few years the State of Timor-Leste has contributed to efforts seeking to alleviate national disasters in many countries. Today the State of Timor-Leste is starting another mechanism, by creating the Development Cooperation Agency. We have started to provide financial support to S. Tomé and Príncipe, which require political reforms, and to Guinea-Bissau under the presence of a UN Peacekeeping mission headed by HE Dr. Jose Ramos-Horta.

Currently, we have the conditions to gradually develop our country and to share our development experience with other fragile States.

The new paradigm of the fight against poverty in Timor-Leste entails acknowledging that no one knows our frailties as well as we do, despite any international standards and readings.

We know the path we want to take and the most adequate strategy for handling our poverty. The *Strategic Development Plan* is the greatest example of this. Instead of universal but abstract concepts for leaving behind poverty, it makes an actual assessment of our needs and obstacles, since what we hear and feel – from Ponte Leste to Ataúro to Oecussi – are the tears, the sweat and the sacrifice of our People, as well as their determination and their aspirations.

As such, despite giving attention to the macroeconomic challenges that we must overcome, we cannot focus only on simple statistical and mathematical calculations for justifying the investments we want to make.

Timor-Leste has its own challenges and a history of struggle and sacrifice, but it also has a history of resilience and of considerable progress appealing to confidence in our future path.

This great project for fighting poverty, which started with the First Constitutional Government, requires a steady commitment by every Timorese citizen, as well as sound State institutions. This will enable us to achieve our common goal of having a developed, fair and dignified country.

And I strongly believe in a ... second Maubere Miracle!

Opening Session of the Pacific Islands Development Forum: 'Leadership, Innovation and Partnership for Green / Blue Pacific Economies', Keynote Address

Nadi, Fiji, 5 August 2013

Your Excellency Commodore Bainimarama, Prime Minister of Fiji
Distinguished Delegates
Ladies and Gentlemen,

It is a great honour for me to take part in this opening session of the Pacific Islands Development Forum. This is my third visit to this beautiful country.

First and foremost, I must congratulate the government of Fiji for hosting this important event, to work towards a prosperous future for the Pacific region through a 'green economy'. I must also thank Your Excellency, Prime Minister, for the warm reception given to me and to my delegation by the Government and the people of Fiji.

This is an important occasion for Timor-Leste to more actively engage with the Pacific Islands, with whom we share so many common fragilities and challenges, but also many opportunities.

Therefore, I thank His Excellency the Prime Minister for inviting me to deliver the key note address at this meeting that aims to develop a safer and more optimistic roadmap for the peoples of the Pacific, for our peoples.

It was not long ago that Pacific Islands gave invaluable solidarity and support to Timor-Leste as the cinders of a quarter of century of illegal occupation were extinguishing. Following our Referendum of 1999, we were once again the victim of violence and destruction and we lost many lives and our infrastructure was destroyed. This almost crushed the hopes of our people, who were already weary from the sacrifices they had made to achieve peace, freedom and independence.

Yet today, we are proud to say that our People, and our Nation, are growing strongly.

We also know, perhaps better than anyone, the importance of not being isolated in searching for solutions to overcome fragility and address the challenges that a country faces in its building process.

Coming from a post-conflict situation with widespread poverty and very limited resources, we lacked governance experience and had no institutions of State. We had no human or financial resources and no infrastructure or capacity to build. We had no laws and yet we had to learn how to live in a democracy. All of this placed us at a terrible crossroad where there was no quick and guaranteed way to respond to the many needs of our people who were suffering and who demanded – and deserved – to have their needs met.

Additionally, from the moment we were 'born' we – as the youngest member of the Community of Nations – had to absorb democratic values and their universal principles, which were conveyed to us by others without having being given the time to digest them.

This resulted in a cycle of crisis, which led to the unrest of 2006 that came to its climax in 2008.

Once again we smelt fire, we saw blood spilt on the ground of our homeland and we reignited hatred, vengeance and violence. This all provoked a break of trust in the still fragile institutions of our State. It also led international experts to rush to the conclusion that Timor-Leste was choosing the way to a failed State.

Your Excellencies

Ladies and Gentlemen,

This is not a history exclusive to Timor-Leste.

We share common circumstances – post-colonialism, fragility and poverty – with many nations of the world, called Least Developed Countries or LCDs, and also with some Pacific nations, some of which are represented here today.

What our experience taught us is that it is not possible to achieve development or assume democratic principles without first building our own identity and determining for ourselves the path we wanted to take.

Every nation has its own context, its own history, and its own culture. Each independence was achieved in a unique form and each development process has its own reality and its own internal factors.

The international community, many times in a hurry to give its generous support but nearly always divided in its approaches that do not respond to the true needs of the aid recipient countries, must not, and cannot, substitute the leadership of a country as it belongs exclusively to its people.

It was in this context that Timor-Leste, the people and society, continuously remind the leaders of the country that those who offered their sacrifices to achieve independence are the ones who are yet to enjoy the benefits of freedom. And, when we analyse our own circumstances, we see that a leadership, that heeds the sentiments and knows the difficulties, of the people, is more capable of guaranteeing the stability and development of a nation. Only when these internal factors are able to determine the specific processes for each country, is it possible to have a sense of belonging or ownership and the need to hold the leadership over decision-making.

As such, we imposed on ourselves and our institutions of the State a political will to cooperate in the search for solutions, or else we would have faced a lack of political discernment in facing and resolving crisis.

Knowing that true freedom does not exist if a people do not hold on to it through democratic means, we learnt also that true development does not exist if it is not a product of the effort of the society itself.

And we embraced our ancestral traditions of conciliating our differences through dialogue. We have rolled out the mat that we call *nahe biti*, with the participation of the entire community, and we involved every Timorese citizen in the resolution of our problems, creating true partnerships towards the common goal of peace and development.

The permanent and genuine dialogue and cooperation between all Sovereign Bodies and Civil Society was fundamental to achieving a turning point, which is reflected in our motto launched in 2009, on the 10th anniversary of the Referendum: 'Goodbye Conflict, Welcome Development'. And so, we put an end to the cycle of crisis that are common in fragile and post-conflict countries.

Today we have a strong and participative civil society and a private sector that, although still emerging, is beginning to realise its responsibility in the development of the nation.

If today Timor-Leste is a viable State, in a secure stage of construction and consolidation, we owe it essentially to our people, who are once again taking part in this process with the dignity that they showed during the struggle, with the goal of making our country a peaceful, united and tolerant nation.

And by consolidating these internal factors we have been able to adopt public policies that provide a framework for sustainable development.

We have achieved some success, from one of the highest economic growth rates in the world to progress in human development to an environment of peace and stability and above all in our friendly relations and partnerships that we have with practically all the countries in the world, especially with the countries closest to us in our region, including the Pacific Islands.

The preparation of our *Strategic Development Plan*, which sets the path for sustainably transforming Timor-Leste from a low income country into a medium-high income country in 20 years, was fundamental to this success.

This Plan gives voice to our women, our youth and our elders; this Plan gives voice to our farmers, our health professionals, our business people and our teachers; this Plan gives voice to consumers, to people who are ill and to students; this Plan gives voice not only to those who live in the capital Díli, but also to those who live in the most remote villages.

This Plan, ladies and gentlemen, reflects the vision of our people and the political will of Timorese leaders, and makes us understand that promoting a 'green economy' means promoting sustainable development.

We decided to harness the great economic potential that we have, thanks to our petroleum wealth and our geographic location, to invest in productive sectors – infrastructure, education, health, agriculture and tourism – with the aim to transform an economy that is much too dependent on oil to a non-oil dependent economy.

The main goals of this strategy are to generate more wealth, create more employment and increase business activity with a consequent increase in commercial and industrial activities.

For us, economic growth can only be considered a favourable indicator of national development if it observes two key principles: inclusiveness and equity.

These principles are the core of the new investment paradigm for Timor-Leste. We need to grow but we want to grow in the right way, by distributing the dividends of this growth across the entire population and throughout the country. We also want to preserve the things that distinguish us: our own culture and our untouched landscape.

Our privileged economic and trade partners are those that share this strategic vision, which belongs not just to the Government but also to all the Timorese people.

Your Excellencies

Ladies and Gentlemen,

In Timor-Leste, as well as in the Pacific Islands, we can find a combination of the best that nature has to offer.

We share the same conviction that the Timorese, and all peoples of the Pacific, will know how to take advantage in a peculiar way of their precarious resources transforming them into major achievements. And because of this, we can achieve our dreams of building sustainable industries for selling our products in local and international markets.

We have tropical forests, stunning mountains and idyllic beaches. We have in the depths of our seas our wealth of corals and other maritime fauna, with incredible biodiversity.

Our tourism will have to be developed alongside other sectors, such as agriculture, rural and infrastructure development, under an integrated plan that will contribute to the sustainable development of the population.

In the near future we will be investing in better mechanisms of disaster risk management through acquiring early warning systems that will enable us to anticipate threats in order to be better prepared to respond. In addition to this, we know that preparation for natural disasters demands a great effort to mitigate our vulnerabilities.

The challenge is enormous: the poverty of our peoples instils in our minds an urgent need for growth. However, we are aware that this growth cannot be achieved by compromising the means future generations need to survive.

Our forests are a tremendously valuable asset that could provide us with easy and immediate wealth, but we are committed to protecting them since otherwise we would have less resilience in the face of natural disasters. In this way, we are preparing, for the coming years, to be able to plant a million trees per year.

We also want to preserve native fauna and flora species, because in this difference resides the speciality of products that we will want to benefit from.

We are focusing on the modernisation of our traditional sectors, such as agriculture and fisheries, but in a considered and sustainable manner, because we are well aware that nature provides us with finite resources that are essential to our daily survival.

We cannot postpone protecting our water resources and our soils just because we want (or need) to obtain immediate income, as this would lead us to depleting those important sources.

Mother nature has its own cycles, which we must respect, as guests on this planet. Safeguarding them today means ensuring a sustainable and lasting economy.

The great potential of ecotourism will be explored with the involvement of our communities who will act in conformity with patrimonial, environmental and cultural preservation objectives, while instilling a modern and innovative approach to our economy.

We are aware that it is the private sector that must drive our economies, which means that States need to stimulate and create the necessary conditions for facilitating investment and enhancing the business environment, allowing goods to be produced that can be traded and exported in a sustainable manner.

At this moment in Timor-Leste the priorities for the Government are the creation of an Investment Agency, the establishment of a Development Bank, legal reforms and the establishment of an efficient legal framework of rights to property and land as well as labour laws.

Additionally, we have started a decentralisation process, seeking to provide greater budgetary balance for the regions, through the equitable distribution of projects and services throughout the territory and through gradual administrative decentralisation, as a mean of stimulating local entrepreneurship with the participation and initiative to take decisions by the communities.

In this new paradigm of sustainable development action and combating poverty, we also want to promote the establishment of Special Economic Zones, making use of land areas that are perfectly harmonised with the vastness of the ocean which encircles them.

The Democratic Republic of Timor-Leste is a half island with an enclave in the other half that belongs to Indonesia. We will seriously invest in that enclave where there will be established a Special Social and Economic Market Zone because this will have a social reach more focussed to the sustainable fight against poverty. For its study and preparation, the Leader of the Opposition, Dr Mari Alkatiri, was appointed the Representative of the State who will also later supervise the implementation of the program and the possibilities of its application to other parts of the national territory.

When conducting a sustained fight against poverty, we know that an integrated approach, where everyone wins, is more likely to succeed.

Under this new paradigm we recognise the potential of a joint approach for an integrated sub-regional development plan. The area covers Timor-Leste and the neighbouring provinces of Indonesia and also with the Northern Territory of Australia.

In the economic area the following sectors are covered:
1. business development that will extend from agriculture, fisheries, manufacturing, energy and natural resources;
2. technology;
3. infrastructure;
4. management;
5. tourism and
6. knowledge through research and development.

In the social area, we will have:
1. cultural and social exchange;
2. health;
3. education and culture and
4. sports.

We are in the preparation stage to establish a Joint Tri-lateral Commission to study and approve the Objectives, Strategies and Action Plans.

In this plan, we intend to protect our natural habitat, preserving our maritime and land biodiversity, preventing illegal fishing and the destruction of our maritime resources. We also intend to exercise effective control over pollution and the impact of climate changes, while investing in alternative and renewable energy projects to safeguard our energy needs.

Today the entire world is paying attention to climate change; however its consequences have never been as evident, as dramatic and as life changing as they are in our region!

Your Excellencies

Ladies and Gentlemen,

Our countries are subjected to increasingly unexpected, even random threats, requiring greater adaptation capacity and a joint response, through dialogue, tolerance and mutual understanding between nations, with an imperative to respect the specific needs of each country and their peoples.

The imminent global challenges in this century are increasingly diverse with the Pacific Islands being particularly vulnerable, as we all know, to climate change as well as to challenges resulting from security in the areas of energy, food and humanity's most precious resource: water.

The economic region of the Pacific Islands has great potential to overcome the difficult obstacles to which it is exposed if every country works together under an integrated plan, with new synergies and strategic partnerships.

I think that by now we all know that our voices will not be heard if we are speaking alone.

It is not with isolated efforts that we will be able to overcome the fact that Kiribati, the Marshall Islands and Tuvalu faces from the permanent and irreversible threat of drowning into the vastness of the ocean. The developed countries, which are the ones that contribute the most to climate change, must by moral obligation think of a plan of financial compensation to enable these countries to safeguard the dignity of their States and their peoples.

And it was the developed economies that caused the great global financial crisis which does not give us much hope that the post-2015 Development Agenda will be achievable in the medium term. And these highly developed countries allowed, in their own nations, very serious social and economic problems being created throwing millions into unemployment and making them fearful for their future, as can be seen, for example, throughout Europe.

We need to change the global macroeconomic policy model that is too rigid and of little use, and that only benefits the wealthy countries to the detriment of the poor.

In this topsy-turvy world, global priorities are still muddled. International policies should focus on **human beings** as an end – rather than as a mean to achieve less dignified goals.

As we know, Timor-Leste is considered by the international community as one of the forty-nine countries that the United Nations calls the 'Least Developed Countries'.

We are also considered by the World Bank as one of thirty 'Fragile States'.

Seeking to understand what has been failing, despite millions of dollars from citizens of the world spent on international assistance, as well as the reason for so much fragility in a world that is globalised and that features enormous technological advances, we have decided to join together with seventeen other countries, including the Solomon Islands and Papua New Guinea, in establishing the g7+, which advocates a 'New Deal' in terms of our relationship with our development partners.

This 'New Deal' requires internal changes in every country. We have been monitoring, reporting and calling attention to the specific challenges faced by fragile States, which up until now did not have the ability to speak loud enough to be heard.

It was in this process of raising our voices that we came to understand the need for a new development paradigm, in which we will play a key part. This paradigm includes correcting the mechanisms used for dealing with poor and weak countries.

Despite the efforts by the international community, the United Nations, the World Bank, the IMF and the OECD, which have been at the forefront of the fight against poverty, the results have left much to be desired, particularly on the African continent.

We must now ask: what is wrong in all of this?

Every year, millions and millions of dollars have been invested but a great part of the world population remains without food, shelter, education, safety or dignity. There are around 1.5 billion – the people living in this situation of extreme poverty!

This leads us to wonder if internal instability in some countries is not intentionally created to protect interests that are not of the peoples of these countries.

This is why the g7+ nations have been working together to make sure that the post-2015 development agenda provides an actual response to their needs in terms of peace and stability and views the perspectives of fragile States as being vital to the overall global dialogue.

More than it being an ethical imperative, changing the paradigm of international intervention is a strategic imperative! Countries receiving assistance must have ownership over the development policies being applied within their territories, otherwise we will forever be 'putting on some shoes that are either too big or too small for our underdeveloped feet'.

Now, the timing is right because there is a dialogue being completed regarding the drafting of the post-2015 development agenda, which will cover the period after the MDGs. The Minister of Finance of Timor-Leste, Emília Pires, is a member of the High Level Panel that has advised the Secretary General of the United Nations on this.

In order to help change these mechanisms, last February Timor-Leste received in Díli leaders from countries throughout the world, including the Asia-Pacific and Africa, for an International Conference on the Post-2015 Development Agenda, the largest international conference ever held in Timor Leste.

I want to take this opportunity to thank the Minister of Foreign Affairs of Fiji, Mr Ratu Inoke Kubuabola, the President of Kiribati, the Prime Minister of the Solomon Islands and other high level dignitaries of the Pacific, for attending this conference that managed to bring together the concerns of countries from the g7+, the Pacific and the Portuguese-speaking African countries (PALOPs).

In the joint document, the 'Díli Consensus', we agreed on our priorities and hopes for the post-2015 development agenda and we have lobbied for an agenda that is more credible, more accountable and more realistic in terms of developing our peoples.

This document also reflects the specific needs of the States of the Pacific where we agreed that the countries that have contributed the most to climate change have to be more involved in its solution including a Marshall Plan for the mitigation, adaptation and reduction of disaster risks.

We have also agreed that, while our specific priorities and needs vary from country to country, we all want the same thing, which is to improve the living standards of our people and to achieve greater human safety.

As such, the post-2015 development framework should guarantee a social contract, promoting integrated actions in four key areas: inclusive economic growth, peacebuilding and Statebuilding, climate change and environmental management.

I am happy to share with you that our participation on this high level panel enabled us to have these recommendations reflected in the final report.

This is important progress in our efforts to be heard on the global stage and it has important implications for the Pacific region, which may also use its influence on the forums they attend, particularly Fiji as the chair of the G77.

We must be the agents of our own change, since it is we who will be the main winners, or losers, in this process.

Last April, Timor-Leste had the honour of assuming the Presidency of the 69th Session of the United Nations Economic and Social Commission for Asia and the Pacific.

As such, I am privileged to be presiding over this session throughout the year and to be working with ESCAP and with the nations of the Asia-Pacific to achieve progress and improve human development. This is another reason Timor-Leste's presence here today is extremely opportune because listening and feeling *in loco* to the needs and aspirations of your peoples are, undoubtedly, more valuable than reading thousands of pages of paper printed in reports – which, after all, do not contribute much towards a 'green economy'!

Your Excellencies

Ladies and Gentlemen,

We need to ensure ownership over the development process. More than development for all, it is time to talk about development by all.

Pacific Islands have special importance in terms of the 'green and blue economy', since they own the world's largest ocean.

This entails enormous economic and commercial potential, but also great responsibility, since protecting the oceans is vital for the wellbeing of the peoples of the Pacific and for all of humanity.

I believe that the large ocean Island States should receive international recognition and greater support, both for protecting this world heritage and for overcoming the specific challenges they face and their vulnerabilities.

If today the role of the forest is well known and advocated in the international arena, then the same must be true of the oceans, particularly the Pacific Ocean, which is a living deposit of biodiversity and a lung for our planet. It is important that the Pacific Ocean benefits from a strengthened protection mechanism and from an awareness-raising strategy that changes the global agenda in an effective and substantial manner.

The defence of a 'green economy' will always be limited if we focus entirely on land and forget the greater area that are the oceans.

The countries in our region are in the frontline to lead this debate, both due to necessity and strategy. This debate must be coordinated and integrated, so that we may have strategic cooperation to ensure better living conditions for our peoples. After all, they are the curators of this enormous heritage of humanity.

Alone we are a drop in the ocean, together we have the power to set a sustainable future for our natural resources, our economies and our peoples.

Thank you very much.

Lecture at the Viet Nam National University on State Building: 'The Timor-Leste Experience in a Southeast Asian Context'

Hanoi, Viet Nam, 3 September 2013

Excellencies
Professor Nguyen Van Khanh, Rector
Distinguished Members of Faculty
Distinguished Lecturers
Ladies and Gentlemen
Dear Students,

It is a great pleasure and an honour to be here today to speak at the Viet Nam National University.

Viet Nam National University is a key institution supporting the remarkable progress of your nation that is playing an important role in our region.

It is always difficult, as you can understand, for someone who never attended university to come here and address such a distinguished audience.

I hope that my talk today about State building in Timor-Leste, Southeast Asia's newest nation, will strengthen the existing bonds of friendship between our two peoples and, especially, between the young generations of Viet Nam and Timor-Leste.

Ladies and Gentlemen
Dear Students,

Today is a unique occasion to allow you to get to know a little about us, the Timorese people, of our past, present and what we desire for the future.

And you will understand that in the end, Viet Nam and Timor-Leste share similar experiences in their history. Both our countries were occupied and dominated successively by foreign powers and, as a consequence of a war to regain their respective sovereignty, both Viet Nam and Timor-Leste experienced devastation and destruction to their economic, social and cultural structures.

After more than 400 years of domination, in April 1974 there was a revolution in Portugal and the colonial power announced that it would grant independence to its colonies.

In the same year that the end was foreseen of the so called 'Viet Nam War', we initiated our own process of decolonisation.

Viet Nam declared its independence on 2 September 1945 (one year before I was born) and I congratulate you on your 68th anniversary, which you celebrated yesterday. On 28 November 1975, we too unilaterally declared our independence. Viet Nam was one of fifteen countries that immediately recognised our independence.

However, nine days later on 7 December, we were invaded and subsequently annexed by Indonesia. And so, in the same year that the war in Viet Nam ended, another war began in Southeast Asia.

While the war in Viet Nam lasted thirty years, the people of Timor-Leste had to endure theirs for twenty-four years. While much of the war here in Viet Nam was fought on the global stage, and filmed on a daily basis by western media and shown on the nightly news, the world largely ignored the war the people of Timor-Leste waged against the brutal occupation.

We began our resistance against the invasion with typical conventional warfare and with thirty thousand weapons against battalions, mortars, cannons and tanks.

I still remember the radio communication on 31 December 1975 between the then Prime Minister, Nicolau dos Reis Lobato, and the Minister of Defense, Rogerio Lobato, who was overseas at the time. Nicolau asked him if he could acquire some supplies and Rogerio replied that Viet Nam would offer plenty of weapons but that the problem was transporting them to Timor-Leste.

Your struggle and your victory were always an inspiration for us, and above all, enlightening us in the most difficult times when we were alone without any help.

As it was impossible for us to be supported from outside, we began wearing out our weapons and ammunition, and we could not bear, in 1977 and 1978, the pressure of the large scale operations of the occupiers that, in addition to controlling the whole population, left the Liberation Armed Forces (FALINTIL) weakened in terms of men and weapons, which were reduced to seven hundred and fifty rifles.

Even worse, the entire Superior Political and Military Leadership was practically decimated, with only three members of the Central Committee surviving, including myself.

It was a terrible situation for our people, with hundreds of thousands having died from bullets, famine, disease and air strikes from the OBV-10 planes that were used by the Americans here in Viet Nam and later sold to Indonesia.

In 1979, having taken on the leadership of the struggle, I tried to understand 'guerrilla warfare'. And among the other wars of liberation, I also studied the guerrilla war of Viet Nam in order to understand the concept, principles and its applicability.

And this was how we began our guerrilla war that lasted twenty-one years, guided by the principle of 'counting on ourselves' for a hard and prolonged war. 'To Resist is to Win' symbolised the integral mobilisation of all Timorese that accepted any sacrifice to liberate the scared land of our ancestors.

One and a half thousand guerrillas, with weapons in the mountains and valleys, the people and above all the youth in the occupied villages and towns, and the patriots in the diaspora, made possible the combination of the three fronts of our struggle: the armed, clandestine and diplomatic.

Throughout difficult years, this strategy proved effective and finally, in 1999, our people were allowed to vote in a referendum on independence.

And so, on 30 August 1999, despite a climate of violence, our people decided and overwhelmingly voted for independence. It was only last week that we celebrated the 14th anniversary of the Referendum which is a national holiday for our nation.

Regrettably, however, the Referendum result brought more killings and spread destruction all over the country. While our people were then free, much of the country had been destroyed and we had to build a new nation from nothing.

Ladies and Gentlemen

Dear Students,

Along with Viet Nam, our story is also one of courage, determination and fighting spirit for freedom. Because, like Viet Nam, we ultimately triumphed. We achieved our independence.

And now, like Viet Nam, we face the challenge of building a new nation from the embers of our brutal history.

Your nation is of course many decades ahead of us. And Viet Nam has made remarkable social and economic progress.

And while the process of Nation building is different for each country, and in each context, we know that there are many lessons that we can learn.

Your history notes that in 1986, the Vietnamese leadership started the 'Doi Moi' approach. Isolated from the world, also in 1986, we initiated a political reform process that allowed us to open the way for the present political system that guides the Democratic Republic of Timor-Leste.

This brings me back to our subject today, Timor-Leste's place in Southeast Asia, and our process of State building.

Ladies and Gentlemen

Dear Students,

Our State building efforts began in late 1999 when our country was under the administration of the United Nations, which helped to establish, from scratch, the institutions of State.

Finally, on 20 May 2002, we became the masters of our fate, and the Democratic Republic of Timor-Leste was reborn as an independent and sovereign nation.

We became the youngest nation in the world and today remain the youngest in East and Southeast Asia.

This means that our Southeast Asian neighbours have had longer to consolidate their State and build their sovereign nations. Timor-Leste is pleased that the countries of ASEAN empathise with our challenge and stand ready to support us.

It is, however, worth reflecting on the fact that Timor-Leste gained its independence around the same time that our closest neighbour, Indonesia, started their democratic reform. This means that, in many ways, we look to the progress of Indonesia as we work to develop our nation.

Timor-Leste was also fortunate to have the assistance of a large number of generous development partners to support our process of building the new State. But we knew that, in the end, the responsibility for our future rests with the Timorese.

But, while we had achieved our independence, we did not have the apparatus of a State or the human resources that we needed. We also had no experience running a government, no infrastructure and no financial capability.

But our people had high expectations on independence and, after many years of sacrifice and struggle, and rightly deserving to experience a new life and better living conditions, demanding immediate results.

We know that this has been a common challenge for the countries of our region. With independence, and strong population growth, the demands for health care, education, development and government services have created pressures across Southeast Asia. And as I will come to discuss, like many countries in our region, Timor-Leste also, at times, faced disruptions to national unity, a fundamental issue for State building.

And so, in our early years, the challenges we faced were enormous and the expectations so high that we struggled with political and social cohesion. Our challenges were compounded by the fact that our people were, socially and psychologically, extremely exposed to the trauma of the past. In this transition, our society lost focus and confused rights with the duties or obligations that we should continue to have to our homeland.

Timor-Leste became gripped by a cycle of violence, which saw conflict erupt every two years. And then, in 2006, we had a serious political crisis that led to confrontations between the police and the military. There was widespread violence, the burning of neighbourhoods and over 10% of our population became internally displaced. During this period of unrest, which continued into 2007, we feared our country would be torn apart.

Many in the international community started to say that we were becoming a failed State. We were told it would take at least a decade to resolve the problems with our internally displaced people. And through this international commentary, much of which did not reflect the realities of our society, we reinforced our belief that it is only the Timorese that can truly understand our context.

We know that conflict and unrest is commonly experienced by post-war nations around the world, especially in Africa. And closer to home, we know from looking at the Southeast Asian experience that maintaining national unity has been an issue for many countries. Even today, some of the nations of our region continue to address internal concerns. But while we may not have been alone in experiencing internal unrest so soon after achieving independence we were shocked by what was happening to our country.

And that difficult time helped us to realise that we had to come together and conciliate our differences and that we had to reflect on the destructive path our people were taking and begin a dialogue with all Timorese people to address the root causes of our problems.

As a nation, we recognised that we could not build a State without building peace. And this meant that we needed to come to terms with our fragility and, then, address it. And so, we started to pull together and began to honestly deal with our problems.

This is something that only we could do ourselves. We had to accept that, with independence, came responsibility and this meant that we had to let go of old rivalries and conflict and look to a shared future. We had to have a broader understanding of the political angles of every issue, so that we could get through to real solutions and results.

In short, it was essential that we took leadership and ownership of our problems, as well as the solutions.

That was also the time when we really began the process of changing mentalities and behaviours. Through the results of these efforts, we provided an example to the rest of the population, by providing them with a vision of what was possible, if we set our minds positively to the future.

It was only through this process of peace building were we able to deal with the issues facing our country and secure stability and security.

This also meant that we had to embark on a process of our State's institutional reform, with the view to strengthening our public agencies and introducing government programs to address social problems.

Although we started, in 2002, with no money and heavily dependent on donor aid, from 2004, we were fortunate that income had started to flow from oil reserves in the Timor Sea. We made sure we had systems in place to be able to provide for the urgent needs of today, while protecting income for future generations. We established a Petroleum Fund that has grown from $1.8 billion in 2007 to over $13 billion today.

We invested in capacity building in the security sector to improve professionalism in the Police and in the Military, bringing about a new stage of cooperation and solidarity among the two institutions.

We provided pensions to our veterans, the elderly, the disabled, widows and orphans and introduced similar social justice measures for other vulnerable groups such as women, children and the youth.

Together as a nation, we forged peace. It was then that we realised that peace building and State building were two sides of one coin, reinforcing and supporting each other.

Ladies and Gentlemen

Dear Students,

Having established a foundation of peace and security, we were aware that many of our regional neighbours developed national plans to help map strategies for development and launch important reforms. This includes Indonesia, Thailand, Philippines, Malaysia and of course Viet Nam.

In light of this common approach in Southeast Asia, we also realised that the country needed a plan to provide a framework for development, set targets to focus our efforts on delivering for our people and give them hope and certainty for the future.

And so in 2011 we released the *Timor-Leste Strategic Development Plan 2011-2030* that provides a comprehensive framework to transform our country from a low income nation to a country with upper-middle income levels by 2030, with a population that is secure, educated and healthy.

For this future, we are asking our people to demonstrate the same dedication and commitment to building the nation, as they did to the struggle for self determination. Where once we dreamt of independence, we now dream of development.

We have begun to implement our Plan and we are already achieving some outstanding results.

Our progress can be measured in many ways. One way is through economic growth, and Timor-Leste has been growing at an average of 11.9% since 2007 and the International Monetary Fund predicts that this level of growth will continue into the future.

But we also know that growth must be balanced and the benefits shared in an inclusive way. We have adopted local development programs to create jobs and improve living conditions of the population in the rural areas and are focusing on service delivery in health, power supply, water and sanitation and access to education and to markets.

Importantly, we are also beginning a process of decentralisation to bring service delivery closer to the people and to give the responsibility for decision making about local issues to local communities.

We have completed the largest infrastructure project in our people's history, by building a national electricity grid with generation and distribution across the country.

And we are embarking on an infrastructure program to provide a basis for our nation's sustainable economic future, which will include a new national port, a major airport upgrade, a national road network and the extensive development of our south coast to become a sub-regional centre for the petroleum industry.

We are heading in the right direction as a nation and we are building our Nation.

We know that we still face many challenges and that the process of State and nation building is ongoing. But we have a plan and we have the same commitment to developing our nation as we did to freeing it.

Ladies and Gentlemen

Dear Students,

We know, as we continue on the challenging road of developing the country that we do so as a part of Southeast Asia. In fact, being part of the fabric of Southeast Asia also gives us great hope and reason for confidence.

At a time of global economic weakness, Asia continues to make incredible progress. It is home to emerging economies, including China, Indonesia and Viet Nam, which are driving world growth, lifting millions from poverty and shifting international economic and strategic weight to our region. And Southeast Asia is a central part of this remarkable Asian transformation.

Improved governance, investment in human and physical development, along with its access to foreign and domestic capital, has helped power this incredible rise of Asia. One only has to look at the remarkable economic progress of Viet Nam, since the 1990s, to get a sense of the possibilities that are before us.

In Timor-Leste, we view our State and nation building mission in the context of the growth and promise of Southeast Asia.

With the future of our country connected to Southeast Asia, we are also, however, aware of the challenges our region faces and we know that its future depends on stable, friendly and positive international relations.

We are concerned about growing regional strategic tensions, many of which are fuelled by a number of complex competing territorial claims. These tensions are rising, at the same time as the region's growing prosperity allows nations to modernise and expand their defence forces.

Last May, at the Shangrila Dialogue on Defence in Singapore, His Excellency the Prime Minister of Viet Nam, in his speech called for the need for Strategic Trust between States and the world decision-makers, because only Trust can dissipate suspicion, misunderstandings and minimise tensions through dialogue.

In Timor-Leste, we look to international leaders to handle our regional tensions in good faith and in the best interests of our common security and prosperity.

We believe that Timor-Leste, in at least a small way, has shown the benefits of pursuing reconciliation and moving on from past conflict. Our nation now enjoys the friendliest of relationships with Indonesia. Rather than being enslaved by the trauma of our history, we are instead honouring our struggle by working towards a better future for our people. We know that Indonesia and Timor-Leste not only share an island, we share a future.

In August 2005, from Viet Nam I travelled to Bali where I met with the President of Indonesia and as part of the Reconciliation process, we agreed on the establishment of a Commission on Truth and Friendship to deal with all the atrocities committed during the war, and to finally put an end to the tragic past between our two nations.

Now, as many of you may know, Timor-Leste has also made an application to join ASEAN. ASEAN has been a global success story in establishing a region of peace, cooperation and development. ASEAN provides a model, and an aspiration, for so many regions of the world.

As Timor-Leste is part of Southeast Asia, we also want to be part of ASEAN and, together, contribute to regional growth, social progress and cultural development in a spirit of partnership. We feel like an integral part of our neighbourhood and have a strong regional sense and solidarity with our Southeast Asian friends – we are one of you.

We also know we must work together on regional issues, including the management of cross border security threats and cooperate on humanitarian assistance, disaster relief and environmental management. This includes the tackling of climate change which is seeing nations like the Republic of Kiribati, the Marshall Islands and Tuvalu slowly sinking into the vastness of the ocean.

Timor-Leste knows very well that our State building effort depends on our regional integration. To cite but one example of this, Timor-Leste continues to rely on Viet Nam to provide rice to ensure our food security.

Also in 2005, during my State visit to your country, I had the opportunity to visit the Institute of Agriculture and was impressed with its programs. We are trying to be self-sufficient in agriculture and with this visit, we will explore the opportunities to learn from the expertise and experience of our Vietnamese brothers and sisters.

Ladies and Gentlemen

Dear students,

As a small nation, subject to world economic, trade and political developments, and committed to being a responsible member of the international community, Timor-Leste's process of State building also includes increasing our engagement beyond our region and across the globe.

Timor-Leste also wants to address the problems with development assistance and international engagement in fragile and developing countries. We have seen so much money being spent for so few outcomes in the name of international aid.

As a small nation, Timor-Leste cannot do this alone. We need to build international solidarity among the Least Developed Countries to make sure that our interests are represented and our voices are heard. If we are not united, individually we will simply be too vulnerable to complex systems and entrenched attitudes that put the lives of our people last.

This is why a new paradigm is imperative. The Global Financial Crisis has brought into focus that the international banking system acts in its own self-interest and nothing more. Financial laws are so susceptible to speculation and manipulation and we have lost trust in this system while at the same time being subject to it.

We need international political and financial policies to put people first, before greed and profit and self-interest, so that we do not increase human misery and isolation.

An important part of this approach is working with the g7+, which is an innovative new collaboration between 18 fragile States.

The group was formed in 2010 to provide a united voice for fragile countries and to advocate for change in global development policies. The g7+ knows, from bitter experience that without peace and stability there can be no development. Not one fragile or conflict affected nation has achieved even one Millennium Development Goal.

This means that it will not be possible to eradicate poverty in the world, without first addressing the issues of fragile and conflict affected countries. That is why the g7+ nations have worked together to ensure that the post-2015 development agenda addresses the need for peace and stability.

This message was repeated loudly and clearly, when the g7+ nations, and some of our neighbours from Asia and the Pacific Islands met in Díli in February of this year, at an international conference, hosted by my Government with the theme 'Development for All'. The Conference agreed on the 'Díli Consensus', which set out our priorities, and hopes, for the post-2015 development agenda.

The Díli Consensus recognised that the standard approaches to development have failed and acknowledged that the challenges we face vary depending upon local context. That means the problems and solutions to achieving human development will differ from a Southeast Asian nation, compared to one of the Pacific island nations and that it will not be possible to eradicate poverty in the Asia-Pacific, and across the world, without first addressing the issue of fragility while ending the very expensive apparatus of war that provokes instability, exclusion, hunger and deaths in many places of the world.

The nations of the world will meet at a special session of the United Nations on September 25 to agree on a new set of sustainable development goals. Timor-Leste is proud of our Finance Minister, Emilia Pires, who was a member of the High Level Panel that advised the United Nations Secretary General on this agenda.

In April this year, Timor-Leste was honoured to take over the Chair of the 69th session of the United Nations Economic and Social Commission for the Asia-Pacific. And so I have the privilege to Chair this session over the next year and work with ESCAP, and the nations of the Asia-Pacific, to make further progress and improve human development.

In this session the challenges that the Asia-Pacific countries face were fundamentally debated with the aim of having a better integration of plans and actions at the regional and sub-regional levels to minimise the imbalance and provide better connectivity to break the isolation of some countries.

In this context, we are pleased that Viettel is now operating in our country.

Ladies and Gentlemen

Dear Students,

In May, we celebrated eleven years of independence and have made great progress in State and nation building. I do not mean to suggest, however, that there is one model that can be adopted to achieve success.

All nations must chart their own course recognising their own context, history and realities. Viet Nam, with its proud history fighting for independence and remarkable economic progress, also provides the world with a model of national progress.

Viet Nam National University has made an invaluable contribution to this progress which has seen a nation of over 90 million people diversify its economy, achieve sustained economic growth and significantly reduce poverty.

I am sure that Viet Nam National University will continue to be called upon to help seize the opportunities of your nation as Viet Nam grows to become a regional economic powerhouse and one of the large economies of the world.

Thank you again for coming today and for listening to the progress of the Timor-Leste State and Nation building process in the context of our region of Southeast Asia.

I hope today sparked your interest in Timor-Leste and encourages you to visit our beautiful country.

Thank you very much.

Conference on 'Harnessing Natural Resource Wealth for Inclusive Growth and Economic Development', Keynote Address

Díli, 18 September 2013

His Excellency Taur Matan Ruak, President of the Republic
His Excellency Anoop Singh, Director of the International Monetary Fund's Asia and Pacific Department
His Excellency, Mr Hiroto Arakawa, Chief Economist of the Asian Development Bank
Members of Parliament
Members of Government
Ambassadors
Distinguished guests
Ladies and Gentlemen,

It is a great pleasure to speak at this conference on 'Harnessing Natural Resource Wealth for Inclusive Growth and Economic Development'.

I would like to thank the International Monetary Fund, the Asian Development Bank, the World Bank Group and the Japan International Cooperation Agency for their important support to this Conference.

We also welcome our international guests who will be able to share with us lessons learned from resource rich nations around our region and the world.

I am very pleased to speak today because the theme of this conference reflects our vision for our nation. It is a vision that is set out in our *Strategic Development Plan 2011-2030* and it is a vision we are already pursuing with determination.

It is absolutely our intention – and our unrelenting focus – to wisely use our natural resource wealth to develop a diversified economy and build our beloved nation for all our people.

Ladies and Gentlemen,

In Timor-Leste we are well aware of the rise in inequality across the world. This is both in developed and developing countries, including the great emerging economies.

In our region of the Asia-Pacific we have seen spectacular growth stories. With access to capital and a focus on human resources many Asian nations have made remarkable progress which has lifted millions of people out of poverty.

Economic growth can only be sustainable; however, if we ensure that there is improvement in the social well being of the people. However, some of the economic growth in our region has often not being balanced and inequality continues to rise.

The Asia-Pacific is still home to nearly two thirds of the world's poor and far too many people face hunger and extreme deprivation. Without addressing poverty and inequality the social cohesion and stability of many growing economies will be put at great risk.

There are many reasons for the growth in inequality but a common thread is the self-interested actions of the wealthy and the powerful.

The world's financial system is a key part of the problem as it perpetuates and reinforces inequality. I think we can say with confidence that global free market finance has failed.

The Global Financial Crisis stripped bare the world of finance and exposed gross inefficiency, unrestrained greed and systemic corruption. To make matters worse, no one in the developed world took responsibility for the Crisis and it was the world's poor and vulnerable that suffered most. And yet, even during the Crisis, Timor-Leste was subject to moralising lectures, for spending our money to improve the desperate lives of our people, by the very same experts who were bringing the world's economy to its knees.

The unrestrained greed and market manipulation by world finance resulted in a huge rise in inequality, as well as in hypocrisy. It also brought poverty and struggle to the people of once proud European nations. We saw hundreds of billions of dollars in bailout funds being given to developed nations while the world's fragile and Least Developed Countries were largely ignored. And we must ask the question, why?

It is perverse that we are urged to put our faith in this same system that has caused such pain and which continues to perpetuate inequality. There must be a better way.

Ladies and Gentlemen,

In Timor-Leste we want to follow a different path. We want to make sure the benefit of our natural resources and our development is spread across our whole nation and to all our people. That is why Timor-Leste is pursuing balanced and sustained growth.

Timor-Leste is a small but emerging economy with open markets and some of the lowest tax rates in the world. We have set an economic and regulatory framework to promote growth and development.

Since 2007, we have enjoyed average rates of economic growth of 11.9% and this strong growth is predicted to continue into the future. This is creating jobs and opportunities for our people and tax revenue to fund important government services including health and education.

We understand that we remain a fragile nation and our economic progress has been possible because of our sustained stability and security. For this important reason, we have also been investing in the professionalism and capability of our security sector to maintain and build peace.

Our sovereign wealth fund, the Petroleum Fund, has grown from $1.8 billion in 2007 to almost $14 billion dollars today. Since January this year, the fund has increased on average by more than $300 million each month, thanks to crisis in Egypt and Syria.

We all recognise the enormous responsibility that we have in ensuring that the wealth from our natural resources is spent to improve the lives and opportunities of our people and build a foundation for our future; while at the same time preserving wealth for future generations.

We are proud that Timor-Leste was the first country in Asia, and the third country in the world, to comply with the Extractive Industry Transparency Initiative. This means that every dollar earned from our oil and gas resources is accounted for and audited so that the funds are managed transparently for the benefit of our people.

Ladies and Gentlemen,

Our people sacrificed so much for the cause of independence and self-determination. They have suffered unspeakable acts of violence and hardship. And while we prevailed against all odds, and with little international support, too many still suffer every day from extreme poverty and miserable living conditions. They deserve more.

When we became an independent nation we started with nothing. We had no money, no experience of nation building and we lacked the core infrastructure necessary to support a modern and productive economy.

And so, when the wealth from our petroleum reserves started to flow we had only one option – to spend money to meet the immediate needs of our people and begin the development of our country.

First, we recognised that without electricity we could not build our country, grow our economy or provide government services. So we embarked on our country's biggest ever infrastructure project and built a national electricity generation and distribution system. This means that power is now provided across the nation.

We know that we have a long way to go. While building good national infrastructure is essential to being able to develop socially and support balanced growth, the challenge is large and ongoing.

We need to build an extensive network of quality and well maintained roads to connect our communities, promote rural development and support industry and tourism.

Providing access to safe drinking water and sanitation is critical to the wellbeing of our people and our national development. And it is important that we have sea port capacity to support our development and a national airport that can meet growing demands.

Importantly, we are also working to establish an undersea optic cable connection from Darwin to Timor-Leste to provide access to high speed broadband internet. This is to make sure that our nation does not suffer from being on the wrong side of the global technological divide and will give our people equal access to knowledge and global connections.

Without providing our nation with core infrastructure we cannot achieve balanced and equitable growth.

Ladies and Gentlemen,

Our vision, which is set out in our *Strategic Development Plan 2011-2030* is to transform our country from a low income nation to a country with upper-middle income levels by 2030, with a population that is secure, educated and healthy.

The first section of our *Strategic Development Plan* is Social Capital. We started our plan with this focus on health, education and training, social inclusion and because we know that the true strength of our nation is our people. We recognise that we cannot build a nation without the human resources to do so.

It is often said that you can judge a society by how well it treats its weakest members. In Timor-Leste we are proud to able to support the most vulnerable member of our community. We have established an effective system of pension and transfer payments to the elderly, the disabled and to our veterans and introduced similar social justice measures for other vulnerable groups such as women, children and young people. We see this as an appropriate way for using our natural resource wealth to tackle inequality and disadvantage.

It is very important that this conference does not neglect an issue of vital importance to equitable growth and that is the circumstances of women and girls.

Growth can never be inclusive if most economic power resides in men. Social progress is no progress at all if it is only men that are benefiting or if women and girls are subject to violence and abuse.

We must always remember that the women of our nation sacrificed and suffered as much as the men in our struggle for independence. Regrettably, this included sexual violence which has been a brutal weapon of war in conflicts across the world.

In measuring inclusive growth and development, I therefore suggest we consider gender equality, and violence against women and girls, as critical indicators of progress and development.

Ladies and Gentlemen,

Government expenditure must also be balanced across the whole nation to ensure that we do not create an enclave economy in Díli.

The government is embarking on a program of decentralisation to ensure the delivery of services is brought closer to all our people and to give the responsibility for decision making about local issues to local communities.

We are also undertaking a major initiative to ensure that our economic growth is balanced across our nation. The *Programa Nasional Dezenvolvimentu Suku*, or *National Program for Village Development*, is a new, nation-wide community development program which will see more than $300 million over 8 years funding basic village infrastructure.

In our rural areas, poor infrastructure is a key constraint to development and access to services and opportunities which helps perpetuate a cycle of poverty and inequality. By supporting communities to plan and build basic infrastructure, this program aims to help to make sure that people are not excluded from development opportunities. It follows the earlier Referendum Package and District Development Programs and is a key policy to ensure balanced and fair economic growth.

We are also moving to establish a Special Economic and Social Zone in Oecussi. Dr. Mari Alkatiri is leading the establishment of this development zone and the concept may be extended to other parts of the country. The Special Zone in Oecussi is a new approach to promote sustainable and balanced development and fight poverty. Through this Zone Oecussi will become a commercial and industrial centre focusing on market opportunities in the region.

Timor-Leste is also implementing the Tasi Mane Project to develop an on-shore oil and gas industry to create jobs and underpin economic growth. The Tasi Mane Project will open up our south coast as a sub-regional centre for the petroleum industry, bringing a direct economic dividend from this industry.

Ladies and Gentlemen,

Before I finish, I would just like to mention that Timor-Leste knows it is not alone in the fight against poverty and systematic oppression. We have reached out to the international community in solidarity and joined with other nations facing similar challenges to ourselves.

In particular, Timor-Leste wants to address the problems with development assistance and international engagement in fragile and developing countries. We have seen so much money being spent for so few outcomes in the name of international aid.

An important part of this approach is working with the g7+, which is an innovative new collaboration between 18 fragile States to provide a united voice for fragile countries and to advocate for change in global development policies. Many of the g7+ members are rich in natural resources and we want to work together to ensure that we are not exploited and to ensure that the benefits of this wealth is distributed fairly to our people.

As a group we want to ensure that natural resource wealth does not fuel conflict as we know from bitter experience that without peace and stability there can be no development.

This message was repeated loudly and clearly, when the g7+ nations, and some of our neighbours from Asia and the Pacific Islands met in Díli in February of this year, at an international conference, hosted by my Government with the theme 'Development for All'. The Conference agreed on the 'Díli Consensus', which set out our priorities, and hopes, for the post-2015 development agenda.

The Díli Consensus recognised that the standard approaches to development have failed and acknowledged that the challenges we face vary depending upon local context.

The nations of the world will meet at a special session of the United Nations on September 25 to follow up efforts made towards achieving the Millennium Development Goals and to discuss the post 2015 development agenda. Timor-Leste is proud of our Finance Minister, Emilia Pires, who was a member of the High Level Panel that advised the United Nations Secretary General on this agenda.

In April this year, Timor-Leste was also honoured to take over the Chair of the 69th session of the United Nations Economic and Social Commission for the Asia-Pacific. I have the privilege to Chair this session and working with ESCAP, and the nations of the Asia-Pacific, to make further progress and improve human development.

We debated the challenges faced by the nations of the Asia-Pacific region with the aim of better integrating plans and actions at the regional and sub-regional levels to address human development and provide better connectivity to break the isolation of some countries.

We are of course honoured to work with Dr. Noeleen Heyzer, United Nations Under Secretary-General and Executive Secretary of ESCAP. Regrettably it was not possible to have Dr. Heyzer here with us today in her capacity as Special Adviser of the United Nations Secretary-General for Timor-Leste. We wish her a quick recovery and we look forward to working with her in friendship and cooperation.

Ladies and Gentlemen,

I wish you all the most productive and constructive conference on Harnessing Natural Resource Wealth for Inclusive Growth and Economic Development.

I trust that the outcomes of this conference will help us to improve our fiscal policy, and the design of our national public investment framework, to transform our nation through a stronger and diversified economy. Using our natural resources wisely will allow us to make sustainable structural changes to our country.

Economic growth by itself is for nothing if it does not support poverty reduction, job creation, better education and health services and the tackling of social exclusion.

Our people fought for independence, not for a few but for every single Timorese person. Let us all work together again to build a better and fairer nation for our people.

Thank you very much.

Workshop on Peacekeeping Transitions: Lessons Learned from the UN Missions in Timor-Leste – 'Timor-Leste on the Verge of the Transition', Opening Address

Nigerian Permanent Mission, New York, 10 October 2013

Excellencies

Ladies and Gentlemen,

It is a great pleasure to speak today at this important workshop on peacekeeping operations and the lessons learnt from the various United Nations Missions in Timor-Leste.

I would like to commend and thank the Government of New Zealand and the New Zealand Permanent Mission for convening this workshop jointly with the Timor-Leste Permanent Mission. And I would also like to thank the Nigerian Permanent Mission for providing the venue for this two day workshop.

We are fortunate that this workshop has many distinguished participants and speakers including Her Excellency Ms Helen Clark, the United Nations Development Program Administrator, the Honourable Ms Anne Tolley, New Zealand Minister of Police and His Excellency Mr Finn Reske-Nielsen, Former Acting Special Representative of the Secretary General for Timor-Leste.

We are also pleased to have here with us, His Excellency Dr José Ramos-Horta, our former President and now the Special Representative of the Secretary-General for Guinea-Bissau, where we, and Dr. Mari Alkatiri, the Leader of the Opposition and former Prime-Minister of Timor-Leste, have just come from.

Ladies and Gentlemen,

To commence the topic of this workshop, allow me to start by describing, in a general picture, the long journey of the UN intervention in our country.

The UN came to play a vital role in a precise moment in the history of our liberation.

For more than two decades, the Timorese people were abandoned to their fate, and year by year, the votes in favour of a *fait acompli* were increasing, until Kofi Annan became the UN Secretary-General. His personal commitment to our case brought to fruition an agreement on the 5th of May 1999, between Indonesia, Portugal and the UN.

UNAMET was the first Mission to our country with a mandate to organise and supervise the popular consultation, which took place on 30th of August that year. Ian Martin and his team did a great job under very difficult conditions.

After the Referendum, and because the May Agreement stipulated a transitional period of administration under the UN, UNTAET led by the late Sergio Vieira de Mello was established.

Feeling marginalised from the process, the Timorese demanded better participation. Consequently, Dr. Mari Alkatiri was appointed Chief Minister, in order to prepare the Timorese to take part in the decisions about our own future.

In this regard, a National Council was established in 2001 with the role of reviewing and endorsing the UNTAET policies which included regulations, budget proposals and plans.

The National Council debated and approved a Transition Plan that would end with the handover of sovereignty.

That Plan provided for the realisation of the first ever elections for a Constitutional Assembly in 2001, to debate and approve the Constitution of the Democratic Republic of Timor-Leste.

UNTAET helped to set up the institutional foundations of our State. It was very important! But, we can note a big mistake – instead of working in the spirit of the Mission by looking at rebuilding some administrative infrastructure for the new State, the Mission was spending large amounts of money paying for UN personnel under so called 'technical assistance'. That technical assistance was regulated by UN criteria that seemed disastrous, although in some specialised areas there were very professional individuals.

But the problem was this:

Timor-Leste was considered so dangerous that the majority of the staff was there for only 4 to 6 months to allow others to come, as part of the rotation of solidarity among humanity from the four continents of the globe.

We dealt with many staff and the only expertise they had was that they had also been posted to missions in conflict affected countries.

On the other hand, in the security sector, INTERFET was crucial in putting an end to the violence by pushing the pro-Indonesian militias out of the country. They did a very good job that resulted in our people gaining confidence and coming back to their communities.

Not being at all involved in the violence before or after the popular consultation, our Guerrilla Forces were so ill-treated that we had to invent a fake list of widows and orphans to get some food for them.

The UN Mission was incapable of making the right decisions due to their lack of understanding of the local reality and the history of the country.

Very soon, the Peacekeeping Forces were deployed. I must tell you that we are still enjoying some bridges that were built by the Bangladeshi and Pakistani forces, as a small contrast to the thousands of military personnel from other countries that were going around our tiny homeland.

On 20 May 2002, UNTAET ended its mission. UNMISET was established, led by Kamalesh Sharma, to continue to provide assistance in many areas, especially in the defence and security sectors, with a mandate extended to 2005.

The State of Timor-Leste was at its beginning, without money, without its own financial capacity, with no experience in governance, without basic infrastructure and with a demanding society that believed that independence would bring benefits to everyone immediately.

These conditions did not allow the Government of Timor-Leste to respond to the demands that were emerging from all sectors of society. This caused social tensions that later dragged into other institutions such as the Military and Police Forces and led to the 2006 crisis.

There are people who defend the argument that the UN Mission and Peacekeeping Operations should not have withdrawn so soon.

I do not share this view because the mere presence of both without changing the policy of simply spending the money of tax payers of other countries, without putting into action concrete plans of assistance, the situation of social tension would have continued.

I say this because following the crisis we sought help and UNMIT and the ISF came to support us – UNMIT with a large UNPOL personnel and the ISF with its big military apparatus. This did not, however, prevent Dr. Ramos-Horta from being attacked and wounded at his residence. After this tragic incident, I was witness for more than a week to the inability of the two international institutions to provide an adequate response to the situation.

We can all recall that at that time, I asked the two institutions to restrict their movements and to allow us, the Timorese, to take the lead on the operations to restore security.

And we did just that without a single bullet being fired. And after that we returned to working on the reform plan for our security and defence forces.

The lesson that can be drawn from the presence of the Peacekeeping Forces and UNPOL is that instead of appearing as forces to secure stability, which is a very expensive exercise, they should have a plan to directly and intensively assist the sectors in need without incurring huge costs.

Meanwhile, I must acknowledge the concrete bilateral support from some countries in the area of defence and security, especially the support given by Australia to our own forces and by New Zealand and Portugal to our police.

It was with this thought of providing concrete support that we sat together with UNMIT to draw up an integrated plan within a specific timeframe that would allow for all to see the concrete results. Although this took some time, what we all should agree is that the Plan had successful results.

Only with the understanding of the international organisations can there be good cooperation with the beneficiary States such as that which took place in Timor-Leste.

In this context, the lesson should be to cooperate with the leadership of the country, so as to ensure ownership of the process and in doing so avoid having so many programs that do not meet the real needs of the country.

Fortunately, the Timorese prepared a *Strategic Development Plan* which allows for international support that can provide a better mechanism for assistance in critical areas of development.

It was in this context that it was agreed with the UN that after UNMIT we could begin to explore a new mechanism for our relationship with the UN, hence having only a non-resident UN Special Adviser for Timor-Leste reporting directly to the UN Secretary-General.

Ladies and Gentlemen,

I would like to reaffirm here our profound gratitude not only to all those countries that contributed to the Peacekeeping Forces but also to the men and women who served in the different UN Missions in Timor-Leste and I repeat what our President of the Republic said at the UN General Assembly last month 'The partnership with the UN throughout the last decade, achieved remarkable success'.

The United Nations family has been an integral part of the early years of the history of our nation and helped to build the foundation of a stable and democratic State. Our people will be always grateful for the contribution of the United Nations and the international community to our country.

Ladies and Gentlemen,

We have emerged from conflict to pursue development with unrelenting focus guided since 2011 by our 20 year *Strategic Development Plan*.

We have a small but emerging economy that is providing balanced and sustained growth.

We have always known that the true strength of our nation is our people which is why our *Strategic Development Plan* is focused on improving health, education and training and social inclusion. We know that we need healthy and educated people to build our nation.

We are developing institutions that operate to strengthen professionalism and accountability in the public administration.

While we know that we have a long way to go, and that many of our people are still not experiencing the life they expected, and that they deserved, on independence, we are heading in the right direction.

The United Nations has been our partner in this process of building peace, and our State, and our successes are also the UN's successes.

In this regard, I wish to acknowledge the work of my dear friend, Atul Khare, as SRSG and to his successor, Ameerah Haq, and to commend the achievements of Finn Reske-Nielsen who worked tirelessly with his team to make the transition as smooth and successful as possible.

Ladies and Gentlemen,

Since December last year Timor-Leste has been a truly sovereign nation – standing on our own two feet.

We know that the process of consolidating the State has still not finished, while we are taking steps to build the nation.

I am pleased to say that following the successful completion of the UNMIT transition, Timor-Leste and the UN have established institutional arrangements to ensure that we maintain positive and supportive relationships.

Our country continues to be supported by UN agencies that are dedicated to improving the lives of our people.

And as I mentioned before, we are particularly pleased that Dr Noeleen Heyzer, Executive Secretary of the United Nations Economic and Social Commission for Asia and the Pacific and Under-Secretary-General, has been appointed as the Special Adviser of the United Nations Secretary General for Timor-Leste. We are working well with her in this special role and look forward to building on the foundation of success and support that we thank the UN for.

Timor-Leste has new confidence in its future. We see the promise of our nation in our people who, having given so much for their liberty, will dedicate themselves to an inclusive development.

Ladies and Gentlemen,

As a member of the United Nations, and leading the g7+ group of 18 fragile and conflict affected nations, I cannot let this occasion go by without recalling that we have just come from Guinea-Bissau.

I understood from my time there that the United Nations is making the opposite mistake of the large amount of funding provided for Timor-Leste and has provided a lack of funds to Guinea-Bissau, which makes the mission of the SRSG, my dear brother, Dr. José Ramos-Horta, a difficult one.

The people of Guinea-Bissau, from all sectors of society who were contacted by Dr. Mari Alkatiri and myself, assumed collective responsibility for what took place in their country since 1980. We understood during our four days there the frustration of all and their intense desire for change.

All were able to understand that the sanctions imposed had a positive role in influencing the collective conscience to accept that the terrible situation could no longer continue. They all expressed this simple word ENOUGH.

They made a declaration of principles to demonstrate to the international community their total commitment to the restoration of constitutional order in their country.

In this document, they appealed to the international community to reconsider the sanctions, with the view of allowing for the initiation of a credible electoral registry as quickly as possible that would be finalised before the end of this year, so as to enable elections to take place at the end of February next year.

According to our calculations, a minimum budget of $USD 5 million is needed to prepare the electoral registry. Timor-Leste has already offered $USD 1 million dollars. I believe that with a fund managed by the UNDP, supported by Timorese, we can at least commence this vital process to guarantee free and credible elections.

When I say a fund managed by UNDP, I wish to stress that these funds should not be solely diverted to technical assistance and civic education. Timor-Leste has people on the ground to help define not only a calendar for action but also the items required such as equipment and operational costs. The next step will be to assist the elections.

If we want to help the people of Guinea-Bissau to have a new future, we have to help now! They are all committed to focus on the electoral process. However, from the Government of Guinea-Bissau, we learned that besides the electoral process, there are also very urgent social needs that must be addressed to allow for stability for the elections.

I urge the international community to take this into account if we want a new State where the rule of law prevails, where social justice can be achieved and where society can participate with new confidence in the future.

The Timor-Leste Permanent Mission in New York will, in due course, deliver to you copies of the signed declaration of principles that I have referred to.

On behalf of the g7+ group, I believe that it is the right time to give a hand to the suffering people of Guinea-Bissau.

Thank you.

Bali Democracy Forum VI – 'Consolidating Democracy in a Pluralistic Society'

Bali, 7 November 2013

Your Excellency, the President of the Republic of Indonesia, Dr Susilo Bambang Yudhoyono
Your Majesty, Sultan Hassanal Bolkiah Mu'izzaddin Waddaulah of Brunei Darussalam
Your Excellency, Dr. R.M. Marty M. Natalegawa, the Minister of Foreign Affairs of the Republic of Indonesia
Excellencies, Heads of Delegations
Ladies and Gentlemen,

It is a great pleasure to again participate in the Bali Democracy Forum. This is the sixth time I have addressed this Forum, having attended every year from the very beginning, and I have watched as it has grown in international significance and global reach.

This Forum is of course a special one. It will be the last one under the Presidency of my dear friend H.E. Dr Susilo Bambang Yudhoyono. Since coming to office almost ten years ago President Yudhoyono has transformed Indonesia.

Indonesia is a thriving and tolerant nation that celebrates its diversity with pride. It is one of the great democracies of the world, and economically Indonesia is now one of the world's leading emerging nations.

Next year, when he departs office, President Yudhoyono will certainly leave his country in a stronger and better position than when he became President.

While I have not come here today to celebrate the achievements of President Yudhoyono – there will be much time for that next year – I would like to again touch on his contribution to building peace and reconciliation with Timor-Leste.

Timor-Leste and Indonesia now enjoy the strongest of relationships. Together we have moved on from our difficult history, to build bonds of solidarity, trust and cooperation. We recognise that Timor-Leste not only shares an island with Indonesia, but that we also share a future and a commitment to democracy and the rights of our people.

We also view the strength of our relationship as an important model of how, with goodwill, a focus on the future and with leadership a history of bitterness and conflict can be overcome.

President Yudhoyono deserves much of the credit for leading us on a path towards a relationship of peace. Of all international leaders, Timor-Leste has no better friend than President Yudhoyono.

Ladies and Gentlemen,

We all know that the world is currently in a difficult situation. Across the globe the various continents are reeling from the near collapse of the world's system. A global system of inefficient decision making around the financial crisis that puts hundreds of millions of people, including in Europe itself, in anguish for their daily survival.

A global system that reflects the intransigency of the decision makers who choose threats and the use of war to fatten a massive military industry, in the guise of 'imposing universal values', instead of favouring dialogue and reconciliation.

I have said it before and continue to say it today that in Africa not a few countries are being torn apart, causing enormous suffering, that even if today we started taking concrete action towards a long term solution we may need half a century to address.

Right from the start I expressed my reservations towards the enthusiasm that was nurtured through the improper use of armed violence in support of the Arab Spring, which is proving by facts that it was unable to install universal values because the Arab Spring fuelled destruction and killings and deepened the disputes and rivalries in society.

As the developing world looks for global leadership we are aghast. The Arab Spring has turned into a nightmare with the transition to peace and freedom thwarted by greed for power, revenge and intolerance.

I was always against the invasion of Iraq and the war in Afghanistan. Western democracies have helped to destroy the millennial history of those peoples and what we see is their self-extermination.

Evidently, before such a result and before the division created within the populations of these countries, no one has the morals to speak about human rights and democracy!

As I have said since the beginning of the BDF, democracy is not an end unto itself; democracy is a social and political process with many components, which should be considered within the context of each reality.

I cannot see in the entire world that there is one example proving that democracy alone solves all political, social and economic problems. What I notice is that all large developed countries are just capable of imposing rules on the whole world with conventions and treaties of all kinds that they themselves do not comply and demand of other countries, particularly the least capable of complying, which has always provoked the beginning of their own agony.

What I notice is the global failure of a system where arrogance prevails and the paranoia of some has led to extreme actions that offend human sensibility.

In old Europe, the old democracy is only ensuring the right to massive protests and demonstrations, without being capable of changing the circumstances of misery of its people. One Europe that is so economically fragile it can only contemplate that democracy, after all, is just the opportunity for political demagogy and dull debates on recovery achieved at the expense of denying bread to the most vulnerable.

Europe is suffering from the Global Financial Crisis which has flowed into the ongoing Sovereign Debt Crisis. The countries of Europe are facing a reckoning after a period of unsustainable financial behaviour. This has led to a rise in instability and insecurity and the emergence of extremism in the midst of pluralist democracies.

With the irresponsible leadership of those in power and the manipulation of the financial system, Europe faces an uncertain future of high unemployment and a lost decade of economic growth.

In the USA itself, millions of households do not have food and people must enlist in order to receive a meal from social security.

As I said before, nowhere in the world is democracy solving every issue, although we recognise it is the system that can ensure individual freedom and the civic rights of the world's citizens.

It is true that across the world we are seeing progress with millions of people being lifted out of poverty, especially in the Asian region as well as in South America and Africa.

However, with the growing middle class we are also seeing growing democratic tensions. As the wealth of people increases they are becoming better educated and enjoying access to the internet and global connectivity. This has profound implications for democracy as it is leading people to ask more of their governments. As they become more prosperous their focus turns to rights and entitlements. We are seeing this not only in mass action from Brazil through to Turkey, but also in other ways in my own country of Timor-Leste.

Ladies and Gentlemen,

We also watch as the leaders of proud democracies do not strive to work together for a better future but instead appeal to the uglier side of human nature and descend into a pattern of mindless negativity, partisanship and conflict that goes so far as to put international stability at risk.

Still, when it comes to civic rights, which are imposed on new democracies or on countries in transition, we see that it is the powerful that shamelessly violate the civic rights not only of their citizens but, more scandalously, the citizens of other countries.

Either we are in the presence of an extreme distrust where everyone is a potential enemy, or we are witnessing the fraudulent use of technology to obtain economic advantage over others, which is even more immoral when those others are weak and small. I would say, with respect for opposing opinions, that both factors are the origin of this lack of ethics, of values of fairness and of principles of equality in regard to rights and obligations.

At the recent Shangri-la Dialogue in Singapore, I appealed to the sensitivities of the powerful to stop 'labelling' people, organisations and countries as enemies. In this new millennium, let us be more human and let us not be too radical when we proclaim, in every set of circumstances, to be defending so-called national interests, while violating the legitimate interests of others.

While we question how democratic a society can be that is ruled by the few in their own interests there are other concerns and challenges that democracy faces.

I ask you all whether we can really say that we are living in a democracy if we are subject to pervasive surveillance. Now that information technology is part of the fabric of our lives we have to consider the impact on democracy when our communications are being watched by others. This is not, however, just a matter of privacy and personal freedom. For nations of the world this question goes to the very heart of what it means to be sovereign. And for a small nation like Timor-Leste, with limited resources, it means that we are subject to prying nations acting in their own national interest.

Democracy also faces other challenges and I regret to say that too many democratic nations are failing to address them.

We are seeing too many democracies around the world captured by a ruling elite, many of which are supported by a broken financial industry. While it is clear that global free market finance has failed, we continue to see the financial industry perpetuating and reinforcing inequality.

The Global Financial Crisis stripped bare the world of finance and exposed gross incompetence, unrestrained greed and systemic corruption. The problem was that while no one in the developed world took responsibility for the Crisis it was the world's poor and vulnerable that suffered the most.

It is as if the world's financial industry transcends, or simply ignores democracy, and acts with unrestrained greed in its own interests which ignores the plight of the world's poor and fans the flames of conflict and fragility.

Strong action must be taken to hold the world's powerful elite to account and to tackle growing and indefensible inequality. Without addressing poverty and inequality the social cohesion and stability of pluralistic democracies will be at risk.

Ladies and Gentlemen,

Let us now look to Asia, where we belong. We are currently in the Asian century and we understand that this relates to economic growth, which also depends on the purchasing power of the developed countries.

The Asian region is not immune to problems of stability and to social and economic inequalities.

The conceptual diversity of political systems can be seen as a weakness so it always deserves our consideration and gradual motivation for changes that, overtime, will come by themselves, and which should never be imposed from outside in convulsions as it was in the Middle East and in an avalanche as it was in Northern Africa.

I also ask what it says about respect for democracy and human rights, and for international solidarity, when we see whole nations, such as the Republic of Kiribati, the Marshall Islands and Tuvalu, slowly sink into the vastness of the ocean as a result of climate change.

That is not to say that there is not progress towards democracy and peace. Close to home Timor-Leste looks to ASEAN as example of the success that regional zones can have in promoting cooperation, progress and development.

Ladies and Gentlemen,

This brings me to the situation in Guinea-Bissau where democracy has been under great threat, for over 30 years, making the country a failed state. Guinea-Bissau was a country that once inspired the Timorese people as it led the Lusophone countries in the struggle for independence. A country with such a proud and dignified history has been shamed by a consecutive leadership motivated by personal, rather than national interest.

I recently visited Guinea-Bissau with the Timorese opposition leader, Dr. Mari Alkatiri, to determine if there was anything that we could do to help put the country back on the path to democracy. We wanted to show how Timor-Leste has overcome a bitter history of animosity to work together for the good of our people in the context of a robust democracy. As a leading member of the g7+ group of 18 fragile and conflict affected nations, we also had a responsibility to support other fragile nations of the world. Our dear brother, Dr. José Ramos-Horta, also has the difficult task of leading the UN Mission in Guinea-Bissau and we wanted to support him in his efforts to steer the nation towards elections and democracy.

While we were there, members of the civil society, intellectuals, women, youth and the political and military leaders of the Guinea-Bissau made a declaration of principles to demonstrate to the international community their total commitment to the restoration of constitutional order and democracy in their country. There was a recognition that the country and its leadership had lost its way and it was now time to act in the national interest.

The coup d'état of April 2012 has resulted in sanctions been imposed by the International Community.

In NY and Washington, we conveyed to the International Organizations that if we want to help the people of Guinea-Bissau to have a new future where the rule of law, social justice and democracy prevails we must act now. Timor-Leste is doing what it can and we are providing $6 million, in equipments and technical assistance and working together with the United Nations Development Programme in Guinea-Bissau to support the electoral process. Nigeria and New Zealand have also committed to provide assistance and I urge the wider international community to support the restoration of democracy in Guinea-Bissau, by sending rice to diminish the suffering of the population. Timor-Leste can be the focal point in Asia for this purpose.

It may seem strange that Timor-Leste, one of the poorest nations in the world, is providing aid to Guinea-Bissau but we remember the generosity of the many nations around the world that supported our nation as we started on the path to peace and stability. And we know, that democracy is worth the investment.

It is worth recalling the key objective of the Bali Democracy Forum, that is to promote 'political development through dialogue and cooperation in strengthening adherence to democratic values and development of democratic institutions.'

Guinea-Bissau may be a long way from Asia but it will equally benefit from the development of a thriving democracy.

Still in Africa, we can see positive development in another member state of the g7+, the Democratic Republic of Congo, where it seems they would put an end to the long armed conflict. I appeal, to the authorities and to the people of DRC, for moderation and restraint from avengeful behaviour. Only dialogue and tolerance would help consolidate peace, obtained at high cost.

Ladies and Gentlemen,

In reality, the subject of this Conference is not only pertinent but also extremely timely – the great challenge for pluralistic societies is how to consolidate democracy.

When it comes to us directly I would like to address the topic under two aspects:
- the political aspect of consolidating the State
- the social and economic aspect of national cohesion.

Regarding the first aspect,

If democracy is the expression of the will of the people, then the elected bodies must, in accordance with the aspirations of the people, do everything so that the State apparatus is strong, which means credible, responsible and fair in the fulfilment of the central objectives of the State.

Because of this, elected representatives must ensure that the national interest prevails over all and any other interests.

The system of checks and balances must be operational, operative and, above all, consistent so that we can ensure the rule of law.

The elected bodies should use democracy as a positive instrument of debate for the construction and/or consolidation of the Nation.

Regarding the second aspect,

Society must adopt a culture of tolerance and honest and frank dialogue for solving differences.

Civil society (NGOs and the press) should assume a critical but responsible attitude, lest it ferment unnecessary and avoidable divisions that, if they develop, can create deep breaches in society and hinder the development of the country.

Citizens should assume a positive patriotic spirit and not fall for manipulations aimed at weakening national sovereignty.

Rulers should be able to present concrete programs to, over time, eradicate poverty and situations of marginalisation or exclusion, which are social factors that are the basis of several convulsions that we see in many developed and developing countries.

Religious faiths should advocate moderation, fraternity and the human values of solidarity and peace of mind.

In this new millennium, let us put an end to war to give space to the blossoming of democracy because if democracy is developed and strengthened, in a process in accordance with the intrinsic conditions of each country, we can envision an environment of peace across the planet for all humankind.

Only constructive dialogue, persistent and careful, can change the current inflexibility of all parties and that has to start at the major circles of decision making.

I urge the participants of this Forum to do all that we can to address the problems the world faces. Leaders must look beyond the language of blame and conflict, and speak of the possibility of progress, of reconciliation and of tolerance.

Ladies and Gentlemen,

Finally, I want to again thank my dear friend H.E. Dr Susilo Bambang Yudhoyono for his leadership and friendship.

I have no doubt this Forum will be a lasting legacy that continues to build peace stability and prosperity in our region and beyond.

Thank you very much!

Lecture at the University of Juba on 'Sharing Experiences'

Juba, South Sudan, 5 December 2013

Rector of the University
Excellencies
Ladies and Gentlemen,

It is a great pleasure and an honour to be here today at Juba University.

I am particularly pleased to address you – the future leaders of South Sudan.

While I have come from half way around the world to speak to you – my homeland is in many ways similar to your own. Timor-Leste is half of an island in Southeast Asia, with the other half belonging to Indonesia. In 2002, Timor-Leste became the youngest nation in the world – just as South Sudan is today.

On independence, Timor-Leste had also emerged from a long and difficult struggle for independence that had left our people traumatised and physically and emotionally scarred. The people of Timor-Leste maintained their resistance against Indonesian occupation for a quarter of a century. We fought a much larger enemy that was supported by some of the world's great powers. While these western nations espoused the universal values of human rights, freedom and democracy; their actions supported a dictator who was brutalising our people. We suffered trauma and heart break. I do not need to tell you of the costs of war.

Despite the cost, we held on to our dream of freedom. Our motto was 'To Resist is to Win' and our occupiers were to learn that, despite terrible suffering, our spirit and our solidarity could not be broken. We were inspired by campaigns against colonial rule in Africa which showed us the way. And so, we fought a guerrilla war in the mountains and valleys of Timor.

Just as with South Sudan, Timor-Leste finally achieved self-determination through a referendum in which our people, despite a climate of violence, overwhelmingly voted for independence.

Between 1999 and 2002 our country was administered by the United Nations as we prepared for self-determination. In many ways this helped our country because it gave us time to form and grow political parties, to develop our civil society and to design a constitution that upholds democracy and human rights under the rule of law. In 2002 we became the newest country in the world.

However, after independence, like many post-conflict countries, we struggled to maintain national unity and a common sense of purpose. Our process of peace building and reconciliation did not go deep enough and we failed to address unresolved conflicts. As a result, in our early years we suffered a cycle of conflict the flared up around every two years. It was not until into 2008 that, as a nation, we finally said enough, and committed to say good bye to conflict and to welcome development. We accepted that our main priority was to move on from our brutal history and to build peace and a resilient State.

Like South Sudan, Timor-Leste is fortunate to have petroleum resources that can be exploited to fund the building of a State and to address the pressing needs of the people. And while both our nations are fragile, we also both enjoy the support of the international community and the benefit of development assistance.

We are also of course not the only nation to work on peace building and State building, after emerging from a long period of conflict. For example, like South Sudan, Timor-Leste is one of forty-nine countries the United Nations labels 'Least Developed Countries'. We are one of the thirty countries labelled by the World Bank as 'Fragile States'.

We are also one of eighteen countries that have come together to form a group – known as the g7+ – to monitor, report and draw attention to the specific challenges faced by fragile states, many of which are home to the 1.5 billion people around the world still living in extreme poverty.

And so, please allow me to touch upon some of the issues that Timor-Leste has faced that may also be of relevance to South Sudan. We all know that the process of State building is different for each country, and in each context, but we also know that we can still learn from each other, and that we can support each other on our path to development.

Ladies and Gentlemen

Students,

When we achieved our independence we recognised that reconciliation was the first thing that we had to do so that we could heal our country.

First, Timor-Leste had to reconcile with our former occupiers, Indonesia. During the occupation Indonesia was a dictatorship but we understood that the Indonesian people also suffered during this time. To the great credit of the Timorese people, we were able to distinguish between the Indonesian people and the Indonesian regime.

Today Indonesia is one of the largest democracies in the world and has a great emerging free market economy. We recognise that Timor-Leste not only shares an island with Indonesia, we share a future, and we now walk together in friendship and solidarity. We view the strength of our relationship as an important model of how, with goodwill, a focus on the future and leadership, a history of bitterness and conflict can be overcome.

What we found, however, was that sometimes reconciliation between our own people has proved more difficult than with our former occupiers.

During the occupation, and in its aftermath, Timorese society was torn apart and our people committed terrible acts of violence against each other. While we tried to reconcile our past, tensions grew between different parts of our country, and this culminated in 2006 with major unrest forcing thousands of people to flee their homes.

And this led to the realisation that we had to come together and reconcile our differences. We had to reflect on the destructive path our people were taking and begin a dialogue with all Timorese people to address the root causes of our problems. As a nation we recognised that we could not build a State without building peace. And this meant that we needed to come to terms with, and then address, our fragility. And so, we started to pull together and began to honestly deal with our problems.

Ladies and Gentlemen

Students,

An important part of the process of securing peace in Timor-Leste was to show our respect for our veterans, the former combatants that gave so much for the independence struggle. Our State has a strong obligation to address the needs of our former freedom fighters. In our transition to self-determination it was important that our veterans were given the support that they needed and were encouraged to make the transition to a new role of building a democratic society.

In October I travelled to Guinea-Bissau which is, like Timor-Leste, a former Portuguese colony. Guinea-Bissau inspired our struggle but, regrettably, it has been heading in the wrong direction with a leadership that has been more concerned with personal self-interest than the well-being of the people. Unfortunately, Guinea-Bissau has also not been able to deal properly with its veterans and has failed to establish a system, and a legal framework, for the State to properly recognise their historical contribution. The State has also not assumed the competence to demobilise the freedom fighters from the struggle. This situation has destabilised the country and contributed to a cycle of instability and coups d'état. We hope that the leadership of Guinea-Bissau can develop a system to deal with these pressures and make clear the role of all parts of society, including the former combatants, to avoid instability and further violence. Because of sanctions, Timor-Leste is working almost alone in helping Guinea-Bissau prepare for its elections. Guinea-Bissau is also a member of the g7+, and a LCD and is a post- conflict country.

Ladies and Gentlemen,

I would also like to emphasise the importance of democracy. Last month I went to Indonesia for the Bali Democracy Forum. This is an important regional and global annual event that promotes democracy and freedom.

I participate in this forum every year and seek to raise important questions about democracy and what it means to be democratic in a situation of fragility. Regrettably, many democracies are heading in the wrong direction. They have been captured by a self-interested and powerful elite that is perpetuating and increased great inequality that is putting the very social cohesion of their nations at risk.

And so, we must do better. We must recognise that while democracy is important the democratic process of each country must reflect its values and its characteristics as well as its context.

As South Sudan reviews its constitution, and heads to elections in 2015, we trust that your nation will be successful in the challenging process of peace building and State building so that the government can continue to address the pressing issues your nation faces and realise the promise of its future.

Ladies and Gentlemen,

As students of this prestigious university, it is you who will be responsible for the future of your nation. Just like in Timor-Leste, where the current generation of leadership must make way for the new generation, your time will soon come in South Sudan where you will have to step up and contribute to your nation's development.

South Sudan has enormous potential and if you show the same commitment and resolve to achieve independence as you do to nation building then you have a very positive future and a very bright future for your children.

One sector that you should look at is agriculture. South Sudan has a huge land area that has the potential to not only be a food bowl for the nation, but to also export. Oil is not a renewable resource, and while the money from oil can build the foundations of a State, you will need sustainable industries to create jobs and support your nation.

Ladies and Gentlemen,

Before I finish, let me mention another area our two nations have in common. We are both fortunate to have the assistance of a large number of generous development partners to support our process of State building.

While we have seen the benefits that international development assistance can bring, we have also experienced the disappointments. We have seen so much money being spent for so few outcomes in the name of international aid. Timor-Leste also wants to address the problems with development assistance and international engagement in fragile and developing countries. As small nation, Timor-Leste cannot do this alone. We need to build international solidarity to make sure that our interests are represented and our voices are heard. If we are not united, individually we will simply be too vulnerable to complex systems and entrenched attitudes that put the lives of our people last. As I mentioned earlier, we are doing this through the g7+, which is an innovative new collaboration between 18 fragile States. The group was formed in 2010 to provide a united voice for fragile countries and to advocate for change in global development policies and we are very pleased that South Sudan is standing together with us in this mission

Ladies and Gentlemen

Students,

I would also like to congratulate South Sudan for holding its 2013 Investment Conference which I addressed this morning. I was last in Juba in 2011, shortly after independence, and I can say that coming back I have seen great progress.

South Sudan has such promise across a number of key sectors including petroleum, agriculture, construction and hospitality. I know that the early investors in this emerging nation will be successful and South Sudan is fortunate to have a Government that understands and promotes the importance of investment, job creation and a diversified economy.

Ladies and Gentlemen,

I would like to finish today to speak of my experience yesterday travelling to the Malou in Jonglei State.

I travelled there yesterday with my Minister for Finance to celebrate the building of a school that the government of Timor-Leste funded.

The visit to Malou was a humbling and emotional experience for us. The true warmth and genuine friendship of the people, in such a remote area, reminded us of our common humanity and what we as people are when the distractions of material wants is stripped away.

It was a privilege for us to have such an authentic experience among your good people and it gave us hope in the promise of your nation under peace. The unrestrained joy and happiness of the villages as they sang and danced gave us pause to reflect on the meaning of our own lives and of the importance of human solidarity.

Ladies and Gentlemen,

Thank you for inviting me to speak to you today; it has been an honour. Timor-Leste looks forward to our continuing friendship with South Sudan. We share such a similar history and feel an affinity with your people.

I wish you all the best in building your nation and I trust that with hard work your future, and South Sudan's future, will be bright.

Thank you very much.

United Nations Economic and Social Commission of Asia and the Pacific Ministerial Conference, on 'Regional Economic Cooperation and Integration in Asia and the Pacific'

Bangkok, 19 December 2013

H.E. Mr Toke Talagi, Premier of Niue

H.E. Dr.Noeleen Heyzer, Under-Secretary-General of the United Nations and Executive Secretary of ESCAP

Excellencies

Distinguished Delegates

Ladies and Gentlemen,

As Chair of the sixty-ninth session of the Economic and Social Commission of Asia and the Pacific I would like to thank Dr.Noeleen Heyzer for organising this very important ministerial conference on regional economic cooperation and integration in Asia and the Pacific.

The Asia-Pacific region has been a global driver of economic growth. It is home to many of the world's emerging economies that have been lifting millions of people from poverty.We are starting to see, however, a slowing in emerging countries as the drag of the global economy takes hold.

The world is still recovering from the damage caused by the Global Financial Crisis and this is impacting the nations of our region. For many countries, especially in Europe, we have seen the Global Financial Crisis become a Sovereign Debt Crisis. This is slowing international recovery and is hurting our region's export markets. It means that the nations of our region are having to look not only to increased domestic growth to make up for this shortfall, but to increased economic cooperation and integration in the Asia-Pacific. That is why this conference is so important.

We avoided the worst of the Global Financial Crisis because our nations worked together and agreed on stimulus measures. Many of these measures have now run their course and it is time to again come together to work towards increased regional and global cooperation. The outcomes of this cooperation may include increased regional trade and investment as well as further stimulus measures in the areas of infrastructure and access to basic sanitation, education and health services that will re-charge growth and improve the lives of our people.

Ladies and Gentlemen,

A critical element in the agenda for regional economic cooperation and integration discussed in the documentation for this meeting is connectivity, including physical transport, energy and ICT infrastructure.

In Timor-Leste we understand well the need for increased regional integration to achieve our national vision of a diversified and sustainable economy that supports a healthy, prosperous and well educated population. While we have enjoyed average rates of economic growth of 11.9% since 2007, we know that without regional cooperation our progress will falter.

And so, we are going to build a new national port and our new international airport to enhance regional trade and investment and promote our tourist industry. To ensure connectivity with the region and the world we will be bringing a sub-sea internet cable to Timor-Leste and we are developing a petroleum hub and supply base on our south coast to support the regional oil and gas industry. As well as these physical projects, Timor-Leste is increasing integration through an extensive regional scholarships program under our Human Capital Development Fund and with our bid to join and contribute to ASEAN and other multilateral bodies.

Ladies and Gentlemen,

When we look to improving regional economic cooperation and integration there is one issue we must keep at the front of our minds. While some countries are becoming increasingly prosperous, others remain stagnant or face great challenges.

Continued and entrenched inequality will also create worrying global and regional risks. This year we have seen major street protests across the world including in such important nations as Brazil, Turkey, Egypt and in Europe itself. In part, these protests have been driven by grievances around economic and political inequality and they demonstrate that social cohesion and stability are being put at risk by rising inequality.

We must ask how we can work towards spreading the growing prosperity of our region to reduce extreme poverty and to achieve inclusive and balanced growth. Given this, a key question is 'How can those countries that are being left behind benefit from the dynamism and growth of the Asia-Pacific?' In answering this question, we must work towards forms of regional economic cooperation and integration which most effectively spread prosperity and development among all countries.

As well as inequality between nations, we must also be alert to the remarkable growth in our region leading to inequality *within* nations. Regrettably, our rising prosperity is not being enjoyed by all and we are seeing vast wealth accumulated by few while millions living in the same country remain in poverty. With the gap widening between the rich and the privileged, and the poor and the vulnerable, it is important to pursue social justice and inclusive economic growth.

We must ensure that all people are free from hunger and have access to health and education and the chance of a fulfilling life. To do this, we must all make sure our economies work to support people rather than operate in the interests of a privileged multinational elite and a corrupt global financial system.

From our perspective, to overcome these challenges, we are in a process of a trilateral cooperation with the eastern part of Indonesia and the northern territory of Australia, in order to establish an integrated development plan in all sectors.

Ladies and Gentlemen,

The context of each nation is different and the circumstances of some countries require unique approaches to development but we must explore the possibility of common potential and the sharing of common goals.

As we approach the expiry of the Millennium Development Goals in 2015, we must recognise that not one fragile or conflict affected country achieved these goals. With over 1.5 billion people living in fragile or conflict affected nations, taking action to support these countries is one of the most pressing international issues of our time.

That is why the g7+ group of 18 fragile and conflict countries was established and is working in solidarity, and speaking with one voice, to build peace and strengthen our States. But now, we need more than 18 countries working together. With the world deciding on the post 2015 development agenda we must make sure that the global community does not forget the need to address security and development in fragile States.

And we must not forget the fragile nations in our own region, such as the Marshall Islands, Kiribati and Tuvalu in the Pacific, and Maldives in the Indian Ocean, that are slowly drowning as a result of climate change.

Ladies and Gentlemen,

Despite the threats and the challenges that we face as a region we should be positive about the promise of our collective future. We have before us a unique opportunity to make development truly inclusive and sustainable and to lead the world's post-2015 development agenda.

Our region continues to drive the world economy and account for much of its economic growth which is creating jobs, opportunities and prosperity.

We, member States and associate members of ESCAP, represent countries with different cultures and histories and at different stages of development. This diversity is not a hindrance but a strength. It gives us opportunities to learn lessons, share good practices and explore approaches to overcoming common challenges. We need to create innovative regional cooperation partnerships, learn from our varied experiences and take responsibility for shared regional development.

Essentially, however, there is a need to enhance regional financial cooperation, because only by mobilising the financing for less developed countries can we boost trade and increase investment for infrastructure and, on the other hand, give positive signals by opening opportunities to private investors.

Last April we launched here the Zero Hunger Challenge. In our region, we can see that there are some countries improving food production but that still lack good access to markets within and beyond Asia-Pacific.

A good financial mechanism will take into account what we face in terms of inequality across our region and within each one of our countries. Only a regional economic integration scheme can narrow the development gaps that the Asia-Pacific region is facing today.

Ladies and Gentlemen,

In finishing my remarks, I would like to mention the inspiration that Nelson Mandela was to Timor-Leste, to our region and, of course, to the world.

In Timor-Leste's darkest moments in our struggle for liberation, as we were fighting in the mountains and valleys of our homeland, Mandela's story gave us hope. He showed us that we were not alone in our struggle and he validated our determination to never give up our dreams of freedom.

Nelson Mandela leaves our world with a remarkable legacy in which forgiveness is stronger than hatred; a world where solidarity is more important than self-interest; and a world where every person should be entitled to develop his or her potential regardless of country, class or gender.

I truly hope that as we mourn his passing, the legacy is not lost. Let us not only make statements of hope but take action for a better world.

Ladies and Gentlemen,

As Chair of the Commission, I congratulate all member States and associate members for your hard work, both during the senior officials segment concluded yesterday, and during two preparatory meetings earlier this year. I also congratulate you all for the draft of the Bangkok declaration on regional economic cooperation and integration in Asia and the Pacific, which will be considered for adoption. I believe that this declaration provides an effective road map to move the agenda for regional economic cooperation and integration forward.

We need to act together because isolated efforts will not succeed. And so, we must be committed to ending extreme poverty, hunger and exclusion with the recognition that economic growth can only be sustainable if the social well-being of all people is improved.

In conclusion, I look forward to working with you towards fostering reconciliation and dialogue to improve peace and social cohesion, that will allow a road map for development, through strengthening economic cooperation and integration in our region.

I am sure that acting together we can achieve a brighter future for our people and for future generations.

Thank you very much.

V Constitutional Government

Dinner to Welcome and Honour Her Royal Highness Princess Maha Chakri Sirindhorn of the Kingdom of Thailand

Díli, 7 January 2014

Her Royal Highness, Princess Maha Chakri Sirindhorn
Excellency, Dr. Noeleen Heyzer, Under-Secretary-General of the United Nations; Executive Secretary of the United Nations Economic and Social Commission for Asia and the Pacific and Special Adviser to the United Nations Secretary General for Timor-Leste
Distinguished Members of Parliament and Government
Ambassadors
Excellencies
Distinguished guests
Ladies and Gentlemen,

It is a great honour and a privilege to welcome Her Royal Highness, Princess Maha Chakri Sirindhorn to Timor-Leste.

On behalf of the People and the Government of Timor-Leste, I thank Your Royal Highness for visiting our country. It is a special honour for us and it inspires confidence and happiness in our people.

Your visit strengthens the close and deep bonds of friendship and solidarity between the Kingdom of Thailand and Timor-Leste.

Last year I had the honour of visiting Thailand on an Official Visit. Under the leadership of the Prime Minister of Thailand, Her Excellency Yingluck Shinawatra, we agreed on enhanced cooperation across key areas important for Timor-Leste's development.

This includes cooperation and support in tourism, agriculture and petroleum as well as Thailand's support for the development of the south coast of our country.

During my Official Visit, I was also pleased that Thailand committed strong support to Timor-Leste's bid to join ASEAN.

Her Royal Highness is well known for her dedication and hard work in support of children, improved education and health care and the protection of the disadvantaged and the vulnerable. She leads by her example, and over her three days in Timor-

Leste she will be busy visiting schools, health clinics, farms, community cooperatives and NGOs. We are honoured that she is interested in our country and our culture.

Ladies and Gentlemen,

On Thursday we will be launching the Zero Hunger Challenge campaign in Timor-Leste with the United Nations Economic and Social Commission for Asia and the Pacific and the Food and Agriculture Organisation.

The Zero Hunger Challenge is a campaign coordinated by the United Nations to eliminate hunger. Its goal is to make sure that every man, woman and child enjoys the Right to Adequate Food and that food systems are sustainable and resilient.

Her Royal Highness is visiting Timor-Leste for the launch of the Zero Hunger Challenge which reflects her strong commitment to alleviating hunger and eradicating poverty. We are pleased that she is joining together with our people in this challenge.

I attended the launch of the Zero Hunger Challenge for the Asia-Pacific in Bangkok last year and I am very pleased that the Challenge is now being launched in Timor-Leste.

We thank the role of the United Nations in tackling this critical issue and, in particular, commend the dedication of Dr. Noeleen Heyzer in leading action to eradicate hunger in the Asia-Pacific region.

Timor-Leste has been working hard to eradicate hunger and poverty. At the World Food Day celebration in 2010 we signed the Comoro Declaration to put an end to hunger and malnutrition. This led to the establishment of the Inter-Ministerial Task Force on Food and Nutrition Security and coordinated work to feed children and communities, promote effective seeds and grain storage and build our livestock and fisheries sectors. The following year we built on our efforts and supported livestock rearing, home and school gardening and the procurement of locally produced agriculture products.

In 2011 Timor-Leste released our 20 year *Strategic Development Plan* which includes strategies and actions to make sure that we achieve our goal of food security by 2020 and that we expand and improve our agriculture, livestock and fisheries industries.

Timor-Leste has invested significantly in agricultural infrastructure, machinery and the provision of seeds and fertiliser. We are releasing new high yielding varieties of maize, rice, cassava and sweet potato and we are improving storage facilities across the country.

Timor-Leste is also making significant investment in rehabilitating and extending irrigation systems and improving water storages. To help feed our children we operate an extensive school feeding program and are promoting school gardens. The

Government is also working hard to develop our fisheries industry through improved transport systems and fishing ports, piers and landing sites.

We know we have a lot more to do – eliminating stunting and hunger is a challenge for us. We also know that working with the assistance of the United Nations, and with the support of the Kingdom of Thailand, we can meet this challenge. I am pleased that the Zero Hunger Challenge will reinforce the work and the plans that Timor-Leste has to eradicate hunger, and I urge you all come together to make sure the challenge is a success in our country.

Ladies and Gentlemen,

Thank you all for coming tonight to welcome and honour Her Royal Highness, Princess Maha Chakri Sirindhorn.

Your Royal Highness, we are privileged by your visit and your support for our People. We all hope that you have a wonderful time in Timor-Leste and enjoy the beauty of our country and the friendship of our people.

Thank you very much.

2014 Jakarta International Defence Dialogue: 'Building Maritime Collaboration for Security and Stability'

Jakarta, 19 March 2014

Excellency, Vice-President of the Republic of Indonesia, Dr. Boediono
Excellency, Minister of Defence of the Republic of Indonesia, Dr. Purnomo Yusgiantoro
Excellencies
Honourable Ministers of Defence
Distinguished Delegates
Ladies and Gentlemen,

First, I would like to thank the Government of Indonesia and the organizers of this prestigious Conference for once again inviting me to be here.

This could be a special moment for the JIDD: if present, it would be the last time we have, in this forum, Dr. Susilo Bambang Yudhoyono as the President of the Republic of Indonesia.

Even without his presence, please allow me to pay tribute to a Leader, who has been the cornerstone of this important forum for discussing regional and global military issues.

Under Dr. Susilo Bambang Yudhoyono's commitement, Indonesia has been playing a precious role in the promotion of debates on universal principles, humanist values and development challenges.

Dr. Susilo Bambang Yudhoyono proved to be a man with a great sense of tolerance, a diplomat of unmatched skill, an extraordinary Indonesian personality and a robust statesman with a strong character.

We hope to continue to count on Dr. Susilo Bambang Yudhoyono's great vision, as he has given us an example of new, positive and continuous approaches, from the conceptual point of view to formulating cooperation and strengthening of relationships.

Ladies and Gentlemen,

In the JIDD, what each of us seeks to visualize, through the discussions that are conducted, is a broader perspective of the challenges of our time, and particularly of the challenges in our region, that may require special attention.

The subject this year is about 'building maritime collaboration for security and stability', which is surely both important and delicate matter.

I have to praise the true spirit of cooperation, with the involvement of 26 countries in a sophisticated search operation, having in mind the suffering of those who are concerned about the fate of their beloved ones. On behalf of the Timorese people, I want to express our solidarity to the Malaysian Government and our profound sympathy to all the relatives in this difficult time.

However, on the other hand, from what we have been following in our region, we are all extremely concerned with the current events in the South China Sea.

The word 'maritime' brings us to the vast ocean or to the sea near to our shores and, if we want to address the issue of 'security and stability', we are talking about common borders, common threats and common challenges.

And when we discuss all these problems (borders, threats and challenges), we all assume that everyone of us is governed by international law, without which relationships between States and Governments cannot be carried out within a framework of rules, set and accepted by all. These rules seek to shape our political behavior in terms of cooperation.

Without establishing this set of principles, to which all of us bow, which is to say that we all vow to enforce it, talking about maritime security and stability would be talking about very vague and general policy issues, while this subject is linked directly with the individual interests of each country, particularly the ones that, in one way or another, think or feel that they face challenges in this area.

In many cases that divide countries, it is plain to see there is a practice of 'double standards', usually by those that have more means to spend on propaganda, on alienation and on the pursue of interests that exceed their rights and breach the interests of others.

More often than not, demagogy normally covers the attempts against the values to which we all in principle are committed.

Otherwise, and stepping away momentarily from the subject of maritime security, we are confused when we cannot find the root causes for many of the world's problems.

Ladies and Gentlemen,

In 2000, when we were undergoing the difficult process of creating a new State from the ashes, the thing we heard and kept repeating to ourselves, in relation to the assistance we were asking for desperately, was the rhetoric of 'everything but arms'.

Today, when we see armed conflicts in so many countries, the question that comes to our minds is: 'Where did those arms come from?', 'Who or which country is benefiting from the selling of those arms?'

We understand that the great powers are concerned with chemical weapons or nuclear weapons and they are busy threatening others with sanctions, but it seems that we all have lost the clear notion that people throughout the world are killing each other every day. The result is that we all become excited only when the reports show millions of refugees, waiting from international organizations' appeal for billions of dollars in humanitarian aid.

If I am wrong I beg you to forgive my great ignorance, but I have never heard of a serious debate on the subject of where the arms provided come from, to various factions in various countries, to shoot each other and to condemn their populations to suffering.

There are special missions created to monitor human rights and to assess domestic violence throughout the world and to quantify underdeveloped and developing countries in these areas. There are costly special courts on genocide. Curiously, nobody is able to identify the origins of the weapons used to conduct the mass slaughter of civilians!

I believe that many of us here are intrigued by this situation that continues to be a reality in several places throughout the world, making difficult the achievement of the Millennium Development Goals.

Ladies and Gentlemen,

Returning to the subject of 'building maritime collaboration for security and stability', as I have said before, only a sound basis of respect for international law can rule cooperative relationships between neighbours and within a regional context.

Otherwise, there will always be an environment of distrust causing frictions and leading to warnings and responses to those warnings, which may lead to confrontations. This situation causes apprehension to those who have little or nothing to do with the problems, since it may lead to possible political, social and economic impacts that will always disturb States, particularly when they are having difficulties in their development processes.

Today, maritime security covers large and small scale activities.

We understand that a trend in our region is to protect commercial maritime interest, amid rising regional tensions and, according to defense analysts, maritime surveillance is the most pressing need in East and Southeast Asia.

In our opinion, maritime cooperation would have a meaning of more deterrence, if we want to put it like that. Timor-Leste has been benefitting from the availability of countries like the United States of America in exercises such as CARAT, even if we are still far from being able to participate with minimum capacity.

Ladies and Gentlemen,

Timor-Leste is an island country (better yet, a half-island country). As such, the sea is of paramount importance when discussing the country's security strategy.

Timor-Leste loses over $50 million a year in illegal fishing. My government is also concerned with the security of its future petroleum exploration facilities in the sea. As such, Timor-Leste wants to strengthen its maritime component to put an end to illegal fishing and to protect its interests and the investments it has.

The strengthening of the maritime police and the naval component, through providing them with proper resources, will surely increase certainty and confidence in regard to our country's maritime security.

Timor-Leste, which has only been an independent State for the past twelve years, is therefore prioritizing its needs, from the human capacity building to the construction of the necessary facilities.

In addition to this, it is obvious that having adequate means, in our exclusive economic zones, will enable us to participate in fighting the trafficking of arms and drugs, as well as illegal trade.

Timor-Leste is currently in the process to joining ASEAN. As small as my country is, we do not harbor illusions of grandeur that we will make enormous contributions to the region's maritime security. However, we recognize the need for active cooperation with all who are close to our maritime borders.

Here, I should say that we are talking with Indonesia in relation to the islands closest to us, and with Australia in relation to the Northern Territory, in order to draft an agreement on an integrated development plan.

Fortunately, everything suggests that there is enormous good will from all parties, which are motivated by the perspective of broader cooperation that results in concrete benefits for the people. We sincerely believe that such a trilateral agreement will cover the entire economic development potential and improve relationships between peoples, so that everyone may live happily on this planet.

Evidently, maritime security will be very important in an area that we may call an economic, social and cultural sub-region.

However, in order for this cooperation to be honest and serious, it is vital that we determine the maritime borders between countries, under international law, in a clear manner without subterfuges of any kind.

It is truly offensive to see how some countries, because they are large, wealthy or heavily armed, are always the ones that are more unfair to their neighbours, particularly when those neighbours are small and poor.

International law is always invoked, in the pronouncements made in relation to other countries. But international law is simply relegated or forgotten, when it is to ensure major economic benefits at the expense of the principle of fair policy and of the universal values of equal rights and obligations between peoples and nations.

As a new country that is still consolidating State institutions and where most people still lack the minimum conditions for living healthy lives, we can only raise our voice to make sure that there must be true justice in the world, particularly in this new millennium.

We only became a full-fledged member of the United Nations in September 2002, while many other countries signed the Charter of the United Nations, when the organization was created and, time to time, it happens that they are called for relevant positions, including in the Security Council.

In a way, we only can get confused and stunned thinking about how international law may prevail, when the ones, that do not respect it, would be the ones making decisions in these important world bodies. The intricate reasons of the 'cold war' have now led to a sophisticated culture of manipulation and fraud, seeking to alienate the unwary and the unprepared.

I have to say, once for all, that we are and will always be committed to standing for the truth, with the same spirit we had, in the past, when many believed that Timor-Leste was a lost cause. We will stand for our rights with the same faith and determination, in order to contribute to justice between nations and better understanding between peoples.

And we believe that the United Nations Convention on the Law of the Sea should play an effective role in solving the differences.

Ladies and Gentlemen,

For a small country as mine, talking about maritime security, whether in terms of joint exercises or information sharing, will never solve and may even permanently hinder the vital issue of the delimitation of the maritime borders.

It is fundamental to us, moreover when neighbours plan to buy drones to secure their ocean resources and to protect their borders.

We firmly believe in the motto 'times change, wills change'. The spirit of the new millennium should proportionate to the leaders of the world a better sense of responsibility towards the humanity.

The international environment, more open to the awareness by all countries, whether they are large or small, strong or weak, of their rights and duties, gives us hope that the leaders of this globalized world want to correct the wrong policies of the past.

I would like to quote the US former Secretary of State for Defence, Robert Gates, who, in a honest way of putting things in regard to a different matter, acknowledged 'the lack of humility to accept there was no forecast on the negative consequences', resulting from decisions made only to display arrogance and power.

Globalization binds small countries and makes them hostage to their own weaknesses, when competing in the global market. However, globalization also presents valuable opportunities, when properly considered, for small countries to denounce the lack of good faith by the large countries, the lack of honesty by the powerful countries and the policy of manipulation by the rich countries.

Globalization and its sophisticated technology is, after all, a two-edged sword.

Let maritime security not be a double-barreled cannon. Let the effort in fighting transnational crimes not allow other interests, particularly in terms of economic dominance, cast a shade over the relationships between countries and the cooperation that should exist between nations.

Excellency, Vice-President of the Republic of Indonesia, Dr. Boediono,
After a very difficult past, Indonesia and Timor-Leste came to embrace, almost at the same time, the path of democratic process.

We commend the very smooth and peaceful transition to democracy, in 1997-1998 which allowed Indonesia to enjoy, once again, another 'pesta demokrasi'.

We wish all the best to this great Nation and to the Indonesian people and express our friendship to all the political parties and our respect to their leaders.

Thank you.

Forum on Trade and Investment Opportunities in Timor-Leste

Kuala Lumpur, 1 April 2014

The Honourable YB Dato' Sri Mustapha Mohamed, Minister of International Trade and Industry
Honourable members of the Malaysian business community
Excellencies
Ladies and Gentlemen,

It is a great pleasure to be here to talk to you about Timor-Leste, Southeast Asia's newest nation and a great place to visit and do business.

May I start, however, by offering my condolences to the families and friends of the passengers of Malaysia Airlines flight MH 370, as well as to the Malaysian people for their loss. In the face of this tragedy, Malaysia is to be commended for managing the situation and for leading a multi-national search effort which has been an outstanding example of leadership and cooperation between the international community.

Yesterday I was honoured to hold bi-lateral discussions with the Prime Minister of Malaysia, the Honourable Najib Razak. Our meeting was held in the spirit of friendship and solidarity between our nations and it led to some very productive outcomes.

Importantly, there was a strong focus on trade and investment. We noted that bilateral trade between our two countries in 2013 was the highest to date, at over $20 million dollars, and that this growth is expected to continue.

We agreed that there was great untapped potential for Malaysian companies to form joint ventures with Timorese companies in areas including health care, infrastructure, agriculture and fisheries and natural resources. To assist this process I agreed with your Prime Minister that we will have an exchange of visits and conduct trade missions to promote closer economic integration.

Following our meeting we were pleased to witness the signing of an MOU between the Ministry of Domestic Trade, Co-operatives and Consumerism of Malaysia and the Timor-Leste Ministry of Commerce, Industry and Environment to establish cooperation in the development of our cooperative sector. This will include promoting participation of the cooperatives of both our countries through the formation of strategic business alliances, joint venture projects, exchanges of expertise and research as well as training and capacity building activities.

During this Official Visit I have also been pleased to meet with senior leaders of Malaysia's oil and gas sector, health care and manufacturing industries. It is clear to me that there is so much scope and opportunity for our two nations to work together to support economic growth and development. And being able to see first-hand Malaysia's remarkable growth and progress provides Timor-Leste with a model of success that we can learn from and from which we can base our future cooperation.

Ladies and Gentlemen,

The birth of our nation brought great hope to our people for a better future of self-determination and freedom. In 2002 we faced the exciting new challenge of learning to live in peace and developing the foundations of a strong and robust State.

We soon learned nation building is a very difficult task. Most of our roads, bridges, schools and hospitals had been destroyed. We had to establish a civil service, a banking system and a court system – all at the same time and all from scratch.

I look back now and sometimes wonder how we did it – because the fact is Timor-Leste has become an international model for reconciliation and national development.

We are a small nation of just over 1 million people but we are fortunate to have a country blessed with natural beauty, rich in natural resources and most importantly, our people are resilient.

Timor-Leste enjoys some of the strongest rates of economic growth in the world. Since 2007, our average growth rate has been 11.9% and the Asian Development Bank predicts double digit rates of growth will continue into the future.

Timor-Leste also has some of the lowest income and corporate tax rates in the world along with generous tax concessions for foreign investors. We also have an efficient and very quick business registration process to support domestic and international business start-ups. We are looking to do whatever we can to support business and build our private sector so that we can continue to grow.

To help realise our potential, and focus our nation building efforts, we produced a 20 year *Strategic Development Plan* in 2011 that provides a framework to transform our country from a low income nation to a country with upper-middle income levels with a healthy, well educated and prosperous population by 2030.

The Plan is based on the premise that to create jobs and build a sustainable future we need to develop a flourishing market economy with a strong and diversified private sector. It identifies three key industries to drive our economic growth: agriculture, tourism and petroleum.

Agriculture is important as over 70 per cent of our population lives in rural areas. We are improving irrigation, road access and seed varieties to actively transform from a subsistence based agricultural system to a market based system. We have seen the great success of Malaysia's agriculture sector and we know there is so much potential for our countries to cooperate together in this important area.

Timor-Leste is also a land of great beauty and promise. Our country is an unspoilt tropical island with stunning beaches and coral reefs. We have steep misty mountain ranges and deep river valleys. It is a great place to visit for people around Asia and beyond.

As you know, with Asia's sustained growth tourism numbers throughout our region continue to increase strongly. For Timor-Leste, this means we need to build more hotels, restaurants and hospitality services. We know that Malaysia has a thriving tourism industry with some of the best international hotels and services so there is great scope to work together to build our own industry. With our tropical beaches, mountain ranges and unique history and heritage, I urge you to consider joining with us to take advantage of our tourism opportunities.

We are also well placed in terms of natural resources. Timor-Leste has significant offshore petroleum resources and substantial onshore mineral resources.

So far, we have only tapped our offshore petroleum resources and all revenue flows directly into our sovereign wealth fund, the Petroleum Fund.

The Petroleum Fund has grown from $1.8 billion in 2007 to around $15 billion today. The Fund is currently growing by several hundred million dollars each month. It underpins our economic growth and our capacity to build our nation and support our people into the future.

Malaysia has a globally significant petroleum industry with technical expertise, experience and capital that would benefit Timor-Leste as we seek to further exploit our natural resources for the benefit of our people.

Because of the importance of our petroleum revenue, which belongs to our people, we are totally committed to transparency. We are proud that Timor-Leste was the first country in Asia and the third country in the world to comply with the Extractive Industry Transparency Initiative.

This means that every dollar earned from our oil and gas resources is accounted for and audited so that the funds are managed transparently for the benefit of our people.

Part of our plan for our petroleum industry is to develop the south coast of our country into a sub-regional industry centre. This development involves three operation clusters along 155 kilometres of coastline. It will include building a Supply Base, with new port facilities and a rehabilitated airport, a refinery with related oil and gas industries and a Liquefied Natural Gas plant.

I know that as we build this new regional hub for the petroleum sector there will be many opportunities to work with Malaysian businesses and benefit from Malaysian investment and expertise.

Ladies and Gentlemen,

While most of the income from our petroleum resources is saved for future generations, we also make withdrawals to fund budget expenditure including our program of infrastructure development and the delivery of education and health services.

We have adopted expansive fiscal policy to help relieve extreme poverty and strengthen our human resources.

We have also planned for a large national infrastructure program including a national port, airports, a road network and a sub-sea internet cable. We are looking to enter into Public Private Partnerships to deliver many of these projects. We know that we will need international firms to deliver major infrastructure projects and so we are looking for partners who can join with us to build our nation.

Timor-Leste will also be establishing Special Economic Zones to encourage and simplify investment. The first to be established will be in the district of Oe-cusse where a new Special Economic and Social Zone will provide incentives, a simple regulatory and tax environment and land to attract foreign investment in industries including tourism, finance and manufacturing.

As you can see, Timor-Leste provides an attractive business environment for foreign investors. With our open economy, expansive fiscal policy, sustained economic growth, comprehensive infrastructure program, low tax rates and strong government support for foreign business we are a good place to consider investing.

Ladies and Gentlemen,

I have come to Malaysia on this Official Visit as part of a tour of all ASEAN countries to advocate for Timor-Leste's accession to ASEAN.

ASEAN is an international model for establishing a region of peace, cooperation and economic growth. As Timor-Leste is part of Southeast Asia we also want to be part of ASEAN and contribute to regional progress. Membership of ASEAN will also allow us to join the economic community that will be established in 2015 and to strengthen trade and investment relations with our Southeast Asian brothers and sisters.

I was delighted when yesterday the Honourable Najib Razak, Prime Minister of Malaysia, pledged Malaysia's support for Timor-Leste's membership of ASEAN. Malaysia plays a very important regional role in promoting peace and cooperation and this endorsement by the Prime Minister is of great value to us.

This is the last ASEAN nation I am visiting as part of my tour of Southeast Asia and the endorsement by the Prime Minister of Malaysia means that we have ended our ASEAN visits on a high note.

Ladies and Gentlemen,

Timor-Leste has established a vibrant and free democracy, a tolerant and peaceful society and the foundations for sustained economic growth.

I hope that some of you look to join us as partners as we continue to build our nation.

Thank you very much.

Address upon Receiving an Honorary PhD in International Relations – 'Timor-Leste and ASEAN: Perspectives and Challenges'

University of Malaysia, Sabah, 2 April 2014

His Excellency Tuan Yang Terutama Tun Datuk Seri Panglima (Dr.) Haji Juhar bin Datuk Haji Mahiruddin, the Head of State of Sabah

Her Excellency Yang Amat Berbahagia Toh Puan Datuk Seri Panglima Hajah Norlidah Datuk R.M. Jasni

The Right Honourable Datuk Seri Panglima Musa Haji Aman, Chief Minister of Sabah, and wife, Yang Amat Berbahagia Datin Seri Panglima Datuk Hajah Faridah binti Tussin

The Right Honourable, YB Datuk Abd Rahim Bakri, Deputy Minister of Defence

Professor Datuk Dr. Mohd. Harun bin Abdullah. Vice-Chancellor, Universiti Malaysia Sabah, and wife, Yang Berbahagia Datin Baidah Ibrahim

The Honourable Federal and State Ministers of Malaysia and Sabah

Distinguished Guests, Principal and Senior Officers of Universiti Malaysia Sabah

Student Representative Council of Universiti Malaysia Sabah

Members of the media

Ladies and Gentlemen,

I would like to start by saying how honoured I am to be here today, in front of such an illustrious audience, receiving this high university award.

University Malaysia Sabah is a prestigious university that has been gaining international recognition. UMS can be characterised with three words – Innovative, Relevant, Sustainable – and is a true temple of knowledge.

As such, it is an enormous privilege for me to address this audience. I must thank the Scientific Council of this University for its generosity in choosing me to share some of my humble knowledge with you. Like many of my countrymen and countrywomen, my perspectives have been forged in our country's struggle for independence, in building it as a State and a Nation, and in finding its place in the world.

The theme 'Timor-Leste and ASEAN: perspectives and challenges' has a special meaning for us Timorese. This is a natural continuation of the path we chose several years ago, seeking to ensure our internal development and stability, as well as contributing to regional stability within this community.

Ladies and Gentlemen,

Timor-Leste, half of a small crocodile-shaped island, with an enclave in the other half, is located in the great archipelago of Indonesia. It is one of around 17,000 islands, one of which includes Sabah. Further to the South, Timor-Leste has Australia and the Pacific islands.

Like many other countries throughout the world, we were a colony for hundreds of years. After conquering Malacca, the Portuguese sent a fleet to the island of Timor, in order to acquire its wealth, in particular sandalwood, honey and wax. They arrived in 1515.

In 2015 we will be proud to celebrate the 500th anniversary of the arrival of the Portuguese in Lifau, in the enclave of Oecusse. We believe that it was this meeting of civilisation and cultures that shaped the destiny of a People, a Country and a Nation – with a history and a culture that are unique in the region!

World War Two, which also affected Timor-Leste from 1942 to 1945, was followed by anti-colonial wars and rushed processes of decolonisation.

Within this context, the Carnation Revolution that took place in Portugal, on 25 April 1974, enabled the Timorese to take on greater responsibility for their people and their land.

As a result of this tense climate of decolonisation and of ideological differences between the Timorese, we began a short-lived civil war that caused a total rupture in the Timorese social fabric.

On 28 November 1975 we unilaterally proclaimed our independence. However, on 7 December of that same year, we were brutally invaded by Indonesia, which had been given a green light by several western powers.

The invasion and the resulting operations of territorial conquest were exercises of total war that had catastrophic effects across the country and caused the death of hundreds of thousands of Timorese citizens. For over two decades, the Timorese people suffered and fought alone, without any military support from overseas. Families, particularly women and children, endured indescribable adversities and abuses.

Our resistance also underwent political changes in late 1986, which consolidated the National Reconciliation efforts and positioned Timor-Leste in the new international setting. Our approach gradually changed, seeking to establish the only possible way towards peace – dialogue with the occupying and oppressor country.

This perception came from the people, from their greatness of spirit and their ability to forgive and to reconcile. Timor-Leste wanted to contribute to the so-called 'New World Order', by rejecting radical thinking and extreme actions.

And so we chose the way of dialogue, with tolerance overcoming vengeance and forgiveness overcoming hatred.

The displays of international solidarity fed the Resistance and gave value to the sacrifices accepted by the people. The Indonesian democratic movement was growing and it heightened internal changes in Indonesia at the time of the Southeast Asia monetary crisis in 1996-1997.

President Habibie opened the 'dossier' of Timor-Leste and, on 5 May 1999, an agreement was signed in New York enabling a popular consultation to hear the voices of a small people situated between two large neighbours, supported by other powerful countries. The human rights of the Timorese depended on economic interests, particularly key industries such as oil.

30 August was a red-letter day for the Timorese. The results left no doubt and confirmed to the sceptics and to the world that the entire Timorese people had longed for freedom for over two decades!

However, the joy of victory was torn apart by the exasperating violence of a few who had benefitted from the occupation and did not want to accept the democratic choice of the majority.

Ladies and Gentlemen,

Achieving our freedom was not the end of the struggle of the Timorese. Instead, it was the start of a new chapter that was at least as difficult as the one of ending the war. We know that peace requires the healing of wounds through pragmatic decisions and policies that put an end to hatred and mistrust and that deal with the difficulties faced everyday by the people.

Building the Timorese State was an enormous challenge, since our infrastructure had been destroyed, our human resources were weak and we had no governing experience. Additionally, there were no State institutions and no legal framework, and the people were suffering, with many families having been separated due to mistaken beliefs or the circumstances of violence.

Timor-Leste received the care and the solidarity of the international community. From September 1999 to the Restoration of Independence we had a strong military and political presence by the international community, including our brothers and sisters from Malaysia. This presence enabled the transitional administration of the territory, under the banner of the UN.

We started creating the necessary institutional frameworks and we created political parties, eleven of which were elected to form the Constituent Assembly that drafted the Constitution of the Republic. Finally, on 20 May 2002, we regained our sovereignty, which meant that we had the power to decide the future of the people and of the country.

Because living in peace means living free from corrosive feelings and reconciling with our enemies and more importantly with ourselves, both individually and collectively, one of the first measures we took was to reunify families and communities across the border.

Our people forgave their Timorese brothers and sisters who had fled to Indonesia and asked them to come back, even those who had defended and fought for integration, so that we might build Timor-Leste together. It is also important to mention that the Timorese embraced the goal of establishing an open relationship of solidarity with the Indonesians, so that both peoples could prosper.

We understood from the experiences of other post-conflict countries that it would be impossible to build our Nation if hatred and distrust were still present in our society.

Reconciliation is a prerequisite for national stability, which is in turn a requirement for development.

We established the CAVR (Commission for Reception, Truth and Reconciliation), the first commission for reconciliation created in our part of Asia. We were pioneers in the promotion of Human Rights, creating a model that seeks the truth about the violence that took place and that helps the people come to terms with the truth.

The people of Indonesia and the people of Timor-Leste added a new chapter to the history of democracy in Southeast Asia. Indonesia left behind its past of autocratic governance and Timor-Leste started its path of national sovereignty and independence. Our peoples also chose democracy, the rule of law and to live in close cooperation and friendship with one another.

The creation in Bali of a Commission of Truth and Friendship, in a joint effort between Timor-Leste and Indonesia, enabled us to continue strengthening our friendship and to contribute to peace in Southeast Asia. I believe that our common history and the difficult processes that we have endured and overcome may be an example of peace and reconciliation in the region and in the world.

The violations and offences that took place were assessed with great courage, particularly on the part of the victims. This enabled a very close relationship between Indonesians and Timorese, which has contributed very significantly to the development of Timor-Leste. Indonesia is more than a close neighbour of solidarity; it is also an example of stability, democracy and economic growth that inspires Timor-Leste.

Ladies and Gentlemen,

After these twelve years as a sovereign State, we can say that our People live in peace, security and stability. This, together with the structural reforms we have made in our public institutions, enabled us to establish the foundation for our economic development.

However, this was a complex progress, with errors and setbacks that had to be corrected gradually.

We entered a vicious cycle of conflict every two years, as if to remind us that peace is an extremely delicate flower that must be watered with great care. It was necessary for the State institutions to cooperate among themselves in the search for solutions. The permanent and ongoing dialogue and cooperation between all Bodies of Sovereignty and Civil Society were essential to the process.

So we finally managed to break that vicious cycle! In 2009, celebrating the 10th anniversary of the popular consultation, we launched the motto: 'Goodbye Conflict, Welcome Development'. The people understood that we should not allow even one more drop of blood to be spilled due to political reasons or divisions in our society.

Since then, Timor-Leste has been living in permanent stability. This has enabled us to assess ourselves socially, politically and economically, so that we could face the challenges of today's globalised world.

Today we have our State institutions operating confidently and improving day by day. Although our private sector is still embryonic one, we have been supporting it in order to diversify our economy, which cannot depend exclusively on oil.

Ladies and Gentlemen,

We have been growing at an average of 11.9% every year since 2007. Our Petroleum Fund is currently worth over 15 billion dollars. We are also improving on several human development indicators and are attracting the international private sector, making use of the privileged relationships that we enjoy in the region and in the world.

We are implementing our *Strategic Development Plan 2011-2030*, which provides a comprehensive framework for transforming Timor-Leste into an upper middle income country by 2030, with a healthy and educated population that lives in safety.

We were the first country in Asia and the third in the world to be granted compliance status with the EITI (Extractive Industries Transparency Initiative), meaning that each dollar from our petroleum revenues is publicly disclosed and that it is cross-checked with the records of the resource companies.

We have created a National Petroleum Authority, employing some of the most academically qualified men and women in Timor-Leste. This Authority is responsible for managing and regulating petroleum activities in the exclusive jurisdiction areas of Timor-Leste and in the Joint Petroleum Development Area with Australia.

We are creating a highly transparent public financial management system, where any person in the world may monitor in real time our budget execution, our procurement and, more importantly, our results.

We have provided pensions to veterans, the elderly, widows, the disabled and orphans. We also introduced similar social justice measures for other vulnerable groups such as children and the young.

We have established local development programs to create employment and to improve the living conditions of the people in rural areas, particularly in regard to health, electricity, water and sanitation and access to education and markets. We have also started building community neighbourhoods in several places.

We have completed the largest infrastructure project in our history in building a national power grid that generates electricity and distributes it to the entire country.

We are also starting an infrastructure program seeking to provide the bases that ensure a sustainable economic future for the nation, including a new national port, significant improvements in our airport, a national road network and the extensive development of our southern coast, so as to become a sub-regional centre for the petroleum industry.

We have created a Human Capital Development Fund to develop our nation's human resources. We are also sending students to several Asian countries so that they may acquire the necessary skills to build our State.

We know that the path is still arduous and that managing the expectations of the Timorese requires us to be very careful, particularly since over half of the population is under 25. We need to make choices between immediate needs and long term goals. Nevertheless, we are moving on the right track as a State and we are defining our role within the Community of Nations.

Ladies and Gentlemen,

At the international level we have several challenges ahead of us, such as the formal membership of ASEAN and the presidency of the Community of Portuguese Speaking Countries (CPLP) in 2014-2016. Timor-Leste wants to have an active presidency and to make the economic component more visible.

In July we will be holding the Summit of the Community of Portuguese Speaking Countries in Díli. These countries share a common past and want to respond collectively to the challenges faced by each, with programmatic actions resulting in social and economic benefits for our populations.

Since this is the first time that Timor-Leste will hold the presidency of the CPLP, we of course feel a great sense of responsibility. Still, we also feel very honoured and very committed to working hard. This will also be a litmus test in terms of our organisational ability, so that we may join ASEAN.

Timor-Leste is strategically located between the CPLP countries and ASEAN, China and the Island States of the Pacific. In today's economically troubled world, it is important to be close to the global economic and financial centres and to explore their potential.

Like ASEAN, CPLP has several facets, including cooperation at State institution level, social and cultural components – namely language –, defence, security and economics. At present, Timor-Leste has the political conditions to promote a serious and honest discussion that leads to a sustainable economic development plan for its member States.

Under our presidency, we want to breathe new life into our policies, which must be in line with the global requirements of today. We also want to make use of our strategic positioning in Southeast Asia, since we have the possibility of creating bridges with Europe, Africa and Latin America.

Ladies and Gentlemen,

These considerations bring us to the international focus of support and work with other fragile States throughout the world. An important part of this is the work with the g7+ group, which is presided over by Timor-Leste and brings together 18 countries from the Caribbean to the Pacific and from Africa to Asia.

During our own Statebuilding process we noticed that the international agencies of support and the United Nations pursued the wrong approaches to development in fragile and post-conflict countries. The international community insisted on a 'one size fits all' policy and felt that it was in a position to say what was best for those peoples, without taking into account the specificities and the necessary timings of each development process.

Instead of being seen as a social process, democracy became an exact science, like an end unto itself, in which elections were supposed to be the cure for every illness.

We continue having difficulty in finding a common understanding with the experts on the poverty of others, who still have to prove that the billions of dollars spent every year with assistance have in fact reduced extreme poverty even if just in one small part of the world.

It is clear that the world does not have a proper solution for the problems that affect humankind, particularly when we all committed to the Millennium Development Goals right at the start of this millennium. Fourteen years later, we see that millions and millions of people continue living in extreme poverty and are dying of hunger and chronic illnesses, becoming easy prey to violence and conflict.

It was within this context that, in April 2010, Timor-Leste invited several post-conflict and fragile countries to an International Conference on Peacebuilding and Statebuilding, in Díli. At this conference we were able to discuss our weaknesses and our potential to assume responsibility for correcting systems and mindsets, so as to deserve renewed trust by our partners, who would commit to respecting the decisions of each country.

The g7+ countries know all too well that without peace and stability it is not possible to have development. No fragile or conflict-afflicted nation has managed to achieve a single Millennium Development Goal.

This means that it will not be possible to eradicate world poverty without first dealing with the issues of fragile and conflict-affected nations. Timor-Leste led the drafting of a 'New Deal', which was presented at the Fourth High Level Forum on Aid Effectiveness, in November 2011, in Busan.

This 'New Deal' was accepted by the World Bank and the IMF in order for each country to determine its priorities in terms of international aid. This seeks to enable each country to have ownership over its own process.

This New Deal is also being considered by the UN in its post-2015 Development Agenda. Timor-Leste is proud to have its Minister of Finance, Ms Emília Pires, as a member of the High Level Panel that advised the Secretary General of the United Nations on this agenda. Last year Timor-Leste hosted in Díli an International Conference on the Post-2015 Development Agenda, receiving leaders from various countries, including the Asia-Pacific and Africa.

These discussions and deliberations had several outcomes, including the 'Díli Consensus', which establishes our priorities and hopes for the post-2015 development agenda. One key aspect in this document is that it states that we need to set a credible, responsible and realistic path towards development.

Ladies and Gentlemen,

ASEAN is an international success story, having established a region of peace, cooperation and development. Since Timor-Leste is part of Southeast Asia, the questions is not *whether* Timor-Leste will become a full-fledged member of ASEAN, but rather *when* it will do so.

We symbolically submitted our formal membership request on 4 March 2011, the year when Indonesia took on the Chair of ASEAN. This request was accepted at the 19th Summit of the Organisation.

Since last year I have been officially visiting each ASEAN country. Malaysia is the final step on this tour. All countries I visited were extremely welcoming and supportive of our integration.

We have established diplomatic relations in Indonesia, Malaysia, Thailand, Singapore, the Philippines and Vietnam. We are currently establishing Embassies in Brunei Darussalam, Cambodia, Laos and Myanmar.

The ASEAN Coordination Council has established a Working Group (ACC Working Group) to discuss all issues related to our request. The ASEAN Secretariat, particularly the Economic Division, sought support from the Asian Development Bank to conduct a study and assess the readiness of Timor-Leste. The main goal was to review the impact, implications and challenges of Timor-Leste's application and its ratification of the ASEAN Economic Agreements.

We are presently implementing the recommendations made by this study. We will follow the same procedures for assessing and complying with other necessary requirements, particularly in terms of Security and of Social and Cultural Aspects.

We are aware of our limitations and of the challenges imposed on us to become an asset to ASEAN. However, being the youngest and poorest country in the region, Timor-Leste sees membership in ASEAN as a way to multiply opportunities for its own development. Ultimately, this will benefit both the member countries and the Community as a whole.

Our country and our economy have been growing steadily year after year. We were one of the top ten nations for the highest levels economic growth in the world in 2011.

The investment plans started at the level of core infrastructure, human capacity and sector development have enabled this growth, mobilising the economy and accelerating the human, social and economic development of the young nation. The plans have also responded to the concerns raised by some ASEAN countries regarding our integration capacity.

We are frequently asked what Timor-Leste can offer to ASEAN. I would respond that, despite our challenges in the area of human resources and in terms of adjusting our legislation to that practiced by the members of the association, we have a 12-year history of Statebuilding and Nationbuilding.

We have made extraordinary progress in view of the time it took us and the truly difficult circumstances in which we achieved it.

Ladies and Gentlemen,

As a member and holding the chairmanship of the 69th session of the Economic and Social Commission for Asia and the Pacific of the United Nations, we understand the great challenges ahead for the region's more underprivileged countries in terms of physical, energy and communication infrastructure, so as to reduce social inequalities and regional economic imbalances within each country and in their relationships with their neighbours.

Timor-Leste, Indonesia and Australia are committed to signing a trilateral agreement towards a sub-regional triangular development area covering the three closest Indonesian provinces, Timor-Leste and the Northern Territory of Australia.

Additionally, under our new development paradigm focused on the people, the enclave of Oecusse will become a Special Zone of Social Market Economy. This will be a special zone with an economy focusing on the market of the region, while looking for potential perspectives to expand beyond it.

Economic development will only have meaning if it benefits the people. Although economic prosperity is a key ingredient for a prosperous society, the building of a nation and the wellbeing of a population cannot be measured only by the material goods to which they have access.

Equity, mutual respect, justice, tolerance and non-interference are principles to be followed by every ASEAN nation, since this has been the formula for the success of the organisation.

The challenge, which obviously will not be exclusive to Timor-Leste, is framing the legal and judicial system in order to achieve greater harmony with the laws of the Community.

Ladies and Gentlemen,

Regional stability would not have been possible without the formation of a strong political alliance that gradually become a block of economic integration, using diplomacy as an art towards common development. ASEAN has played a key role in ensuring common security, by neutralising decade-old points of tension and promoting peace and stability, making an impact that is felt far from our region.

We salute the signing of the peace agreement between the Government of the Philippines and MILF, in which the Malaysian Prime Minister, the Honourable Najib Razak, played a key role.

Several regional organisations of discussion and forums, where dialogue is a common denominator, became consolidated and institutionalised. Presently, more than reflecting on the future, they are shaping that very future. ASEAN, APEC, ARF (where Timor-Leste has been a full-fledged member since 2005) and, more recently, the Bali Democracy Forum, the Shangri-la Initiative and the Jakarta International Defence Dialogue are good examples.

Timor-Leste is monitoring their progress closely. Although we are the youngest nation in the region, we already have a strong sense of regionalism and we have been adopting public policies that fit in this development framework. We started this by prioritizing policies promoting reconciliation and the promotion of internal security and national stability.

We want to make an active contribution in order to reduce the array of possible threats and the many challenges ahead of us, including the management of transnational security threats, as well as to cooperate in terms of humanitarian assistance, disaster relief, environmental management and response to climate change.

Dialogue, the asset of diplomacy, is the only weapon that can deal with the problems of our time.

As such, sharing security challenges in our region will contribute to improve strategic trust between countries in the region. In the present situation, building trust between countries should be a more important and safer investment than preparing for war. Timor-Leste is watching the developments in the South China Sea with concern, but it trusts that ASEAN can contribute to the easing of tensions.

China and USA are two giants that will play a vital role in the prosperous and safe development of Asia and the Pacific in the future. A positive and cooperative relationship between these two powers is vital to the integrated and sustainable development of all small and large countries in the region and in the world.

Regarding strategic issues and maritime challenges in the region, we must bear in mind that we require an effort of collective cooperation in order to ensure peaceful coexistence and to overcome differences between nations. The interests of one party must not hinder the legitimate development expectations of another party. Diplomacy – together with considered defence capabilities – is essential to maintain peace and stability, based on cooperation between States. This cooperation must defend the genuine interests of the peoples, rather than the interests of the countries and of their leaders.

Being such a small country, we do not harbour illusions of grandeur that we will make enormous contributions to the region's maritime security. However, we recognise the need for active cooperation with all who are close to our maritime borders.

Ladies and Gentlemen,

In view of the above, there is a clear national consensus in Timor-Leste on joining ASEAN. The establishment of the ASEAN Community in 2015, with the coming together of nations under a strong commitment towards sustainable development, peace, stability and prosperity, is the path in which Timor-Leste believes. It is also the cornerstone of our foreign policy.

We see ASEAN as a dynamic and united community, with leaders that safeguard the collective interests of the nations, guided by ethical considerations and valorising assistance rather than dependence between States. As a result of its experience and its relationship with the International Community, particularly as a recipient of aid, Timor-Leste views ASEAN as a model of integration that preserves the emancipation of its countries and the dignities of their peoples.

Lastly, and because I believe that ASEAN's great success is based on mutual respect, without pretentions of dominance or condescendence, Timor-Leste is pleased to hear those who say that we are not yet ready to join this organisation. This responsible, open and honest dialogue leads us to believe that we are building serious strategic alliances. On our part, we are committed to overcoming any obstacles.

All of this, Ladies and Gentlemen, adds a new chapter to the history of Southeast Asia and provides a great lesson for the rest of the world. More importantly, it gives hope to the world's fragile and underdeveloped countries that are still walking their path towards development.

In the geostrategic chessboard of Southeast Asia, all pieces are important – even the smaller ones, with small economies and populations. Their importance is not so much in terms of military, political or economic capacity, but rather in terms of the stability they can provide in the region. As we know, currently the main agents of threats are not necessarily States. Instead, they are agents from countries where poverty and inequalities persist.

Address at a Western Australia Business Lunch Hosted by DLA Piper

Perth, 4 April 2014

Andrew Darwin, Chief Operating Officer and Managing Director, DLA Piper
Allan Drake-Brockman, Perth Managing Partner, DLA Piper
Stephen Webb, Partner, DLA Piper
Stephanie Airey, DLA Piper
And I associate myself with the acknowledgements given by Andrew Darwin
Excellencies
Ladies and Gentlemen,

It is a great pleasure to be here in Perth and to have this lunch with you to talk about Timor-Leste's progress and opportunities.

I have just come from an Official Visit to Malaysia where there was much enthusiasm for investing in Timor-Leste. In my discussion with the Malaysian Prime Minister, the Honourable NajibRazak, we also agreed to make trade and investment a core part of our bi-lateral relationship.

At this time, I also give my condolences to the families and friends of the passengers of Malaysia Airlines flight MH 370 and I commend the international cooperation of the search effort.

Ladies and Gentlemen,

Timor-Leste is only 12 years old as a self-governing State. When our nation was born we had to start from scratch. We had no State institutions and no experience of governance, we had no court system nor legal framework, no infrastructure, no health or education services, no banking system and no funds. We had to secure peace in a society brutalised by war; and we had to build a State.

Looking back, it is amazing how much we have achieved. We now live in peace, in a tolerant and free democracy that upholds the rule of law and human rights. Timor-Leste now enjoys some of the strongest rates of economic growth in the world. Since 2007, our average growth rate has been 11.9% and the Asian Development Bank predicts strong growth to continue.

To realise our potential, and focus our efforts, we produced a 20 year *Strategic Development Plan* in 2011 that provides a framework to transform our country from a low income nation to a country with upper-middle income levels with a healthy, well-educated and prosperous population by 2030.

To achieve our objectives we need to create more jobs and build a sustainable and diversified market economy. We are fortunate to have petroleum resources and revenue which flows directly into our sovereign wealth fund, the Petroleum Fund. This Fund has grown from $1.8 billion in 2007 to around $15 billion today – and it continues to grow.

Because of the importance of our petroleum revenue we are totally committed to transparency and are proud that Timor-Leste was the first country in Asia, and the third country in the world, to comply with the Extractive Industry Transparency Initiative. This means that every dollar earned is accounted for and audited.

Part of our plan for our petroleum industry is to develop our south coast into a sub-regional industry centre. This development includes building a Supply Base, with new port facilities and a rehabilitated airport, a refinery with related oil and gas industries and a Liquefied Natural Gas plant.

Western Australia is a powerhouse of the resources industry and, with our low cost base, we look to integrate our south coast development into the regional industry.

As many of you know, Timor-Leste is also a land of great beauty. Our country is a tropical island with stunning beaches and coral reefs. We have deep river valleys that carve through our mountain ranges. And so, we are also developing our tourism industry to tap into the expanding Asian market.

We have also planned for a large infrastructure program including a national port, airports, a road network and a sub-sea internet cable. We know that we will need international firms to deliver our major projects and we are looking for partners who can join with us to build our nation.

Timor-Leste will also be establishing Special Economic Zones to encourage and simplify investment. The first to be established will be in the district of Oe-cusse to attract foreign investment in industries including tourism, finance and manufacturing. Further zones will then be established elsewhere in Timor Leste.

Ladies and Gentlemen,

Timor-Leste provides an attractive business environment for foreign investors. With our open economy, expansive fiscal policy, sustained economic growth, large infrastructure program, low tax rates and strong government support for foreign business we are a good place to invest.

Tomorrow I will be leaving for an Official Visit to China and meetings with the President, Premier and the Chairman of the Standing Committee of the National People's Congress. We know that much of Australia's economy is tied to the fortunes of China. Timor-Leste is also benefiting from an increase in interest and investment from China. The former Prime Minister of Timor-Leste, Mari Alkatiri, has been charged with responsibility for our Special Economic Zones and he will be joining me next week at the invitation of the Chinese government to visit the Xiamen Special Economic Zone.

As the centre of the global economy shifts to our region, Timor-Leste plans to be part of this great Asian growth story.

We urge you to consider the opportunities for business investment that our nation provides and I invite you all to visit our beautiful country.

Later during this lunch we will hear from four companies that are engaged with investments and developments in Timor-Leste and I thank the ANZ Banking Group, Sang Tai Hoo, the Buckeridge Group and DCC Capital for presenting to us.

Thank you for coming today and for your interest in our young nation.

Special Event SAS Charity Dinner*

Perth, 4 April 2014

His Excellency, Malcolm McKusker AV CVO QC, the Governor of Western Australia and Mrs McKusker
The Honourable Julie Bishop MP, Minister for Foreign Affairs
Senator, the Honourable David Johnston, minister for Defence
The Honourable Joe Francis, MLA, Western Australian Minister for Veterans Affairs
The Honourable Alannah Mc Tiernan MP
The Honourable Tony Simpson, Western Australian Minister for Local Government
The Honourable Melissa Park, Member of Parliament
The Honourable Chris Ellison
The Honourable Peter Blaxell, Chairman SAS Resources Fund
Lieutenant Colonel Greg Daly, Commanding Officer and Mrs Daly
Air Chief Marshall (Ret) Angus Houston AC AFC
The Honourable Graham Edwards AM, State President of the RSL
Members of the Australian Defence Force
Current and former members of the Special Air Service Regiment
Family of members of the Special Air Service Regiment
Ladies and Gentlemen,

It is a great privilege to be with you tonight at this dinner to honour the Special Air Service Regiment and to support the families of SAS members.

When I was invited by the SAS Resources Fund to speak at a fund raising dinner I made it a priority to come to Perth. It is important not only to me, but to the people of Timor-Leste, to give thanks to the SAS for their service to our nation.

I can speak personally about the courage and the dedication of the SAS.

While there was elation at our people's overwhelming vote for independence in 1999, the aftermath brought chaos. In the violence that followed the vote many died, our country was destroyed and many of our people fled to the mountains. When I returned to this turmoil, the SAS were by my side.

We will always remember that, at this very difficult time, when we were taking our first steps as a free people, the SAS and the Australian Defence Forces were with us.

Ladies and Gentlemen,

As you know, the Australian military and its special forces have a long history of operations in our country which began during the Second World War.

It was during the Second World War that Australia first established elite special forces units. Two of the first units served in what was then Portuguese Timor. In December 1941 the 2/2nd Independent Company, represented here tonight by their families and supporters, landed in neutral Portuguese Timor. The following February the Japanese invaded. The 2/2nd conducted a guerrilla style campaign in our mountains and valleys and held down an entire Japanese Army division for almost twelve months. In September 1942 the 2/4th Independent Company joined the 2/2nd in this guerrilla campaign and carried out successful ambushes, bombing raids and surveillance.

These Australian special forces were clearly brave, remarkable men. But they could not have been so effective without the support of the thousands of Timorese villagers who risked their lives to provide food and shelter, carry supplies and act as guides and scouts for the Australian soldiers. I know in Australia you call the good men of Papua New Guinea who did the same thing the Fuzzy Wuzzy Angels and in Timor-Leste they were called Criados. By January 1943 the 2/2nd and 2/4th had withdrawn back to Australia and the Timorese men, women and children paid an awful price with up to 60,000 killed during the Japanese occupation which lasted until the end of the war.

That is why, thirty years later, many Timorese felt hurt and betrayed when Australia supported Indonesia's occupation of our country in 1975.

It was comforting to hear many former members of 2/2nd and the 2/4th Independent Companies acknowledging the debt they owed the Timorese when they spoke out during our campaign for a fair share of resources in the Timor Sea some years ago.

We should also remember the link between those original special forces units, the Commandos, that served in Timor in II World War and today's SAS. I understand that the success of the 2/2nd and the 2/4th was later used as a model for training of the SAS.

Ladies and Gentlemen,

As I have already mentioned, the Australian Defences Forces and notably the SAS returned to our county in 1999. On 20 September 1999, the International Forces for East Timor, known as INTERFET, was deployed to Timor and was led by Australia. INTERFET commanded by my good friend, then Major General Peter Cosgrove who, now Sir Peter, with the help of the SAS and Australian and international soldiers, did an outstanding job in helping to restore order and security to our country. The contribution of INTERFET is remembered well by our people, and by me.

The Timorese people have a special sensibility not only to express their feelings but also to preserve their memories.

Right after the announcement of the result of the referendum, because of the violence and killings in Díli, many people took refuge in the UNAMET compound.

A baby was born in that compound and named Pedro UNAMET expressing not only the mother's anguish but also giving thanks for the fact she could deliver her child safely.

The same happened in the enclave of Oe-cusse when a woman was giving birth while Australian INTERFET tanks were rolling past her door. And so, in gratitude to the Australian forces, she named, at that very moment, her new child INTERFET.

As with that mother, the Timorese people will always remember the important role the SAS played during that time.

Ladies and Gentlemen,

As is the case in many post-conflict countries, Timor-Leste struggled with stability in its early years and in 2006 we descended into unrest and violence.

Again, the Australian military, working with the New Zealand military, returned as part of the International Stabilisation Force. They joined Malaysian Forces and the Portuguese para-military GNR to help restore peace and order. The ISF left Timor-Leste in 2012 and we have enjoyed many years of peace and stability. Ladies and Gentlemen, we have said goodbye to conflict and we are now building our State and developing our country.

Timor-Leste will always acknowledge the contribution made by Australia during our journey to peace and stability and we will always honour the involvement of the SAS. We want to celebrate our shared history, remember the sacrifices of our people and retain the links and the memories.

We know that Australians are proud of their military history and the service of their soldiers around the world. We would be pleased to welcome more Australians to Timor-Leste to see first-hand not only the conditions faced by their soldiers but the success of the country they have helped build.

Today, I was pleased to be given a tour of the SAS Barracks and I was very impressed by what a saw. I was also honoured to lay a wreath at the memorial at the SAS barracks in memory of the fallen soldiers, both men and women, of the Australian defence forces.

Ladies and Gentlemen,

In Timor-Leste during the resistance we saw the great dignity and resilience of our people in the face of terror. We witnessed remarkable acts of sacrifice and saw ordinary people cope with terrible adversity and deprivation. Through all the horror and the violence we were reminded of the enduring hope and the essential goodness of humanity.

During the occupation the Timorese people stood up to fight for their homeland and for self-determination. They did this knowing the costs of resistance and knowing that many would die for their right to live in freedom. In the early years of our resistance we suffered awful losses as we were just learning how to wage war while at the same time we were overwhelmed by the occupier. The resistance was almost decimated. But like the Australian special forces that fought in Timor in World War II we mobilised a small force and waged a guerrilla war. And from this we built our struggle and brought our people together to fight for liberation.

Today in our country we remember the martyrs of this struggle who died so we could be free. We also honour the veterans of our struggle who gave so much for their people. Some complain that we provide too much support to our veterans and to their families, they say that we cannot afford it – but who would we be as a people if we did not honour those that fought for our freedom and make sure that their families do not live in poverty.

I want to acknowledge here the RSL of Western Australia which is hosting a group of our Veterans visiting here in a few weeks and on ANZAC Day as well. They are here with an invitation from the National President of the RSL, Mr Steve Doolan.

Today in Timor-Leste we are drawing on the same reserves of courage and determination we showed in war towards building our nation. We want a healthy, well-educated and prosperous population.

Timor-Leste has already achieved a great deal. Our country now enjoys sustained peace and stability, with a successful democracy, the rule of law and a tolerant and free society. Our economy is one of the fastest growing in the world and we are taking big steps to alleviate extreme poverty and improve the lives of our people.

We also know that much still needs to be done. Many of our people suffer every day from poverty, poor living conditions and disadvantage. We need to improve our health care and education, our housing and sanitation, as well as basic infrastructure including roads and communications. We have a long term plan that provides a framework for our development but to succeed we will need to draw on the strengths we showed during the resistance.

We also know that Timor-Leste enjoys many friends that are working together with us as we build our country. This includes the Australian people and the Australian Government and I would like to take this opportunity to thank the Honourable Julie Bishop for her dedicated support of Australia Timor-Leste relations. I understand that at an event held in Canberra last year, Minister Bishop said in her speech regarding the relationship between our two nations that 'the best is yet to come'; I hope so Minister, and look forward to overcoming areas of challenge and working together.

Ladies and Gentlemen,

In Timor-Leste we have great respect for the way that Australia honours its Veterans and remembers all those that served and died in battle. The attendance at this dinner is an example of the importance that your nation rightly places on supporting your soldiers and their families.

In Timor-Leste we know as good as any the brutality, the despair and the utter heart break and hopelessness of war. War is not an adventure. It is full of madness and horror. The invasion and occupation of Timor-Leste had a catastrophic impact on our people who were held hostage by violence for a generation.

We know that the costs of war are not just borne by the soldiers. There is also a great cost to families both during and after conflict. The impact on families is often hidden while they bear the brunt of trauma and grief. And the greatest sacrifice is borne by the loved ones of soldiers that do not return.

Tonight, we are honoured to be joined by the wives of four members of the SAS that served in Timor-Leste and that have since died in combat. We honour:

Mrs Leigh Locke, wife of Sergeant Matthew Locke, MG, deceased
Mrs TA Diddams, wife of Sergeant Blaine Diddams, MG, deceased
Mrs Naomi Nary, wife of Warrant Officer Class Two David Nary, deceased
Mrs Taryn Linacre, wife of Sergeant Craig Linacre, deceased.

While she was able to attend tonight I would also like to honour Mrs Kylie Russell, wife of Sergeant Andrew Russell, deceased.

I cannot stand here and tell you that we can measure the contribution of these SAS members – it is not possible to value. On behalf of Timor-Leste I give thanks for their service to our nation and together we all say, lest we forget.

Ladies and Gentlemen,

We honour the members of the SAS and tonight we honour their families and loved ones. I salute the SAS Members living and fallen. Timor-Leste gives thanks to the contribution of SAS members in not only protecting me on my return to my homeland, but in putting their lives at risk to protect the Timorese people.

I also pay tribute to the SAS Resources Trust and its supporters for the great work in giving comfort to the families of SAS members.

Thank you for inviting me tonight. It is a special honour.

Thank you very much.

* With the Minister of Defence and Security

Boao Forum for Asia Annual Conference 2014 – 'Asia's New Future: Identifying Growth Drivers', Keynote Speech

Hainan Province, China, 8 April 2014

H.E. Mr Li Keqiang, Premier of China
The Hon. Tony Abbott MP, Prime Minister of Australia
His Excellency, Jung Hong-won, Prime Minister of the Republic of Korea
H.E. Thongsing Thammavong, Prime Minister of Laos People's Democratic Republic
His Excellency, Hage Geingob, Prime Minister of Namibia
H.E. Muhammad Nawaz Sharif, Prime Minister of Pakistan
H.E. Arkady Dvorkovich, Deputy Prime Minister of Russia
H.E. Deputy Prime Minister Vu Duc Dam, Deputy Prime Minister of the Socialist Republic of Vietnam
H.E. Yasuo Kukuda, Chairman, Boao Forum for Asia
H.E. Zhou Wendzhong, Secretary General, Boao Forum for Asia
Excellencies
Ladies and Gentlemen,

It is a great pleasure and an honour to speak to you at this most important Asian Conference.

With the theme of this year's conference 'Asia's New Future, Identifying Growth Drivers', we will be exploring the dynamics of the great geo-political transition of our time. Now, more than ever, it is critical that we engage in dialogue, including at conferences such as this, to ensure that the transition to Asia's new future is peaceful and beneficial for all.

We are part of a great shift in global economic and strategic weight to Asia. In this new Asia, we will see the world's financial capitals in our region, not only Hong Kong and Singapore, but also Shanghai and Mumbai, Jakarta and Tokyo, Seoul and Shenzhen. As Asia powers global production, as well as consumption, we will become the centre of international focus as strategic geo-politics is played out in our region.

The Global Financial Crisis, which exposed the moral bankruptcy and endemic failure of the international financial system, has hastened this shift to Asia and continues to cause havoc on both sides of the Atlantic.

The drivers of growth in the new Asia, however, continue unabated. Emerging economies continue to grow and drive global growth. In coming decades, and in South East Asia alone, we will see Indonesia become one of the world's largest economies. Asia's rise will produce a massive regional middle class of hundreds of millions of people driving huge increases in consumption and production.

And of course, unrelenting technological progress is not only transforming productivity and how we do business but is changing the global social fabric and connecting us all in ways unthinkable in the past.

Central to the transition to the new Asia is the rise of China. We look to the achievements of China with awe and admiration. With outstanding leadership, and guided by the traditions of an ancient culture, China is harnessing the energy of its people and by the end of this decade will become the largest economy in the world. The dragon is roaring and no one will be unaffected by the rise of a modern and advanced superpower as it shakes the world bringing peaceful development and widespread prosperity.

The rise of China, along with Asia, is bringing benefits to our small nation of Timor-Leste which has been enjoying peace, good governance and some of the highest rates of economic growth in the world.

Ladies and Gentlemen,

The rise of Asia is lifting hundreds of millions of people out of poverty, at a level never seen before in human history, and is driving global growth and innovation. But as we transition to the new Asia we must be aware of the challenges.

Some of our economic growth has not been balanced and extreme poverty remains. Inequality is rising which presents risks to our social fabric and progress. While the Asia-Pacific region is home to many of the world's great economic powers, it is also home to nearly two-thirds of the world's poor. The lack of infrastructure, such as road networks, energy and telecommunications, is the most challenging issue in the Asia-Pacific, especially in land locked countries.

Problems are also most acute in fragile and conflict affected nations, not only in other parts of the world but also in our region. Not one fragile nation has achieved a single Millennium Development Goal, and the global development agenda needs to turn its focus to these countries.

At the same time the rise of the Asian middle class will see increased consumption impacting the sustainability of resources while the existential challenge of climate change must be addressed.

And of course, we cannot deny growing regional strategic tensions at the same time as the region's growing prosperity allows nations to modernise and expand their defence forces.

And so, we must look to a new paradigm of global engagement which is driven by the common good and international law and not the self-interest of the rich and the powerful.

Now, as much as ever, we need dialogues such as this conference so that we can build and strengthen positive relationships of respect and friendship; and together navigate a path towards a new Asia of cooperation, stability and prosperity for all.

Thank you very much.

Boao Forum for Asia Annual Conference 2014 – 'Asia's New Future: Identifying New Growth Drivers', Session 12, 'Reviving The Silk Road: A Dialogue with Asian Leaders'

Boao, China, 10 April 2013

H.E. Thongsing Thammavong, Prime Minister of Laos People's Democratic Republic
H.E. Muhammad Nawaz Sharif, Prime Minister of Pakistan
H.E. Yang Jiechi, State Councillor, People's Republic of China
H.E. Zhang Guobao, Chairman, the Advisory Board, National Energy Commission of China
H.E. Surakiart Sathirathai, Former Deputy Prime Minister and Minister for Foreign Affairs of Thailand
Excellencies
Ladies and Gentlemen,

It is a special pleasure to be here as part of such an illustrious international panel to discuss Reviving the Silk Road; an initiative that has the potential to drive global growth and cooperation.

At this Boao Conference we are identifying growth drivers for Asia's New Future. These include technological progress, the rise of emerging markets, the expanding Asian middle class and the benefits of an interconnected and globalised world. The great value of Reviving the Silk Road is that it leverages off these emerging economic trends with a concrete initiative to strengthen trade as well as international peace, cooperation and friendship.

The initiative plans to revive the ancient overland and maritime routes that extended from China to Europe and Africa through Central, Southeast and South Asia. These routes, which were driven by the trade in fine Chinese silk, opened up the world and became important channels for trade and people to people exchange as well as the transfer of culture and ideas.

During a visit to Kazakhstan last October the President of China, H.E. Xi Jinping, proposed reviving the overland route from China through Central Asia to Europe. Taking in a population of over 3 billion people along this route the potential gains are vast. With parts of Central Asia suffering from a lack of modern rail and road networks, the Silk Road initiative has the potential to drive infrastructure development and super-charge growth and prosperity.

In a speech to the Indonesian Parliament in October last year President Xi Jinping also proposed the revival of the Maritime Silk Road between ASEAN nations and China. Later this proposal was extended through to South Asia and on to Africa and has been warmly received by countries along the route.

The maritime Silk Road dates back centuries to when Chinese seafarers made great voyages that reached as far as Africa's west coast. The Silk Road maritime routes travelled through some of the world's great ports establishing a road of friendship as well as of development.

Of course, for Timor-Leste, the revival of the fabled Maritime Silk Road is of most significance. China is Southeast Asia's largest trading partner and trade and investment continues to grow at a fast rate. ASEAN nations together have a population of around 600 million people and an economy larger than India's. With planned economic integration towards a single market with labour and capital mobility and improved transport and communication connectivity the economic potential of a revived Maritime Silk Road route from Southeast Asia to China is enormous.

Ladies and Gentlemen,

We have seen the impact of economic growth for people in our region. With its outstanding public leadership and vision, China is growing and soon it will become the largest economy in the world. This growth has lifted hundreds of millions of people out of poverty in what has been the greatest exercise in poverty alleviation in human history.

Through reviving both the overland and maritime Silk Roads the Chinese economic miracle can be spread across our regions with the potential for large scale improvement in the lives and circumstances of millions of people.

And so, the Silk Road can be revived as a road of sustainable development. As it winds through Asia we should make sure we see an improvement in peoples' lives – in health, in education, in the environment and in social well-being. And we should make sure that no countries along the road are neglected or left behind.

The initiative will also provide a framework in which countries, especially developing countries, can look to build much needed infrastructure including roads, railways, ports, telecommunications and oil and gas pipelines.

It is, of course, important to look beyond the economic, trade and infrastructure benefits of the initiative. The Silk Road has also symbolised tolerance and peace as it has supported people to people links as well the transfer of ideas, art and culture.

From this perspective, the Silk Road can be revived as a path of international solidarity and not just of trade. In promoting cooperation and dialogue the Silk Road initiative can support the development of a new model of international engagement which rejects the old ways of putting powerful and national interests ahead of human solidarity.

And the Silk Road can also be revived as a road of culture, art and heritage and not just of commerce. In this way we can bring meaning to the journey through spreading dialogue and the exchange of ideas.

Looking at the Silk Road through such alternative perspectives will allow us to achieve not only economic growth but promote and nurture tolerance, peace and understanding. All the countries along the route must make sure that we truly maximise the potential of the Silk Road for the benefit of all and not just the advancement of the few. We must work towards common prosperity and development and tackle rising inequality, national fragility and the oppression of the vulnerable and marginalised.

A revived Silk Road also provides a further opportunity to improve regional and international security and stability. In our unstable world, in which threats and conflict are more often than not caused by extremism and criminality, the Silk Road can provide a framework for international cooperation to combat terrorism and transnational crime.

Ladies and Gentlemen,

Timor-Leste is a half island nation in Southeast Asia that has overcome conflict to establish a foundation of sustained high economic growth and stability. However, our future depends upon our connectivity. To achieve our vision of a healthy, well-educated and prosperous nation, with a sustainable and diversified economy, we need strong regional integration and cooperation.

That is why we are building new ports and upgrading our airports to make sure we are connected to the world to support trade and build a tourism industry. We will bring a sub-sea internet cable to our shore so that we are not caught on the wrong side of the digital divide. And we will bring a gas pipeline from our largest known petroleum field to our coast to build our onshore petroleum industry and drive our economy.

Without international connectivity Timor-Leste simply cannot progress and prosper. That is why the initiative of the Maritime Silk Road has such value to our country.

And in being a part of the Maritime Silk Road we would hope to also bring benefits to our neighbours. Being on the crossroads of Asia and the Pacific, Timor-Leste would like to play a role in linking the island States of the Pacific to Asia. And we can also act as a bridge between Asia and the Portuguese speaking countries of Africa. We know that a Maritime Silk Road will enable us to make these connections a reality.

Ladies and Gentlemen,

A revived Silk Road can be a new growth driver for the prosperity and peace of the Asian region and beyond. It has the potential to share and spread development opportunities and promote tolerance, peace and understanding.

I urge us all to work together in cooperation and solidarity so that we can realise that great benefits that a revived Silk Road can bring to our nations and our peoples.

Thank you very much.

Address at the Hunan (China) Timor-Leste Investment Co-operation Conference

Changsha, China, 11 April 2013

His Excellency, Mr He Baoxiang, Vice Governor
Ambassadors
Ladies and Gentlemen
Dear friends,

It is a great pleasure to be here in Changsha and to have this opportunity to talk to you about Timor-Leste and the progress and opportunities of our young nation.

During my Official Visit to China I have also had the honour to meet with the Chinese leadership, including His Excellency, the President Xi Jinping, His Excellency, the Premier Li Keqiang and His Excellency, the Chairman of the Standing Committee of the National People's Congress, Zhang Dejiang.

In our meetings one of the central issues of discussion was how China and Timor-Leste can further strengthen our economic and trade relationship and promote business and investment between our countries.

I am very pleased with the cooperation between our Ministry of Agriculture and Fisheries and Longping High Tech Ltd. I would also like to give personal thanks to Professor Longping, who is known as the Father of Hybrid Rice, for his contribution to agriculture in Timor-Leste as well as to global food security.

It was also good to hear from the leaders of Hunan Province who are pleased to be helping Timor-Leste and our agricultural development and thank you for all your contribution. I would also like to give thanks for their wonderful hospitality and the warm welcome. Hunan Province has been hosting a number of our Ministers before my arrival and has worked closely with us to organise today and I thank them for their support.

Today we will be discussing Timor-Leste's economy and investment environment. I look forward to hearing from China Development Bank as it presents an advisory opinion on our *Strategic Development Plan 2011-2030*. China has such deep understanding of development that we have much to learn from its experiences.

We are also fortunate to be joined today by our former Prime Minister, Dr Mari Alkatiri. The State of Timor-Leste has given him the trust and responsibility for the establishment of Special Economic Zones. Dr Alkatiri will be delivering a presentation on our plans for Special Economic Zones in Timor-Leste including our first which will be in the enclave of Oecusse. I believe you will enjoy the presentation.

We will also hear in detail about the economic and investment potential of Timor-Leste which will include a speech by our Minister for Commerce, Industry and Environment.

Given that we have so many interesting speakers and presentations to follow I will not take up more of your time.

Before I finish, however, I will say what a great place Timor-Leste is to invest and to do business. We live on a peaceful tropical island with stunning beaches and mountain ranges.

Timor-Leste has an open economy with very low tax rates and strong government support for foreign business. We have a plan for our future, which you will hear more about today, which includes a large infrastructure building program. Timor-Leste also enjoys strong and sustainable economic growth as well as a growing sovereign wealth fund, our Petroleum Fund, which helps us to finance our development.

We have come to China on the invitation of the Chinese Government and to learn more about your economic miracle. And so, we look to China as partners in the development of our country. I urge you to consider the opportunities for business investment that our nation provides and I invite you all to visit our beautiful country.

Thank you for coming today and for your interest in our young nation.

Address at the g7+ Ministerial Meeting

Togo, 29 May 2013

Your Excellency Kwesi Ahoomey-Zunu, the Prime Minister of Togo
Your Excellencies Ministers
Ladies and Gentlemen,

It is a great pleasure to be here in Togo for this g7+ Ministerial meeting.

I would like to thank the Togolese Government for hosting this important meeting and for the warm welcome we have all received. It is wonderful to see so many Ministers here and such commitment to the goals of the g7+.

This is our third Ministerial Meeting since we established the g7+ in April 2010. We can all be proud of how far we have come since we met in a small room in Díli and decided that for too long our nations had walked alone, as others made decisions affecting our common future.

We now walk together. We have shared our stories and histories, from across Asia, Africa and the Pacific. And while each nation is unique, we are bound by similar challenges, and a shared desire to contribute the discussions on the global development agenda.

The g7+ is now a credible voice, and our vision has been accepted in international forums including, of course, the United Nations.

No one knows better than us what it means to experience internal conflict or to build peace and a State in a fragile environment.

We have seen exciting progress in some g7+ member nations. The Afghani people have again shown their resilience after holding a successful election – an important step in strengthening their State. In Guinea Bissau the leaders of this troubled nation have had the courage to recognise the errors of the past and jointly commit to a future in which national interests are put above personal interests. This recognition has led to successful national elections that we hope will see the country moving to fulfill its legitimate aspirations.

Regrettably, however, some of our members continue to experience great challenges.

The lives of people in the Central African Republic, South Sudan and Somalia are still threated by daily conflict and violence.

When Timor-Leste lapsed into crisis several times after independence, I was saddened and surprised at how quickly we could lose our way.

Last December I was in South Sudan where I talked about how hard it is to build lasting peace and a strong State.

Again I was saddened and surprised when only few weeks later South Sudan faced its own crisis and debilitating outbreak of violence.

I commend the parties in South Sudan for discussing the establishment of a transitional government, and agreeing to put the pursuit of peace above retribution and division.

The situation is also distressing in the Central African Republic and Somalia. I am sure I speak on behalf of all g7+ nations when I say we will do all we can to help these nations get back on their feet. We have all survived conflict and know how bad it can get. We also know that, with reconciliation, dialogue and compromise, it is possible to build a sustainable peace.

Brothers and Sisters,

While people in our fragile countries continue to suffer, the global elite and powerful continue to set the rules of global finance and governance.

We live in a world characterised by a broken and corrupt financial system where the sweat and the blood of our people benefits the international super wealthy. It is a world where the division in our countries helps the powerful drive down the conditions of the poor as they shift their money around to avoid paying tax and contributing to improved human wellbeing.

Regrettably, the global elites benefit from perpetuating division, intolerance and hatred.

The world today is facing a big crisis – the crisis of confidence! It comes from international financial institutions failure (and we can see in the result of the European Parliament elections) to the political behavior of the powerful (as we see in the disaster of the Arab so called Spring, to Syria and Ukraine)

In our underdeveloped world, the crisis is about leadership! Nowadays, leadership is not about a leader, but about a national understanding and compromise of men and women on the collective interests of the country and the aspirations of their people.

The world today needs change and we have to be active agents of this change!

I salute President Obama in his foreign policy review, saying that the U.S. military intervention should not be seen as the only way or the primary option for the U.S.

I also agree with President Obama that an active diplomacy with all stakeholders is what the world needs.

From our side, fragile and conflict affected countries, we have to participate with a more active engagement in solving our internal problems, to be able to be ourselves in an united effort to change the world.

And so, we must recognise that no one else will stand up for the interests of people from fragile and conflict affected countries except for ourselves. If we stand alone we have no voice and can be ignored, but together we can speak with legitimacy and credibility.

This is most important as the world decides on the post 2015 global development agenda.

We have learnt from our experience with the Millennium Development Goals that resilience and progress in fragile and conflict affected countries cannot be achieved with a development agenda based on general and standard assumptions.

There is no grand narrative of social progress that works in all countries regardless of their context, their history and their culture. There is no single solution, or perfect model or even a checklist of actions, which is transferable from one country to the next. Despite the focus of the development agenda continually changing, as each new failure is recognised, extreme poverty persists... while we see trillions of dollars spent in military interventions, to impose democracy.

It may not be convenient for global institutions, or high profile people or political movements to admit, but we cannot achieve global development goals unless we first achieve peace in fragile countries. And we cannot achieve peace in fragile countries unless the people of those countries lead and own the peace building process, as the only way to build the state and develop the Nation.

While this may all be self evident to all of us here it has also been proven by the results. Not one low-income fragile or conflict affected country has yet achieved a single Millennium Development Goal. And while over one and a half billion people live in areas affected by fragility, conflict or organised criminal violence, and with conflict causing human, social and economic costs that last for generations, the global development agenda is failing to properly address the challenges of our countries.

The Millennium Development Goals did not focus enough on reaching people in fragile countries – in our countries – and they failed to recognise the devastating consequences of conflict on development.

I was invited to participate, in the coming weeks, in an international gathering in London, to campaign against 'sexual violence in conflicts'.

For me, while I support this campaign, I have to say that it will be a waste of time and money, because the real cause of the problem is the conflict itself, the war itself, the violence itself.

If the real issue is not addressed, we continue to see the international community pledging for billions of dollars to spend in humanitarian assistance, without solving the problem.

Last March, in a Defense Dialogue in Jakarta, I challenged the international community to produce a report on who or which country is being benefitted with the sale of sophisticated weapons to groups, militias and rebels.

This is a real problem to be addressed, not only the consequences of the conflict.

And this problem belongs to us – we have to play our role by influencing and helping all the stakeholders to seat at the same table and to discuss with openness, frankness, and honesty to safeguard the interests of our people.

We saw for ourselves in Timor-Leste how widespread conflict can wipe out years of development progress. And we learnt how important it was for peace building and State building efforts to be guided by the realities of our national context.

That is why I urge the g7+ family members to work together to make sure the post 2015 global development agenda does not again stay silent on the needs and importance of fragile and conflict affected nations.

We must make sure that we are not left behind and that our voices are heard as the world decides on the direction and focus of the international development agenda.

The new proposed Sustainable Development Goals, which are to set targets for the coming 15 years, will determine the allocation of hundreds of billions of dollars and the focus of global development efforts. It is vital that we push for targets that will actually make a difference for our people.

Brothers and Sisters,

Please let me finish by stressing the importance of formalising the arrangements of the g7+.

We must make sure that we have the institutional strength and capacity to unite together and to properly pursue our agenda. We must be resilient.

The g7+ has brought us together in solidarity to speak with a common voice to the international community. It gives us the chance to actively participate in the global development dialogue, which has been largely controlled by the donor nations.

To continue to pursue, and advocate, an independent agenda, in an often hostile environment, we need the strength of an institutional backbone. It is only with a standing organisational structure that we will have the capacity to properly and professionally advocate for change.

That is why I commend and support the initiative of developing a g7+ charter and working to institutionalise the g7+ secretariat.

It is in this way that we can fully develop and pursue a new vision of alternative possibilities for the international development agenda and for our countries.

Brothers and Sisters,

I urge us all to work with dedication and purpose over the two days of this Ministerial Meeting. We must agree on a plan of action to guide the future agenda of the g7+ and ensure results for our peoples.

And I would like to give thanks again to the Togolese Government for hosting us and for their warm hospitality.

Thank you very much.

International Scientific Conference on the Investigation, Education, Cooperation and Development in the Community of Portuguese Language Countries – 'Timor-Leste's Policy During its Leadership of the CPLP: A Globalised Vision for the Future'

Universidade Nacional Timor Lorosa'e (UNTL), Díli, 16 July 2014

His Excellency Mr President of the Republic, Taur Matan Ruak
Magnificent Rector of the UNTL, Professor Doctor Aurélio Guterres
Magnificent Rector of Universidade do Minho, Professor Doctor António Cunha
Magnificent Rector of Universidade de Aveiro, Professor Doctor Manuel Assunção
Magnificent Vice Rector of Universidade de Coimbra, Professor Doctor Joaquim Ramos de Carvalho
Excellency Mr President of the Instituto Universitário de Educação de Cabo Verde Professor Doctor Florênço Mendes Varela
Distinguished Members of the Parliament
Members of Government
Distinguished Faculty Members
Distinguished Guests
Dear Students
Ladies and Gentlemen,

First, I would like to take this opportunity to congratulate the Universidade Nacional Timor Lorosa'e in organising this conference at such a pertinent time and I thank the International Scientific Community for its support and for gracing this national initiative with its presence.

It is for me a great honour to address this auditorium and I am thankful to see so many Timorese students with an interest in better understanding the Community of Portuguese Language Countries, a group that has – as fundamental areas of its dynamic scope – education, investigation and cooperation. But it goes beyond this.

To begin, taking into account that I was asked to speak about Timor-Leste's policy towards the leadership of the CPLP, allow me to remind you here of those historical factors that moulded Timorese culture and identity.

Timor-Leste gathered throughout its history distinct elements that today foster its political identity.

To our own indigenous culture, with its heterogeneous ethnic and language diversity but also with a unique history supported by our own shared legends and animistic beliefs, absorbed through colonial experience a religion and cultural heritage that reached us at the hands of the Portuguese, in an encounter that we will celebrate in 2015 when we will mark the 500 years of the arrival of the first Lusitanian caravel to Lifau, in Oecussi.

Both the catholic faith and the Portuguese language took up roots in our existence, assuming more visible presence during period of the Indonesian occupation and becoming an important instrument for the Timorese resistance.

It was from this meeting of cultures and civilisations that our small half-island, with an enclave inside the other half, within an archipelago composed of over 14 thousand small and large islands of Indonesia that our Country, Timor-Leste, affirmed itself as a People, the Maubere, and as a Lusophone Nation.

It is important to remember that here the 'maubere miracle' of independence took place thanks also to the persistence of the 'administrative power', Portugal, its State, its governors and its People.

In addition, during the difficult years of our bloody struggle we received support from our other brother countries. It was due to a magnificent coming together of wills, and also of the States and People of the PALOP and Brazil, that our voice was cast into the international arena, and these countries tirelessly promoted the right to independence of the Timorese, maintaining their steadfast political and diplomatic solidarity.

Timor-Leste's presidency of the CPLP is, as such, also a moment to thank the solidarity of the nations and peoples of Angola, Brazil, Cape-Verde, Guinea-Bissau, Mozambique, Portugal and São Tomé e Príncipe. And this gesture will be consecrated as we name the Comoro Bridge for the CPLP, which will be inaugurated on the 22nd, with the presence of the Heads of State and Heads of Government of this Community.

Excellencies

Ladies and Gentlemen

Dear students,

The Community of Portuguese Language Countries was founded in 1996 in response to circumstances very different from today. At that time, composed of only 7 countries, it encompassed such disparate and challenging national settings, such as the civil war in Angola, the recent peace attained in Mozambique, and the growing regional integration of Portugal within the transformation of the CEE into the European Union.

It realised its founding axis on the Atlantic Ocean, pulling Maputo towards the West, rather than adventuring in search of new oceans.

The CPLP has been developing its own mechanisms of political and diplomatic focus, according to the themes dominating the international agenda, in particular by the United Nations system.

As I already mentioned, one of the key results of this unmatched effort was to end in a long process towards self-determination and independence for Timor-Leste, becoming part of the CPLP in 2002, enabling this Organisation a global dimension in a globalised world.

In truth, next week's X Summit of the Heads of State and of Government of the CPLP in Díli is not only an historical moment because Timor-Leste will take charge for its first time, and be responsible for presiding over this Organisation, but also because this is the first time since its foundation that this Meeting takes place in the Asia-Pacific region, shifting the geopolitical space of the Atlantic into the Indo-Pacific.

For us Timorese becoming part of the CPLP was key because it allowed us over the past 12 years to become an active part of the international community, creating stronger linkages of fraternity, feeling a sense of belonging in a world where talk, emotions, and negotiations are all done in Portuguese, with homes in Africa, America and Europe. Timor-Leste also offers a broader horizon to the Community and to each of its member-peoples.

In particular, Timor-Leste now welcomes the representatives of the Member-States of our Community, in a region that is the economic, financial and strategic axis of the world.

Timor-Leste continues to develop its natural process of international relations, deepening its relations with neighbouring States and establishing conditions for future integration into ASEAN, one of the most dynamic and globally integrated regions.

It is within this context, ladies and gentlemen, we must put into perspective the program that the Timorese presidency may propose to this Community, which reflects the future we want.

Acknowledging the year in which the CPLP will reach adulthood, turning 18 tomorrow, on the 17th June, it is appropriate to reflect on the changes taking place around the world and on the change that has taken place at international junctures.

This includes the extension of borders superimposing on traditional physical borders and also Timor-Leste's independence, with its international repercussions.

This includes the events of September 11th 2001, the wars in Iraq and Afghanistan and, more recently, the tumult in the Arab world and the technological revolution and spread of the internet. And, naturally, we cannot ignore the economic rise of China bringing with it the growth of Asia, Africa and Latin America.

On the other hand, we witnessed the recent world financial crisis which although its origins were in the Anglophone countries, altered the global political and economic outlook, affecting almost all countries, many of which are still in the process of economic recovery, and that demonstrated the fragility of the global economic system and the need to restructure it.

The increase of international trade, the liberalisation investment flows, the shifts of mega economic trends, with pressure also felt on energy resources and on nature. As a result of this process of globalisation, multinational firms have grown and this has had significant implications for almost all of the world's governments.

This entire context changed each region across the four continents of the CPLP nations and changed the dynamic of regional economic integration.

It is important also to highlight the spaces where the Member-States of the CPLP are situated, with the action and influence of Angola and Mozambique in the Community for the Development of Southern Africa (known also as SADC), of Guinea-Bissau and Cape Verde in the Economic Community of West African States (CEDEAO), of São Tomé e Príncipe in the Economic Community of the Central African States (CEEAC), of all these PALOP in the African Union, of Brazil in the Common Market of the South (MERCOSUL) and of Portugal in the European Union.

Meanwhile, these different regional frameworks and the geographic discontinuity do not make our efforts towards dialogue and cooperation between the nations of the CPLP less valid. Quite the contrary, these are opportunities on which we can capitalise and are platforms for globalisation, as respect for differences and feelings of belonging to a Community of Peoples and Cultures can benefit each one of these countries.

In other words, the CPLP can be understood as a platform on which each member-State can manage its own process for participation in global trade through regional integration, as long as it is an Organisation that serves its Peoples.

Excellencies

Ladies and Gentlemen

Dear students,

We see here that which unites us as a Community: a shared past of historical links, a common identity and a common assimilation of universal values which have given way to unique shows of solidarity and fraternity between peoples who express themselves in the same language – a crucial pillar for our education systems and the training of our peoples.

Nevertheless, what can we do together to overcome the challenges imposed by a globalisation that has polarised individual actions, in which each of our countries must face our own challenges and also in the way we relate to the region in which we are located?

What can we do to transform the asymmetries of our countries, in the current phase of development, with proposals of clear evolution, enabling action and interdependency of efforts of all States and countries, to guide the sustainable development of our peoples?

How can we ensure a successful future for the CPLP as a community, maximising the benefits associated with globalisation and mitigating its risks?

Ladies and Gentlemen,

To start off with, we must identify our weaknesses, with sobriety, and examine our capacity, with frankness – because only this way will we be able to appreciate the contribution that each of us can give.

The Timorese presidency in adopting the theme 'The CPLP and Globalisation' wishes to set a new course for the policies of the CPLP, which are being updated according to the global demands of humanity.

'Let us plant the flag of the CPLP in the business of the world and let us be also the messengers of peace, of the defence of human rights and social justice wherever we are represented.' This is the motto that Timor-Leste wishes to imprint in the core of this Organisation.

Excellencies

Ladies and Gentlemen

Dear students,

The Timorese presidency proposes to establish a program of action that allows giving continuity to the work of preceding presidencies, focussing on already defined priorities, identified around three axes:

- The political and diplomatic concentration
- Cooperation
- The promotion of the Portuguese language

In the first axis, the presidency of Timor-Leste will progress and maintain political-diplomatic actions within the international agenda, be they at the United Nations, or in other international forums, and we will promote possible dialogue and coordination of the positions of member-States of the CPLP about the key challenges facing the world.

I would like to now highlight that the Timorese presidency will contribute as much as possible towards the process of stabilising Guinea-Bissau, with whom

Timor-Leste has already opted to get more directly involved, initially within the framework of the g7+.

As you will already know, we have supported Guinea-Bissau financially and with a technical team under the leadership of our Secretary of State for Administrative Decentralisation with vast experience attained during the several electoral episodes in Timor-Leste, the electoral process in Guinea-Bissau.

Also the United Nations mission in Guinea-Bissau, until very recently, under the leadership of our former President of the Republic, Dr José Ramos-Horta, whom accompanied the efforts of the Bissau-Guinean people in the undertaking of their electoral process.

The Timorese mission of support obtained high results in voter registration and, as you know, the elections – parliamentarian and presidential – were a success, through a massive democratic demonstration that served also as a sign of the wishes of all the Bissau-Guinean people for peace and stability.

These brothers, whom inspired us during our struggle for liberation, were the first to recognise our independence, and as they reinstituted their constitutional normalcy, will continue to be a target of our solidarity and support.

We know that elections are the mere starting point. For a State unable to provide for the basic needs of its people, there are many challenges ahead – financial, social and administrative – it is fundamental to realise the promise of peace and national unity.

We believe that we, with the other partners of the CPLP, can support the consolidation of the gains already achieved in these brother countries.

In the second axis, about cooperation, we will strengthen this which has become one of the key pillars of the CPLP.

As you are aware, Timor-Leste is currently implementing a series of projects, in particular at the bilateral level, in regards to the CPLP countries, in practically all sectors, highlighting here the areas of education, justice, defence, health, public works, tourism and natural resources, to mention but a few only.

We wish to give continuity and support for cooperation projects in the areas of development, creating new synergies and focussing naturally in sectors that aim towards the economic growth of our peoples.

In the third axis, the promotion of the Portuguese language, I take this opportunity to highlight that the promotion of this official language will emerge stronger during the Timorese presidency.

Here it is fundamental to mention that Timor-Leste paid a high cost to belong to this language which was also the language of our resistance. A banning of its use, for over two decades, had a tremendous impact in the development of a new generation and also of our education systems.

On the one hand, Portuguese never stopped being the official language of Timor-Leste, but on the other hand, it was never the language of the majority of the people. And, for obvious reasons, Timor-Leste lagged behind in efforts to widen its scope and encouraging tis appropriation by our citizens. Of all member-States, Timor-Leste has the most need to increase the use of and mastery of this language.

Notwithstanding, the Portuguese language, more than the symbolic value attributed because of the crucial role it played during our period of struggle for independence, it is also an important instrument of geopolitical identity.

Portuguese is today recognised by many as an instrument of our own uniqueness in the region and, increasingly, it is becoming among the agents of global progress, as a language for the sciences and technology, with steady growth and adequate positioning to compete in the global labour and knowledge markets.

With over 250 million Portuguese language speakers, this is also the fifth most spoken language in the world and the third most spoken in the western world.

We will thus continue efforts to promote new initiatives aimed at strengthening and promoting the position of the Portuguese language in the world system, including making national efforts, with the expansion of the teaching of the language in the private schools, including Catholic schools and at private universities.

The International Institute of Portuguese Language (IILP) which was even established prior to the founding of the CPLP, and was adopted by it as one of its key fundamental organs, has come to play a key role in the teaching, promotion and internationalisation of the Portuguese language, and it is one of the objectives of the Timorese presidency to strengthen this institute and seeks new partnerships which can promote our language in common.

As such, I am delighted to inform you that following up on the sequence of initiatives already promoted in Brasilia in 2010 and in Lisbon in 2013, the Timorese presidency will organise in Díli in 2016 the Third International Conference about the Portuguese Language in the World System, thus continuing focussing in the promotion and diffusion of the Portuguese language through global strategies.

I believe this Conference today will also provide important clues about the key role of the Portuguese language in investigation, education, cooperation and development, in such a way that we will be able to draft the guidelines for that which might be debated at the Conference to take place in 2016 in Díli.

Excellencies

Ladies and Gentlemen

Dear students,

Other important initiatives will mark the next two years, following up on the preceding presidencies, such as the Youth Forum and the Civil Society Forum which will be held in 2015.

In the meantime, in reference to the theme 'CPLP and Globalisation' that will guide our programs, we believe this multilateral forum has now the opportunity to promote cooperation in the economic domain.

We shall as such make the best use of the potential each country has in the sectors of development, encourage the exchange of experience and competencies that will lead to inclusive and sustainable development, always aware of our linguistic ties and our common legal tradition.

We want to promote from the onset cycles of conferences that develop themes on entrepreneurship, business, investment, industry, tourism, in particular ecotourism and community tourism, and focus on economic cooperation in the hydrocarbon sector.

The CPLP countries increasingly occupy key places in regards to deposits of energy resources. Brazil and Angola are within the top 20 producers of oil in the world. In Mozambique, the recent finds of natural gas seem to indicate that in the short term, Mozambique will be a world leader in the production of natural gas with reserves equal to those in Qatar. São Tomé e Príncipe also has tremendous potential with its joint maritime zone share with Nigeria to be able to become an exporter of mineral resources. Timor-Leste and Equatorial Guinea (with the presumed adhesion to the CPLP during this Summit) are two of the most mineral revenue dependent countries.

Realising the importance of natural resources (in particular oil and gas and petroleum) for the CPLP countries, this is an area in which the countries in the community will be exposed to external risks, such as those demonstrated by the low international prices during the recent world financial crisis. This suggests this is an area where there can be greater scope for cooperation in terms of funds management, of mechanisms to mitigate the impacts, of fighting tax evasion and in the exchange of experience in the various areas.

In this context, and in close collaboration with the Entrepreneurial Confederation of the CPLP, the Timorese presidency shall organise in early 2015, the first Global Economic Forum.

Timor-Leste is committed to begin consolidating a new path towards economic cooperation, seeking to gather the consensus of the member-States to this, also whilst keeping in our common agenda the new paradigm for the fight against poverty, and thus strengthening our pillar of cooperation.

This is a challenge, considering the heterogeneous characteristics and the economic, social and political realities that each of our States faces, but the benefits may prove advantageous both in terms of the expansion of markets and increased investment and above all in terms of the transfer of knowledge and experience that may lead to the development of new ideas and contribute to this new global economic paradigm.

We have added advantages for being an exclusive club of only eight nations to date; as such the debate can be more honest and programmatic.

The purpose of the CPLP is to improve the quality of life of its peoples. A global vision for our common future is to mobilise political-diplomatic will and efforts but also human, scientific, technologic and financial resources which will allow the development and progress of each one of the citizens of our Community.

On the 21st there shall be a meeting of Finance Ministers of the CPLP and other specialists in economics, under the theme 'The Impact of Globalisation on Public Finance in the CPLP'. And on the 24th, a Seminar about the 'Economic Globalisation and Opportunities for Investment: the CPLP and the Asian-Pacific Region'.

Excellencies

Ladies and Gentlemen,

I wish this International Scientific Conference will bring also important reflection for the CPLP debates and for the creation of new opportunities for development in the area of education.

Education and training continue to among the highest priorities for Timor-Leste to improve the life opportunities of our people and so they can realise their potential.

Without quality education we will not be able to reach the objective of development and economic growth for Timor-Leste.

Thank you very much.

Seminar on Economic Globalisation and Investment Opportunities: The CPLP and the Asia-Pacific Region – 'Timor-Leste's Presidency of the CPLP: a Vision towards the Future'

Díli, 24 July 2014

Your Excellencies
Ladies and Gentlemen,

I would like to start by thanking everyone here for attending this event: the international representatives who have visited us, our partners in Timor-Leste and the national private sector.

It is also an immense pleasure to host the Prime Minister of Portugal, Mr Pedro Passos Coelho, who is starting today the first Official Visit by a Portuguese Head of Government to our country. This represents one more step in the relationship of friendship and solidarity that has always existed between Timor-Leste and Portugal.

As you know, yesterday Timor-Leste received the rotating Presidency of the Community of Portuguese-Speaking Countries from the President of the Republic of Mozambique. Timor-Leste will hold this Presidency during the biennium 2014-2016.

It was with great honour, but also with responsibility, that we accepted this role. The inauguration of Timor-Leste's Presidency of the CPLP is made even more special because it has brought the highest representatives from the other Portuguese-speaking nations throughout the world to this far away country, a remote half island in the Asia-Pacific.

Created in 1996, the CPLP was born out of a shared cultural identity, seeking to create a space for solutions towards the individual and collective development of our Peoples.

During these almost twenty years of history, the CPLP has focussed primarily in three key areas: diplomatic solidarity, technical cooperation and the development of the Portuguese language, which was the basis for the CPLP.

However, as we prepare to take on the Presidency of this institution with tremendous potential, we believe that the CPLP can and should do more.

Being a group of countries that represents today over 250 million people and that features incomparable natural resources and a cumulative geostrategic position that provides access to the major economic growth regions in the world, Timor-Leste has chosen as the theme for its Presidency 'The CPLP and Globalization'.

We want this biennium to be characterised by greater economic and business stimulus between member States and their respective key partners. This intention is a key element in the Action Plan for the Presidency that we presented yesterday at the Díli Summit.

As such, our Presidency will seek to encourage the development of business projects between member States strengthening the national private sector and making use of the transfer of technology and expertise within the Community to promote new strategic partnerships enabled by our integration in different key regions within the globalised economic system.

We want to focus on the hydrocarbon sector, by studying the creation of a consortium between companies from the member States, so as to ensure that the enormous reserves available to us are translated into fair wealth for our nations.

With this goal of nurturing the economies of the CPLP countries, we have started a comprehensive reflection on the mechanisms and instruments that are available to us or that may be created in order to ensure that our development process leads to the improvement of the living situations of our Peoples.

We officially started that reflection at a meeting held on Monday – the findings of which have just been presented by the Minister of Finance – that brought together the Ministers of Finance of the CPLP and their representatives with key partners from other international forums and organisations, so as to discuss the impact of the financial crisis on the public finances of the CPLP.

That meeting already conveyed the intention by the Government of Timor-Leste to make this debate as broad as possible, expanding the influence of the CPLP through dialogue with other agents. We believe that the economic stimulus of this influence must be achieved by having the CPLP open to the outside rather than close in around itself.

We are experiencing this intention today, at this Seminar. In today's globalised world, replicating the fraternity that exists within the CPLP in other spaces of dialogue will strengthen our position in the world.

We rely on everyone in attendance for this process of reflection and debate. The next key event will be the organisation, at the start of 2015, of the Global Economic Forum, to which you are all invited. This will be undertaken in close collaboration with the Business Confederation of the CPLP, which is here today.

Your Excellencies

Ladies and Gentlemen,

The globalisation of our economies has changed significantly our position within the international framework. The dilution of borders, as a result of the advances in information and communication technologies, has led to the fast expansion of markets and to an enormous interdependency by economies as different as the ones, for instance, of the CPLP countries.

By itself, globalisation creates critical challenges that require greater competitiveness within the international arena. Additionally, it can often nurture individualistic trends, with each isolated State trying to respond to its own pressures. However, this global dynamic also provides exceptional opportunities for boosting strategic synergies that can generate actual social and economic benefits.

Leaving aside the challenges, globalisation can also provide greater access to the world!

The most unique aspect of Timor-Leste's Presidency of the CPLP was clear before we even started setting targets and goals for this period. For the first time in 18 years of existence, the Community was relocating its epicentre from the Atlantic to the Asia-Pacific.

Today, Asia includes two of the three largest economies in the world. These economies have, with great vision, succeeded in combining technological progress, skilled human resources and access to capital in order to become great emerging centres in the international system. Asia's growth is lifting hundreds of millions of people from poverty, while serving as an economic engine for the rest of the world.

This century, which is the great Asian Century, is unquestionably marked by the emergence of China in international markets. China, which is a key partner of Timor-Leste, succeeded in expanding its reach across the entire world and in maximising the potential offered by the new global networks.

In preparation of Timor-Leste's membership in ASEAN, which is also a unique international success story, I visited every ASEAN country and found that they all wanted new investment partnerships.

In view of Asia's current vibrant situation, Timor-Leste wants to make use of its unique geostrategic standing and provide a platform of complementariness between Asia-Pacific and the European, African and Latin American regions to which the CPLP countries have access.

Your Excellencies

Ladies and Gentlemen,

We know from experience that nowadays strategic partnerships are the cornerstone of an economy that seeks to enter the globalised system. Timor-Leste is, as you all know, a young country that, in trying to find its place in the world, has always sought to learn from other experiences and to apply them to its own intrinsic realities.

We are committed to several regional and international organisations and forums that use dialogue as a catalyst for peace, stability and collective development. The g7+ has been one of the most rewarding experiences within this framework, as a result of the exchange and solidarity that it generates between fragile and conflict-afflicted countries. Having 20 countries speak in one voice, the g7+ has advocated a 'New Deal' to ensure that the new post-2015 development agenda puts the perspectives of the fragile States at the centre of the debate.

From the very start, we have been walking side by side with our development partners. The success, albeit modest, that we have been experiencing in these initial years of independence demonstrates that we are on the right track.

Since 2007 we have been growing at an average of 11.9% per year. While this is undoubtedly positive, it will only have actual meaning if it is translated into sustainable and inclusive growth, which is the main goal of our *Strategic Development Plan 2011-2030*. The Plan seeks to develop a diversified economy based on three key sectors: tourism, agriculture and petroleum. In order to achieve this, we know that we need a stronger private sector.

Aware that our private sector requires support, we are investing in the building of infrastructure, such as a port, a new international airport and a road network, in order to facilitate trade and attract investment. We also have low tax rates that are attractive for foreign investors.

The priority that we attribute to the consolidation of the institutions enables us to have a structure that generates trust. We are noted for our transparency – indeed, we were the first country in Asia and only the third in the world to achieve compliant status with the EITI (Extractive Industries Transparency Initiative). We have a sovereign wealth fund, our Petroleum Fund, which has already exceeded $15.7 billion.

We know that it is vital to build the capacity of our human resources and to create jobs for our youth. As such, we are investing in large projects, such as the development of the South Coast and the two projects that you will learn about this morning: the integrated sub-regional development plan involving the nearest provinces in Indonesia and the Northern Territory of Australia, and the Special Zone of Social and Market Economy.

By expanding its horizons, Timor-Leste is strengthening a network of sharing. We want this network to be your network as well.

Your Excellencies

Ladies and Gentlemen,

Globalisation reduces the distances between us, expands our paths and liberalises connections. It does so within a dynamic network that facilitates the sharing of expertise and experiences, while boosting international trade and investment.

Timor-Leste's vision for the CPLP entails walking those new paths together, in order to achieve development and to provide a better future for our peoples.

Thank you very much.

2014 Timor-Leste Development Partners' Meeting

Díli, 25 July 2014

Excellencies

Ladies and Gentlemen,

Welcome to the 2014 Timor-Leste Development Partners' Meeting.

I particularly want to welcome our brothers and sisters from the Community of Portuguese Language Countries, the CPLP.

We deliberately scheduled the Development Partners' Meeting to immediately follow the CPLP Summit so we could benefit from the contributions of our friends from Portuguese speaking nations around the globe.

Portugal, of course, has a long and proud history of participation in our Development Partners' Meetings, but this is the first time that representatives from many of the CPLP members have participated in our annual meeting with our development partners.

We are honoured to have you here and look forward to broadening our perspectives and our development potential as a result.

Ladies and Gentlemen,

Two days ago, we hosted the Heads of State and Government Summit of the CPLP.

That event marked two other historic milestones.

It was the first time the CPLP Summit has been held in the Asia-Pacific region and it saw Timor-Leste assume the Presidency of the CPLP for the first time.

Next year, in 2015, we will celebrate the 500 year anniversary of the arrival of the first Portuguese to Lifau, in our enclave of Oecusse. The Portuguese language has enormous significance for our people and our culture.

Portuguese was the language of our resistance struggle. Since independence, our shared familiarity, cultural heritage and language, have forged a pathway linking us to our CPLP friends across three continents. In a fractured world, our language has created strong links of fraternity and a strong sense of belonging.

During our CPLP Presidency we hope to deepen the economic cooperation between member States and open up trade opportunities in the Asia-Pacific and across the globe.

Our main objectives will be to work together to achieve shared prosperity, to reduce poverty and bring progress and stability across the Portuguese speaking world.

Ladies and Gentlemen,

The CPLP leaders' Summit and Development Partners' Meeting in Díli demonstrate the promise of international cooperation and friendship.

Regrettably, our camaraderie is not mirrored across the globe.

Last week we were all horrified to learn of the shooting down of Malaysian Airlines flight MH17 and the brutal death of so many innocent people. We have with us today representatives from countries that suffered loss from this awful event including our dear friends from Australia and New Zealand. On behalf of the people of Timor-Leste I extend to them our deepest condolences.

I have already written to the Malaysian Prime Minister to pass on our condolences to the people of Malaysia who are still dealing with loss of family and friends on missing flight MH146.

The tragedy of flight MH17 reflects the sad state of global affairs today. We all hoped the end of the Cold War would lead to a new world order of cooperation and progress, but we now have a world of disorder and distrust.

We watch helpless as the Middle East tears itself apart with unfathomable sectarian violence and centuries old disputes. We witness terror and death across Israel and Gaza, in Syria and Iraq and in Afghanistan and Libya. We see fragility and conflict across the region with the future unknown to all of us. The high hopes of the Arab Spring have long ago blown away in the dust.

Across parts of Africa we still witness conflict and fragility which bring with it entrenched poverty and famine. At last year's Timor-Leste Development Partners' Meeting we were pleased to welcome the Deputy Minister of Finance from South Sudan. Tragically, the proud people of this new but fragile nation have fallen back into conflict and face terrible violence and starvation.

And across the globe we still have 1.5 billion people facing poverty, hunger, disease and exclusion. Even with the remarkable growth of the Asia-Pacific this region is still home to nearly two–thirds of the world's poor people.

Next year marks the expiry of the Millennium Development Goals. While many goals are on target to be met globally, not one fragile or conflict affected nation is on track to achieve even one Millennium Development Goal.

The common factors, fragility and conflict, were not addressed in the Millennium Development Goals. You cannot have development if you do not first have peace. We witness with despair the sad reality of this in South Sudan right now.

In the West, the greed and corruption of the international financial system resulted in the Global Financial Crisis. Initial hopes that the global reaction would lead to a fairer system in which people were put before the profits of the powerful, have also ended in despair as we witness elite interests, with huge financial resources, capture and dominate governments.

The recovery from the financial crisis has benefited the global elite who are skilled at evading national laws and taxation systems to avoid making a contribution to the common good. This disturbing trend has resulted in rising inequality in the West, the entrenched economic segregation of the Least Developed Countries and even the richest of the world's nations ignoring international law.

This unrestrained self-interest threatens the very existence of some nations with climate change resulting in some countries of the Pacific slowly sinking into the vastness of the ocean.

Ladies and Gentlemen,

Fortunately there are signs of hope. Our nearest neighbour Indonesia, and the world's third largest democracy, just held a successful election with around 190 million voters across thousands and thousands of islands. After ten years of inspired leadership by His Excellency Susilo Bambang Yudhoyono building a modern democracy of tolerance and progress, we will soon see another peaceful transition to a new President of this great nation.

Just as close to our hearts, but so much further away, we have seen successful elections held in Guinea-Bissau breaking a devastating cycle of coups d'etat. Timor-Leste is honoured to have supported the electoral process in Guinea-Bissau financially and with a technical team. The United Nations mission in Guinea-Bissau, until very recently, was also under the leadership of our former President, Dr José Ramos-Horta, whom accompanied the efforts of the Guinea-Bissau people in the undertaking of their electoral process.

It was our brothers and sisters from Guinea-Bissau that inspired our struggle for liberation and that were the first to recognise our independence. As Guinea-Bissau restores constitutional government it will continue to have the support and solidarity of Timor-Leste and the CPLP.

We have also seen other signs of progress and promise. The Association of Southeast Asian Nations, ASEAN, has established a sub-regional zone of cooperation and peace between nations and Timor-Leste looks forward to joining this important regional forum. The incredible rise of Asia, which has been led by China, has also lifted hundreds of millions of people out of poverty and given hope to the people of a continent. This has led many in our region to claim that we are now living in the Asian Century, but I also see the great potential of Africa, and of South America, and I think it is truer to say we are seeing the rise of the South.

Ladies and Gentlemen,

To bring about a positive future we must all work together in friendship and with an attitude of tolerance and understanding. We must take the positive spirit of this Development Partners' Meeting to all our international relations.

Timor-Leste is a development success story thanks to the determination of our people and the support of our international friends. Since our crisis of 2006 we, as a people, have pulled together. In tackling the root causes of our fragility we were able to embark on a process of peace building and State building. We had learnt only too well that conflict can wipe out years of development progress. And today, we enjoy peace and stability, which you can all witness from the vibrancy and positive energy on our streets and in our towns.

We were fortunate that income started to flow from oil reserves in the Timor Sea and we made sure we had systems in place, to be able to provide for the urgent needs of today, while protecting income for future generations. We established a Petroleum Fund, which has grown from its opening balance of $205 million in September 2005 to almost $16 billion today. In order to lower risk and increase returns, we also made a decision to diversify the investments of the Petroleum Fund beyond US Treasury Bonds to include international bonds and equities. This investment strategy has been a success and in 2013 the investment income generated by the Petroleum Fund was US$865 million.

Timor-Leste was also the first in Asia, and third in the world, to be compliant with the Extractive Industry Transparency Initiative (the EITI), so that every dollar that comes in, from petroleum revenue, is publicly disclosed and transparent.

We invested in capacity building in the security sector to improve professionalism in the Police and in the Military, bringing about a new stage of cooperation and solidarity among the two institutions. Timor-Leste continues to enjoy the support of our development partners in building this most critical foundation of our development future.

In the pursuit of social justice as well as stability we have established a strong system of social support and are providing pensions to our veterans, the elderly, the disabled, widows and orphans. We know that our growth must be shared and that without peace and internal reconciliation, there can be no inclusive development.

Having established a foundation of peace and security, we turned our attention to long term planning and entered a new phase of our development. At the Timor-Leste Development Partners' Meeting in 2011 our *Strategic Development Plan 2011-2030* was released setting a framework to transform Timor-Leste from a low-income country to a medium-high income country by 2030, with a healthy, educated and safe population. We have begun to implement our Plan and we are already achieving some outstanding results.

Our progress can be measured in many ways. One way is through economic growth, and since 2007 Timor-Leste has averaged double digit rates of economic growth with the International Monetary Fund predicting continued strong growth into the future.

But we also know that growth must be balanced and the benefits shared in an inclusive way. With the assistance of our development partners, we have established local development programs to create jobs and improve living conditions of the population in every village across our country, especially with assistance in health, power supply, water and sanitation and access to education and to markets. We are also moving towards the establishment of local government and have begun with pre-decentralisation reforms to build the administrative capacity of our regions.

Our economic growth also means an expanding private sector, which is creating more jobs for our people and paying more taxes to fund the provision of basic public services. We know that our future depends on a strong and diversified private sector to work in partnership with the government to build our country.

Our progress can also be measured by looking at health and education. Our child mortality rates have also seen a sharp decline from 83 to 64 per thousand live births, between 2003 and 2009/2010. Life expectancy at birth has also increased from 59.5 in 2006 to 64.6 in 2011. In the education sector we have worked to lift the number of children enrolled in school and we are strengthening our education institutions.

We have completed the largest infrastructure project in our people's history, by building a national electricity grid with generation and distribution across the country. We are embarking on an infrastructure program to provide a basis for a nation's sustainable economic future, which will include a new national port, a major airport upgrade, a national road network and the extensive development of our south coast to become a sub-regional centre for the petroleum industry. Just this week, I was pleased to officially open the CPLP bridge that joins Díli to our international airport and the west of our country.

Under the leadership of our former Prime Minister, Dr Mari Alkatiri, we are also establishing Special Economic Zones in Timor-Leste including our first which will be a Special Economic and Social Zone in the enclave of Oecusse.

Ladies and Gentlemen,

Our domestic progress has also given us the opportunity to look beyond our own shores and allowed us to increase our international engagement. Just as the international community has done so much to support our people, now we want to be able to contribute something in return.

Part of our focus is working with other fragile countries around the world. An important part of this is working with the g7+ that now consists of 20 fragile and conflict affected States. It was under the framework of the g7+ that Timor-Leste began its support for Guinea-Bissau. The g7+ plays a global role as voice for fragile countries and to advocate for change in global development policies. This includes the g7+ nations working together to ensure that the post-2015 development agenda addresses the need for peace and stability, and that the perspectives of fragile States are central to the global dialogue.

While Timor-Leste continues to pursue membership of ASEAN we are also deepening our relations with the great island nations of the Pacific. We make sure Timor-Leste is always represented at the highest levels at the Pacific Islands Forum and I was pleased to participate in the 2011 Forum in New Zealand. In 2013 I was also honoured to attend the inaugural Summit of the Pacific Islands Development Forum in Fiji. Since 2013, Timor-Leste has also held the chair of the Economic and Social Commission for Asia and the Pacific and, of course, this week we have assumed the Presidency of the CPLP for the next two years.

Ladies and Gentlemen,

While we have made great progress from the time of the Restoration of our Independence in 2002, we know that so much more needs to be done and we must stay on track in implementing the *Strategic Development Plan*.

At the 2013 Development Partners' Meeting the Government announced the establishment of a Development Policy Coordination Mechanism to facilitate the implementation of the *Strategic Development Plan*. This Mechanism consists of four Strategic Sectors that are directly aligned with the four pillars of the *Strategic Development Plan*.

To allow the Development Policy Coordination Mechanism to be effective a tool has been developed to drive delivery and ensure policy implementation. This tool is the SDP Matrix and it provides a structure and process to achieve accountability for results. With the New Deal for Engagement in Fragile States the g7+ demands accountability from development partners for the results that are achieved through development assistance. Consistent with this approach, it is also important that Timor-Leste requires accountability for results from ministries that spend public money.

The work of the Development Policy Coordination Mechanism in using the SDP Matrix will be vital to the successful realisation of the *Strategic Development Plan*. The development of the SDP Matrix was a highly inclusive and collaborative process with the intensive involvement of ministries as well as development partners. Later today we will release the SDP Matrix and this document will help guide our discussions during this 2014 Development Partners' Meeting.

Ladies and Gentlemen,

Despite our turbulent past, Timor-Leste has established a vibrant and free democracy, a tolerant and peaceful society and the foundations for sustained economic growth and development progress.

We thank all of you here today, our development partners, who have been such an important part of our success story to date. We look forward to continuing to work together so that we can achieve sustained development, positive international cooperation and a better future for the Timorese people.

Thank you very much.

70th Session of The United Nations Economic and Social Commission for Asia and the Pacific, Keynote Address

Bangkok, 7August 2014

His Excellency, Mr Tshering Tobgay, Prime Minister of Bhutan
His Excellency, Lord Tu'ivakano, Prime Minister of Tonga
His Excellency, Mr Manasvi Srisodapol, Deputy Permanent Secretary, Ministry of Foreign Affairs of Thailand
Her Excellency, Ms. Shamshad Akhtar, Under-Secretary-General of the United Nations and the Executive Secretary of ESCAP
His Excellency, Mr Shun-ichi Murata, Deputy Executive Secrtary of ESCAP
His Excellency, Mr Adnan H Aliani, Secretary of the Commission
Ministers
Excellencies
Distinguished Delegates
Ladies and Gentlemen,

In April last year, I was honoured to take over the Chair of the 69th session of the United Nations Economic and Social Commission for Asia and the Pacific.

And so I have had the privilege to Chair this Commission over the past year and work with the ESCAP secretariat, and the countries of the region, to make further progress towards sustainable development.

It is a privilege to again address the annual Commission session, the highest intergovernmental forum for policy dialogue on development issues in the Asian Pacific region.

Being Chair of the Commission has allowed me to work with you to shape approaches to economic and social challenges facing our region.

Last year, in this Hall, I made a call for us to work together to draw a road map for a joint approach to regional and sub-regional integrated development. I am pleased to be able to say that we have made significant progress.

Already in its 69th session, the Commission has adopted 17 resolutions that harness regional opportunity. The resolutions have supported opportunities for inclusive growth, addressing structural and development gaps, ending hunger, building resilience against external shocks both from natural disasters and financial crisis and have helped secure the sustainable future we all want.

In this session the Commission has also fostered regional consensus to set a path for enhanced energy security, and member countries have adopted a landmark agenda for shaping the future of sustainable energy in the region.

We have adopted a ground breaking agenda on population, development and rights, which issued a strong reaffirmation that gender equality and sexual and reproductive health rightsare indispensable to sustainable development, and must be a key part of the post-2015 development framework.

In December last year, Asia-Pacific countries unanimously endorsed a landmark declaration outlining the road map towards a regional economic community. Together with government leaders, ministers and senior officials from 36 countries, we adopted the 'Bangkok Declaration on Regional Economic Cooperation and Integration in Asia and the Pacific,' resolving to work closer together to build an integrated market, seamless transport and energy connectivity, financial cooperation and enhance resilience to address vulnerabilities and risks of natural disasters.

This year, the Commission has been the regional platform for Asia-Pacific countries to foster consensus on the shape of the post-2015 development agenda. We have sought an agenda that keeps the promise and the commitment to fight poverty, hunger, and other forms of deprivation, but also faces head-on the problems of rising inequality, fragility and conflict, exploitation, climate change and environmental pressures.

Excellencies

Ladies and Gentlemen,

While I am pleased with the significant progress we have made through ESCAP, our region and the globe continues to face many challenges. Last year, when I accepted the Chair of the 69th session of ESCAP, I spoke of concerns for a world of disunity and disorder. Regrettably, since that time, we have seen a deterioration in the state of world affairs.

Last month we were all shocked to learn of the shooting down of Malaysian Airlines flight MH17 and the death of so many innocent people. In many ways, the tragedy of flight MH17 reflects the current state of international relations in which a cold war mentality continues to infect global perspectives. We see countries blindly pursue their own short term self-interest rather than working together for a common good.

In the Middle East the hopes and promise of the Arab Spring are now just an idealistic memory blown away like desert sand in the wind. Across the region we see a rise in fundamentalism, intolerance and unfathomable sectarian violence.

We watch in horror the terror and death in Israel and Gaza and despair that peace remains elusive. I believe many of us received the open letter from the President of Indonesia, His Excellency, Susilo Bambang Yudhoyono, on this issue. Allow me, ladies and gentlemen, to quote His Excellency:

> *Although I am a Muslim, I realise full well that this conflict is not a religious conflict. I do not associate my call and thoughts with Islam, Judaism, Catholicism, Christianity and any other faiths or religious beliefs. The problems that we are facing now relate to the issue of humanity, morality, law, and war ethics, as well as actions from any side that have gone way beyond what is acceptable. This humanitarian tragedy and unbearable human misery are also attributed to the sense of responsibility from the leaders, which directly or indirectly have made this humanitarian tragedy an enduring problem.*

In East Asia, the powerhouse of the world economy, we are despondent as tensions rise between our close friends and we all know that there is, or there should be, a better way…to build collective understanding for more reciprocal cooperation and shared benefits.

Across the globe, according to the United Nations, there are still 2.2 billion people already facing, or heading towards, poverty, hunger, disease and exclusion. Even with the remarkable growth of the Asia-Pacific our region is still home to nearly two–thirds of the world's poor.

Meanwhile, we are watching a dangerous rise in inequality with wealth and power being accumulated by the few, to the detriment of the rest of humanity. After the greed and corruption of the international financial system caused the Global Financial Crisis we are seeing the entire population of the developed world struggling with enormous economic burden, as a result of dramatic austerity measures, where the recovery only benefits the very perpetrators of the financial meltdown. And so, elite interests, with huge financial resources, have been able to avoid paying their share of tax and have been able to capture and dominate governments. We must remember that the problem is not just inequality within nations but also between nations with the entrenchment of economic segregation of the world's Least Developed Countries. Even with the situation like this, world leaders only focus to escalate tensions and support war.

Nowadays, everybody who follows the news hears of people talking about stopping the war. I believe we should start changing our mindset and instead of talking about war we should all be making a big campaign for peace. And instead of saying 'I am against war', we should say 'I am for peace' because peace is more than the end of war, or the absence of war; peace means in political environments, peace for inclusive development, and peace in the relations amongst societies and between nations.

And, in the middle of the humanitarian crisis provoked by war in so many places, last week the Pacific Islands Forum was held in Palau and the threat of climate change again dominated the agenda. The weak global response to climate change threatens the very existence of some nations that risk being swallowed by the rising waves of the Pacific Ocean.

Excellencies

Ladies and Gentlemen,

While there may have been deterioration in international affairs over the past year we also have reason for hope.

As well as the good work of this Commission we have also witnessed great progress throughout our own region.

In India and Indonesia we have seen the world's first and third largest democracies hold successful elections. Indonesia is Timor-Leste's closest neighbour and has being enjoying ten years of inspired leadership by His Excellency Susilo Bambang Yudhoyono building a modern democracy of unity and progress. We will now see another peaceful transition to President Joko Widodo and we wish him all the best for his great nation. We believe that the political leaders will put the interests of the people first in order to create a climate of tolerance and unity as the guiding principle for development.

We are all in Bangkok where instability has led to political changes. On behalf of the people of Timor-Leste, and I believe on behalf of all the members of ESCAP, and knowing that there is already a road map presented by the National Council of Peace and Order to make sure that the transition to the democratic process can proceed with the involvement of all the components of society, I can say that we understand that with every social, economic and political process each country always faces big challenges. What is important is that everybody undertakes proper introspection in order to serve the interests of the State, the country and all of the population. In the end we wish all the best to the people of Thailand.

In China progress continues to astound us all as this nation lifts hundreds of millions of people out of poverty, drives regional and global economic growth and makes sweeping governance reforms. With it, we see economies throughout the Asia-Pacific growing at remarkable rates to improve the quality of life for so many in our region.

And technological progress continues to drive positive change and connect us all in ways unthinkable even in the recent past.

Ladies and Gentlemen,

To address the challenges of our region and to realise our opportunities we must continue to work with dedication and commitment. ESCAP provides the forum to bring us all together to forge a common partnership for progress.

Next month the United Nations General Assembly will consider the proposed Sustainable Development Goals and the future global development agenda.

Timor-Leste has been working hard, through the g7+ group of 20 fragile and conflict affected nations, to make sure that this agenda reflects the needs of fragile States and recognises that without peace there can be no development.

We are pleased that one of the proposed Sustainable Development Goals is to 'Promote peaceful and inclusive societies for sustainable development, provide access to justice for all and build effective, accountable and inclusive institutions at all levels'.

We must all work together to make sure that the outcome of the deliberations in New York next month will be to set a global framework to ensure sustained and inclusive development for all. In this, the role of ESCAP, as the most inclusive intergovernmental platform in Asia and the Pacific, is crucial.

Excellencies,

Ladies and Gentlemen,

Despite global challenges, I remain positive about our future. We need to continue to focus on our shared interests and the importance of tolerance, cooperation and peace. We need to continue taking collective regional and international actions to build resilient, just and vibrant societies.

The Commission plays an important role undertaking policy research and analysis on critical and emerging issues and bringing them to the attention of member States for policy discussion and decisions.

The Commission also has a role building the capacities of member States on those issues through technical cooperation at the regional level and by forging partnerships with other development partners within and outside the United Nations system.

I now renew my call for us to work together to chart the path for the sustainable development of our region. I look forward to seeing this reflected in the outcome of the 70th ESCAP Commission Session and I wish you all success in your deliberations. I joined the Prime Minister of Bhutan today and know he will be an excellent Chair of the session.

Last but not least I would like to pay tribute to Dr Noeleen Heyzer for her hard work and dedication to ESCAP. Dr Heyzer is now the Special Adviser of the United Nations Secretary General for Timor-Leste giving us very useful insights into our task of strengthening our State and improving our service delivery as well as reducing poverty and inequality between rural and urban areas. Thank you Noeleen.

To the new Executive Secretary of ESCAP, and the Under-Secretary-General of the United Nations, Ms. Shamshad Akhtar, I wish you all the best in your current endeavour. Today you presented a very comprehensive vision and inspirational description of the important issues we all have to address together.

Thank you very much.

Address at the World Summit 2014: 'Peace, Security and Human Development'

Seoul, 10 August 2014

Your Excellencies the Heads of State and Government
Your Excellencies the Heads of Delegation
Your Excellencies the First Ladies
Distinguished leaders of the Universal Peace Foundation
Dr Charles Yang, Chairman
Dr Thomas Walsh, President
Mr Tageldin Hamad, Secretary-General
Ladies and Gentlemen,

First and foremost, I want to express my sincere thanks for being invited to this World Summit for the second consecutive time.

I congratulate the Universal Peace Federation for their faith and tenacity, and particularly Mother Moon for her commitment and Father Moon for his legacy, in making sure that many important global issues continue to be on the agenda of so many international leaders that are here today. I believe the testimonies of the distinguished individuals in attendance will contribute to raising awareness about international concerns that afflict humankind.

Currently, the idea of achieving peace, security and human development for all countries and for all peoples of the world is nothing but a simple mirage, and this is because it is not yet even a dream or a legitimate aspiration.

And if, in these meetings, we cannot find solutions for all the problems of the world; if we cannot immediately relieve the suffering of the victims of the horror of the war, of poverty and of the countless abuses perpetrated in a troubled world – where moral values are subjugated to the economic interests of a powerful minority – we can, at least, continue to be attentive and to try raising collective concerns.

We want to contribute with our experiences, our perspectives and our clear desire to change the current world disorder, so that the primacy of the Human Person is put at the core of the political agenda of the global decision-makers.

Ladies and Gentlemen,

I represent a small country that, like so many others over the history of Humankind, suffered atrocities perpetrated over centuries, in successive events that brought us to this day.

Timor-Leste became independent on 20 May 2002, after 24 years of a hard struggle. Being a country that had just emerged from a prolonged conflict with Indonesia, as well as conflict among ourselves, we opted for dialogue, tolerance and reconciliation.

We knew that all our people wanted was to live in peace, because peace was the only condition in which to feel free. Immediately after the end of the war, we started a difficult and lengthy process to achieve a true reconciliation within Timorese society. This process led to the establishment of a Commission of Truth, Mutual Acceptance and Reconciliation, where all the victims of repression could testify without fear.

All the testimonies of violations of human rights are now sealed and safe in the Office of that Commission, which produced its Report which was titled 'Enough!'. 'Enough' is a strong word that will remind everybody of the commitment of the entire society not to repeat the conflict of the past, for the sake of the Timorese people.

Following this report, we believed we could go beyond our borders and, thanks to the goodwill of the Indonesian leaders, the two States established a Commission of Truth and Friendship. For two years, a joint team worked hard to hear all the witnesses and the possible perpetrators of the violations of human rights. The final report was signed by the Heads of State and Government of both countries, putting an end to the painful past, with a solemn agreement that the Timorese and Indonesian people will never again be harmed.

I have to say, to uphold this policy of reconciliation, we needed to fight against pressure from the international community that demanding trials in the International Court of Justice, in accordance with a principle of 'no impunity', for the 'perpetrators of crimes against humanity'.

We fought against this hypocrisy in the mind-set of the world leaders that, even today, are supporting other conflicts and wars, without any sense of responsibility, just as they supported the war in Timor-Leste.

Both Timor-Leste and Indonesia wanted to clear the way for true and genuine reconciliation and tolerance amongst communities and people, rather than feed hatred and revenge that would only destroy the country and impede the efforts of the population to improve their living conditions.

As a result of this forward looking policy, Indonesia and Timor-Leste now enjoy a solid relationship between people and between States, based on cooperation, friendship and a collective vision for the future.

Today, Timor-Leste is a development success story, thanks to the determination of our people and the support of our international friends. Timor-Leste has established a vibrant and free democracy, a tolerant and peaceful society and the foundations for sustained economic growth and development progress.

At the same time, we are witnessing the amazing transition in our neighbour Indonesia, from an autocratic regime to a sound democracy, with an emerging economy and a pluralistic and tolerant society. Indeed, Indonesia has become one of the main development partners of Timor-Leste.

More than a close neighbour, Indonesia is an inspiration for our Nation. Under the wise leadership of His Excellency Susilo Bambang Yudhoyono, we witnessed the construction of a modern democracy that encompasses progress and the promotion of peace at national, regional and international level. We wish that the peaceful transition to President Joko Widodo will contribute to the success of this great nation.

Ladies and Gentlemen,

At the end of the millennium, when we Timorese were deciding our own future, the world proclaimed the end of the cold war and the advantages of globalisation and the technological and communications revolution.

We are now on the eve of 2015 and no LDC, essentially the fragile and conflict affected countries, will achieve a single millennium development goal.

Instead, in some countries in Africa, abductions, bombings, war and killings are the daily news that feed the hunger, fulfil the poverty and sustain the persistence all kinds of deprivation.

We continue to watch helplessly as the Middle East tears itself apart as a result of endless sectarian violence and disputes that have gone on for far too long. We watch scenes of horror and death as well as bloody confrontations in Syria and Iraq, in Afghanistan and, very recently, in Ukraine.

We are also watching Libya on a continuous descent into chaos. In addition to the calamity that is the loss of human lives, an environmental disaster also appears to be looming. Throughout the region we see frailty and conflict, making it impossible for anyone to predict the future. The high hopes of the Arab Spring have become a hell in which it is mostly the innocent who have become the victims.

We were caught with disbelief and deep sadness by the events in Israel and Gaza and despair that peace remains elusive. His Excellency, the President of Indonesia, wrote an open letter to the world leaders and I ask you to allow me to read a paragraph of Dr. Susilo Bambang Yudhoyono:

> *Although I am a Muslim, I realise full well that this conflict is not a religious conflict. I do not associate my call and thoughts with Islam, Judaism, Catholicism, Christianity and any other faiths or religious beliefs.*
>
> *The problems that we are facing now relate to the issue of humanity, morality, law and war ethics, as well as actions from any side that have gone way beyond what is acceptable. This humanitarian tragedy and unbearable human misery*

are also attributed to the sense of responsibility from the leaders, which directly or indirectly have made this humanitarian tragedy an enduring problem.

And yet, there is no single reason in the entire world that justifies the massacre of innocent civilians, including women and children. Nor could the threat of so-called 'weapons of mass destruction in Iraq' justify the endless war that destroyed that country, and which is now heading to a fatal self-mutilation.

In the name of 'universal values' and 'moral principles', the world's decision-makers chose war to impose democracy, provoking conflicts to teach human rights. And it seems that the world is preparing a diversion from the tragedy in providing humanitarian assistance. With billions of dollars spent sustaining war, and millions of dollars spent on emergency needs to temporarily solve the problems of refugees, the World avoids looking deeply into the roots of the problems.

Inequality, exclusion, disease, hunger and poverty all stimulate anger, despair and revolt, which contribute to intolerance, to radical behaviours towards others and to extremism of actions by individuals seeking to achieve feelings of psychological compensation in accordance with their sense of injustice.

Ladies and Gentlemen,

If peace doesn't necessarily mean the absence of war, security certainly cannot mean a strong and well equipped army, ready to be deployed to any corner of the planet.

Security, for every single person and every single country, comes from the sense of a peaceful social environment, security means a tolerant and stable political atmosphere and security means a sense of freedom as the result of good regional and international cooperation.

And while in our region, including under ASEAN, nations are cooperating and promoting peace – which, led by China, has enabled Asia's rise and the lifting of hundreds of millions of people from poverty – we must still be worried with the tensions in the east and south of the China Sea.

I just came from the 70th Session of the United Nations Economic and Social Commission for Asia and the Pacific (ESCAP) in Bangkok in which debates were focused on how to reduce the inequalities in the Asia-Pacific Region. And I continue to appeal to all parties to seek beneficial solutions through dialogue, instead of increasing the capability of winning through rising tensions. Asia-Pacific is a large region, where every single person seeks peace and security to develop himself or herself, their family, the community, the country and, consequently, the whole region.

Your Excellencies

Ladies and Gentlemen,

Before I conclude, I would like to share with you that Timor-Leste has been working hard within the scope of the g7+, a group of 20 fragile and conflict-affected countries. In addition to sharing experiences and knowledge and seeking to put the needs of those countries on the international development agenda, we continue repeating that there can be no development without peace.

Unfortunately, theatres of war are common place today. Often, the unjustified use of violence or the isolation of countries with international sanctions are the instruments for the supposed instilment of universal values and democracy. However, death, destruction, misery and isolation do not build democracies or Nations.

Furthermore, in the imbalance of today's multipolar system, crises can lead to unpredictable results!

The spirit of solidarity and cooperation should prevail in the world. If Timor-Leste is today a success story and a peaceful country that is growing fast, it is in part due to the international aid we received during the final stage of our struggle for independence and, particularly, during our early years of Statebuilding.

Ultimately, ladies and gentlemen, it is sad to recognise that, today, we can do unimaginable feats, thanks to advances in knowledge and technology, but we still cannot search within ourselves to find peace!

Our campaign should not be anymore 'I am against war', because it will lead us to try to end the war, whatever the consequences. Our campaign should be 'I am for peace', because peace doesn't mean the end of a war or the absence of war; peace means peace of mind, peace in the social behaviour, peace in the solidarity of communities, peace in political environment and peace in the relations between people and between nations.

We need a World of Peace!

Thank you very much.

Address to a Business and Investment Lunch Hosted by DLA Piper

Melbourne, 19 September 2014

Andrew Darwin, Chief Operating Officer and Managing Partner, Australia, DLA Piper
Stephen Webb, Partner, DLA Piper
The Honourable Harold Mitchell AC
Bishop Hilton Deakin
Justice John Dowd AO
Distinguished guests
Ladies and gentlemen,

Thank you all for coming. I would particularly like to thank Harold Mitchell for coming today, and for his friendship with Kirsty and myself over the last decade.

He may be half the man he was on the outside but Harold's heart is as big as it ever was!

While I am only going to speak briefly, as there are other speakers today, including the Timor-Leste Minister for Petroleum and Minerals Resources, my message today is that Timor-Leste is ready for foreign investment and that we want to invite more Australians to do business in Timor-Leste.

It is now 15 years since our people bravely voted for independence and we set out on our path of nation building. It has not always been easy, and we have had to overcome many challenges along the way.

We have had to work hard to heal the wounds of war in our nation and in our neighbourhood. We are now at peace in our country and our relationship with Indonesia is a model for international reconciliation. It was only last month that our good friend, the President of Indonesia, His Excellency Dr Susilo Bambang Yudhoyono, visited Timor-Leste and proclaimed that Indonesia and Timor-Leste now enjoy the best bi-lateral relationship in the region. And, more recently, a group of retired Indonesian generals and widows came to pay tribute to the victims of the war, to our national heroes in Metinaro and to the deceased Indonesian soldiers.

We still face the challenge of having to build our national infrastructure. We also started from scratch as most of our roads, bridges, schools, hospitals and other buildings had been destroyed. And we started with no institutions of State, we had no governing body with experience running a country and we had a legal vacuum with no functioning legal system. Being 12 years old, we are making progress, although there is still much to be done.

Ladies and gentlemen,

While we are a small nation of just over 1 million people we are fortunate to be rich in natural resources. This has helped to charge our economy and since 2007 we have enjoyed average non-oil GDP growth of over 10%.

To help realise our potential, and focus our nation building efforts, we produced a 20 year *Strategic Development Plan* in 2011 with a framework to transform our country from a low income nation to a country with upper-middle income levels with a healthy, well educated and prosperous population.

The Plan is based on the premise that to create jobs and build a sustainable future we need to develop a strong market economy and a diversified private sector.

To help achieve this goal we have set some of the lowest income and corporate tax rates in the world while having a very low cost base for doing business. We have also adopted an expansive fiscal policy to help relieve poverty and strengthen our human resources.

Our sovereign wealth fund, the Petroleum Fund, has grown from its opening balance of $205 million in September 2005 to almost $17 billion today. The Fund is growing everyday and underpins our economic growth and our capacity to support our people into the future. By diversifying the investment of the Fund beyond bonds, to around 50% in equities, we have achieved over the last 3 years a return of $2.7 billion and, in the first 6 months of 2014 alone our return is around $900 million.

We are investing in a large infrastructure program including a national port, airports and a national road network and we are looking for international partners who can join with us to build our nation.

We are also committed to major nation building projects. This includes developing our south coast into a regional petroleum sector hub which the Minister for Resources and Energy will talk more about shortly.

We have also established a Special Economic Zone in the district of Oe-cusse where we will provide incentives, a simple regulatory and tax environment and land to attract foreign investment in industries including tourism and finance.

Friends, we are part of the Asian growth story and we are on Australia's doorstep – Díli is only one hour from Darwin by air.

Timor-Leste provides a peaceful and beautiful place to oversee investments. We enjoy stability and one of the safest capital cities in the world.

With traditional emerging markets becoming crowded with competition, our country provides sophisticated investors with the opportunity for high returns across a wide range of industries. While we are part of the Asian growth story we also provide the chance for early entry into an economy with limited competition that is on Australia's doorstep.

And we have a culture Australians can relate to. Many of our people have deep connections to Australia and Victoria has the largest overseas Timorese population with over 10,000 Timorese Australians living in this State.

Timor-Leste also provides a great opportunity to invest to transform. Investments can have national significance and make a substantial contribution to improving the lives of the Timorese people.

Ladies and gentlemen,

I know we have focused on business today but I want to share with you another important part of the relationship between Timor-Leste and Australia, and that is between our veterans. Our countries share a military history that goes back to the Second World War. And recently, through the invitation of the National President of Australian RSL, the Timorese veterans from the resistance struggle came to Australia and marched under the RSL banner on ANZAC Day. More than that, they saw how Australia respects and treats its veterans and they came back to Timor-Leste incredibly impressed.

And so, I invited representatives of Australian veterans to Timor-Leste who attended FALINTIL Day, our veterans day, and we were all moved when our Timorese children's choir sang Waltzing Matilda in perfect 'Australian' at a function at the President's Palace. This relationship is now strong and we look forward to further exchanges and building this relationship of solidarity.

Ladies and gentlemen,

Timor-Leste has established a tolerant and peaceful society with a vibrant democracy that upholds the rule of law.

With our open economy, expansive fiscal policy, large infrastructure program, low tax rates and strong government support we have established a platform for sustained economic growth.

We are looking for international partners to work with us to build our economy and help us provide a better future for our people.

Thank you for coming today, I hope we meet next in Timor-Leste.

High-level Ministerial Lunch Meeting on Peace and Capable Institutions as Stand-alone Goals in the Post-2015 Development Agenda

New York, 22 September 2014

Distinguished guests
Ladies and gentlemen,

We are all here because we are committed to advancing human development, eradicating poverty and securing a sustainable future.

The world took a great step forward in 2000 when the United Nations agreed on the Millennium Development Goals.

The MDGs focused the global development effort on achieving eight goals that addressed poverty, education, gender, child mortality, maternal health, disease, environmental sustainability and development funding. Since the adoption of the Millennium Development Goals we have experienced unprecedented human progress.

We have seen hundreds of millions of people lifted from poverty, and improved health and education outcomes across many countries of the world.

However, it is important to note, that much of this progress is not because of the global development effort, but because of the rise of Asia and, in particular, of China.

It is even more important to note, that there are still 2.2 billion people living in poverty in fragile and conflict affected nations – nations that will not achieve even a single Millennium Development Goal by 2015.

The common factor in many of the nations left behind, despite the MDG initiative, is conflict. Sometimes a truth is so obvious that it is easily overlooked. The truth we have learned through bitter experience in Timor-Leste is that you must have peace – before you can even begin to rebuild a state.

Ladies and gentlemen, there was not a Millennium Development Goal that addressed this fundamental truth.

We must ensure we do not ignore the obvious, as we work together to formulate the post 2015 development agenda.

I am very pleased to see that a peace related goal is one of the 17 Sustainable Development Goals suggested by the Open Working Group.

Sustainable Development Goal 16 is to: 'Promote peaceful and inclusive societies for sustainable development, provide access to justice for all and build effective, accountable and inclusive institutions at all levels.'

This is a very welcome move, but I believe it should be Sustainable Development Goal number 1, as none of the other 16 goals will be achievable without peace and effective state institutions.

Let me share with you some hard 'truths' we learned in Timor-Leste to explain what I mean.

Firstly, while we have made remarkable progress in many areas, we are not on track to reach the targets set under even one of the Millennium Development Goals. This is perhaps in part, because we are a very young nation. We are younger even than the Millennium Development Goals, having only achieved our independence in 2002 after a war of resistance that lasted nearly a quarter of a century.

But it is also because following independence, and despite extensive assistance from the international community, we found ourselves trapped in a cycle of violence and unrest. In 2006, we faced our greatest crisis as sections of our police and army resorted to armed conflict and took us to the brink of civil war. The crisis wiped out years of development progress and we realised that our problem was not that we were poor but that our institutions were weak

Children stopped going to school, health clinics were deserted because people were too scared to make the journey to the clinic, our economy was stagnating because the government went into shut down and international investors fled. We had 150,000 people living as displaced people in their own country because they were too scared to go back to their villages.

After much national reflection, we decided we had to make our number one priority the peaceful resolution of our differences. We realised that there can be no development if there is chaos. We realised that without peace, we would betray the dreams of all those who died in our quest for independence. And we realised that without peace, we would be failing our children.

So we started a dialogue. We convinced our rebel soldiers in the mountains to surrender peacefully. Our friends here at the United Nations said it would take a decade but within two years, the tents were gone and our people had all returned home to their villages.

And we began to rebuild our State institutions. We still have a long way to go.

But you only have to compare Díli of eight years ago with the Díli of today to know we are on the right track and that we have made remarkable progress.

Ladies and gentlemen

As we embarked upon the process of consolidating peace and building our institutions we discovered that our experience was not unique. There were other nations around the world which were fragile, or affected by conflict, that were not on track to achieve a single Millennium Development Goal.

We came together to speak with one voice as the g7+ group of fragile and conflict affected nations. The g7+ now represents 20 nations that have learnt, through bitter experience that a global development framework will not work without a focus on peace building and State building.

Sadly, the crisis in South Sudan is the most recent example of the hope of development progress being destroyed by conflict, and the failure of state institutions.

And then there is the Ebola crisis gripping West African nations that highlights the critical need for capable institutions to address what could become a global health crisis.

I want to state here that Timor-Leste will contribute $1 million to assist the West African g7+ member nations dealing with the Ebola crisis.

And we see disturbing events in the Middle East unfold which prove the need for peace and properly functioning governments.

We also have to ask the question – who profits from conflict in developing nations? The answer of course, is ultimately those corporations that manufacture and sells the arms. We need some collective action in the United Nations to properly monitor and investigate who profits from conflict.

Ladies and gentlemen,

If we are serious about having sustainable development goals that will have a transformative impact on human development and global peace and security, then we need a stand-alone goal that addresses peace building and effective, accountable and inclusive institutions.

I urge the international community to embrace this goal so we can ensure that no nations, and no people, are left behind by the global development agenda.

And so, as we look into the future, I hope that securing global, regional and national peace will be our consuming agenda.

Because there can be no sustainable development without peace.

Thank you very much.

International Conference: INTERFET, Reflections on the 1999 East Timor Crisis

Melbourne, 20 September 2014

Lieutenant General Kiki Syahnakri (Rtd)
Major General Surasit Thanadtang
Lieutenant General Ash Power, AO, CSC (Rtd) (former Colonel Operations INTERFET)
Major General Mark Kelly, AO, DSC (Rtd) (former Chief of Staff INTERFET)
Major General Orlando Ambrocio (Rtd) (former Commander of the
Philippines Humanitarian Support Mission to East Timor)
Major General Jim Barry, AM, MBE, RFD, ED (Rtd)
Colonel Marcus Fielding (former Brigade Major West Force, INTERFET)
Admiral Chris Barrie, AC (Rtd) (former Chief of the Australian Defence Force)
Doctor John Blaxland (former Intelligence Officer West Force, INTERFET)
Colonel Kevin Burnett, ONZM (Rtd) (former Commanding Officer New Zealand Battalion)
Lieutenant General Mark Evans, AO, DSC (Rtd) (former Commander West Force, INTERFET)
Colonel Neil Thompson, CSC (Rtd) (former Commander Response Force, INTERFET)
Excellencies,
Distinguished participants
Ladies and gentlemen,

It is a privilege to speak at this Conference marking the 15 year anniversary of the arrival of INTERFET in Timor-Leste.

I commend Military History and Heritage Victoria, the School of International, Political and Strategic Studies, the College of Asia and the Pacific and the Strategic and Defence Studies Centre, Australian National University, for co-hosting this event.

This conference gives us the opportunity to reflect on the events that led to the Restoration of Independence in Timor-Leste and the fiery re-birth of our nation.

It reminds us of the strength and resilience of our people and of a time when humanitarian values of peace and freedom guided the behavior of nations.

While we know that the crisis of 1999 revealed some of the worst of humanity, it also revealed humanity as its best – as demonstrated by the resilience and strength of our people, and by the decision of the international community to intervene to stop the violence.

Ladies and gentlemen,

I want to share with you my perspective on the crisis of 1999, and the need for the intervention of International Forces East Timor, known with great affection as INTERFET.

To understand the significance of the INTERFET intervention it is necessary to consider the history of our struggle for independence and to locate that struggle in the context of broader international events.

The Timorese undertook a long and difficult path to liberation. For almost five centuries we were subject to the Portuguese colonial rule, a situation which led to numerous unsuccessful revolts. Our history registered the biggest and the last one in 1912, the Manufahi Revolt, which we celebrated in 2012. This same spirit of resistance was on display during the devastating Japanese occupation of our land during the Second World War.

The Second World War was the first significant major event that brought the Timorese and Australian people together. In December 1941 the 2/2nd Independent Company landed in neutral Portuguese Timor and the following February the Japanese invaded. The 2/2nd conducted a guerrilla style campaign in our mountains and valleys that was in many ways was replicated by the Timorese resistance decades later. In September 1942 the 2/4th Independent Company joined the 2/2nd before both companies withdrew back to Australia by January 1943.

The Australian soldiers were clearly brave, remarkable men. But they could not have been so effective without the support of the thousands of Timorese villagers who risked their lives, with many losing their lives as well, to provide food and shelter, carry supplies and act as guides and scouts for the Australian soldiers.

Ladies and gentlemen,

In April 1974, the Carnation Revolution put an end to the dictatorship and to the colonial empire in Portugal. This led to the recognition of the right to self-determination for the African colonies as well as for Timor-Leste, so on 28 November 1975, we made a unilateral declaration of independence. Nine days later we were invaded by the Indonesian Armed Forces.

The past is a very different place and was a period of high international tension in Southeast Asia. The United States and Australia were engaged in the Vietnam War, responding to western fears of the spread of communism. By the end of 1975 the war was lost and communist governments came to power in Vietnam, Cambodia and Laos.

Like so many people living in poor countries around the world, the Timorese also became victims of the Cold War. Our people were forsaken by the major western powers that gave Soeharto the green light to invade East Timor and, for two decades, remained silent or supported our annexation. And so, for 24 years, we fought a war without any external military support, while developed nations supplied weapons, tanks, aircraft and training to the occupying forces to destroy the resistance of the small and ill-equipped guerrilla army, with less than 1,500 personnel. Unlike other liberation struggles, in Africa and Asia, we did not have a land border with a friendly country or an external provider of weapons. We were fighting literally alone, solely dependent on our capability to counter the annihilation operations.

However, our strategy was to fight not only in our lands, but also in the hearts and minds of the international public. We took our campaign to countries around the world and to the United Nations. Our weapons in this campaign included newspaper and magazine articles, photos, films, public talks and protests. We built one of the largest solidarity movements in the world.

Importantly, we took our campaign to Indonesia. We never considered the Indonesian people our enemies as we knew they were also suffering under the dictatorship that, ironically, was a good ally of the western powers. We prioritised developing relationships of solidarity including with the pro-democracy movement inside Indonesia.

Ladies and gentlemen,

We were fortunate to have the support of many Australians. We knew that despite the unjust policies of successive Australian Governments, the Australian people did not support the illegal occupation of our country. Many Australian solidarity movement activists suffered intimidation, but they continued to support us.

We owe them a great debt as without their support, I would not be here today and Timor-Leste would not be an independent nation. We have honoured many of them with the Order of Timor-Leste.

The late Brian Manning and Dennis Freney were two honoured very recently, in a ceremony at the Presidential Palace in Díli.

Brian Manning, and other Australian supporters, ensured that we had six radio transmitters that allowed the resistance to communicate with the outside world. This operation was illegal in Australia and continued until the end 1978, because our radio transmitter was captured in that year, terminating the only link between the outside world and the resistance. However, in 1984, I received a new radio transmitter and we re-established the link to Darwin. It was more difficult to work in Darwin than in the mountains of Timor-Leste and I was informed so many times they had to change their locations to avoid confiscation and arrest. And then the day came and we lost again our only radio link to the outside world.

Dennis Freney was the pioneer of the first movement of Australian solidarity with Timor-Leste. Mr Freney helped establish several branches throughout Australia of the Campaign for the Independence of East Timor. Despite surveillance, monitoring and persecution by intelligence and security agencies, Mr Freney worked tirelessly so that the world got to know that our resistance was strong.

We also honoured the late Dr. Andrew McNaughton, a medical doctor who visited Timor-Leste many times during the 1990s. In October 1998, Dr Andrew McNaughtan smuggled out the entire Indonesian army personnel records. These records showed that troop numbers had increased, disproving claims of military withdrawal. He also worked tirelessly to tell the stories of the Australian soldiers who fought in Timor in Second World War and the Timorese who helped them.

One such soldier, now deceased, was Cliff Morris, an Australian dairy farmer from New South Wales. At the age of 21 he had fought in Timor-Leste during the Second World War as a commando with 2nd/4th Independent Company. In 1976 Mr Morris was one of four Australians who were arrested, convicted and fined for trying to sail to East Timor with medical supplies. Cliff Morris said the reason he supported our people was because he owed his life to them during Second World War. Sadly, Mr Morris died in 1998 and never saw an independent Timor-Leste.

Just today, I was also privileged to award the Order of Solidarity to four Australian activists at a ceremony at Queen's Hall at the Victorian Parliament. Three were in attendance, Jill Jolliffe, Fabio Cavadini and John Sinnott, while we honoured the memory of Michelle Turner who sadly passed before she could see an independent Timor-Leste. All made selfless and important contributions to our cause of freedom.

I cannot discuss INTERFET without mentioning some Australians who are unknown to us, but whose contributions are absolutely vital to making sense of the events of 1999. We do not know their names, and perhaps we never will, but these Australians ensured that there was a constant series of leaks of intelligence and diplomatic material that revealed the truth of our situation and provided momentum for action. I expect some of these leaks will be discussed today as we all look for the truth of this dramatic episode in our regional history.

Ladies and gentlemen,

While the Cold War had worked against us, towards the end of the millennium international events began to turn in our favour. In 1997, the Asian Financial Crisis spread through our region and gripped many countries of East Asia. Indonesia was hit particularly hard and its economy collapsed with plunging exchange rates and sky rocketing inflation. This led to widespread rioting and protests and as Indonesia started to falter, the resistance gained renewed hope and mass demonstrations were held across Timor. With the economic crisis engulfing Indonesia, after 30 years in power, President Soeharto was forced to step down on 21 May 1998.

And so, while the Asian Financial Crisis brought hardship to Indonesians, it also ushered in sweeping political changes that today remain of global significance. Just as the Timorese were on the cusp of achieving their independence, Indonesia's transition to democracy – and its emergence as a great nation – had begun.

After so many years of struggle, the combination of international and domestic pressure, internal upheaval and the costs of war gave us a chance at freedom. It was this path of history that led our people to be given, on 30 August 1999, the opportunity to vote on their future under a referendum called a 'popular consultation', to be conducted by a United Nations Mission in East Timor.

Like so many dramatic events in world history, this was a day so many people thought would never come. During the struggle, we followed with anxiety the referendum process in Western Sahara that, for no reason, is still being postponed today. I mention this because, while in Jakarta, under house arrest, the UNAMET Chief asked me to postpone, due to the increasing violence, and my answer was 'no', reminding him of the Western Sahara case and that, for two decades, we accepted all the sacrifices and we were ready for the last one.

I would suggest that this should give us all pause, when we consider responses to our new world of disorder, and remind us that if history has taught us anything it is that the future is unpredictable. And that if you don't take the right decision, at the right time, you will wait for too long to repair the damage, if you are able to at all. From the fall of the Soviet Union, the emergence of the Asian Financial Crisis, the development of the internet, the September 11 attacks, the Global Financial Crisis to the Arab Spring – these events that dramatically changed the world were unexpected by most, while we see the western powers battling with new and more difficult challenges.

Ladies and gentlemen,

Our independence Referendum was an uplifting event for our people that brought the promise of self-determination after many years of struggle. While we knew the wishes in the hearts of our people, we also knew best the situation on the ground in our country and the risks of a vote for independence.

On 30 August the Timorese people came out to vote in a collective act of courage and determination. The Referendum had a turnout rate of 98.6% and 78.5% voted for independence. The Timorese people had achieved what so many had told us was no more than a dream.

Today, the Referendum stands as a testament to the bravery and the dignity of our people. We knew that a vote for independence would provoke vengeance and retaliation. After the result was announced on 4 September widespread violence broke out, spreading across our country. People were killed as a scorched earth campaign of destruction was carried out, leaving most of our country in ruins.

This was a bittersweet moment for our people as our joy turned to despair. Just as our dreams of freedom were becoming a reality we faced further brutality and fear. Our people were desperate. We were not certain if the international community would intervene with peacekeeping forces, so desperately needed.

We, Falintil, chose not to participate in the voting process, knowing that it could provoke even more violence, than the terrible violence that had preceded the referendum many months before the vote. This was a strategic decision, not an easy one, but one that was the right one. We, in no way, wanted to risk the referendum being abandoned, or impugned; and Falintil stayed in barracks.

Despite the chaos and bloodshed that followed the referendum, our resistance soldiers still remained in barracks. While the armed FALINTIL guerillas could hear the pleas of anguish from their people, they did not-could not leave the barracks. That time in the barracks demonstrated the extraordinary discipline of our soldiers. It was a time of great torment for our people and our soldiers, but we had learnt the hard lessons of history and knew that, if we responded to the violence, the situation in our country would have been portrayed as a civil war. That time of doing nothing, was the ultimate test of our resistance.

We knew that the world was watching and that there was great international concern for our situation. And it was clear that we needed help to deal with our humanitarian and security crisis, and that we needed help to restore order. As our country went up in flames, the pressure for something to be done increased.

As I am speaking in Melbourne, I must pay tribute to the more than 40,000 people who marched here in this city on 10 September 1999. They were followed by tens of thousands more around Australia, all demanding respect for our right to self-determination. I must also thank the Australian union movement and its members who stood with us and undertook effective action in support of our cause.

And, of course, I must thank the Australian Government for committing to lead the international peacekeeping effort to restore order in our country.

Ladies and gentlemen,

Following an invitation and authorisation from Indonesia, on 15 September the United Nations Security Council passed Resolution 1264 calling for a multi-national force to restore peace and stability. On 20 September 1999 INTERFET began deploying to our country. A coalition of 22 countries contributed to INTERFET. At its peak more than 11,000 personnel were involved.

I am pleased that we have the key players from many of nations participating at this conference including New Zealand, Thailand and the Philippines.

INTERFET was, of course, led by force commander, Major General Peter Cosgrove, now Sir Peter Cosgrove, Governor-General of the Commonwealth of Australia, who shall join us shortly, to give his account of INTERFET.

Major General Cosgrove and I established a good working relationship. I soon realised that he was a man of moral integrity and a great leader. However, it took a serious incident for both of us to get to that point. It was the matter of the modus operandi between INTERFET and FALINTIL, and it was this modus operandi, that aided and enabled the success of the INTERFET Mission. FALINTIL had not only accepted to be cantoned, but had embraced it, knowing it was an essential plank in INTERFET's securing of the peace. The incident I shall now recount put the mission at risk.

It was 11 pm, November 18th, 1999. I had fallen into bed, after another exhausting day, when Commander Riak was ushered in. His distress was evident as he told me that a group of some 20 Falintil soldiers had been moving from their cantonment of Bobonaro to cantonment at Alieu, and when their truck broke in Díli, they were surrounded by some seven tanks and truckloads of INTERFET soldiers who confiscated their weapons, in a heavy handed manner.

I knew I had to take action and I did.

Early next morning a helicopter touched down in Alieu with an INTERFET official on board, to try and talk me out of my protest visit to Díli. I declined to meet and headed off with my men. I had a pistol in its holster strapped to my leg and my men had their arms. If anyone was going to disarm my men, they had to disarm me. We drove in convoy until we were intercepted by INTERFET at Dare (ironically where the Sparrow Force memorial is). Major-General Cosgrove tried to talk me out of proceeding, but we kept going. We got further down the road towards Díli, to a place called Lahane, where we stopped to refuel. The INTERFET vehicles set up a roadblock. We got out and marched past, with INTERFET following behind. Our people came out in droves. They were happy to see us, singing out 'Viva Falintil'. It was both tense and festive. Major-General Cosgrove appealed to me not to proceed. I responded. 'In my country we do not negotiate on the side of the road. I will talk to you at the UN compound, which is where we are heading.'

We marched into Sergio's office at UNTAET Headquarters. Major General Cosgrove followed. I then outlined the incident and its impact. Major General Cosgrove explained that it had arisen due to a misunderstanding, and in future greater attention would be given to identifying any armed group. I responded saying, 'Your men are the saviours of our people, General, but please don't forget that the heroes are my men, the Falintil. I will not accept that they be treated like armed bandits or petty criminals'.

Honour and order was then restored, on a handshake. The strategy was on track.

Thanks to Major General Cosgrove's inspired leadership INTERFET now enjoys a legendary quality in Australia's military history.

INTERFET had been warmly welcomed by the Timorese and is remembered well by our people. It freed us from a dark period of awful violence and fear. It ended a humanitarian crisis and allowed our people to come down from their hideouts in the mountains and begin the process of building a new democratic state.

INTERFET was an outstanding success that brought peace and restored order over a country and provided the stability to allow the United Nations mission, UNTAET, to effectively begin its operations.

We must also record for historical purposes what I cited above, and it is that the success of INTERFET was also thanks to the cooperation and support of FALINTIL. The support that was given was of a strategic nature. It was to actively engage in our cantonment, and if we left not to carry our weapons. We were mature enough to know that needed to be done for the sake of the nation. That was our very reason for existence and we were not going to abandon our cause at this final stage of our independence struggle. We knew that INTERFET needed to have full capability to succeed.

The FALINTIL soldiers, who had for years fought in the most difficult of conditions to free their people, welcomed the INTERFET force and assisted them in their mission.

I also want to acknowledge that despite the ensuing carnage the late Sergio Vieira de Mello, Major General Peter Cosgrove, Lieutenant General Kiki Syahnakri, and I met at the border to discuss and agree on the best way to secure the peace. This was critical to the success of the Peace Keeping Operation, as without such collaboration and cooperation, it could not work. All parties are needed at the table to succeed, and this is what we secured. The dynamics of this and the relationships is a 'lesson learned' for other peace keeping operations.

The other acknowledgement is to Australia's SAS, who toured my country with me, by car or in helicopters, ensuring my safety. What wonderfully trained soldiers they are, and men of great caliber and a credit to Australia.

The Timorese people have a special sensibility not only to express their feelings but also to preserve their memories. A perfect example of this occurred in our enclave of Oe-cusse where a woman was giving birth in her home when INTERFET tanks rolled past her front door. And so, in gratitude to the peace the INTERFET forces had secured, she named, at that very moment, her new child INTERFET. And so today, there is a teenager running around Oe-cusse who is known to his friends by the nickname 'Inter'.

Ladies and gentlemen,

In many ways INTERFET laid the foundations for the special relationship we have with Australia today.

For many of our people the sight of Australian soldiers in 1999 put right the historical wrong of recognising the Indonesian annexation of East Timor. The Australians of INTERFET were well liked on the streets of our country. Their down to earth manner and professional approach gave our people confidence and they started to look at Australia in a new and positive light.

It was also a result of the INTERFET intervention that many Australians began to establish links with districts in Timor-Leste. Local councils in many parts of Australia have established 'friendship city' arrangements with various places in Timor-Leste and many schools have begun to build links with schools in Timor-Leste. We now enjoy so many people to people links, which have built deep bonds of friendship and solidarity between our countries. I wish to acknowledge our Ambassador to Australia, H.E. Abel Guterres for his initiative regarding this.

Ladies and gentlemen,

The success of INTERFET provides a model for peace keeping operations.

Today we live in a confused world – a new world of disorder. We face conflict and turmoil across the globe that the international community seems unwilling or unable to resolve. We have seen that the use of force is not always the most effective way to approach deep rooted tensions and conflict that, at their core, are fuelled by poverty, injustice, ignorance and marginalisation. Regrettably, we see powerful nations acting to achieve short-term solutions to defend their strategic interests, rather than taking meaningful engagements to address the root causes of conflict and fragility.

INTERFET has proved to be a shining light in the history of international military engagements to bring peace and order. It is therefore a model that should be looked at as global leaders consider international military interventions. In many ways, however, INTERFET benefited from a set of unique circumstances. These included an invitation from the Indonesian Government, establishment in accordance with international law and with the Security Council endorsement, a local population that welcomed international intervention, a broad regional and international coalition, adequate forces to get the job done and, importantly, outstanding leadership. It was also a just and proper cause.

Ladies and gentlemen,

This conference provides us with the opportunity not only to reflect on the crisis of 1999 but to consider different perspectives for the benefit of a proper accounting of Timorese history and of the INTERFET intervention.

One thing that we must all remember is the role INTERFET played in building the foundation for the reconciliation amongst the Timorese and with Indonesia, which helped the establishment of a tolerant and peaceful society in Timor-Leste. This was the only condition needed for a vibrant and free democracy contributing to a growing economy that is improving the lives of its people.

Thank you very much.

Order of Solidarity Medal Awards Ceremony, Queen's Hall, Parliament House, Victoria

Melbourne, 20 September 2014

Excellencies,
Honoured guests,
Ladies and gentlemen,

I am very pleased to be here in Melbourne surrounded by so many familiar faces and the local Timorese community.

As you know, we are here to honour some outstanding individuals who helped us on our long journey to independence -Fabio Cavadini, Jill Jolliffe and John Sinnott are with us today.

We are also here to honour the memory of Michelle Turner who sadly passed before she could see an independent Timor-Leste.

Today allows us to show our deep appreciation and the respect we have for the contribution of these individuals to our struggle for independence.

During the darkest hours of our resistance so many had abandoned us. If it was not for the selfless work of our friends in the solidarity movement we would have had trouble continuing our struggle. We will always remember that so called 'ordinary' Australians stood with us. Australians from all walks of life – journalists, social workers, teachers, unionists, mothers, fathers, students – each one had a role in ensuring that our cause was heard.

Ladies and gentlemen,

The world is said to be divided into 'realists' and 'idealists'. According to the realists, international relations are driven by power. According to the idealists, international relations should be guided by agreed principles of justice.

The fact that I am here today, as the democratically elected Prime Minister of Timor-Leste, is proof that sometimes the realists get it wrong – that the powerful do not always prevail over the weak. It is proof that, in the end, good will prevail and that we must continue to work in solidarity for what we know in our hearts of be right.

The reason I am here today owes an enormous amount to the efforts of some fine Australian idealists – Michelle Turner, John Sinnott, Jill Jolliffe and Fabio Cavadini, and other idealists like them from around the world.

While the people of Timor fought a bitter guerilla war, a war of resistance, our friends in the international community fought a diplomatic and political struggle.

Our strategy was to fight not only in our land, but to also fight internationally, for the hearts and minds of the people of the world.

One international battleground was the United Nations – an organisation dreamed up by idealists following the Second World War. My dear friend Jose Ramos-Horta, who has recently been awarded Australia's highest honour, led our campaign in the United Nations. Thanks to his efforts, and the many nations that supported us, our cause stayed on the United Nations agenda for 24 years and eventually the United Nations paved the road to our independence.

Our other international weapon was people – people like Michelle, Fabio, Jill and John who were prepared to take up our cause because they believed a great injustice had been done to our people.

As we have heard, Michelle Turner was introduced to our cause by her grandfather who was an Australian solider kept alive by Timorese during the Second World War. She was drawn to record the story of Australia's veterans who had served in Timor-Leste, and then the personal stories of the suffering endured by many Timorese.

Jill Jolliffe has devoted her life to the Timorese cause since she was in Díli just before the Balibo Five journalists were murdered in 1975. She has interviewed hundreds of people, written countless articles and books, all aimed at keeping our story alive and seeking justice for our people and the Balibo Five.

Fabio took our struggle to the world through the medium of film. He was part of the team that made the first Australian film to comprehensively examine the terrible death toll and the resolute resistance in my country following the Indonesian invasion in 1975.

John Sinnott helped run the Australia-East Timor Association. He sold books, addressed political meetings, and raised money to support political prisoners in Díli – of which I was a direct beneficiary.

None of these people had to do what they did. It wasn't their families being torn apart, being starved or killed. It wasn't their country that was invaded. And yet they chose to act, to call out to the world, each in their own way, about the great injustice that was occurring in my country.

I am humbled by their courage and their commitment. The world needs more people like them.

We can also say that their support represented the Australian people who always believed in our cause. The same Australia that accepted so many of our people as refugees and that today continues to work with us in friendship to improve the lives of our people.

Friends, our people's struggle goes on. Achieving the restoration of our Independence turned out to be but the first step in achieving true freedom for our people – a freedom from poverty and the freedom to realise our full potential as a nation and as a people.

We cannot do this alone. Today, we continue to need the help of our international friends. We still need you to stand in solidarity with us as we develop Timor-Leste.

Many Australians are working with us to bring better education, health care and food security to our people. They are some of our most important partners in our future.

Ladies and gentlemen,

Together we have shown the world that ideals matter – that sometimes the weak can prevail against the strong – that idealism can triumph over realism.

We cannot thank you enough for what you have done for our people.

And now, thanks in large part to your efforts, our people live in freedom and peace.

This award symbolises our gratitude and our thanks.

Obrigado barak.

United Nations Third International Conference on Small Island Developing States: 'The Sustainable Development of Small Island States through Genuine and Durable Partnerships'

Apia, Samoa, 1 September 2014

His Excellency, Tuilaepa Lupesoliai Sailele Malielegao, Prime Minister of Samoa and President of the Conference
His Excellency, Ban Ki-moon, Secretary-General of the United Nations
His Excellency, John Ashe, President of the UN General Assembly
His Excellency, Wu Hungbo, Under Secretary General for DESA and Secretary-General for the Third International Conference on Small Island Developing States
Excellencies, the Representatives of the various United Nations Organisations
Heads of States and Heads of Government of Ministers
Small Island States around the world
Distinguished Participants
Ladies and gentlemen,

It is a great honour to speak at this III UN International Conference of such importance to humanity's collective and sustainable future – 'the sustainable development of SIDS through genuine and durable partnerships'. I would like to thank the people and the government of Samoa for hosting this event and for the warm welcome and wonderful hospitality.

Like all the small States, Timor-Leste was colonised for centuries and only very recently achieved its sovereignty. In this short period of 12 years of independence, Timor-Leste is building the nation and is classified as a 'fragile' and 'vulnerable' State. I cannot argue with this, but it is important to make the distinction between the institutions of the State, and people who make up the State. I have to admit that our State institutions are still fragile, but our people are resilient, and they are determined to build a better future for our children.

In Timor-Leste we may be distant from the global centres of power, but this gives us the opportunity, and the time, to look closely at what is happening in the world.

It allows us to come with a different perspective that is not bound by economic and political orthodoxies.

It is a perspective in which it is impossible to ignore the 2.2 billion people facing poverty and living in fragile and conflict affected nations that will not achieve even a single Millennium Development Goal by the target date of 2015.

It is a perspective that allows us to see that we are so much stronger as nation States when we come together to form partnerships and alliances, when we recognise our common challenges and our common vulnerabilities.

That is why my small nation of Timor-Leste has been working in partnership with 19 others, called 'fragile and conflicted affected nations', to make sure our voices are heard in debates about how to encourage sustainable development in the post 2015 agenda.

Our partnership is called the g7+ and it includes small island States, most of which are here at this conference.

The g7+ partnership is a voluntary association of countries that are, or have been affected by conflict and are now in transition to the next stage of development. The main objective of the g7+ is to share experiences and learn from one another, and to advocate for reforms to the way the international community engages in fragile and conflict-affected States.

For example, we are loudly advocating for the new set of global sustainable development goals to include a stand-alone goal on 'peaceful and inclusive societies, rule of law and capable institutions.' We know from bitter experience that you cannot have development unless you first have peace and stability.

The g7+ is also advocating for action on climate change. One of the largest threats to global stability, as well as to the very existence of many small island States, is climate change. Regrettably, no issue better demonstrates the concentration of power, and the neglect and self-interest of the wealthy, than the world's response to the threat of climate change.

The Díli Consensus document released at the end of an international development conference in Timor-Leste, in March 2013, recognised the lived reality of climate change and concluded by noting that:

> *We are not part of the cause of climate change; nor can we manage its inevitable effects on our own. We must hold to account the countries that contribute most to the problem, and marshal international support for climate change mitigation, adaptation and disaster risk reduction. While solutions continue to elude us in our global negotiations, this is all the more reason to put climate change firmly on the development agenda and to build resilience against those impacts that can no longer be averted.*

The President of Palau earlier raised an important question, 'who will be committed with us?' It is important that in the Climate Summit this month in New York we can have the right answer.

And today the Prime Minister of the Cook Islands put the issues in such a clear way, to help us all to understand the problem of the lack of global commitment.

Ladies and gentlemen,

Climate change is not only about rising sea levels and changed weather conditions. It is about food security, poverty, health and access to clean water. Environmental degradation, increased food and resource insecurity, population pressures, and internal and external migration are just some of the factors that will imperil already vulnerable fragile States and stoke global tensions.

Climate change is therefore a full frontal threat to the stability of many small island nations. What the world must understand is that climate change also threatens international security and that we can give up on our sustainable development ambitions if we do not have a foundation of stability and peace.

Respected friends,

Ahead of us we have an opportunity to ensure the post-2015 development agenda is truly transformative and that this time no one is left behind. I urge us all to grasp the opportunity this Conference presents to agree on specific actions to drive change. And, if you allow me, I would recommend we avoid overly ambitious plans, taking into account the global consequences of the international financial crisis. And so, we have to adopt more realistic, phased and feasible programs. It should respect equitable distribution of aid depending on the need and priorities of each country and I fully support the establishment of better mechanisms of monitoring, accountability and implementation as the Prime Minister of Papua New Guinea and the representative of the European Union referred today. We also heard the Prime Minister of Tuvalu express both the anxiety and the hope of the Small Island States.

Then SAMOA will really be the pathway towards making this happen.

Then, just as the President of Seychelles believes in his people, we can also go home to our strong, resilient people, and harness their energy to build stronger institutions and global partnerships. And this partnership should be based on mutual trust and accountability from both the donors and the recipients.

We must act together with strength, courage and unity. Sustainable development, global progress and the very future of the people of some small island States depends upon it.

Last night, at the Conference Cultural Opening Ceremony, we were shown the best example of how we can all work together as true partners when we watched the incredible acts of over 500 young and talented Samoans performing in harmony. We must all follow their inspiring lead.

Fa'afetai Lava.

United Nations Climate Change Summit

New York, 23 September 2014

His Excellency, Ban Ki-moon, Secretary-General of the United Nations
Distinguished Participants
Ladies and gentlemen,

The way the world responds to climate change is of critical importance to international development and our shared future.

I commend the Secretary-General for his great leadership in urging the world to take collective action.

This Summit provides the catalyst towards a global binding agreement in 2015.

Climate change is not only about rising sea levels and changed weather conditions. It is not just an environmental issue.

It is about our security and our very survival.

The impacts of climate change threaten our food, energy, water, resource and social security.

The risks associated with these security challenges are compounded where there are existing stresses on water supply, agricultural productivity, health and education systems, and where there are demographic pressures and limited employment and business opportunities for our young people.

Climate change amplifies all of our existing and future development challenges.

Just last year, the Initial National Communication on Climate Change in Timor-Leste concluded that climate change poses a severe threat to future growth and development in Timor-Leste.

While we are introducing measures to mitigate the effects of climate change to protect our economy and infrastructure, it is coordinated global action that is also needed.

But regrettably, no issue better demonstrates the concentration of wealth and the self-interest of the rich and powerful.

Which is why the nations of the world most at risk of the affects of climate change are speaking with one voice on this issue that is not of our making.

Most recently, I attended the United Nations Small Island States meeting in Apia, Samoa, led by H.E. the Secretary-General where we called for universal action to be taken on climate change.

In 2012 I promised the President of Kiribati, that I would raise this matter in every global forum, until we get action. I do so today, as I have done since I made my promise.

We need action not words. This issue is no longer the sole domain of scientists and environmentalists.

The evidence is in front of us.

For our brothers and sisters living in the Pacific Islands climate change is threatening to literally wipe them out of existence.

We need a political solution. Ladies and gentlemen, we must achieve a binding global agreement for urgent and meaningful action on climate change.

Sustainable development, global progress and our very future depends upon it.

Thank you very much.

69th Session of The United Nations General Assembly

UN, New York, 25 September 2014

Your Excellency the President of the United Nations General Assembly
Your Excellency the Secretary-General of the United Nations
Your Excellencies the Heads of State and Government
Ladies and Gentlemen,

In September 2000, before becoming an independent country and while under UNTAET's administration, we came to this Great House as observers, in order to familiarise ourselves with the grand designs for the new century, in the shape of the Millennium Development Goals.

Twelve years after Timor-Leste was admitted into this prestigious Organisation, here we are again to take part in a review of what has been done and of what has not been done, looking at reasons and impacts. Ultimately we want to revise the manner of operation and redefine plans and strategies.

However, other speeches made both here and at the Security Council Summit show the other face – the most troubling one – of world problems, which is the general unquietness of the spirits and the pressure to use force in order to punish.

As such, I add my voice to all those who spoke before me, stating my deep concern in relation to the particularly difficult time in which the Community of Nations is living.

The United Nations has been an unequivocal forum for approaching international issues and continues to be the hope of millions of people throughout the world.

In the year 2000, the challenges came from the condition of extreme poverty, educational needs, enormous scarcity in terms of doctors and medication and lack of food production that affected the populations of many underdeveloped countries.

Fourteen years later, little has been achieved under this effort by the Community of Nations. The fragile or conflict affected countries are the furthest away from achieving their MDGs. Worse still, the challenges of the year 2000 have taken on a new path, increasing the problems related with the rise of tensions and conflicts in many parts of the world.

An organisation's true greatness and its ability in terms of global leadership are measured in difficult times such as these, where the search for peaceful solutions through more intense dialogue may well determine the future of humankind.

In order to respond to these challenges, we require an Organisation that operates effectively. We require an Organisation that is more active and less stereotyped – an Organisation that strengthens cooperation with other organisations, particularly regional ones, and that acts with great respect for the sovereignty and the idiosyncrasies of each State.

Every action carried out so far has just been a continuation of past measures that, in most cases, failed to achieve results that can be considered to be positive.

We are witnessing an increasing loss of trust and we are faced with a crisis of values. More important than the incomprehensible identity of issues that force us to react, we must seek to understand the true causes of the problems. When faced with a threat that does not respect borders and that jeopardises our commitment towards tolerance and peace, it is vital that we can better understand the interdependency of problems, so as to locate the civilizing gap that prevents us from talking to each other and from finding consensus.

We have always advocated that the use of military force does not establish universal values or build democracies. Misguided approaches that fail to recognise the various and diverse elements of the threats or, worse still, which are based on contradictions and on conflicts of interest, only serve to fuel the fire of radicalism and of extremist actions. As such, we must reflect and think things over ... because as things stand, we are merely sliding off into the darkness of war, upholding the medieval principles of an 'eye for an eye, tooth for a tooth'.

This is why I reiterate at this Great House that our collective efforts to preserve world peace and security must reject ill-conceived plans that are only motivated by the strategic interests of domination by the large powers. Instead, we need a plan that is more suited to the reality of each situation and that provides a true response to the main causes of the current crisis.

This common agenda should not insist on manipulating facts in order to produce collective reactions, but rather admit past mistakes due to the urge to impose peace through war. Only by correcting our way of thinking and acting will we truly be giving peace a chance!

Your Excellencies

Ladies and Gentlemen,

The responses to the crises faced by humankind cannot be exacerbated by the desire to end war by waging war. Instead, they must be based on the desire to build a world of peace, supported by dialogue and by an effort – herculean, if need be – to respond to the root causes of problems that lead to terrorism, racism, extremism and intolerance.

When dozens of millions of people throughout the world suffer the horrors of conflict and the countless abuses perpetrated in this century of globalisation, the actions by the international community should prioritise the establishment of the best mechanisms for resolving the problems of exclusion, discrimination and marginalisation of groups, sects and ethnicities.

We must also ensure, from the very start, that the societies emerging from the ashes of these conflicts and committed to leaving the memories of the past behind are entitled to a vital transitional period, respecting their behaviours, their ways of thinking and acting, and their own internal rules and commitments.

Otherwise we will just be sowing the seeds for new conflicts, which we may end up reaping later on.

The war in Iraq, which has destroyed the legacy of a centuries-old civilisation, as well as the bloody conflicts in Afghanistan, Libya, Syria and the Ukraine, should make the international community draw its conclusions about the international standards applied in these contexts. The uncertainty and the bloody anguish that surround Israel and Palestine, with those two peoples destined to live side by side, should alert us once and for all to the fact that fear and insecurity for the future lead to hate, which is the root of all evils.

Your Excellencies

Ladies and Gentlemen,

Timor-Leste knows only too well the consequences and the scars of war.

In addition to the hundreds of thousands of Timorese killed, we also witnessed the near complete destruction of our country. A State born without the ability to ensure and promote the fundamental rights and liberties of its citizens is a fragile State that is unable to carry out its main mission.

Immediately after the war we started to reconcile the Timorese society. We wanted to achieve peace, since without peace we could not feel free.

We have also embraced Indonesia in order to achieve true and genuine reconciliation. Instead of feeding hatred and vengeance, we nurtured solidarity and tolerance between our communities. In this manner, we cultivated a sound relationship of co-operation between our States and our Peoples.

Western democracies are prone to paying for costly international tribunals for judging genocides. They also tend to feel shocked by the human rights violations that occur in developing countries. The issue with Indonesia cannot be seen only in terms of the actions by its military and its generals. Instead, it must be seen within a broader perspective, in which the governments of the western powers sold sophisticated weapons like rifles, warships, fighters, ammunition, tanks and cannons to the Indonesian military, in addition to providing it with training, so that it could decimate the Timorese.

That is why we Timorese and Indonesians preferred instead to record the truth of the facts, to close this painful chapter in our past and to look to the future, which required and continues to require much effort to develop both nations and to improve the living conditions of both peoples.

With its pluralistic and tolerant society, Indonesia is more than a close neighbour. Indeed, it is an inspiration for Timor-Leste. Under the wise leadership of His Excellency President Susilo Bambang Yudhoyono we have witnessed the establishment of a modern democracy that harmonises progress with the promotion of national, regional and international peace. We sincerely hope that the peaceful transition to President Joko Widodo will bring more success to this great Nation.

And I say this in a year when Timor-Leste is celebrating the 12th Anniversary of its Independence. We have learned from our weaknesses and today we are living in an atmosphere of social and political peace.

We are very familiar with the challenges that are inherent to the efforts of developing a nation and of building peace and security.

We are very thankful for the support that the United Nations and all donor countries have provided to Timor-Leste. Nevertheless, these years of partnership have also taught us important lessons, which we have been sharing with the world, particularly the fragile States. We are encouraging them to own their processes and to be committed to the future of their citizens.

Your Excellencies

Ladies and Gentlemen,

We have also started to be more internationally active. We have been working hard within the scope of the g7+, a group that brings together 20 fragile and conflict-afflicted countries. In addition to sharing experiences and knowledge and seeking to put the needs of these countries on the global development agenda, we continue repeating, as many leaders have been doing since yesterday, that without Peace there can be no development. In turn, without development there can be no room for democratic transition, since democracy is a dynamic process of assimilating principles and values, rather than a process that can be measured by elections alone.

And this brings us to the subject of the general debate at this 69th Meeting of the United Nations General Assembly on the post-2015 development agenda.

Inequality is increasing dangerously throughout the world, with wealth being concentrated in the hands of a few to the detriment of us all. Even after the world has learned of the greed and the corruption of the international financial system, which led to the Global Financial Crisis, we are now seeing how the faltering economic recovery is only benefitting those who were responsible for the financial meltdown.

Despite the best efforts by the Secretary-General and his team in the UN, we are almost in 2015 and we know that 2.2 billion people throughout the world are already in or are entering the ranks of the extreme poor, without even knowing what the Millennium Development Goals are.

Here I must draw attention to the incorrect practice by international organisations to view each of the United Nations' 193 member countries in the same manner, regardless of whether they are large or small; rich or poor; young or in a transitional period or centuries-old; developed, with emerging economies or underdeveloped. And these development indexes create scales of values that are both unfair and demotivating to the majority of least developed countries.

As such, all of us in attendance here today have a historical opportunity to share our thoughts on the enormous challenges ahead of us, so as to outline a truly transformative agenda in which no country is left behind.

However, the issue that deserves our collective apprehension and that requires urgent measures is the mitigation of the environmental threats that continue to increase and that are hindering the legitimate perspectives of emerging and developing countries.

Yesterday's Summit on Climate Change raised expectations in relation to actual action plans being implemented in some countries. These plans will be expanded more globally next year, in Paris. Some developed countries have also committed to providing capital for the adaptation fund, which has a vital importance for developing countries.

Ms Emília Pires, the Minister of Finance of Timor-Leste, was a member of the High Level Panel that advised the Secretary-General of the United Nations on this agenda. In the year 2013 and up until last August, Timor-Leste had the honour of assuming the Presidency of the 69th Session of the Economic and Social Commission for Asia and the Pacific. As such, we had the privilege of presiding over this session for one year, working with ESCAP and the nations of the Asia-Pacific region in order to achieve progress and to improve human development.

Timor-Leste is committed to this noble ideal and to this so-deserving mission of helping to nurture a culture of peace in our region, through the gradual and persistent reduction of social inequalities within each country and between countries.

However, and while in our region, including within the scope of ASEAN, there is presently strong cooperation and countries are promoting peace – which has enabled the rise of the Asian region, led by China, lifting hundreds of millions of people from poverty – we cannot but be concerned by the developments in the east and south of the China Sea.

This brings us to a key issue, and one that has vital importance for Timor-Leste. I am speaking of the need to set maritime borders between countries in a clear and serious manner, in line with international law.

Back in 2002, when we began to walk our own path in freedom, we saw a globalised world in which the arrogance of the powerful and the ambition of the rich prevails, and who prey upon the inexperience or the ignorance of the poor and the weak to act dishonestly and in bad faith, in a serious insult to universal values.

And I must affirm that big multinationals have always played an improper and disloyal role, acting with dishonesty and bad faith when dealing with poor countries.

Timor-Leste, a young, small and poor country, is caught off-guard in this sophisticated culture of manipulation and deceit. Nevertheless, we want to continue believing that international mechanisms, such as the United Nations Convention on the Law of the Sea, contribute to justice between nations and understanding between peoples, so as to defend sovereign rights and the truth.

Today, these commitments are vital in order to start rebuilding trust in the world system and to prevent tensions from increasing. The strengthening of dialogue and tolerance and the promotion of a new diplomacy must be translated from a set of good intentions into actual deeds in the international arena.

But what is truly intriguing is the fact that no decent country has yet advocated the need to promote inquiries that would ascertain the origin of the weapons used in the massacres of civilians, particularly women and children, so as to identify the true beneficiaries of this world crisis, who are the ones selling weapons to uncontrolled bands throughout the world.

Your Excellencies

Ladies and Gentlemen,

Before I conclude, I would like to share with you that this year Timor-Leste has assumed the rotating presidency of the Community of Portuguese-Speaking Countries.

In this space, we want to use diplomacy and cooperation to nurture our joint economic potential by making use of our regional ties. We also want to disseminate a message of peace, human rights and social justice throughout all the forums in which we are represented.

Guinea-Bissau is a member of this community, and a country with which Timor-Leste has been closely involved, including within the scope of the g7+, and particularly when it realised that Guinea-Bissau had been left to its fate and was at the mercy of international sanctions. After a devastating cycle of coups, we felt that the people of Guinea-Bissau needed peace and stability and we saw how their leaders were striving to achieve a collective commitment that would benefit the People and the Country.

Timor-Leste had the honour of providing financial support and of sending a technical team for assisting the whole electoral process in Guinea-Bissau. This process, which featured massive democratic participation, was a success and restored constitutional order in the country. Still, as we all know, elections are but a starting point, and a State without the means for ensuring the basic needs of its people faces countless challenges that jeopardise the promise of peace and national cohesion.

In line with the subject of the debate in this General Assembly, I must say that it is now urgent to create the conditions to enable Guinea-Bissau to move from fragility to resilience, by supporting its State agencies. Guinea-Bissau needs to rehabilitate its public administration and its State agencies, as well as to reform its defence and security sector by modernising its forces. Furthermore, Guinea-Bissau requires a financial boost in order to jumpstart its economy.

Within the scope of the CPLP, we want to have an active collaboration with the authorities of Guinea-Bissau and with the international partners, namely ECOWAS, so as to hold an International Conference on Aid to Guinea-Bissau as soon as possible. This conference should start by focusing on matters of extreme urgency, such as salaries, food security, fuel and health. Timor-Leste has already contributed with $6 million, which corresponds to one month of public sector salaries.

I also urge every country in attendance to join Timor-Leste and the CPLP countries, consistent with the highest values of international solidarity, in supporting the consolidation of the achievements made so far by the people of Guinea-Bissau. Indeed, this is something that will also convey a promise of peace to the entire African continent.

And I cannot talk about Africa, a continent that is already wounded on the inside and massacred by hunger and poverty, without mentioning the scourge of the Ebola virus, which is presently challenging the international health system itself. This epidemic, which is unprecedented in our time, requires a vital and undelayable commitment by the International Community.

I hereby declare that Timor-Leste will provide $1 million as immediate support, within the spirit of solidarity that guides the g7+, which includes Sierra Leone, Liberia and Guinea. Next year we will also be allocating an equal amount to help fight this epidemic.

Your Excellency the President of the General Assembly
Your Excellency the Secretary-General
Your Excellencies
Ladies and Gentlemen,

The great challenge in today's world is freeing people from fear. I am talking about the fear of difference, insecurity, hunger, poverty and disease. The fear of losing power or the fear of becoming a slave to power.

In today's unbalanced and unequal world, we need to have the courage to speak a language of trust and tranquillity. We need to pacify minds, to encourage dialogue and to free people from doubt and from feelings of injustice, so that they acquire greater tolerance and greater respect for differences and for diversity.

We need to free people from the yoke of poverty and from the deplorable conditions in which they are living, so as to ensure their right to development. We still have time to write a different and more humane tale for today's generation and for future generations.

Timor-Leste wants to make an active contribution to a Better World, where each country may live in tolerance, harmony and tranquillity, within a true atmosphere of friendship and solidarity that promotes peace. This peace must start in the minds and behaviours of the people at every level of society, so that they can have a positive influence on the policies of the global centres of decision-making.

This is the only way for us to believe that the baby from the Marshall Islands, who touched all our hearts two days ago, may be certain that her future is guaranteed and that she will be able to live in those small islands that comprise her country.

That is all.

Acceptance Speech for the Conferral of the Highest Indonesia Medal of Honour, 'Bintang Republik Indonesia Adipurna' by H.E. President of The Republic of Indonesia

Bali, Indonesia 10 October 2014

Excellency, President of the Republic of Indonesia, Dr. Susilo Bambang Yudhoyono
Excellencies, Members of the Indonesian Government Distinguished guests

It is with profound emotion that I am here, on behalf of the People of Timor-Leste, to receive the highest medal of honour of the Republic of Indonesia, the 'Bintang Republik Indonesia Adipurna'.

It was an honour to deserve from the legitimate representatives of the Indonesian State and from our brothers and sisters, the Indonesian People, this appreciation for the small contribution that I made in strengthening relations between our two nations.

Since 1974, I have been involved in a process where my Homeland and my People have asked everything of me that I could give, to serve their rights and sovereignty, as a People equal to other Peoples of the world.

It was a journey of 40 years, painful in the beginning and difficult in the last decade and a half, but they were also 40 years of learning in regard to respecting other human beings, in order to understand other peoples and identities, in the need to comprehend the latest policies of the world and the basis of relations that should exist between nations.

The effort to understand all this, while still at war with Indonesia, gave me strength to guide our resistance, breaking with the conventional taboos of hatred and vengeance as the ultimate expressions of petty sentiments of victory.

And the result of all this was that we were capable of disentangling honesty from tendencies of manipulation, true from false standards, and in that way, we could choose our own path to the future, upholding universal values and principles and denouncing at the same time new forms of neo- colonialism.

This effort was matched by the Indonesian authorities and I want to emphasise here, by His Excellency, Mr. President on an unusual scale.

In this solemn moment, I want to make known to all those here the following passage, in our different journeys that placed the interests of our people above all else. In the beginning of 2002, Mr. President, I was in Jakarta when Your Excellency called me, as 'Menko Polkam', and said 'Xanana, we heard that you do not want to be the President of Timor-Leste. On behalf of the Indonesian generals who fought in the war in Timor-Leste and on behalf of the Government of Indonesia, I ask you to accept to be the President of the Republic. We need you, at least for the first five year mandate, because we believe that with you being the President of Timor- Leste, we can work to build new relations between the two peoples and two States'.

I do not need, Mr. President, to repeat here the various meetings where true brotherhood proved fundamental to our relations, breaking the rigid and conventional climate of relations between States.

Today, the Republic of Indonesia and the Democratic Republic of Timor-Leste are two sovereign States that respect each other and place as a fundamental basis for their relations of cooperation, the spirit of brotherhood and the principle of equal to equal, and above all, the value of sincerity in our acts for the greater interests of our Peoples.

We have in you, Excellency, the best friend of the people of Timor- Leste.

I wish from the bottom of my heart that this act cements the already solid relations between the two sovereign States and between our two peoples.

Thank you very much for the honour and privilege that Your Excellency has bestowed on me on behalf of the Government of the Republic of Indonesia.

www.ingramcontent.com/pod-product-compliance
Lightning Source LLC
Chambersburg PA
CBHW052130070526
44585CB00017B/1771